T0178708

Digital Color Imaging

# Digital Color Imaging

Edited by

Christine Fernandez-Maloigne
Frédérique Robert-Inacio
Ludovic Macaire

First published 2012 in Great Britain and the United States by ISTE Ltd and John Wiley & Sons, Inc.

ISTE Ltd
27-37 St George's Road
London SW19 4EU
UK

www.iste.co.uk

John Wiley & Sons, Inc.
111 River Street
Hoboken, NJ 07030
USA

www.wiley.com

Library of Congress Cataloging-in-Publication Data

Numerical color imaging / edited by Christine Fernandez-Maloine, Frederique Robert-Inacio, [and] Ludovic Macaire.
    p. cm.
Includes bibliographical references and index.
  ISBN 978-1-84821-347-0
  1. Color--Mathematics--Research. 2. Image processing--Mathematics--Research. 3. Color vision--Research. I. Fernández-Maloine, Christine. II. Robert-Inacio, Frédérique. III. Macaire, Ludovic.
  QC496.N86 2012
  535.601'51--dc23
                                                                                    2012008577

British Library Cataloguing-in-Publication Data
A CIP record for this book is available from the British Library
ISBN: 978-1-84821-347-0

Printed and bound in Great Britain by CPI Group (UK) Ltd., Croydon, CR0 4YY

# Table of Contents

**Chapter 4. Linear Prediction in Spaces with Separate Achromatic and Chromatic Information**
Olivier ALATA, Imtnan QAZI, Jean-Christophe BURIE and
Christine FERNANDEZ-MALOIGNE

**Chapter 5. Region Segmentation**
Alain CLÉMENT, Laurent BUSIN, Olivier LEZORAY
and Ludovic MACAIRE

**Chapter 6. Color Texture Attributes** . . . . . . . . . . . . . . . . . . . 193
Nicolas VANDENBROUCKE, Olivier ALATA, Christèle LECOMTE,
Alice POREBSKI and Imtnan QAZI

# Foreword

The relationship that scientists have with color is one that is particularly worthy of examination. The study of color has its roots in physics, and more specifically in optics, and to a lesser extent in biology, in the context of the physiology of perception. Due to this double connection both with physical science and life science, the study of color holds a unique position in physics that is shared only with the field of acoustics (for exactly the same reasons). We will however see that scientists have approached these two fields very differently.

Other fields associated with the human perception of physical phenomena could also benefit from the same approach, but so far at least this has not been followed through. Other senses – touch, taste, and smell – do not seem to have achieved the same theoretical underpinnings and methodology, or the same body of experimental research to put them firmly into the realm of physics.

As with acoustics, and more specifically musical acoustics, when studying color, the scientist is faced with a highly demanding task. Not only must he understand how the signals are generated and propagated, but he must also explain the interpretation that ultimately occurs in the body of the listener or viewer. *In caude venenum*! This final stage proves to be the most intractable in the face of a rigorous approach.

The researcher must contend with uncertainty and imprecision, with the variable and the relative and, worst of all, the subjective. He must attempt to justify beauty, harmony, ugliness, and disharmony. Curiously, while it is primarily mathematicians who have attempted to bring order and harmony to sound, it is the physicists who have dealt with the problem of color. Maybe this can be explained in retrospect by the large spectral range occupied by sound (over ten octaves), compared to the visible spectrum, which barely covers a single octave, and by the selectiveness of the sensors.

The ear is an instrument that is near linear in frequency that transmits all the signals it receives, while the retina is a three-channel projector where a great deal of mixing takes place. Thus, sound provides a huge diversity of signals that can be used to extract order and rules, which is the natural domain of the mathematician. Colors however must be explained and the means by which they are reduced to such a compact form is in the domain of the physicist.

Great men of physics have been fascinated by this problem, starting with Newton who was the first (1666) to separate white light into its component colors and then recombine them to recreate the original light, thereby demonstrating that white light consists of different colors. After him, Young (1777), Dalton (1794), and Helmholtz (1850), among others, carried out a wide range of studies in color perception, leading in particular to the identification of the three components of color vision and the identification of color blindness within the population. Lord Rayleigh, Lorentz, Mie, and Planck dedicated themselves to explaining the colors of natural phenomena, including the sky and clouds as well as powders and metals. Maxwell not only built the foundations of the wave approach to radiation, but he also showed how the visible spectrum fits into the broader electromagnetic spectrum. Playing with spinning tops, he showed the laws of color balancing that are the basis of metamerism and used this insight to discover the color perception space (1857). Finally, it is less widely known that he was also responsible for producing the first color photograph by superimposing three black and white photographs taken with appropriate filters.

These approaches on the nature of color taken by famous physicists, as well as a large number of less famous and unknown researchers, were not taken in the absence of any psychological or even philosophical consideration, which in any case is incredibly subjective. Long before this, the ancient philosophers had already placed color at the center of their visions of harmony, in interpretations that were built around an intimate mixture of reality and mathematics. In the same way as with music, color was given a key role in the harmony of the universe.

Aristotle had adopted a vision based around the antagonism between "light" and "darkness", between which there lay seven carefully chosen gradings ranging from white to black. This antagonism of conflicting colors persisted in representations up until the 20th Century and contributed on a large-scale to the antagonism of complementary colors used by painters and photographers. Aristotle chose the seven colors of the rainbow as the basis for his decomposition, which he placed between white and black. Plato distanced himself from this approach, confining the effects of color to within the eye, and proposing his own primary colors with different hues and saturation. Later, Pythagoras looked for other harmonies within the positions of the planets, which led to a more universal equilibrium within which colors and music both played roles.

Fifteen centuries later, in the classical era and in parallel with the work of physicists, a concurrent trend toward physical analysis started to develop. This was led largely by philosophers, attempting to bring color within the sphere of human experience, in terms of perception, sensitivity, and subjectivity. This began with the postulates of Locke, who in the 17th Century separated color from the object it was associated with, and was followed by the writings of Goethe that drew on a spectrum of experimental work to "prove" the limitations of Newton's approach, which was too physical in that it ignored the role of the individual and the context in color perception, and was not subtle enough to describe simultaneous contrast and variations in hue; finally, Schopenhauer refused to ascribe any objective qualities to color, viewing it simply as the result of subjective antagonism between light and darkness in the perception of the observer, whose retina becomes fatigued from overstimulation.

It was from these often divergent works, which at times led to conflict between physicists and philosophers, that the artists of the 19th Century drew inspiration for their palettes: first Turner and the adherents of the English school of painting, followed by Seurat and the entire Impressionist family, and especially the works of Chevreul (1839).

When approaching an academic text such as the present work, the reader should keep in mind the complexity of the representation and modeling of color, models that are the pinnacle of twenty-five centuries of historical study. We encourage the reader to examine the impact of ancient theories of color on modern day practices in digital processing of color images, in their filtering and restoration, the extraction of significant components, lines, shapes, and textures, their compression and transformation. This book will help the reader to grasp the importance of the mathematical tools that are required for the treatment of this complex data: differential equations, graphs, Markov fields, spectral analysis, etc. It will also draw attention to the importance of a suitable choice of color space for color representation: RGB, L*a*b, HSV, etc. This choice is determined both by physical constraints and by the requirements of psycho-physiology; the reader will discover the importance of metrics associated with similarity and confusion, or alternatively with contrasts.

The reader will also be struck, on reading these chapters, by the role of experimentation, the relevance of experiment and empirical approaches, and the importance of the ultimate adjudicator, the human observer, who is required to classify and categorize, above and beyond what can be achieved with scores and norms. The book will reveal why operations that the human eye has no difficulty at all with, discrimination and detection, today require a vast and complex arsenal if they are to be automated, and why their results still often remain limited or conditional. Finally, through this, the reader will understand why the compelling avenues of research presented here are still ripe for further exploration, challenges that still inspire the authors of this work.

Henri MAÎTRE
April 2012

# Chapter 1

# Color Representation and Processing in Polar Color Spaces

## 1.1. Introduction

A wide range of technological representations for color have been established over the last few decades. We recommend some classic references to the reader interested in developing a thorough appreciation of this multiplicity [CAR 95, POY 03, SHI 95, TRE 04]. Today, it is widely accepted that no single color space is suitable for all fields and all applications. We will, however, show that the specific choice of representation has a strong impact on the image processing methods and algorithms that we will discuss. In particular, this chapter will focus on the processing of color images represented in polar coordinates. The hue, saturation, intensity (HSI) triplet is very closely related to how the human vision system operates, and this makes it highly intuitive. We, therefore, intend to work in a geometric framework whereby the RGB (red, green, blue) color cube is transformed into polar coordinates, and this will require us to adapt our subsequent processing of these color coordinates.

Chapter written by Jesús ANGULO, Sébastien LEFÈVRE and Olivier LEZORAY.

We will begin by recalling intuitively the three variables represented by this triplet, and will then show a sample calculation for the geometric transformation of Cartesian RGB coordinates into polar HSI coordinates. The manipulation of hue and associated operators is particularly important. We will treat in detail various examples of filtering and segmentation methods that can be used to best exploit the HSI triplet form. These image processing approaches are largely nonlinear techniques or extensions of color images of operators and transformations with their roots in concepts of mathematical morphology.

### 1.1.1. *Notations used in this chapter*

Throughout this chapter, we will use a different notation for the color axes, which will be denoted in capital letters (RGB, HSI, etc.), from that used for coordinates of color points $\mathbf{c}$ (the latter being a vector), which will be represented by lowercase letters: $r, g, b, h, s, i, \ldots$

A gray scale image is a numerical function $f(\mathbf{x})$: $E \to \mathcal{V}$, where $E$ is the support space of the image (in general $E \subset \mathbb{Z}^2$ for discrete 2D images), $\mathbf{x} \in E$, where $\mathbf{x} = (x_1, x_2)$ is a point or pixel and $\mathcal{V}$ is an ordered set of gray levels in a closed bounded interval $\mathcal{V}_{[v_{min}, v_{max}]} = [v_{min}, v_{max}]$ (or, more generally, $\mathcal{V} \subset \mathbb{Z}$ or $\mathbb{R}$). Practical applications consist of digital images taking values from a discrete set of gray levels encoded using $N$ bits, and so consequently $v_{min} = 0$ and $v_{max} = 2^N - 1$. However, for computational simplicity, it is always possible to consider the reduced interval $[0, 1]$.

Recall also that the $(\mathcal{V}, \leq)$ pair, where "$\leq$" corresponds to the natural order of scalar values is a complete totally ordered lattice or chain. The family of gray level images, written as $\mathcal{F}(E, \mathcal{V})$, also forms a complete lattice.

Digital processing of color images is generally performed in a 3D space, for example, using the red, green, and blue (RGB) primary colors. Thus, a color image is defined as a multivariate image $\mathbf{f}(\mathbf{x}) = (f_R(\mathbf{x}), f_G(\mathbf{x}), f_B(\mathbf{x}))$, where $f_R$, $f_G$, and $f_B$ are the gray level images for the red, green, and blue components. More precisely, the color image $f\colon E \to \mathcal{V}^{RGB}$ takes values from the product space $\mathcal{V}^{RGB} = [\mathcal{V}^R \times \mathcal{V}^G \times \mathcal{V}^B]$, where typically $\mathcal{V}^R = \mathcal{V}^G = \mathcal{V}^B = \mathcal{V}$. Despite $\mathcal{V}$ being a chain, the product space $\mathcal{V}^{RGB}$ is not a complete lattice since we have not supplied a complete ordering between the color points $\mathbf{c} = (r, g, b)$, $\mathbf{c} \in \mathcal{V}^{RGB}$. Following a color space transformation, for example into a HSI representation, the image can also be given by the corresponding variables in that space, $f(\mathbf{x}) = (f_H(\mathbf{x}), f_S(\mathbf{x}), f_I(\mathbf{x}))$; we can therefore write $f\colon E \to \mathcal{V}^{HSI}$, where $\mathcal{V}^{HSI} = [\mathcal{V}^H \times \mathcal{V}^S \times \mathcal{V}^I]$. In a similar way, a color point can also be represented in terms of its coordinates along the $HSI$ axes, i.e. $\mathbf{c} = (h, s, i)$, $\mathbf{c} \in \mathcal{V}^{HSI}$. The levels of luminous intensity and saturation, $\mathcal{V}^I = \mathcal{V}$ and $\mathcal{V}^S = \mathcal{V}$ are chains. On the other hand, the hue image $f_T(\mathbf{x})\colon E \to \mathcal{C}$ is a special case since it is a function defined on the unit circle $\mathcal{C} \equiv [0, 2\pi]$, and therefore has no associated ordering.

## 1.2. The HSI triplet

### 1.2.1. *Intuitive approach: basic concepts and state of the art*

Although the colorimetric models defined by the CIE (International Commission on Illumination) are widely used, it has been known since the work of Munsell [MUN 69] that it is easy and intuitive to use the terms hue, saturation and intensity to represent a color and hence to work in a 3D polar coordinate system. More precisely:

– hue $H$ is the way in which a region appears similar to a perceived color. This is an angular parameter, with the origin $0°$ commonly being assigned to the color red: $T \in [0°, 360°] \equiv [0, 2\pi]$;

– saturation $S$ is the proportion of color relative to the luminous intensity or mathematically, a measure of the distance of the color from the achromatic axis. Pure colors are the most saturated. This variable normally takes values between 0 and 1: $S \in [0, 1]$;

– brightness, lightness, or luminance, which we will refer to here as "intensity" $I$ to avoid any ambiguity, is the way in which a region is perceived to emit more or less light. It can be given a range of different mathematical definitions starting from the concept of luminous intensity (taking into account the radiant intensity and the spectral sensitivity of the human eye) per unit area. A geometrical model can also be used to define the intensity as the norm of a particular vector in space. As with saturation, its levels are normalized between 0 and 1: $I \in [0, 1]$.

It can therefore be observed that the HSI color space can be easily used to separate purely achromatic information, associated with the intensity, from chromatic information as represented by the hue/saturation pair. In addition, as we will show later on, saturation plays an important role in the "weight" attributed to the chromatic information contained within an HSI triplet. This representation is thus particularly appropriate to digital processing of color images, assuming that the formulation of the HSI triplet is correct.

The two most widely used "hue/saturation/intensity" color spaces are the HSV and HLS spaces, and their equations as a function of RGB (invertible expressions) involve an approximate Cartesian-polar coordinate transformation [SHI 95]. The traditional geometric interpretations of the HSV and HLS spaces are as a hexa-cone and a double-hexa-cone (see Figure 1.1). If the vertical axis is taken to be the diagonal of the unit RGB cube, then this looks loosely like two hexagonal pyramids with their bases glued together. But, with these pyramids many coordinates cannot be calculated. As the intensity tends to zero along the V axis, it is not possible to have a high level of saturation, as is the case along the L axis for values close to 0 or close to 1. To avoid excursions outside the domain over which the variables are defined, the validity of every operation that is applied must be verified. To avoid having to do this continuously, the cone is transformed into a cylinder, by dividing the saturation by the luminance in some way. This has important implications when defining a saturation threshold; specifically, a constant saturation threshold is represented by a hyperbola [HAN 03b].

In view of these shortcomings, significant improvements have been proposed in the literature [CAR 95, LEV 93]. Motivated by this lack of clarity, and in particular lack of mathematical precision, a series of studies led by Serra [ANG 07c, HAN 03b, SER 02] shed light on the limitations of classical representations: the expressions for luminance and saturation are often not norms (in the mathematical sense), and this causes errors in the computation of mean values or distances. Moreover, the intensity and saturation components in HSV and HLS are not independent. These shortcomings can be overcome using a range of alternative representations, depending on the different methods used to define luminance and saturation. In this context, rather than listing all the alternatives available in the literature, we have decided to justify, using basic geometric concepts, a consistent calculation of the HSI triplet using the norms $\mathcal{L}_2$ and $\mathcal{L}_1$.

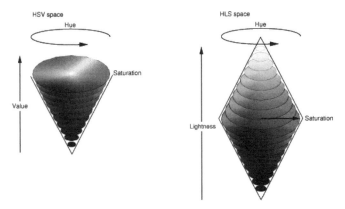

**Figure 1.1.** *Geometric representation of HSV (hexa-cone) and HLS (double-hexa-cone) polar color systems*

### 1.2.2. *Geometric approach: calculation of polar coordinates*

Here, we will assume RGB data to be a given; i.e. we will not dwell on how suitable it is for representing physical space, complete with illumination, objects and their reflectances and absorptions. Our working geometrical space will consist of the achromatic axis, corresponding to the principal diagonal of the RGB unit cube, and the chromatic plane, defined as the plane perpendicular to this axis at the origin and which contains all the color information (see Figure 1.2). Any color vector $\mathbf{c} = (r, g, b)$ can be decomposed into a vector sum of its projection onto the achromatic axis $\mathbf{c}_d$ and its projection onto the chromatic plane $\mathbf{c}_p$; i.e. $\mathbf{c} = \mathbf{c}_d + \mathbf{c}_p$. It can easily be shown that:

$$\mathbf{c}_d = \left( (r + g + b)/\sqrt{3}, (r + g + b)/\sqrt{3}, (r + g + b)/\sqrt{3} \right) \quad [1.1]$$

and:

$$\mathbf{c}_p = \left( (2r - g - b)/3, (2g - r - b)/3, (2b - r - g)/3 \right) \quad [1.2]$$

This last expression is obtained from the classic equation: $\mathbf{v}_\Pi = \mathbf{v} - \langle \mathbf{v}, \mathbf{n}_u \rangle \cdot \mathbf{n}_u$ ,which gives the projection of a vector $\mathbf{v}$ onto a plane $\Pi$ defined in terms of its unit normal vector $\mathbf{n}_u$.

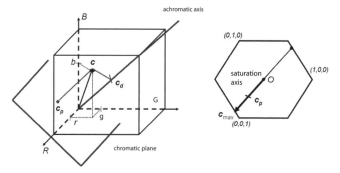

**Figure 1.2.** *Unit RGB cube and geometric space for calculation of HSI polar coordinates*

We will now express the chromatic plane in polar coordinates $(\theta, \rho)$, taking the chromatic projection of the color red $\mathbf{r} = (1, 0, 0)$, written as $\mathbf{r}_p$, as the angular origin:

$$\theta = \arccos \left( \frac{\langle \mathbf{r}_p, \mathbf{c}_p \rangle}{||\mathbf{r}_p|| \cdot ||\mathbf{c}_p||} \right) \quad [1.3]$$

The positive direction for this angle $\theta$ represents the transition from red to green and then to blue. Clearly, the radial coordinate is given by the norm of the projection, i.e. $\rho = ||\mathbf{c}_p||$. Any point $\mathbf{c}$ can be expressed in an equivalent manner through its Cartesian coordinates $(r, g, b)$ or its spatio-polar coordinates $(||\mathbf{c}_d||, ||\mathbf{c}_p||, \theta)$. Luminance and saturation are then defined as being proportional to the norms of these projections, reduced to the interval $[0, 1]$. Furthermore, we know that $||\mathbf{c}_d||_2 \propto ||\mathbf{c}||_2$.

To simplify calculations based around the $\mathcal{L}_1$ norm, we can also make use of the fact that $r$, $g$ and $b \geq 0$. Nevertheless, this equivalence will result in different equations depending on whether the $\mathcal{L}_2$ or $\mathcal{L}_1$ norm is used. In particular, for the case of $\mathcal{L}_2$ we obtain:

$$
\begin{cases}
i_2(\mathbf{c}) &= \frac{1}{\sqrt{3}}\left(r^2 + g^2 + b^2\right)^{1/2} = \frac{1}{\sqrt{3}}||\mathbf{c}||_2 \\[2mm]
s_2(\mathbf{c}) &= \frac{3}{2}\left((2r-g-b)^2 + (2g-b-r)^2 + (2b-g-r)^2\right)^{1/2} \\[2mm]
&= \frac{1}{\sqrt{6}}\left(9||\mathbf{c}||_2^2 - 3||\mathbf{c}||_1^2\right)^{1/2} \\[2mm]
h_2(\mathbf{c}) &= \arccos\left(\frac{r-g/2-b/2}{(r^2+g^2+b^2-rg-rb-gb)^{1/2}}\right) \\[2mm]
&= \arccos\left(\frac{3}{\sqrt{6}} \cdot \frac{(3r-||\mathbf{c}||_1)}{\left(9||\mathbf{c}||_2^2-3||\mathbf{c}||_1^2\right)^{1/2}}\right)
\end{cases}
$$

[1.4]

However, this HSI representation, which is the most mathematically suited to quantitative calculations, has the significant disadvantage of having a non-trivial inverse relationship from the HSI $\rightarrow$ RGB. Using the $\mathcal{L}_1$ norm and a suitable approximation for hue, the following simpler equations are obtained [ANG 07c, SER 02]:

$$
\begin{cases}
i_1(\mathbf{c}) &= \frac{1}{3}(max + med + min) = \frac{1}{3}||\mathbf{c}||_1 \\[2mm]
s_1(\mathbf{c}) &= \begin{cases} \frac{3}{2}(max - i_1) & \text{if } i_1 \geq med \\ \frac{3}{2}(i_1 - min) & \text{if } i_1 \leq med \end{cases} = \frac{3}{4}\left(|r - i_1| + |g - i_1| + |b - i_1|\right) \\[4mm]
h_1(\mathbf{c}) &= \frac{\kappa}{6}\left(\xi + \frac{1}{2} - (-1)^\xi \frac{3}{2}\frac{i_1 - med}{s_1}\right)
\end{cases}
$$

[1.5]

where $max = maximum(r, g, b)$, $min = minimum(r, g, b)$ and $med = median(r, g, b)$, along with:

$$
\xi(\mathbf{c}) = \begin{cases}
0 & \text{if } r > g \geq b \\
1 & \text{if } g \geq r > b \\
2 & \text{if } g > b \geq r \\
3 & \text{if } b \geq g > r \\
4 & \text{if } b > r \geq g \\
5 & \text{if } r \geq b > g
\end{cases}
$$

and the constant $\kappa$, which can be used to express the hue in different units: $\kappa = 1$ implies that the hue varies from 0 to 1, $\kappa = 2\pi$ for a representation in radiant, $\kappa = 360$ for degrees. The equations for inverse transformation from HSI $\rightarrow$ RGB using the $\mathcal{L}_1$ norm are given in [ANG 03a, SER 02]. The calculations for the direct and inverse transformations using other (pseudo)-norms are given in [HAN 03b].

Throughout the rest of this chapter, we will assume that the HSI triplet has been calculated in an appropriate manner, using the possible norms, and consequently that the magnitudes of hue, saturation, and intensity produce mathematically correct values.

## 1.3. Processing of hue: a variable on the unit circle

As indicated earlier, the hue component is angular in nature. We must therefore pay particularly close attention to it. In what follows, we will represent hue over the normalized interval $[0, 1]$, but it is also possible to use another scale of representation (such as $[0, 2\pi]$ or $[0, 360]$).

The operators of mathematical morphology (but also other nonlinear image processing techniques including rank filters such as the median filter) require that the values associated with each pixel can be ordered if they are to produce the required outcome. The question of hue ordering is therefore crucial. However, in contrast to the case with intensity and saturation represented as scalar values, there is no universal ordering relation in the case of hue.

### 1.3.1. *Can hue be represented as a scalar?*

The most trivial solution for hue ordering involves manipulating their values as scalars. However, if this strategy is followed, then we must, for example, state that the color red ($h = 0$) is to be systematically considered as smaller than the color green ($h = 0.66$). The fixed origin at $t = 0$ and the discontinuity observed for the color red (corresponding to values $h \in [0.0 + \varepsilon] \cup [1 - \varepsilon, 1]$) are the root of a number of issues. In addition to a lack of flexibility (since the order of the different colors should be specific to a given application context), there is unexpected and inappropriate behavior inherent in a vector approach within the corresponding region of the hue circle. As an illustration of this problem, Figure 1.3 shows the result of a morphological dilation based on scalar hue ordering, for an image that contains the full gamut of possible hues. The discontinuity observed for the color red can be observed in the middle of the second row of this figure (artificial contour effect).

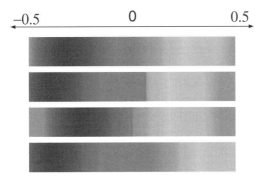

**Figure 1.3.** *From top to bottom, a color image (500 × 70 pixels) consisting of fully saturated hues, its morphological dilation with a 51 pixel-long horizontal structuring element (with scalar ordering) and the hue orderings are defined in equations [1.6] and [1.8], under the assumption that $h_0 = 0.0$. (For a color version of this figure, see www.iste.co.uk/fernandez/colorimag.zip)*

### 1.3.2. *Ordering based on distance from a reference hue*

The difficulty illustrated in Figure 1.3 has for a long time led many authors to ignore this component when discussing color image processing in a polar space. The first attempts at solving this problem were made by Peters [PET 97]. He proposed that the hues $h$ be ordered as a function of their distance $D$ from a reference hue written as $h_0$:

$$\forall\, h, h' \in [0, 1], \;\; h \le h' \Leftrightarrow D(h_0, h) \le D(h_0, h') \qquad [1.6]$$

where $D(\cdot, \cdot)$ is defined as:

$$\forall\, h, h' \in [0, 1], \;\; D(h, h') = \begin{cases} h - h' + 1 & \text{if} \quad -1 \le h - h' < -0.5 \\ h - h' & \text{if} \quad -0.5 \le h - h' < 0.5 \\ h - h' - 1 & \text{if} \quad 0.5 \le h - h' < 1 \end{cases}$$

$$[1.7]$$

The choice of reference hue $h_0$ is thus crucial. Various strategies can be used to define $h_0$, as we will see later on.

Since hues intrinsically lack an ordered relationship, the choice of an arbitrary order (for example *green* > *yellow* > *blue*, etc.) is of limited practical interest. Conversely, the use of a distance measurement introduces a flexibility that is essential for adapting the ordering to an application context, through the definition of an appropriate origin or reference hue. This is why this solution has been widely adopted and has motivated a range of different enhancements.

Thus, Hanbury and Serra [HAN 01a, HAN 01b] proposed a variant that uses morphological operators with a more intuitive character, since under the previous definition, a morphological erosion would have a tendency to enlarge objects of the reference color $h_0$ rather than shrinking them (see Figure 1.3, row three). This variant is defined by:

$$\forall\, h, h' \in [0, 1], \quad h \leq h' \Leftrightarrow h' \div h_0 \leq h \div h_0 \qquad [1.8]$$

where, in contrast to equation [1.6], hues close to $h_0$ are considered to be the largest and the angular distance $h \div h_0$ from $h$ to $h_0$ is modified as follows:

$$\forall\, h, h_0 \in [0, 1], \quad h \div h_0 = \begin{cases} |h - h_0| & \text{if} \quad |h - h_0| < 0.5 \\ 1 - |h - h_0| & \text{if} \quad |h - h_0| \geq 0.5 \end{cases} \qquad [1.9]$$

The final row of Figure 1.3 shows the result of a hue dilation based on the order defined by equation [1.8]. Since the vectors are ordered as a function of their distance from $h_0 = 0.0$, the artificial contour previously observed in the region associated with the color red is avoided.

We should emphasize one particular theoretical weakness in these approaches based on a distance from a particular hue or, generally, a reference vector. Since such solutions do not satisfy the condition of antisymmetry (i.e. two distinct hues can be at an equal distance from the reference hue), the use of the term "ordered" is erroneous because it is, in reality, a pre-order. To satisfy the property of antisymmetry, it is possible to choose an arbitrary direction around the unit hue circle to resolve such conflicts [HAN 02]. For example, if $h \div h_0 = h' \div h_0$ and $h \neq h'$, then the hue first encountered in the chosen direction is considered the smaller one.

### 1.3.3. *Ordering with multiple references*

The use of a variable reference hue can be used to introduce a complete lattice structure on the unit hue circle and thus apply morphological operations that take hue information into account. However, this approach does also have a number of drawbacks. When an image consists of one dominant color, while it is easy to order this hue with respect to the others, it is more difficult to order the secondary hues among themselves: in other words, how should the hues representing yellow and green be ordered within an image represented primarily by the color red? The choice is implicitly determined by the position of the different colors on the hue circle, and their resulting distance from the principal hue. Moreover, the use of a single reference hue seems inadequate when the image to be processed consists of not one but several dominant colors (a situation that is frequently encountered in practice).

Aptoula and Lefèvre [APT 08a, APT 09] suggest the use of several references to determine hue ordering. By defining $k$ reference hues in the form $R = \{h_i\}_{1 \leq i \leq k}$, it is then possible to order two hues as a function of their distances from each of the $k$ references, and define the larger one as the one that is closest to one of the representative colors:

$$R = \{h_i\}_{1 \leq i \leq k}, \quad \forall\, h, h' \in [0, 1], \quad h \leq_T h' \Leftrightarrow \min_i \{h' \div h_i\}$$

$$\leq \min_i \{h \div h_i\} \qquad [1.10]$$

where the binary relation $\leq_T$ represents the proposed ordering based on multiple references. We observe that this method is equivalent to that given in equation [1.8] in the case of a single reference hue (Figure 1.4 (left)). However, if on the other hand the set $R$ contains several references, then the hues closest to these references will be favored in the ordering process (Figure 1.4 (center)). In other words, the hue circle is divided into different regions (arcs of a circle), each one with its own *extrema*.

To illustrate the practical interest in this approach, consider the example given in Figure 1.5a. This image consists of two uniform regions colored blue and yellow, containing green and magenta-colored blotches. The principal hue in this case is blue in Figure 1.5b, it can be seen that a hue dilation based on a single reference will only have the required effect (suppression of the blotches) in the upper half of the image (since the green and magenta blotches are closer to blue than the color yellow is). On the other hand, the use of multiple references (blue and yellow) make it possible to achieve the required result (see Figure 1.5c) over the full extent of the image.

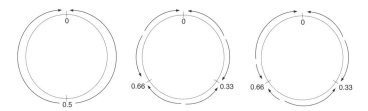

**Figure 1.4.** *From left to right, the hue circle with arrows indicating the direction of increasing hue: for the case of a single reference ($h_0 = 0.0$), multiple references ($h_0 = 0.0$, $h_1 = 0.33$, $h_2 = 0.66$), and multiple references weighted with arbitrary importance*

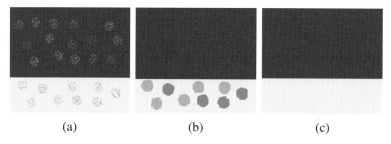

(a)                    (b)                    (c)

**Figure 1.5.** *(a) Original image (297 × 252 pixels); (b) its morphological dilation based on the order [1.8] and $h_0 = 0.66$, and (c) using the order [1.10] with $h_0 = 0.66$ and $h_1 = 0.33$. The dilations are obtained through the use of a structuring element of size 5 × 5 pixels. (For a color version of this figure, see www.iste.co.uk/fernandez/colorimag.zip)*

As with equation [1.8], the relation $\leq_T$ is also a pre-order. However, due to the presence of multiple references, the solution discussed earlier, involving the imposition of arbitrary directions around the unit hue circle [HAN 02], is no longer applicable. To satisfy the property of antisymmetry, it is, for example, possible to make use of the relative weightings of the reference hues in such a way that a hue close to a strongly weighted reference is considered as larger. Any remaining ambiguities can be resolved by considering the ordering between scalar values [APT 08a, APT 09]:

$$h <_T h' \Leftrightarrow \begin{cases} \min_i \{h' \div h_i\} < \min_i \{t \div h_i\}, & \text{or} \\ \min_i \{h' \div h_i\} = \min_i \{h' \div h_i\} & \text{and } \phi(\text{ref}(h)) < \phi(\text{ref}(h')), & \text{or} \\ \min_i \{h' \div h_i\} = \min_i \{h' \div h_i\} & \text{and } \phi(\text{ref}(h)) = \phi(\text{ref}(h')) & \text{and } h < h' \end{cases}$$

[1.11]

where $\text{ref}(h) = \arg\min_{h_i \in R} \{h \div h_i\}$ is the reference hue that is closest to the hue $h$ and $\phi(\cdot) \colon [0, 1] \to \mathbb{R}$ is the function that assigns a relative weighting to a reference hue.

### 1.3.4. *Determination of reference hues*

The approaches outlined above require the selection of one or more reference hues for their implementation. It is possible to leave this choice to an expert in the relevant field, but an automatic decision-making method is preferable.

Thus, the mean hue $\bar{h}$ of a set of hues $R = \{h_i\}_{1 \leq i \leq k}$ can be calculated as follows [FIS 93]:

$$\bar{h} = \arctan \left( \frac{\sum_{h_i \in R} \sin h_i}{\sum_{h_i \in R} \cos h_i} \right)$$

[1.12]

However, in the circular case, the mean can be a statistical measure whose relevance is weak. It is thus preferable to replace it with the most frequent hue as determined from the hue histogram, from which the principal mode can be identified [ANG 03a, HAN 03a]. The hue histogram is also useful for identifying multiple reference hues, with each one being associated with a significant mode within the histogram [APT 09]. To guarantee a level of robustness in these approaches, it may be useful to filter the histogram (suppression of elements smaller than the mean value, histogram smoothing, etc.). The reference hue associated with each histogram mode is then identified as the maximum, median, or mean hue within the mode.

Note that the automatic calculation of multiple reference hues may lead to an excessive number of references. To deal with this problem, it is possible to take into account the relative importance $n_i$ of each reference hue $h_i$ in the ordering given by equation [1.10]. To measure the importance of a section $h_{\alpha,\beta}$ of the histogram, we can calculate its length $l_{\alpha,\beta}$ or preferably its integral $w_{\alpha,\beta}$, which are defined respectively as [APT 09]:

$$l_{\alpha,\beta} = h_\alpha \div h_\beta \qquad\qquad [1.13]$$

$$w_{\alpha,\beta} = \sum_{h_j \in [h_\alpha, h_\beta]} P(h_j) \qquad\qquad [1.14]$$

where $P(h_j)$ is the probability of encountering the hue $h_j$ as given by the normalized histogram. The weight $n_i$ for each reference is then obtained by normalization, so that for example:

$$n_i = w_i / \sum_{h_j \in R} w_j \qquad\qquad [1.15]$$

Ordering with respect to multiple weighted references can then be written as:

$$R = \{(h_i, n_i)\}_{1 \leq i \leq k} , \forall\, h, h' \in [0,1]$$
$$h \leq h' \Leftrightarrow \min_i \left\{ (h' \div h_i) \times 1/n_i \right\} \leq \min_i \left\{ (h \div h_i) \times 1/n_i \right\}$$
$$[1.16]$$

The factor $n_i$ ensures that hues relatively close to a significant reference are considered as greater than those close to a hue of lesser importance (see Figure 1.4, right). This increases the robustness in the presence of a noisy histogram, limiting the contribution of less significant references. Note that $n_i$ can also be used to enforce antisymmetry (see equation [1.11]).

Due to their nature and the way they are calculated as the projection angle of the color vector onto the achromatic axis, hues are only considered relevant in the case of significant saturation. If the saturation is very small (color close to the achromatic axis), then a small variation in color leads to a large variation in the angle associated with the hue. This observation has led to the introduction of new methods for calculating reference hues, taking the associated level of saturation into account. Thus, the mean hue can be calculated as [HAN 03a]:

$$\bar{h} = \arctan \left( \frac{\sum_{h_i \in R} s_i \sin h_i}{\sum_{h_i \in R} s_i \cos h_i} \right) \qquad [1.17]$$

where for each pixel index $i$ considered, $s_i$ is the saturation associated with the hue $h_i$. The contribution of each pixel to the construction of the hue histogram can be weighted by its saturation value [APT 09].

Note, however, that the hue ordering discussed here, and the resultant choice of reference hue, is not always necessary. Operations such as gradients or "top-hats" as discussed in the next section make this type of calculation unnecessary.

## 1.4. Color morphological filtering in the HSI space

Mathematical morphological filtering methods can be applied to a complete lattice structure with the assumption of an ordering relation. The associated operators can thus be immediately applied to binary or gray scale images. Any set of pixels can be considered as totally ordered by assuming a natural intensity-based ordering. On the other hand, the extension of mathematical morphology to color images, and, more generally, to multivariate images, is not straightforward.

The scope of this section does not include giving an exhaustive exposition on the application of mathematical morphology to color images. The interested reader is referred to recent state-of-the-art publications [ANG 07a, APT 07]. Here, we will discuss two possible methods of handling color operators in the HSI space. The first involves marginal application of a scalar operator to each component in the HSI space, and then defining a technique for combining these marginal results. Naturally, this type of marginal technique only makes sense for certain differential morphological operators such as the top-hat function. The second approach involves building total ordering within the HSI and then generalizing the color erosion and dilation operators. The most natural and widely-used strategy makes use of lexicographical cascades, where the part associated with hue ordering is achieved using the methods discussed in the previous section.

### 1.4.1. *Chromatic and achromatic top-hat transforms*

Let us begin by reviewing the alternatives in the definition of the residue for opening and closing operations, known as the top-hat transform [SER 88, SOI 99]. The white top-hat is the residue between a numerical function $f \in \mathcal{F}(E, \mathcal{V})$ and its morphological opening, i.e.:

$$\rho_B^+(f)(\mathbf{x}) = f(\mathbf{x}) - \gamma_B(f)(\mathbf{x})$$

The black top-hat is the residue between a closing operation and the numerical function, i.e.:

$$\rho_B^-(f)(\mathbf{x}) = \varphi_B(f)(\mathbf{x}) - f(\mathbf{x})$$

Recall that opening and closing are the two fundamental morphological filters [SER 88], obtained respectively by erosion $\varepsilon_B$ followed by dilation $\delta_B$, and by dilation followed by erosion, i.e. $\gamma_B(f) = \delta_B(\varepsilon_B(f))$ and $\varphi_B(f) = \varepsilon_B(\delta_B(f))$. Opening acts on positive (bright) structures within the image, filtering out those with a support smaller than the structuring element $B$; closing acts in an equivalent manner on negative (dark) structures. The circular centered top-hat [HAN 01b] measures spatial variations of an angular function $a \in \mathcal{F}(E, \mathcal{C})$ (defined on the unit circle) with supports that are smaller than the structuring element $B$, i.e.:

$$\rho_B^{\circ}(a)(\mathbf{x}) = \{-\sup[\nu_B^{\circ}(\mathbf{z})], \mathbf{z} \in B_{\mathbf{x}}]\}$$

where $\nu_B^\circ(\mathbf{x}) = \{-\sup[a(\mathbf{x}) \div a(\mathbf{y})], \mathbf{y} \in B_\mathbf{x}\}$, and where $B_\mathbf{x}$ is the structuring element centered on a point $\mathbf{x}$. These three functions are normalized to the unit interval $\rho_B^+(\mathbf{x}), \rho_B^-(\mathbf{x}), \rho_B^\circ(\mathbf{x}) \in \mathcal{F}(E, \mathcal{V}_{[0,1]})$.

We can now define color top-hat operators that are separable in the HSI space [ANG 07c], i.e. those that, for a color image $f \in \mathcal{F}(E, \mathcal{V}^{HSI})$, are obtained from the hue, saturation, and intensity components separately. The results are then combined, leading to residues that contain the chromatic and achromatic details. Recall that intuitively a region is considered to be chromatic if its saturation is sufficiently high for the associated hue value to be perceived by the eye, whereas an achromatic region will be perceived as black, white, or grayish.

*Chromatic top-hat.* This operator extracts chromatic variations with spatial support that is less than $B$, associated with high saturation regions lying within achromatic regions and with regions of varying hue within saturated regions:

$$\rho_B^C(f) = [f_S(\mathbf{x}) \times \rho_B^\circ(f_H)(\mathbf{x})] \vee \rho_B^+(f_S)(\mathbf{x}) \qquad [1.18]$$

where "$\times$" represents pixel-by-pixel multiplication of the values of the two functions and where $\vee$ is the pixel-by-pixel supremum.

*White achromatic top-hat.* This is used to characterize variations within bright regions of spatial support smaller than $B$ (i.e. regions of the image that are smaller than $B$ having a high intensity) and variations within achromatic regions on a chromatic background (i.e. non-saturated regions smaller than $B$):

$$\rho_B^{A+}(f)(\mathbf{x}) = |\rho_B^\uparrow(f)(\mathbf{x}) - \rho_B^C(f)(\mathbf{x})| \qquad [1.19]$$

where $\rho_B^\uparrow(f)(\mathbf{x}) = \rho_B^+(f_I)(\mathbf{x}) \vee \rho_B^-(f_S)(\mathbf{x})$ gives bright global variations.

*Black achromatic top-hat.* In an equivalent manner, this extracts variations within dark regions of spatial support smaller than $B$ (or regions of the image that are smaller than $B$ and have a low luminous intensity) and variations within achromatic regions on a chromatic background:

$$\rho_B^{A-}(f) = |\rho_B^{\downarrow}(f) - \rho_B^C(f)| \qquad [1.20]$$

where $\rho_B^{\downarrow}(f)(\mathbf{x}) = \rho_B^-(f_I)(\mathbf{x}) \vee \rho_B^-(f_S)(\mathbf{x})$ gives dark global variations. The term $\rho_B^-(f_S)$ appears both in $\rho_B^{\uparrow}(f)$ and in $\rho_B^{\downarrow}(f)$ to obtain symmetric definitions.

Figure 1.6 compares chromatic and achromatic top-hats and shows that for certain highly chromatic images, the result of $\rho_B^C$ is invariant under hue rotations and is more robust to noise than $\rho_B^{A+}$. The examples in Figure 1.7 illustrate the practical uses of color top-hats in the HSI space for the differential extraction of chromatic/achromatic details in cartographical images.

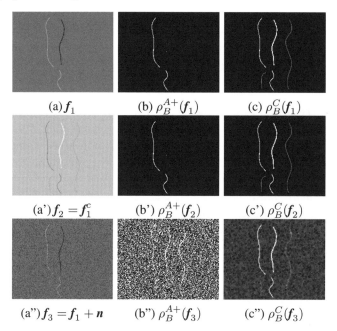

(a)$f_1$    (b) $\rho_B^{A+}(f_1)$    (c) $\rho_B^C(f_1)$

(a')$f_2 = f_1^c$    (b') $\rho_B^{A+}(f_2)$    (c') $\rho_B^C(f_2)$

(a")$f_3 = f_1 + n$    (b") $\rho_B^{A+}(f_3)$    (c") $\rho_B^C(f_3)$

**Figure 1.6.** *Comparison of achromatic $\rho_B^{A+}$ and chromatic $\rho_B^C$ top-hats for the extraction of spatial variations of smaller extent that the structuring element B in a strongly chromatic image $f_1$ (first row), the corresponding image following hue rotation $f_2$ (second row) and following addition of Gaussian color noise $f_3$ independently to each color component (third row). The structuring element B is a $5 \times 5$ pixel square. (For a color version of this figure, see www.iste.co.uk/fernandez/colorimag.zip)*

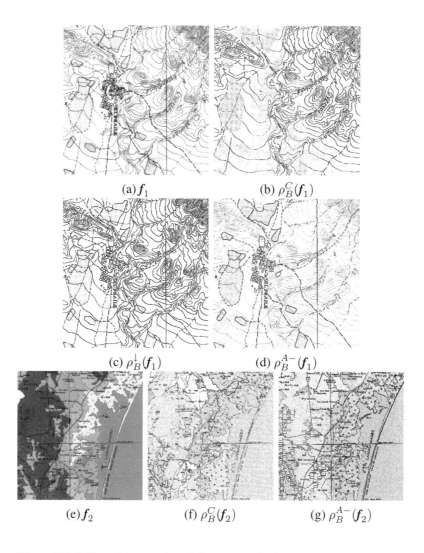

(a) $f_1$

(b) $\rho_B^C(f_1)$

(c) $\rho_B^{\downarrow}(f_1)$

(d) $\rho_B^{A-}(f_1)$

(e) $f_2$

(f) $\rho_B^C(f_2)$

(g) $\rho_B^{A-}(f_2)$

**Figure 1.7.** *Differential extraction of chromatic and achromatic details (structures with spatial support smaller than B) in cartographical images using chromatic and achromatic top-hat transforms. The structuring element B is a $5 \times 5$ pixel square. The top-hat images are shown in negative form for easy visualization*

This marginal combination of operators is entirely pertinent for the residues since the associated images are numerical functions and therefore there is no problem of false colors. Similar operators can be defined in the HSI space or in alternative color representations where the information associated with the different components is well separated and easy to interpret.

### 1.4.2. *Full ordering using lexicographical cascades*

The concept of ordering by lexicographical cascades belongs in the family of conditional ordering, according to the classical taxonomy of Barnett [BAR 76]. The approach is based on assigning priorities to the various components in the ordering of the vectors [SER 92].

If we consider a color point in the generic color space UVW or $\mathbf{c}_k = (c_k^U, c_k^V, c_k^W)$, and if we assume that the relative importance of these components can be written as: $U > V > W$, where $k$ is simply an index, the color point $\mathbf{c}_i$ is smaller than the point $\mathbf{c}_j$ according to the total lexicographical order $\Omega_{UVW}^{lex}$ if the following relation is satisfied:

$$\mathbf{c}_i \leq_{\Omega_{UVW}^{lex}} \mathbf{c}_j \Leftrightarrow \begin{cases} c_i^U < c_j^U \text{ or} \\ c_i^U = c_j^U \text{ and } c_i^V < c_j^V \text{ or} \\ c_i^U = c_j^U \text{ and } c_i^V = c_j^V \text{ and } c_i^W \leq c_j^W \end{cases} \qquad [1.21]$$

The total order $\Omega_{UVW}^{lex}$ can also be defined as follows: $\mathbf{c}_i \leq_{\Omega^{lex}} \mathbf{c}_j$ if, and only if, in the difference vector $\mathbf{c}_i - \mathbf{c}_j \in \mathbb{Z}^3$ the first value on the left that is different from zero is positive. It can be seen that all permutations of the three components produce valid total orderings, and it is also clearly not necessary to always use the same direction for each marginal ordering that the cascade is formed from; for example the second condition $\mathbf{c}_i \leq_{\Omega^{lex}} \mathbf{c}_j$ since $c_i^U = c_j^U$ and $c_i^V > c_j^V$, which will be written as $\Omega_{U-VW}^{lex}$.

In most cases, the comparison between two vectors will be determined uniquely by the first condition in the lexicographical cascade, i.e. by the first color component $U$. The second component is only considered when $c_i^U = c_j^U$. Different variants can be used to more finely weight the relative importance of the components, while preserving the principle of total ordering [APT 08b]. One simple approach involves linearly reducing the variation in the first component to reduce the probability of encountering equality in the first condition, thus ascribing a slightly greater importance to the second component [ANG 05]. In practice, the first component is divided into integer values, $c_i^U \in \mathcal{V}_{[v_{min},v_{max}]}$, using the constant $\alpha \in \mathbb{R}_+$, $\alpha > 1$, in other words:

$$c_i^U|_\alpha = \left\lceil \frac{c_i^U}{\alpha} \right\rceil$$

so that the number of levels is reduced for $c_i^U|_\alpha \in \mathcal{V}_{[v_{min}/\alpha,v_{max}/\alpha]}$. The associated vector ordering, written $\Omega_{U|_\alpha VW}^{lex}$ is known as the lexicographical order modulo $\alpha$. This is not a total ordering since for two points $\mathbf{c}_i \neq \mathbf{c}_j$ we may have $c_i^U|_\alpha = c_j^U|_\alpha$, $c_i^V = c_j^V$ and $c_i^W = c_j^W$. To complete the definition of the ordering, a fourth condition is required in the lexicographical cascade to ensure that $c_i^U < c_j^U$. We note that orderings produced by bit interlacing [CHA 98] and its variants correspond to lexicographical orderings modulo values that are powers of two of the divisor components. It is also possible to use more complex weighting models for the different components [APT 08b], taking into account the properties of the color space under consideration, and even spatial information.

Once the total color order has been formulated, the morphological operators can be generalized in a natural manner. In particular, dilation and erosion of a color image $f \in \mathcal{F}(E, \mathcal{V}^{its})$, using the order $\Omega$ and with a structuring element of the form $B \subset E$, are defined respectively by:

$$\delta_{\Omega,B}(f)(\mathbf{x}) = \{f(\mathbf{y}) : f(\mathbf{y}) = \vee_\Omega [f(\mathbf{z})] \, \mathbf{z} \in B_\mathbf{x}\} \qquad [1.22]$$

and:

$$\varepsilon_{\Omega,B}(f)(\mathbf{x}) = \{f(\mathbf{y}) : f(\mathbf{y}) = \wedge_\Omega [f(\mathbf{z})] , \mathbf{z} \in B_\mathbf{x}\} \qquad [1.23]$$

where $\vee_\Omega$ and $\wedge_\Omega$ are the *supremum* and the *infimum* respectively, with respect to the ordering $\Omega$, and where $B_\mathbf{x}$ is the structuring element centered on pixel $\mathbf{x}$. Thus, in a similar manner, we can also extend more powerful operators such as geodesic transformations, for example, opening by reconstruction [VIN 93] for a reference image $f$ and a marker image $\mathbf{m}$, $\gamma_\Omega^{rec}(f, \mathbf{m})$.

The ordering family $\Omega_{U|_\alpha VW}^{lex}$ is of limited interest for the RGB color space since it is difficult to assign a priority to one of the red, green, or blue components with respect to the others. Conversely, this family is particularly suitable when used in the HSI color space (see examples shown in Figures 1.8 and 1.9).

*Priority assigned to intensity*: $\Omega_{I|_\alpha S-(H \div h_0)}^{lex}$. This order acts on colors in terms of their luminance, making the assumption that bright and saturated colors have larger values. The hue is ordered based on the distance from one or more origins $h_0$ (see previous section), and is assigned to the third level to minimize its importance. In certain treatments, a reversal of order for saturation $\Omega_{I|_\alpha -S-(H \div h_0)}^{lex}$ is more useful for acting specifically on bright or dark, but unsaturated, colors.

*Priority assigned to saturation*: $\Omega_{S|_\alpha I-(H \div h_0)}^{lex}$. The most saturated colors (or alternatively, those with a higher intensity) have larger values, since hue plays a minimal role.

*Priority assigned to hue*: the direct approach involves constructing a lexicographical ordering with, at the first level, the hue order based on the distance from one or more chosen origins, i.e. $\Omega_{-(H \div h_0)|_\alpha SI}^{lex}$. However, this order rarely yields interesting results. The hue is too noisy in the case of low saturation. These two components of chrominance should not be treated independently. One solution to this problem involves modifying the hue as a function of saturation (ordering $\Omega_{-(h \div h_0)_{sat-weight}|_\alpha SI}^{lex}$). This adjustment may either involve a change in position of the hue on the unit circle as a function of the saturation and the chosen origin [ANG 03a, HAN 01a], or defining a chromatic origin $(s_0, h_0)$ (typically $s_0 = v_{max}$) and using this to compute a hue-saturation angular distance for $(s_i, h_i)$ and $(s_j, h_j)$ from $(s_0, h_0)$. In this case, the colors with the greatest values are those with a (saturated) hue that is closest to $h_0$, with the intensity playing a minimal role in this case. This can nevertheless be used in conjunction with saturation to define the importance that should be ascribed to the different reference hues [APT 09].

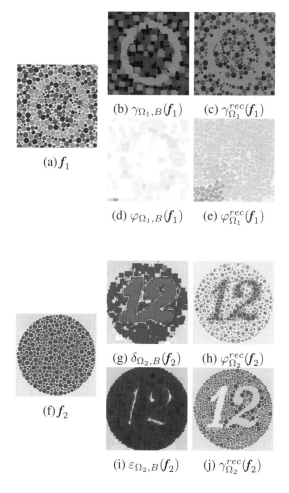

**Figure 1.8.** *Examples of color opening/closing by reconstruction on Ishihara test images. First column: original images* $\mathbf{f}_1$ *and* $\mathbf{f}_2$*; second column: marker images; and third column: images reconstructed by opening or closing. The HSI lexicographical orderings are* $\Omega_1 = \Omega^{lex}_{I|_{\alpha=10}S-(H\div h_0)}$*,* $h_0 = 0\circ$*; and* $\Omega_2 = \Omega^{lex}_{S|_{\alpha=10}I-(H\div h_0)}$*,* $h_0 = 0\circ$*. The structuring element B is a* $15 \times 15$ *pixel square. (For a color version of this figure, see www.iste.co.uk/fernandez/colorimag.zip)*

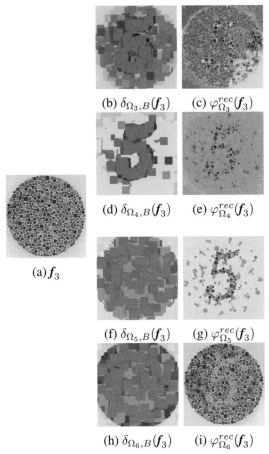

(b) $\delta_{\Omega_3,B}(\boldsymbol{f}_3)$     (c) $\varphi^{rec}_{\Omega_3}(\boldsymbol{f}_3)$

(d) $\delta_{\Omega_4,B}(\boldsymbol{f}_3)$     (e) $\varphi^{rec}_{\Omega_4}(\boldsymbol{f}_3)$

(a) $\boldsymbol{f}_3$

(f) $\delta_{\Omega_5,B}(\boldsymbol{f}_3)$     (g) $\varphi^{rec}_{\Omega_5}(\boldsymbol{f}_3)$

(h) $\delta_{\Omega_6,B}(\boldsymbol{f}_3)$     (i) $\varphi^{rec}_{\Omega_6}(\boldsymbol{f}_3)$

**Figure 1.9.** *Examples of color opening/closing by reconstruction on Ishihara test images. First column: original images $\boldsymbol{f}_3l$; second column: marked images (dilation); and third column: images reconstructed by closing. The HSI lexicographical orderings are $\Omega_3 = \Omega^{lex}_{-(H \div h_0)SI}$, $h_0 = 0.26$ (green, closer to yellow than to red); $\Omega_4 = \Omega^{lex}_{-(H \div h_0)_{sat-weight}SI}$, $h_0 = 0.26$; $\Omega_5 = \Omega^{lex}_{-(H \div h_0)_{sat-weight}SI}$, $h_0 = 0.14$ (yellow, closer to red and orange than to green); $\Omega_6 = \Omega^{lex}_{-(H \div h_0)_{sat-weight}SI}$, $h_0 = 0.07$ (orange, closer to red and yellow than to green). The structuring element $B$ is a $25 \times 25$ pixel square. (For a color version of this figure, see www.iste.co.uk/fernandez/colorimag.zip)*

## 1.5. Morphological color segmentation in the HSI space

Segmentation of color images is a very large subject, with a wide range of different methodologies and algorithms. The interested reader can find an excellent state-of-the-art in Chapter 5 of this work. In this section, we will give consideration to a number of segmentation techniques for images represented in the HSI space, based around the concepts of mathematical morphology.

### 1.5.1. *Color distances and segmentation by connective criteria*

#### 1.5.1.1. *Basic concepts*

1.5.1.1.1. Color distances

Let $\mathbf{c}_k = (c_k^U, c_k^V, c_k^W)$ be a color vector in a color space $UVW$. We can define the color distance between two vectors in terms of the norm $\|\mathbf{c}_i - \mathbf{c}_j\|_\Delta^{UVW}$ in the color space $UVW$. A norm $\mathcal{L}_2$ is commonly used to compare two different colors:

$$\|\mathbf{c}_i - \mathbf{c}_j\|_2^{UVW} = \sqrt{\left(c_i^U - c_j^U\right)^2 + \left(c_i^V - c_j^V\right)^2 + \left(c_i^W - c_j^W\right)^2}$$

When considering a HSI type color space, the standard norm $\mathcal{L}_2$ is not particularly suitable due to the definition of hue over a unit circle, as discussed in section 1.3. Thus, any color distance in an HSI space should make use of this angular difference. However, hues are unstable for low-saturation colors and it is preferable to weight the hues by saturation [ANG 05, APT 09, CAR 94, HAN 01a]. This results in the following $\mathcal{L}_1$ and $\mathcal{L}_2$ norms in the HSI space:

$$\|\mathbf{c}_i - \mathbf{c}_j\|_1^{HSI} = \left|c_i^I - c_j^I\right| + \frac{(c_i^S + c_j^S)}{2}\left|c_i^H \div c_j^H\right| + \left|c_i^S - c_j^S\right| \quad [1.24]$$

$$\|\mathbf{c}_i - \mathbf{c}_j\|_2^{ITS} = \sqrt{\left(c_i^I - c_j^I\right)^2 + 2c_i^S c_j^S \cos\left(c_i^H \div c_j^H\right) + \left(c_i^S\right)^2 + \left(c_j^S\right)^2}$$

$$[1.25]$$

1.5.1.1.2. Connective criteria

Serra introduced the concept of connective criteria for segmentation [SER 06]. This concept can be used to divide an image into different regions based on a particular criterion. Whatever the chosen connective criterion, it is always possible to divide an image into regions that satisfy that criterion.

DEFINITION 1.1.– *A criterion* $\sigma\colon \mathcal{F} \times \mathcal{P}(E) \rightarrow [0,1]$ *is a connective criterion when, for any image* $f \in \mathcal{F}(E,\mathcal{V})$, *the sets* $A$ *such that* $\sigma(f,A) = 1$ *form a connection, i.e.:*

*– when $\sigma$ is satisfied over the class $S$ of singletons and the empty set:*
$\forall f \in \mathcal{F}, x \in S \Rightarrow \sigma[f\{x\},\emptyset] = 1$;

*– when for all functions* $f \in \mathcal{F}$ *and for all families of partitions* $\{A_i\} \in \mathcal{P}(E)$ *for which the criterion $\sigma$ is satisfied, we have* $\cap A_i \neq 0$ *and* $\wedge \sigma[f, A_i] = 1 \Rightarrow \sigma[f, \cup A_i] = 1$.

To put it another way, when a connective criterion $S$ is satisfied by an image $f$ over a family $\{A_i\}$ of spatial regions, if all these regions have a point in common, then, the connective criterion is also satisfied for $\cup A_i$.

In what follows, we will describe three useful connective criteria and discuss their use for color image segmentation.

### 1.5.1.2. *Quasi-flat zones*

The flat zones of an image $f$ are the maximal connected components with constant [SAL 92]. Since this criterion is highly restrictive, Meyer proposed to extend this concept to quasi-flat zones [MEY 98], which are the maximal connected components whose internal variation does not exceed a given threshold $\lambda$.

DEFINITION 1.2.– *Two pixels* $\mathbf{x}_p$ *and* $\mathbf{x}_q$ *from a color image* $f \in \mathcal{F}(E,\mathcal{V}^{its})$ *belong to the same quasi-flat zone of $f$ if there exists a path* $(\mathbf{x}_{p_1}, \cdots, \mathbf{x}_{p_n})$ *between these two points such that* $p_1 = p$, $p_n = q$, *and* $\forall i \in [1,n[, \|f(\mathbf{x}_{p_i}) - f(\mathbf{x}_{p_{i+1}})\|_\Delta \leq \lambda$.

### 1.5.1.3. *Homogeneous zones*

The concept of homogeneous zones [LEZ 06, MEU 07, MEU 10] is a connective criterion for morphological segmentation of vector images, which is a variation of path-based connections (watersheds) and threshold-based connections (quasi-flat zones). A homogeneous region is defined as follows.

DEFINITION 1.3.– *Two points $\mathbf{x}_p$ and $\mathbf{x}_q$ belong to the same homogeneous zone of an image* $f \in \mathcal{F}(E, \mathcal{V}^{hsi})$ *if* $\|f(\mathbf{x}_p) - f(\mathbf{x}_q)\| \le k \times \Psi(Seed(\mathbf{x}_p))$, *where* $Seed(\mathbf{x}_p)$ *is the seed pixel for the region containing* $\mathbf{x}_p$ *and* $\Psi(\mathbf{x}_p) = \frac{1}{|V(\mathbf{x}_p)|} \sum\limits_{\mathbf{x}_{p_v} \in V(\mathbf{x}_p)} \|f(\mathbf{x}_p) - f(\mathbf{x}_{p_v})\|_\Delta$.

$f(\mathbf{x}_p)$ represents the color of pixel $\mathbf{x}_p$; $V(\mathbf{x}_p)$ represents the set of neighbors of the point $\mathbf{x}_p$; $\| \cdot \|_\Delta$ is a norm $\mathcal{L}_\Delta$; and $k$ is a real number representing the coarseness of the resulting partition. Homogeneous regions produce non-embedded partitions (a non-stratified hierarchy). To construct a stratified hierarchy, the principle of inclusion must be respected. For this, the homogeneous regions can be redefined in terms of a region adjacency graph.

DEFINITION 1.4.– *Two nodes $v_i$ and $v_j$ of a graph $G$ belong to the same homogeneous region if* $\|f(v_i) - f(v_j)\|_\Delta \le k' \times \Psi(Seed(v_i))$ *where* $Seed(v_i)$ *is the seed node for the region containing* $v_i$ *and* $\Psi(v) = \frac{1}{\delta(v)} \sum\limits_{u \sim v} \|f(v) - f(u)\|_\Delta$.

$f(v)$ is the mean color vector computed from the initial partition, $v \sim u$ is the set of nodes $v$ that are neighbors of $u$, and $\delta(v) = |v \sim u|$ is the degree of node $v$.

Figure 1.10 shows a number of levels of a stratified hierarchy of partitions based on three connective criteria with a norm $\Delta = \mathcal{L}_2$ in the HSI space: quasi-flat zones ($\lambda \in \{1, 5, 10\}$), homogeneous stratified zones ($k = 1$, and $k' \in \{2, 3, 4\}$). [MEU 10] investigated the influence of the color space on these three connective criteria, and the HSI representation was found to be particularly well suited.

### 1.5.1.4. *Jump connections*

Both the connective segmentation criteria we have just considered make use of the vector nature of the HSI space, since they are based on a global color distance. Alternatively, by using a chromatic/achromatic information separation in the HSI space, it is possible to segment each

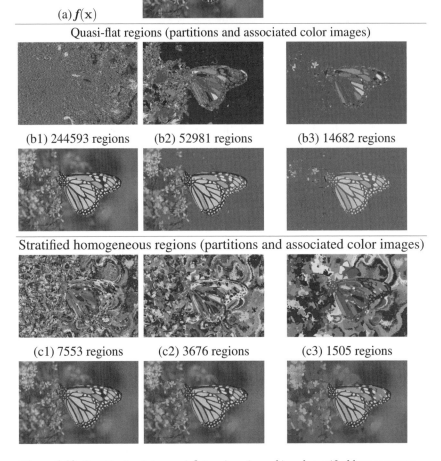

**Figure 1.10.** *Partitioning into quasi-flat regions (rows b) and stratified homogeneous regions (rows c). For each type of partition, the first row shows the partition and the second the associated color image. The original image is shown in (a). The partitions were obtained in a HSI space*

variable separately and then to come up with a method for combining the marginal partitions. This color approach is based on a formalization of the psycho-visual approach taken for segmentation by the human eye, based on variations in hue within saturated regions and intensity variations within poorly-saturated regions. The principle is as follows:

– the luminous intensity, hue, and saturation are segmented individually;

– the intensity and hue partitions are combined with the help of the saturation. This is used to locally select either the intensity or the hue as the relevant class for use in the segmentation.

From the range of possible segmentation methods, we propose to segment the $f_I(\mathbf{x})$ and $f_H(\mathbf{x})$ components (after defining a hue origin $h_0$) using the jump connection criterion [SER 06].

DEFINITION 1.5.– *A jump connection $A_{k,a}^{jump-area}(f)$, with jump parameter $k$ and area $a$, results in the following segmentation of the scalar image $f \in \mathcal{F}(E,V)$. All points $\mathbf{x}$ are placed into the same partition class if $f(\mathbf{x})$ differs by less than $k$ from one extremum. These classes are drawn from the image plane $E$, and the process is iterated until the space $E$ has been fully partitioned. Those regions with an area of less than $a$ pixels are eliminated by region fusion.*

Then, to combine the two resultant partitions, the saturation image must be reduced to a set $X_S$ containing the highly-saturated pixels, the hue partition restricted to $X_S$, and the intensity partition to $X_S^c$. Finally, these two results are fused. More specifically, one class of the synthetic partition is either the intersection of one class of the intensity partition with the low-saturation region $X_S^c$, or the intersection of one class of the hue partition with the high-saturation set $X_s$. If $A_{k,a}^{jump-area}(f_I)(\mathbf{x})$, $A_{k,a}^{jump-area}(f_H)(\mathbf{x})$, and $A_{HSI}^{jump-area}(f)(\mathbf{x})$ represent the intensity and hue classes, and the color synthesis class at a point $\mathbf{x}$, it follows that:

$$A_{HSI}^{jump-area}(f)(\mathbf{x}) = \begin{cases} A_{k,a}^{jump-area}(f_I)(\mathbf{x}) \cap X_S^c & \text{if} \quad \mathbf{x} \in X_S^c \\ A_{k,a}^{jump-area}(f_H)(\mathbf{x}) \cap X_S & \text{if} \quad \mathbf{x} \in X_S \end{cases} \quad [1.26]$$

Of course, the simplest procedure for determining the set $X_S$ involves thresholding the saturation to some particular level $u$: $X_S = Th_u(f_S)$. However, this type of selection does not offer any control over the shape of the set $X_S$, risking a result that is irregular, containing holes, small isolated regions, etc. It is preferable to work on a smoothed image or, since we are interested in partitions, on a mosaic saturation image. We use for saturation the same algorithm of segmentation as for the intensity and hue, to obtain $A_{k,a}^{jump-area}(f_S)(\mathbf{x})$. Each class is then set to the mean saturation value of its pixels to obtain $f_S^{mosaic}$. An optimal automatic thresholding algorithm applied to the histogram can be used to obtain the optimum value of the achromatic/chromatic separation to be used for each image. A complete example is shown in Figure 1.11.

(a) $f$

(b) $f_I$    (c) $f_H$    (d) $f_S$

(d) $A_{k=20,a=50}^{jump-area}(f_I)$    (e) $A_{k=20,a=50}^{jump-area}(f_H)$    (f) $f_S^{mosaic}$

(g) $X_S = Th_{u=35}$    (h) $A_{HSI}^{jump-area}(f)$    (i) Edges of $A_{HSI}^{jump-area}(f)$

**Figure 1.11.** *Segmentation of an image $f$ by using the saturation $f_S$ to select from intensity (achromatic) partitions $f_I$ and hue (chromatic) partitions $f_H$. The marginal partitions $A_{k,a}^{jump-area}$ are obtained using a mix involving jump connections of range $k$ and fusion of regions of sizes smaller than a pixels. (For a color version of this figure, see www.iste.co.uk/fernandez/colorimag.zip)*

It should be noted that this method is not easily generalizable to other color representations, since it is the specific role of saturation that makes it possible to easily combine the chromatic and achromatic partitions. Note also that the jump connection method cannot be applied directly to a vector image, since this approach is based on the extraction of regional *extrema* within the image.

### 1.5.2. *Color gradients and watershed segmentation*

Watershed segmentation is a fundamental morphological tool for image segmentation [BEU 92]. The watershed concept is closely linked to that of the regional *minimum* and catchment basins. Consider the relief of the numerical function $g(\mathbf{x}) \in \mathcal{F}(E, \mathcal{V})$ when subjected to rainfall. Let $M$ be a regional *minimum* of $g$. The catchment basin associated with $M$, written as $CB(M)$, is a set of points $\mathbf{x}$ such that a drop of water falling onto $\mathbf{x}$ eventually reaches the bottom of the valley associated with $M$. The $CB$ can be used to associate a portion of the image with each local *minimum*: the valley associated with it. The set of catchment basins associated with each regional *minimum* defines a partitioning of the image into disjoint regions. Since the criterion that "all points of $A$ are flooded from the same *minimum*" is a connective criterion, the watershed segments the space over which $E$ is defined into catchment basins connected by arcs, along with a set of pointwise connected components representing the watersheds themselves.

The watershed is not generally calculated from the original image, but rather from its gradient; or, to be more specific, the modulus of its gradient. It should be noted that in mathematical morphology, the concept of gradient always implies a scalar function. In this way, the watershed represents peaks in gradient surrounding regional *minima*, i.e. zones of high intensity in the gradient which are associated with the edges in the initial function. Evidently, strong transition regions are associated with boundaries or contours of homogeneous regions within the image. By definition, the number of regions is equal to the number of regional *minima* in the gradient image, and this corresponds to the number of areas with constant levels in the original image. Since realistic photographic images contain a large number of gradients *minima*, the result is an over-segmentation. To avoid this problem, the idea is to apply the watershed algorithm to a smaller number of *minima*, associated with only the most significant regions. The simplest method of doing this involves interactively introducing markers for these regions of interest. Hierarchical approaches also exist based on the watershed algorithm, and these can be used to process regions in which the choice of marker is not obvious, as is often the case in images of real-world scenery, video-surveillance images, etc. We choose to draw attention to three such approaches, which are: (1) the waterfall algorithm [BEU 94], which from one level of the hierarchy to the next, eliminates those contours that are completely surrounded by stronger contours; (2) hierarchies based on extinction values, and especially volume-based criteria [MEY 01, VAC 95], which combine the size and the contrast of a given region to produce a good criterion for evaluating the visual significance of regions; (3) approaches that use learning or random sampling for marker extraction [ANG 07b, DER 10, HAN 09, LEF 09, LEZ 02].

Whatever approach is used, if the watershed algorithm is to be applied to an image, then we must first determine its gradient. The classical definition of the morphological gradient of a scalar function $f \in \mathcal{F}(E, \mathcal{V})$ is given by the following scalar function:

$$\varrho(f)(\mathbf{x}) = \delta_B(f)(\mathbf{x}) - \varepsilon_B(f)(\mathbf{x}) = \{\vee[f(\mathbf{z})], \mathbf{z} \in B_{\mathbf{x}}\} - \{\wedge[f(\mathbf{z})], \mathbf{z} \in B_{\mathbf{x}}\}$$

(where $B$ is a structuring element of unit size (typically a $3 \times 3$ pixel square)).

When $\mathbf{f} \in \mathcal{F}(E, \mathcal{V}^{hsi})$ is a color image, the color gradient (once again, taking a modulus-based view) can be formulated in a number of different ways [ANG 03b]. Here, we will give a number of alternative definitions for the morphological gradient of a color image $f = (f_I, f_H, f_S)$ in the HSI space:

– intensity gradient: information associated with luminous intensity transitions, i.e.:

$$\varrho_I(\boldsymbol{f})(\mathbf{x}) = \varrho(f_I)(\mathbf{x}) \qquad\qquad [1.27]$$

– hue gradient: circular centered version of the morphological gradient, rewritten in terms of increments, i.e.:

$$\varrho_H(f)(\mathbf{x}) = \vee[(f_H(\mathbf{x}) \div f_H(\mathbf{y})), \mathbf{y} \in B_\mathbf{x}] \qquad [1.28]$$

– chromatic gradient: the use of hue alone leads to errors in achromatic regions due to their low saturation, and so it is useful to weight the hue gradient by the saturation, such that:

$$\varrho_{HS}(f)(\mathbf{x}) = f_S(\mathbf{x}) \times \varrho_H(f)(\mathbf{x}) \qquad [1.29]$$

– achromatic gradient: this is the intensity gradient in highly achromatic regions and for chromatic/achromatic transitions:

$$\varrho_{IS}(f)(\mathbf{x}) = (1 - f_S(\mathbf{x})) \times \varrho(f_I)(\mathbf{x}) + \varrho(f_S)(\mathbf{x}) \qquad [1.30]$$

– supremum-based color gradient: the pixel-by-pixel maximum of the gradient of each component is the easiest method (although a non-selective method) of obtaining global color information, i.e.:

$$\varrho_\vee(f)(\mathbf{x}) = \vee[\varrho(f_I)(\mathbf{x}), \varrho_H(f)(\mathbf{x}), \varrho(f_S)(\mathbf{x})] \qquad [1.31]$$

– saturation-weighted color gradient: barycentric combination of the intensity and hue gradients according to the achromatic or chromatic nature of the region, as follows:

$$\varrho_{wS}(f)(\mathbf{x}) = f_S(\mathbf{x}) \times \varrho_H(f)(\mathbf{x}) + (1 - f_S(\mathbf{x})) \times \varrho(f_I)(\mathbf{x}) \qquad [1.32]$$

– full color gradient: the aforementioned gradient is combined with the saturation gradient to take better account of chromatic/achromatic transitions:

$$\varrho_{HSI}(f)(\mathbf{x}) = \varrho_{wS}(f)(\mathbf{x}) + \varrho(f_S)(\mathbf{x}) \qquad [1.33]$$

– norm-based color distance gradient $\mathcal{L}_\Delta$: rather than using a combination of marginal color component gradients, a vector version of the morphological gradient allows for the use of an arbitrary color metric to obtain the color gradient:

$$\varrho_{\mathcal{L}_\Delta}(f)(\mathbf{x}) = \vee[\|f(\mathbf{x}) - f(\mathbf{y})\|_\Delta, \mathbf{y} \in B_\mathbf{x}] - \wedge[\|f(\mathbf{x}) - f(\mathbf{y})\|_\Delta, \mathbf{y} \in B_\mathbf{x}]$$

$$[1.34]$$

Other gradients have also been proposed using an approach independent of the color space being used [LEZ 05, LEZ 07, LEZ 08]; however, the advantage of those based around the HSI space is their interpretation in terms of different types of segmented regions and also in terms of invariance properties with respect to variations in hue, saturation, and intensity.

Figure 1.12 illustrates these different morphological gradients for a color image.

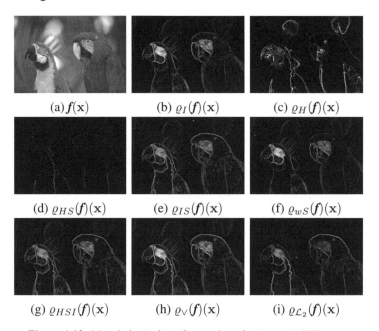

(a) $f(\mathbf{x})$    (b) $\varrho_I(f)(\mathbf{x})$    (c) $\varrho_H(f)(\mathbf{x})$

(d) $\varrho_{HS}(f)(\mathbf{x})$    (e) $\varrho_{IS}(f)(\mathbf{x})$    (f) $\varrho_{wS}(f)(\mathbf{x})$

(g) $\varrho_{HSI}(f)(\mathbf{x})$    (h) $\varrho_\vee(f)(\mathbf{x})$    (i) $\varrho_{\mathcal{L}_2}(f)(\mathbf{x})$

**Figure 1.12.** *Morphological gradients of a color image in HSI space*

A watershed algorithm can be built upon any of these different morphological gradients. Figure 1.13 shows such a comparison of different segmentations obtained using a watershed algorithm starting from markers on the gradients shown in Figure 1.12. We observe that depending on the HSI variables that are used, the different choices of gradient will reveal contours associated either with intensity variations or with hue or general color gradients. Particular gradient definitions are more suitable for different segmentation applications where only one type of region (for example highly chromatic regions) is required from the segmentation. For applications where global image segmentation is required, independent of the nature of the image, empirical studies of their performances for a range of images representative of the algorithm must be used to choose between the different gradient definitions. In general terms, systematic studies such as [ANG 03a] reveal that the gradients $\varrho_{wS}(f)(\mathbf{x})$ and $\varrho_{HSI}(f)(\mathbf{x})$ tend to lead to the best results. This shows the importance of taking into account the information supplied by each one of the components of the HSI color representation if a good segmentation is to be achieved.

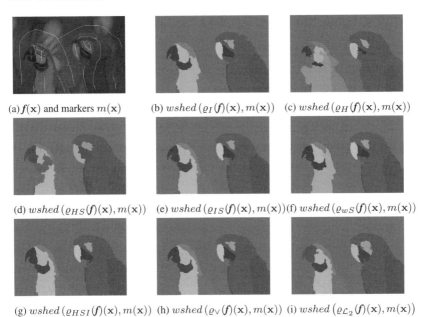

(a) $f(\mathbf{x})$ and markers $m(\mathbf{x})$    (b) $wshed\,(\varrho_I(f)(\mathbf{x}),m(\mathbf{x}))$    (c) $wshed\,(\varrho_H(f)(\mathbf{x}),m(\mathbf{x}))$

(d) $wshed\,(\varrho_{HS}(f)(\mathbf{x}),m(\mathbf{x}))$    (e) $wshed\,(\varrho_{IS}(f)(\mathbf{x}),m(\mathbf{x}))$ (f) $wshed\,(\varrho_{wS}(f)(\mathbf{x}),m(\mathbf{x}))$

(g) $wshed\,(\varrho_{HSI}(f)(\mathbf{x}),m(\mathbf{x}))$ (h) $wshed\,(\varrho_\vee(f)(\mathbf{x}),m(\mathbf{x}))$ (i) $wshed\,(\varrho_{\mathcal{L}_2}(f)(\mathbf{x}),m(\mathbf{x}))$

**Figure 1.13.** *Watersheds for a color image, based on markers added to the initial image, using different definitions of the morphological color gradient in HSI space*

## 1.6. Conclusion

The representation of color images in polar HSI spaces is closely related to the interpretation of color in the human brain. In addition, from a mathematical point of view, this space produces colorimetric variables that are particularly suited to digital processing of color images.

Drawing on these two observations, this chapter has discussed a series of nonlinear methods for image filtering and color segmentation that act upon images represented in polar HSI coordinates.

Our aim has been to demonstrate that the appropriate use of all three HSI components improves the performance of image processing when compared to the use of luminance alone. Moreover, manipulation of the chromatic part, i.e. the hue/saturation pair, requires methods that are adapted to the space they are defined over; in particular, the hue channel is a rich source of information provided that it is defined and manipulated appropriately over the unit circle. In addition, saturation plays a very specific role in mediating the relative influences of luminous intensity and hue.

The operators and algorithms studied in this chapter stem largely from mathematical morphology. Through them, we have illustrated the different ways of generalizing morphological operators based on the concepts of the *supremum* and *infimum* to the specific case of the HSI color space; however, we have also discussed color gradient operators and color top-hats in the HSI space, which do not require any concept of ordering. Similarly, we have shown that color segmentation can be treated in the context of mathematical morphology, either using concepts of color connections in HSI, or directly through the watershed transformation as applied to color gradients.

In terms of the more general problem of color segmentation, Chapter 5 in this work deals in detail with non-morphological segmentation methods. The reader may also refer to Chapter 4 where a similar approach is taken (although this time an entirely linear one) for the analysis of color textures in HSI spaces.

## 1.7. Bibliography

[ANG 03a] ANGULO J., Morphologie mathématique et indexation d'images couleur. Application à la microscopie en biomédecine, PhD thesis, Centre de Morphologie Mathématique, Ecole des Mines de Paris, 2003.

[ANG 03b] ANGULO J., SERRA J., "Color segmentation by ordered mergings", *Proceedings of IEEE International Conference on Image Processing (ICIP '03)*, vol. 2, p. 125-128, 2003.

[ANG 05] ANGULO J., "Unified morphological color processing framework in a lum/sat/hue representation", *Proceedings of International Symposium on Mathematical Morphology (ISMM '05)*, p. 387-396, Kluwer Academic Publishers, 2005.

[ANG 07a] ANGULO J., "Morphological colour operators in totally ordered lattices based on distances, application to image filtering, enhancement and analysis", *Computer Vision and Image Understanding*, vol. 107, p. 56-73, 2007.

[ANG 07b] ANGULO J., JEULIN D., "Stochastic watershed segmentation", *Proceedings of 8th International Symposium on Mathematical Morphology (ISMM '07)*, p. 265-276, 2007.

[ANG 07c] ANGULO J., SERRA J., "Modelling and segmentation of colour images in polar representations", *Image and Vision Computing*, vol. 25, p. 475-495, 2007.

[APT 07] APTOULA E., LEFÈVRE S., "A comparative study on multivariate mathematical morphology", *Pattern Recognition*, vol. 40, p. 2914-2929, 2007.

[APT 08a] APTOULA E., Analyse d'Images Couleur par Morphologie Mathématique. Application à la Description, l'Annotation, et la Recherche d'Images – Colour Image Analysis with Mathematical Morphology, Application to Image Description, Annotation, and Retrieval, PhD thesis, University Louis Pasteur, Strasbourg, France, 2008.

[APT 08b] APTOULA E., LEFÈVRE S., "On lexicographical ordering in multivariate mathematical morphology", *Pattern Recognition Letters*, vol. 29, no. 2, p. 109-118, February, 2008.

[APT 09] APTOULA E., LEFÈVRE S., "On the morphological processing of hue", *Image and Vision Computing*, vol. 27, p. 1394-1401, 2009.

[BAR 76] BARNETT V., "The ordering of multivariate data", *Journal of the Royal Statistical Society A*, vol. 139, p. 318-354, 1976.

[BEU 92] BEUCHER S., MEYER F., "The morphological approach to segmentation: the watershed transformation", DEKKER M., DOUGHERTY E. (eds), *Mathematical Morphology in Image Processing*, p. 433-481, 1992.

[BEU 94] BEUCHER S. "Watershed, hierarchical segmentation and waterfall algorithm", *Mathematical Morphology and its Applications to Image and Signal Processing (Proceedings of ISMM '94)*, p. 69-76, Kluwer Academic Publishers, 1994.

[CAR 94] CARRON T., LAMBERT P., "Color edge detector using jointly Hue, Saturation and Intensity", *Proceedings of IEEE International Conference on Image Processing (ICIP '94)*, p. 977-981, 1994.

[CAR 95]  CARRON T., Segmentations d'images couleur dans la base Teinte Luminance Saturation : approche numérique et symbolique, PhD thesis, University of Savoie, 1995.

[CHA 98]  CHANUSSOT J., LAMBERT P., "Total ordering based on space filling curves for multivalued morphology", HEIJMANS H.J.A.M., ROERDINK J.B.T.M. (eds), *Mathematical Morphology and its Applications to Image and Signal Processing (Proceedings of ISMM '98)*, p. 51-58, Kluwer Academic Publishers, 1998.

[DER 10]  DERIVAUX S., FORESTIER G., WEMMERT C., LEFÈVRE S., "Supervised segmentation using machine learning and evolutionary computation", *Pattern Recognition Letters*, vol. 31, no. 15, p. 2364-2374, November, 2010.

[FIS 93]  FISHER N., *Statistical Analysis of Circular Data*, Cambridge University Press, 1993.

[HAN 01a]  HANBURY A., SERRA J., "Mathematical morphology in the HLS colour space", COOTES T., TAYLOR C. (eds), *12th British Machine Vision Conference*, Manchester, UK, p. 451-460, December, 2001.

[HAN 01b]  HANBURY A., SERRA J., "Morphological operators on the unit circle", *IEEE Transactions on Image Processing*, vol. 10, p. 1842-1850, 2001.

[HAN 02]  HANBURY A., SERRA J., "Mathematical morphology in the CIELAB space", *Image Analysis and Stereology*, vol. 21, no. 3, p. 201-206, March, 2002.

[HAN 03a]  HANBURY A., "Circular statistics for colour images", *8th Computer Vision Winter Workshop*, Valtice, Czech Republic, February, 2003.

[HAN 03b]  HANBURY A., SERRA J., "Colour image analysis in 3D-polar coordinates", *Proceedings of DAGM Symposium*, vol. LNCS 2781, p. 124-131, Springer, 2003.

[HAN 09]  HANBURY A., MARCOTEGUI B., "Morphological segmentation on learned boundaries", *Image and Vision Computing*, vol. 4, no. 27, p. 480-488, 2009.

[LEF 09]  LEFÈVRE S., "Segmentation par ligne de partage des eaux avec marqueurs spatiaux et spectraux", *Colloque GRETSI sur le Traitement du Signal et des Images*, 2009.

[LEV 93]  LEVKOVITZ H., HERMAN G., "GLHS: a generalized lightness, hue and saturation color model", *Graphical Models and Image Processing*, vol. 55, p. 271-285, 1993.

[LEZ 02]  LEZORAY O., CARDOT H., "Cooperation of color pixel classification schemes and color watershed: a study for microscopical images", *IEEE Transactions on Image Processing*, vol. 11, p. 783-789, 2002.

[LEZ 05]  LEZORAY O., MEURIE C., ELMOATAZ A., "A graph approach to color mathematical morphology", *ISSPIT (IEEE International Symposium on Signal Processing and Information Technology)*, p. 856-861, 2005.

[LEZ 06]  LEZORAY O., MEURIE C., BELHOMME P., ELMOATAZ A., "Multi-scale image segmentation in a hierarchy of partitions", *EUSIPCO (European Signal Processing Conference)*, CD Proceedings, 2006.

[LEZ 07]  LEZORAY O., MEURIE C., ELMOATAZ A., "Mathematical morphology in any color space", *IAPR International Conference on Image Analysis and Processing, Computational Color Imaging Workshop*, IEEE Computer Society, p. 183-187, 2007.

[LEZ 08]  LEZORAY O., MEURIE C., ELMOATAZ A., "Graph-based ordering scheme for color image filtering", *International Journal of Image and Graphics*, vol. 8, no. 3, p. 473-493, July, 2008.

[MEU 07]  MEURIE C., LEZORAY O., "A new method of morphological hierarchical segmentation", *VIE (IEEE and IET Visual Information Engineering)*, 2007.

[MEU 10]  MEURIE C., LEZORAY O., KHOUDOUR L., ELMOATAZ A., "Morphological hierarchical segmentation and color spaces", *International Journal of Imaging Systems and Technology*, vol. 20, no. 2, p. 167-178, 2010.

[MEY 98]  MEYER F., "From connected operators to levelings", *Mathematical Morphology and its Applications to Image and Signal Processing*, p. 191-199, 1998.

[MEY 01]  MEYER F., "An overview of morphological segmentation", *International Journal of Pattern Recognition and Artificial Intelligence*, vol. 15, p. 1089-1118, 2001.

[MUN 69]  MUNSELL A., *A Grammar of Color*, Van Nostrand-Reinhold, 1969.

[PET 97]  PETERS A., "Mathematical morphology for angle-valued images", *Proceedings of SPIE, Nonlinear Image Processing VIII*, vol. 3026, p. 84-94, April, 1997.

[POY 03]  POYNTON C., *Digital Video and HDTV, Algorithms and Interfaces*, Morgan Kaufmann Publishers, 2003.

[SAL 92]  SALEMBIER P., SERRA J., "Morphological multiscale image segmentation", *SPIE Visual Communications and Image Processing*, p. 620-631, 1992.

[SER 88]  SERRA J., *Vol I: Image Analysis and Mathematical Morphology, Vol II: Theoretical Advances*, Academic Press, 1982,1988.

[SER 92]  SERRA J., "Anamorphoses and function lattices (multivalued morphology)", DOUGHERTY E. (ed.), *Mathematical Morphology in Image Processing*, Marcel-Dekker, p. 483-523, 1992.

[SER 02]  SERRA J., Espaces couleur et traitement d'images, Rapport Technique CMM-Ecole des Mines de Paris, N-34/02/MM, 2002.

[SER 06]  SERRA J., "A lattice approach to image segmentation", *Journal of Mathematical Imaging and Vision*, vol. 24, no. 1, p. 80-130, 2006.

[SHI 95]  SHIH T.-Y., "The reversibility of six geometric color spaces", *Photogrammetric Engineering & Remote Sensing*, vol. 61, p. 1223-1232, 1995.

[SOI 99]  SOILLE P., *Morphological Image Analysis*, Springer-Verlag, 1999.

[TRE 04]  TREMEAU A., FERNANDEZ-MALOIGNE C., BONTON P., *Image numérique couleur - De l'acquisition au traitement*, Wiley, 2004.

[VAC 95]  VACHIER C., MEYER F., "Extinction value: a new measurement of persistence", *IEEE Workshop on Nonlinear Signal and Image Processing*, p. 254-257, 1995.

[VIN 93]  VINCENT L., "Morphological grayscale reconstruction in image analysis: applications and efficient algorithms", *IEEE Transactions on Image Processing*, vol. 2, no. 2, p. 176-201, 1993.

Chapter 2

# Adaptive Median Color Filtering

## 2.1. Introduction

Filtering an image involves the removal of non-pertinent or corrupted information. In this way, a filtering operation aims to remove the noise present in an image, which is why it is sometimes referred to as denoising. A range of techniques have been set up for filtering grayscale images. Most of these are developments from the field of signal processing and are extensions to the 2D of techniques developed for 1D signals. Color image filtering presents the challenge of computing the filtered value from a set of pixels described by their spatial coordinates and color (generally represented as a triplet of values) [BAR 76, PLA 97]. However, the different color components are correlated, and this is especially true in the RGB (red-green-blue) space as commonly used for data acquisition and display on a screen. Several approaches can be used to deal with this correlation, such as the Karhunen-Loeve transform [PIT 90]. However, this correlation means that a marginal approach is not appropriate [AST 90] and leads to artifacts (such as false colors) that degrade the image quality. After introducing the various forms of noise and their origins, this chapter will discuss a selection of

Chapter written by Frédérique ROBERT-INACIO and Eric DINET.

vector methods that can be used to handle these color vectors in a global manner, as well as spatially adaptive filters which have the additional property of determining the most appropriate size of filtering window. In this chapter, we will give a brief summary of a range of implementations of the median filter. Different approaches exist to determine *a priori* if a pixel is noisy. They can be based on deterministic methods or they can make use of fuzzy logic. In addition, the size of the filtering window can be determined in a range of different ways: by combining several filters that are attenuated as a function of distance from the pixel being filtered, by making use of gradient information, determining statistically the homogeneity of the neighborhood of the pixel being filtered, etc. We will then present a generic method for spatially adaptive filtering, in which the most appropriate size of filtering window with respect to the context of the current pixel is determined for each pixel of the image individually. In other words, this window should make use of as much information as possible while preserving the important data within the image. In most cases, the aim is to retain as much contour and color difference information as possible. The filters, whether linear or nonlinear, produce an output image $I_{out}$ by combining neighboring parts or values or the input image $I_{in}$. The filtering window used for pixel $x = P(i, j)$, with color vector $c = c(i, j)$ is written as $W_x$ or $W_x(i, j)$.

## 2.2. Noise

Noise is a common phenomenon within images. It consists of a layer of parasitic information that introduces random perturbations to the digitally acquired scene, altering or adding in details to the data. For example, during acquisition of color images in digital photography, noise is particularly prominent in dimly lit regions or uniform areas. This results in both a loss of sharpness in the details and a degradation of homogeneous regions.

Noise can affect color images in many ways. Chrominance noise is visible in the form of random color blotches, whereas luminance noise results in darker or brighter pixels, which give the image a granular feel.

**2.2.1.** *Sources of noise*

There are many different sources of noise. Some of these are closely linked with the sensor; others with the process of image acquisition; and still others are associated with the signal processing phase where the output signal from the sensor is transformed into an image that can be visualized. The influence of noise on an image depends on the acquisition parameters: illumination level of the scene, ISO sensitivity, temperature, etc. For further details, the reader may refer to Chapters 4 and 5 of the book *Digital Color Imagery* [FER 12].

*2.2.1.1. Sensor noise*

Generally speaking, this type of noise is introduced during the transformation of the luminous signal into an electrical signal. It takes the form of electronic noise and photon noise, which takes the form of temporal variations in the output signal which has its origin in the discrete nature of photons and electrons. There are many different sources of noise, and some of these can be specific to the technology used. In the interests of clarity, we will only mention the most commonly encountered types of noise that have the most significant impact on color images. The interested reader may refer to the following publication for more details: [MAI 03, TRE 04].

*Thermal noise* or Johnson-Nyquist noise is generated by the natural thermal motion of electrons. The level of this motion increases with temperature, leading to a dark current. This noise is proportional to the square root of the number of electrons produced through thermal agitation in the absence of any external illumination. It is therefore independent of the number of photons hitting the photosite. Finally, dark current is not spatially uniform. There are several methods of reducing this noise: sensor cooling, inclusion of an infrared filter, mean dark current subtractions, or hot pixel removal.

*Salt and pepper noise* is impulse noise that reveals itself through the presence of white or black pixels distributed randomly over the image. It stems from failures of certain elements within the sensor, through data transmission errors, or the presence of dust on the sensor surface.

As sensitivity characteristics of photoreceptors vary slightly in terms of their quantum efficiency as a function of fill factor, the non-uniformity of photoreceptors response introduces noise. This *fixed pattern noise* has an amplitude that is proportional to the illuminating light level.

Shot noise or *quantum noise* is photon noise produced when the number of incident photons is sufficiently low for its statistical variation to be visible. This photon distribution is modeled as a Poisson process. Thus the number of photons arriving on the photoreceptor has a dispersion around a mean value $\lambda = I.A.T$ ($I$: intensity of light source, $A$: photoreceptor area, $T$: integration time), with a standard deviation $\sigma = \sqrt{\lambda}$. There is no physical way of eliminating this noise since it is intrinsic to the quantized nature of light.

*Read noise* is produced by the electronic components prior to digitization. This noise is thermal in origin, and arises from the structure of the output amplifier. The greater the amplification of the symbol (by changing the ISO sensitivity for example), the more significant this noise becomes. It is independent of the number of incident photons.

### 2.2.1.2. *Noise in the image acquisition process*

This noise source is due to the projection of the light signal onto a photosensitive surface via a lens system. During this phase, geometric distortions may be introduced, especially around the edges of the sensor, as well as chromatic aberrations, blurring or vignetting. We have included this type of acquisition error under the umbrella term noise, even though it is not strictly a form of noise, since it degrades the image quality. However, it is not random, but completely predictable. We will not therefore consider it in the course of this chapter.

### 2.2.1.3. *Signal processing noise*

*Quantization noise* or analog/digital conversion noise is a nonlinear process. Each photoreceptor sends an analog signal as output, which must be transformed into the closest digital level taken from a finite set of discrete values. This approximation leads to signal quantization noise. This quantization noise follows a uniform distribution, with a maximum value that depends on the quantization size. It can be made negligible by increasing the number of bits used to encode the quantized values.

### 2.2.2. *Noise modeling*

In theoretical terms, the easiest-to-use hypotheses, and hence the most commonly used ones, are that noise is additive, with a mean value of zero, independent of the value being measured. Noise is considered to be a stationary and ergodic phenomenon. It is thus characterized by a power density, a variance, and an autocorrelation function. In practice, noise is different for every pixel. It is therefore very difficult to determine a universal model. Strictly speaking, the noise model must be tailored to each individual sensor and the image acquisition conditions, but in general terms, the full range of noise associated with the sensor is modeled in terms of additive, white, stationary, Gaussian noise.

So, if $A$ is the image to be acquired, containing the useful information, and $b$ is a random field representing the noise, the image $I$ to be processed can be considered as the result of:

– an addition: $I = A + b$, in which case the noise is said to be additive;

– a product: $I = A \times b$, in which case the noise is said to be multiplicative;

– a convolution: $I = A * b$, in which case the noise is said to be convolutive.

To model the most common forms of noise, the associated probability densities used have the form:

$$f(c) = C exp\left(-K |c|^{\alpha}\right) \qquad [2.1]$$

where $C$, $K$, and $\alpha$ are constants and $c$ represents the intensity measured by the photoreceptor. For example:

– $\alpha = 1$: exponential noise;

– $\alpha = 2$: Gaussian noise;

– $\alpha \to \infty$: uniform noise.

### 2.2.2.1. *Impulse noise*

Impulse noise is characterized by a probability density $f$ representing the probability that an image pixel will be noisy. The impulsive characteristic of this noise is associated with the appearance of aberrant values that represent a significant departure from the range of values found within a given range of the pixel being filtered. Whatever its origins, this type of noise generally affects an RGB color image by randomly and independently modifying one of the three channels.

### 2.2.2.2. Gaussian noise

Equation [2.2] gives the probability density for the normal distribution with a mean of $\mu$ and a standard deviation of $\sigma$, and this can be used to model Gaussian noise. When $\mu = 0$, we have additive white Gaussian noise:

$$f(c) = \frac{1}{\sigma\sqrt{2\pi}} exp\left(-\frac{1}{2}\left(\frac{c-\mu}{\sigma}\right)^2\right) \qquad [2.2]$$

For a given luminous intensity interval in the scene, the Gaussian model is justified [FAR 06] even if the photon transfer calibration curve for a CCD technology indicates that the dominant noise (thermal noise and photon noise) follows a Poisson distribution.

### 2.2.2.3. Poisson noise

The arrival of photons on the photoreceptor follows a Poisson distribution, and the probability of detecting $n$ photons when on average $N$ would be expected is given by the following equation:

$$p(n) = \frac{N^n e^{-N}}{n!} \qquad [2.3]$$

which represents a Poisson distribution with mean $N$ and standard deviation $\sqrt{N}$. However, for large values of $N$, $p(n)$ is of the order of $exp\left(-\frac{(n-N)^2}{2N}\right)$, which represents a Gaussian distribution of mean $N$ and standard deviation $\sqrt{N}$. This, therefore, justifies the approximation of the noise model in terms of Gaussian white noise.

In the following section, we will discuss a range of nonlinear filter models used for noise removal.

## 2.3. Nonlinear filtering

In multi-spectral image processing, and more specifically in color image processing, a vector approach is generally considered more appropriate than marginal methods. This is due to the correlation present between the different channels. In vector approaches, each pixel is associated with an $n$-dimensional vector, where $n$ is the number of channels (three in the case of color images). The characteristic quantities of these vectors, such as their direction or norm, are then considered. Such an approach is used to perform processing operations as varied as noise removal, contour detection, or segmentation. The majority of vector filtering methods require a function to be defined that will be minimized. This function can be used to quantify the error resulting from substituting the vector of the current pixel with a vector close to the pixel being filtered. Minimizing this function therefore involves minimizing the error between the pixel under consideration and its neighbors, and can thus be used to eliminate any noisy vectors.

The median filter is one of the most commonly used filters. The main reason for the success of the median filter is due to two of its intrinsic properties: contour preservation and its ability to remove impulse noise [HOD 85, KOS 01]. A range of approaches have been presented in the literature, some iterative [AST 90] and some recursive [ABB 99]. The main difficulty in implementing a median filter in a given color space lies in defining a total ordering relationship over the elements of the filtering window [BAR 76]. Several vector solutions have been proposed [AST 90, KHR 99] to introduce partial order over a set of color vectors, along with more or less effective solutions used to define a total ordering relationship over the entire color space, such as through the use of bit mixing [CHA 98].

In this section, the filtering window $W_x$ under consideration is a square window of fixed size $s$ (with $s$ odd), centered on $x$. Let $\{x_1, ..., x_N\}_{W_x}$ be the set of $N = s^2$ pixels contained within the sliding window $W_x$ with color vectors $\{c_1, ..., c_N\}_{W_x}$. Moreover, since the pixels are numbered in terms of their scan order, $x = x_{\frac{N+1}{2}}$.

### 2.3.1. *Vector methods*

In next three sections, we will discuss three different median color filters [LUK 05]. These are vector filters, i.e. the color components for each pixel are considered together as vectors, as opposed to considering them separately and marginally.

#### 2.3.1.1. *Vector median filter (VMF)*

A distance measure $D_i$ is associated with each vector $c_i$:

$$D_i = \sum_{j=1}^{N} ||c_i - c_j||_L \qquad\qquad [2.4]$$

for $i = 1...N$, where $||c_i - c_j||_L$ is the distance separating $c_i$ and $c_j$ according to the $L$-norm. The filtered value after passing through this basic vector median filter $VMF(W_x)$ is then defined by:

$$I_{out}(x) = VMF(W_x) = c_M \qquad\qquad [2.5]$$

where $c_M$ is the vector such that $D_M = min_{i=1...N}D_i$.

The result of filtering using a window with a fixed size equal to 3 for the $L_2$ norm is shown in Figure 2.5f.

#### 2.3.1.2. *Directional median filter*

An angular measure $A_i$ is now associated with each vector $c_i$ [TRA 93, TRA 96, LUK 05]:

$$A_i = \sum_{j=1}^{N} \alpha(c_i, c_j) \qquad\qquad [2.6]$$

for $i = 1..N$, where $\alpha(c_i, c_j)$ is the scalar value (obtained using $cos^{-1}$ for example), representing the angle between $c_i$ and $c_j$. The value filtered using this basic directional median filter $BVDF(W_x)$ is then given by:

$$I_{out}(x) = BVDF(W_x) = c_M \qquad\qquad [2.7]$$

where $c_M$ is the vector such that $A_M = min_{i=1..N}A_i$.

The result of filtering using a window with a fixed size equal to 3 is shown in Figure 2.5g.

### 2.3.1.3. *Directional-distance filter (DDF)*

A scalar value $\Omega_i$ mixing angular and distance measures is associated with each vector $c_i$:

$$\Omega_i = D_i^{\,1-\omega}.A_i^{\omega} \qquad\qquad\qquad [2.8]$$

for $i = 1...N$. Then:

$$\Omega_i = \left( \sum_{j=1}^{N} ||c_i - c_j||_L \right)^{1-\omega} . \left( \sum_{j=1}^{N} \alpha(c_i, c_j) \right)^{\omega} \qquad [2.9]$$

where $\omega$ is a real value between 0 and 1 whose role is to control the relative influence of $D_i$ and $A_i$ in the equation. The value filtered by this directional-distance filter $DDF(W_x)$ is then given by:

$$I_{out}(x) = DDF(W_x) = c_M \qquad\qquad\qquad [2.10]$$

where $c_M$ is the vector such that $\Omega_M = min_{i=1...N}\Omega_i$.

The result of filtering using a window with a fixed size of 3 for the $L_2$ norm and with $\omega = 0.5$ is shown in Figure 2.5h.

### 2.3.1.4. *Equality*

For each of the three filters discussed above, the color vectors are sorted based on a criterion involving the norm and/or the angle, and it can be anticipated that equalities may be encountered during evaluation of this criterion. These correspond to color vectors that are considered equivalent in terms of this criterion. Thus the choice of one or the other of these vectors is not obvious. It follows that the choice is generally determined by the scan path. In other words, the value ($D_i$, $A_i$, or $\Omega_i$) associated with the criterion can be used to order the color vectors, with those whose values are equal being arranged in the order in which they are encountered. Thus, color vectors equivalent to $c_M$ lie just before or after $c_M$ in the order that is defined.

### 2.3.1.5. *Comparison of vector methods*

The vector median filter (see section 2.3.1.1) is particularly effective in the face of impulse noise, since it is largely concerned with intensity-based criteria, whereas the directional median filter (see section 2.3.1.2) is a spherical estimator that is good at preserving the chromaticity of color vectors. The directional-distance filter (see section 2.3.1.3) is a combination of the first two filters, and it combines the advantages of those two filters. In all three cases, the examples shown in Figure 2.5f, g, h, have been computed using the smallest possible filtering window, to keep the filtering as light as possible. However, degradations are visible in all three cases. When the norm criterion is applied, the degradation tends to be *low frequency* (the image is more blurred), whereas the angular criterion tends to lead to *high frequency* degradation (introduction of erroneous detail). The combination of both of these (the $DDF$ filter) is a good compromise.

### 2.3.2. *Median filter using bit mixing*

Since there is no total ordering defined for vectors within a color space, bit mixing is a method that can be used to sort the content of a window $W_x$ [LAM 00]. This method is different from the lexicographical order, but it still privileges one of the color components over the others, although to a lesser extent. For each color vector $c_i$, let us consider the associated scalar value $k_i$. For example, if $c_i$ is a vector in the RGB space represented as three eight-bit values, $k_i$ is a 24-bits integer as defined in Figure 2.1 [CHA 98]. The most strongly weighted bit of the resultant integer represents the privileged color component. Thus in Figure 2.1, it is the red component that is the dominant one.

The values of $k_i$ are sorted in this way, and the resultant value $BMF(W_x)$ filtered using bit mixing is defined as:

$$I_{out}(x) = BMF(W_x) = c_M \qquad [2.11]$$

where $c_M$ is the color vector corresponding to $k_{\frac{N+1}{2}}$.

The median filter can then be implemented since the total order required to sort the color vectors is determined through the use of bit mixing. The filtered value is then the color vector corresponding to the 24-bit median value. The result of filtering using a window with a fixed size equal to 3 is shown in Figure 2.5e. This filter will tend to blur the image. Note that the total order established through bit mixing can also be used to implement morphological filters such as dilation and erosion applied to color images.

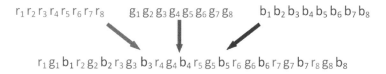

**Figure 2.1.** *Basic concept of bit mixing*

## 2.4. Median filter: methods derived from vector methods

### 2.4.1. *Vector filtering*

The vector methods discussed in section 2.3.1, based on local image statistics, are widely recognized for their efficiency in eliminating impulse noise. However, they are applied blindly to each pixel within the image, without any *a priori* information on whether the current pixel is noisy or not. For this reason, such filters have a tendency to soften contours and reduce the level of detail, thus degrading the image quality. Moreover, these methods may prove very expensive in terms of computation time. Integration of fuzzy logic into the filtering process opens up the possibility of providing complementary information that can influence the result of this processing, thereby reducing the processing time.

Let $W_x$ be a square window of odd size $s$ centered on $x$, the pixel to be filtered. The $N$ color vector present in this window is indexed from $1$ to $N$ by scan order: $W_x = \{c_1(x), c_2(x), \ldots, c_N(x)\}$. The color vector for the pixel $x$ to be filtered is therefore $c_{\frac{N+1}{2}}$.

2.4.1.1. *Fast Similarity-based Vector Filter: FSVF*

Let $\mu$ be a measure of similarity:

$$\mu: S_c \times S_c \to \mathbb{R} \qquad\qquad [2.12]$$

that evaluates the degree of similarity between two color vectors from $S_c$ (generally the RGB color space) using the norm $\|.\|_L$.

Let $\mu_L$ be the function defined over $[0; +\infty[$ and such that:

$$\mu_L(\|c_1 - c_2\|_L) = \mu(c_1, c_2) \qquad [2.13]$$

where $c_1$ and $c_2$ are two color vectors from $S_c$. $L$ is generally chosen to be equal to 1 or 2. The properties of $\mu_L$ are as follows:

1) $\mu_L$ is non-increasing and convex over $[0; +\infty[$;

2) $\mu_L(0) = 1$;

3) $lim_{t \to \infty} \mu_L(t) = 0$.

$\mu$ must give a value equal to 1 when two pixels are the same color, and must tend to 0 when the pixels are very different colors. For example, we could consider the function $\mu_L$ defined by:

$$\mu_L(t) = \begin{cases} 1 - t/h & \text{if} \quad t \le h \\ 0 & \text{if not} \end{cases} \qquad [2.14]$$

where $t$ is a real, positive variable and $h$ is a real, positive number. $h$ can be used to parameterize the strength of the filter and as $h$ tends to 0, we recover the vector median filter.

To define the cumulative sums of the similarity values for pixel $x = x_{\frac{N+1}{2}}$, it is useful to re-index the pixels by swapping the numbers 1 and $\frac{N+1}{2}$:

$$M_1 = \sum_{j=2}^{N} \mu(c_1, c_j) \qquad [2.15]$$

$$M_k = \sum_{j=2, j \neq k}^{N} \mu(c_k, c_j) \qquad [2.16]$$

Thus, the degree of similarity between the color vectors associated with pixels $x_k$ and the color vector of $x_1$ is not taken into account in the cumulative sums $M_k$ for $k = 2 \ldots N$. The pixel $x_1$ is then only replaced by one of the pixels $x_k$ if it is really noisy, i.e. if $M_1 < M_k$ for $k = 2 \ldots N$. In this case, the color vector $c_1$ of the central pixel $x = x_1$ is replaced by the color vector $c_k$ that maximizes $M_k$.

### 2.4.1.2. *Center-weighted vector median filter: CWVM*

The center-weighted vector median filter [MA 07] is popular since it is good at preserving structures in color images due to its resaturation. It is defined as follows. The output of the $CWVM$ filter is given by:

$$I_{out}(x) = c_m \qquad\qquad [2.17]$$

where $m = argmin_{1 \leq i \leq N}\{R_i^k, \quad k \in [1, \frac{N-1}{2}]\}$ is the integer value defining the weighted value and:

$$R_i^k = (2k - 1)\left\|c_i - c_{\frac{N+1}{2}}\right\| + \sum_{j=1, j \neq \frac{N+1}{2}}^{N} \|c_j - c_i\| \qquad [2.18]$$

$k$ can be used to weight the influence of the central pixel relative to its neighbors. When $k = 1$, this filter is equivalent to the vector median filter ($VMF$).

### 2.4.2. *Switching vector and peer group filters*

Many variants of *switching filters* exist. These are intended to eliminate impulse noise. Their general approach is based on identification of impulse noise [CAM 08, MOR 08]. For example, it is possible to perform an analysis of the neighborhood of the pixel to be filtered, thereby determining a family of pixels with common color characteristics. All that is then required is to analyze the central pixel to determine its degree of membership to this family. Those pixels for which the degree of membership is low are considered to be noisy. In other words, a cluster is defined over the neighborhood of the pixel being filtered. The degree of membership of a pixel to this *cluster* is estimated to have a higher or lower value regarding the similarity degree between this pixel (color vector) and the cluster features. In the case of switching filters, a color vector identified as noisy will be replaced by an alternative color vector from its nearby neighborhood.

Thus, a peer group filter can be defined by considering the difference between the peer group for a pixel and the peer groups of its neighbors, to establish a detection rule. Let $h > 0$ and let $C$ be the set associated with a pixel $x$ of the color vector $c_x$ in a color space $X$:

$$C(x, h) = \{c_y \in X, \|c_x - c_y\| \le h\} \tag{2.19}$$

$C(x, h)$ is the sphere with center $c_x$ and radius $h$ in the vector color space. Over the filtering window $W_x$ centered around $x$, the peer group associated with $x$ is defined as:

$$P(x, h) = \{y \in W_x, c_y \in C(x, h)\} \tag{2.20}$$

where $c_y$ is the color vector associated with pixel $y$.

When using peer groups for the filters discussed above, it is important to ensure that they contain a minimum number of pixels $m$. A peer group will therefore be considered valid for a value $m$ if it contains at least $m + 1$ pixels. It will then be written as $P_m(x, h)$. Note that any peer group contains at least one pixel, $x$, irrespective of the value of $h$. A pixel $x$ is thus considered to be noise-free to degree $m$ if the peer group $P(x, h)$ is valid for the chosen value of $m$, in other words if $P_m(x, h)$ exists. The parameter $m$ defines the performance of the filter, since it controls the number of elements in a peer group. Thus, small values of $m$ will conserve the original characteristics of the image better, but the filter will not be very effective. It is therefore important to seek a compromise between suppression of impulse noise and preservation of fine structure within the image.

### 2.4.2.1. *Peer group filter: PGF*

Using such peer groups, pixels are divided into two categories: noisy pixels and noise-free pixels. This classification is achieved in two iterations. The first iteration is used to separate noisy pixels from those that either *are not* or *may be* noisy, by considering the existence or otherwise of a peer group $P_m(x, h)$ with cardinality at least equal to $m$. If this exists, the pixel is not noisy and the pixels belonging to $W_x$ whose color vector does not belong to $C(x, h)$ are indeterminate. If the peer group does not exist, the pixel is noisy and all other pixels of $W_x$ are indeterminate.

The second stage can be used to determine which of the indeterminate pixels have a peer group that corresponds to noise-free pixels. In this case, the indeterminate pixel becomes a noise-free pixel, while if the opposite is true then it is declared to be noisy. For noise-free pixels, it is clear that pixels belonging to their peer group are also noise-free. This observation can be used to improve the filter performance in terms of processing time. The final stage involves replacing noisy pixels with a pixel from their peer group $W_x$ either by using the $VMF$ filter or by computing the arithmetic mean ($AMF$) of the vectors in $W_x$.

### 2.4.2.2. *Iterative peer group switching vector filter: IPGSVF*

This filter is said to be iterative since it acts in a manner broadly similar to $PGF$ filters, but the phase in which indeterminate pixels are classified is repeated several times. The algorithm is as follows:

**for all** pixel $x_i$ **do**
   **if** $\exists P_m(x_i, d)$ **then**
      $x_i$ is not noisy
   **else**
      $x_i$ is indeterminate
   **end if**
**end for**
**repeat**
   **for all** indeterminate pixels $x_i$ **do**
      **if** $\exists P_m(x_i, d) \subset W'_x$ **then**
         $x_i$ is not noisy
      **else**
         $x_i$ is indeterminate
      **end if**
   **end for**
**until** there are no new noise-free pixels
**for all** indeterminate pixels **do**
   pixel is noisy
**end for**

$W'_x$ represents the set of noise-free pixels in $W_x$.

### 2.4.3. *Hybrid switching vector filter*

The $VMF$ and $BVDF$ filters consider either an angular criterion or a distance criterion to determine the color of the pixel being filtered (see section 2.3.1.5). The hybrid switching vector filter [DAN 08, TSA 99] mixes the properties of both these filters to isolate noisy filters. The first stage of the processing involves the use of a direction-based noise detector and then the second stage, where the actual filtering takes place, consists of a directional and modular filter. Let $W_x$ be a square filtering window of odd dimension $n$ centered on $x$. The following function can be used to estimate the angle between two color vectors $c_1$ and $c_2$ associated with two pixels $x_1$ and $x_2$ (see section 2.3.1.2):

$$\alpha(c_1, c_2) = cos^{-1}\left(\frac{\|c_1.c_2\|}{\|c_1\| \times \|c_2\|}\right) \qquad [2.21]$$

The quantity $\delta(x_i) = \sum_{x_j \in W_x} \alpha(c_i, c_j)$ can be used to detect the presence of noise. The larger $\delta(x_i)$ is, the greater the probability that $x_i$ is noisy. Therefore all we need to do to determine whether a pixel is noisy or not is to apply a threshold to the values of $\delta(x_i)$.

In this way, the filtering process is applied only to those pixels marked as noisy. The first stage involves implementing a $BVDF$ filter (see section 2.3.1.3). The resultant median color vector is written as $c_\theta$. The second stage uses a $VMF$ filter (see section 2.3.1.1), resulting in a color vector $c_m$. The color vector of the noisy pixel is then replaced by a color vector of modulus $|c_m|$ and with the same direction as $c_\theta$. In this way, the color of the central pixel is replaced by the closest possible color from among the other pixels contained within the filtering window $W_x$, in terms of both modulus and angle. On the other hand though, this filter technique has the disadvantage of introducing false colors (colors that are not necessarily present in the original image).

### 2.4.4. Fuzzy filters

Fuzzy metrics for pixel classification were introduced with the aim of improving the performance of certain types of filters. Such a pixel classification divides the pixels into three categories: noisy pixels, noise-free pixels, and indeterminate pixels (which may or may not be noisy). In the following sections, we will discuss the evolution of a number of filters from section 2.4, based on the introduction of a fuzzy metric.

2.4.4.1. *Fuzzy metric*

A fuzzy metric $M$ over a set $Y$ is defined over $Y \times Y$ and satisfies the following conditions:

1) $M(x, y, t) > 0$

2) $M(x, y, t) = 1$ if and only if $x = y$

3) $M(x, y, t) = M(y, x, t)$

4) $M(x, z, t) \geq M(x, y, t) * M(y, z, t)$

5) $M(x, y, .) : ]0, +\infty[ \rightarrow [0, 1]$ is continuous

where $*$ is a continuous $t-$norm. $M$ evaluates the proximity between $x$ and $y$, with $M(x, y, t)$ close to 0 when $x$ is far from $y$. $t$ is generally chosen to be equal to 1 or 2.

2.4.4.2. *FVF: fuzzy variant filter*

The fuzzy version of $FSVF$ (see section 2.4.1.1) is obtained by replacing both the norm $\|.\|_L$ and $\mu_L$ with the following fuzzy metric [MOR 05]:

$$M^\alpha(c_i, c_j) = \prod_{l=1}^{3} C^\alpha\left(c_i(l), c_j(l)\right) \qquad [2.22]$$

where $c_i$ and $c_j$ are color vectors with components $(c_i(1), c_i(2), c_i(3))^t$ and $(c_j(1), c_j(2), c_j(3))^t$, with:

$$C^\alpha(a, b) = \left(\frac{min\{a, b\} + K}{max\{a, b\} + K}\right)^\alpha, a, b \in [0, 255] \qquad [2.23]$$

for 24-bit RGB-encoded images.

The similarity measure $\mu_{fuzzy}$ is then defined as follows:

$$\mu_{fuzzy}(c_i, c_j) = M^\alpha(c_i, c_j) \qquad [2.24]$$

The parameters $K$ and $\alpha$ can be used to adjust the filter. The parameter $K$ influences the uniform character of the filter. The larger the value of $K$, the more non-uniform is the filter. The best value for most types of noise is $K = 2^{10}$. As $\alpha$ increases, the lower bound of the fuzzy metric decreases and the preponderance of the central pixel (the pixel being filtered) is reduced. Thus, $\alpha$ influences the strength of the filtering. The number of pixels replaced over the course of the filter operation is an increasing function of $\alpha$. The parameter $\alpha$ must therefore be larger in the case of noisier images.

### 2.4.4.3. *Fuzzy Rank-ordered Filter: FRF*

Consider a window $W_x$ of odd size $n$ centered on the pixel $x$ being filtered. $x$ is a pixel associated with a vector $c$ of three components in the RGB space. The color distances $d(c, c_i) = \|c - c_i\|$ are computed for every pixel $x_i$ that falls within the window centered on $x$. These distances are ordered in a sequence of increasing values of $r_j(x)$:

$$\forall j, k \in [1..n^2], j < k \Rightarrow r_j(x) \leq r_k(x)$$
$$r_1(x) = d(x, x) = 0 \qquad\qquad [2.25]$$
$$\forall j \in [1..n^2], \exists i \in [1..n^2], r_j(x) = d(c, c_i)$$

It then becomes possible to calculate for any positive integer value $m \leq n^2 - 1$, the following the rank-ordered difference (ROD):

$$ROD_m(x) = \sum_{j=1}^{m} r_j(x) \qquad\qquad [2.26]$$

$ROD_m(x)$ is the sum of the distances between $x$ and its $m$ nearest neighbors in terms of color. This value is assumed to be larger in the case of a noisy pixel than in the case of a noise-free pixel. Substituting in the $L_2$ norm for calculating the value using metric $M_\infty$:

$$M_\infty(x_i, x_j) = min_{l=1..3} \frac{min\{c_i(l), c_j(l)\}}{max\{c_i(l), c_j(l)\}} \qquad\qquad [2.27]$$

an increasing sequence of values $s_j(x)$ is defined for $M_\infty$, in the same way as the sequence $r_j(x)$ for the $L_2$ norm. The value $FROD_m(x)$:

$$FROD_m(x) = \prod_{j=1}^{m} s_j(x) \qquad\qquad [2.28]$$

can be used to determine the degree of similarity between $x$ and its $m$ closest neighbors in the sense of $M_\infty$. This quantity $FROD_m$ can be used to classify the pixels, dividing them *a priori* into three populations: noisy pixels, noise-free pixels, and those that it has not been possible to classify. The fuzzy $FRF$ filter [CAM 10] is then implemented by calculating this quantity $FROD_m$ once again for the indeterminate pixels, but this time excluding those pixels from its peer group that have already been marked as noisy. A further thresholding stage can then be used to decide if the pixels are noisy or not. Finally, those pixels classified as noisy during the first or the second classification phase are then replaced by the value obtained from a $VMF$ filter.

### 2.4.4.4. *CWVM: fuzzy version*

If we consider a filtering window $W_x$ consisting of $N$ pixels, centered on a pixel $x$ of color $c$, the output of the fuzzy $CWVM$ filter (see section 2.4.1.2) [MA 07] is given by:

$$I_{out}(x) = \frac{\sum_{i=1}^{N} (\mu(c, c_i).c_i)}{\sum_{i=1}^{N} (\mu(c, c_i))} \qquad [2.29]$$

where $\mu$ is the fuzzy function measuring the similarity between the two color vectors. Let $c_1$ and $c_2$ be two color vectors. The function $\mu$ may take one of several different forms. For example: $\mu_1(c_1, c_2) = exp\left(-\frac{\|c_1 - c_2\|^2}{2\sigma^2}\right)$, where $c_j(i)$, $j = 1, 2$, $i = 1...3$ are the components of the color vectors $c_1$ and $c_2$, and $\sigma$ is a parameter controlling the strength of the filter.

### 2.4.4.5. *Fuzzy modified peer group filter: FMPGF*

The following fuzzy metric (see section 2.4.4.2) is used to define the reference groups (see section 2.4.2.1) for two color vectors $c_i$ and $c_j$:

$$M(c_i, c_j) = \prod_{l=1..3} \frac{min\{c_i(l), c_j(l)\} + K}{max\{c_i(l), c_j(l)\}} + K \qquad [2.30]$$

Thus, a peer group over the filtering window $W_x$ is defined for all $x \in W_x$ as follows:

$$P(x, d) = \{x_j \in W_x, M(c, c_j) \geq d\} \qquad [2.31]$$

where $c$ and $c_j$ are the color vectors associated with $x$ and $x_j$, respectively.

$FMPGF$ filters are defined in the same way as $PGF$ filters, but using this fuzzy metric to determine the peer groups.

## 2.5. Adaptive filters

The main drawback of filtering methods that use a fixed-size reference window is that the content of the pixel being filtered is not taken into account [CIU 98, SMO 02]. In other words, those pixels that lie within homogeneous regions (i.e. ones that do not contain contour information) can be filtered using large windows, whereas filtering should be performed using windows of very limited size when close to contours to preserve as much detail as possible. In Figure 2.2, the yellow star represents a homogeneous region. The colored squares are examples of maximum-sized filtering windows centered on pixels within this homogeneous region and lying entirely within that region. The size of a filtering window thus depends on the distance of the pixel being filtered from the boundary of a homogeneous region.

**Figure 2.2.** *Homogeneous region (yellow) and filtering windows (shown in green, blue, and red). (For a color version of this figure, see www.iste.co.uk/fernandez/colorimag.zip)*

This is the motivation behind generic methods for determining a filtering window size in a context-adaptive manner. The generic method described in this section can be used in combination with the methods discussed earlier, enabling them to adapt to the individual characteristics of each image being filtered.

### 2.5.1. *Spatially adaptive filter: generic method*

To remove noise in an optimal manner, the size of the window should be adapted to suit its content and prevent the output image from blurring.

Implementation of a spatially adaptive filter takes place in three main stages [ROB 06]. The first stage involves extracting the information regions that should be preserved in the form of a binary image. These regions will not be filtered and will remain intact in the resultant image. We will refer to this operation as the *contour map*, since the information to be preserved is generally associated with the presence of contours in the original image. In the second stage, the size of the filtering window is computed for every pixel not belonging to the contour map. Thus, each region bounded by the contours is assimilated into a homogeneous region as defined by the contour map. Within such a region, the filtering window centered on a given pixel is chosen to be as large as possible, so that the filtering can be as strong as possible without damaging the regions that need to be preserved intact. Finally, once the size of the filtering window has been determined, all that remains is to apply a previously chosen filter method to produce the output image.

### 2.5.1.1. *Contour map*

Determination of the contour map is the first stage in calculating the size of the filtering window. This stage involves building up a binary image, which will then act as a mask during the size calculation of the filtering window. It serves to inject *a priori* information into the filtering stage. This additional information is similar to that added for fuzzy filters. Generally, this stage is based around detection of contours or significant color differences, since the resultant regions contain highly pertinent information [ROB 08]. However, any form of extraction of significant information, however that is defined, is acceptable for this stage, as discussed in section 2.5.2.

When the significant information takes the form of color differences (the norm of the difference between two color vectors), the contour map is computed using the algorithm developed in [DIN 07]. A map of color differences is computed based on the pixel abscissas ($X$ direction) by considering the current pixel $A$ and its right-hand neighbor $B$, and then a color difference based on the pixel ordinates ($Y$ direction) by considering the current pixel $A$ and its neighbor $C$ above it. In the same way as when computing the modulus of a gradient, the Euclidean norm of the difference between the color vectors is determined, making use of a particular norm ($L_2$, $L_\infty$, etc.). Figure 2.3 shows the pixels used for calculating this color difference map.

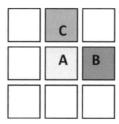

**Figure 2.3.** *Pixels neighboring A that are used to calculate the directional maps: A and B for the X map and A and C for the Y map*

The resultant map is then the thresholded to obtain a binary image. This binary image is the map of the information that must be preserved, representing the areas with the greatest color differences. The threshold value used for the calculation can be used to parameterize the filter as a function of image content.

### 2.5.1.2. *Adaptive-size filtering window*

At each contour pixel, the filtering window size is equal to one, i.e. the filtering window is reduced to just one pixel. For the other pixels, the half-size $k$ of the filtering window is given by the Chessboard distance map [BOR 86] calculated from the contour map:

$$n = 2.k + 1 \qquad [2.32]$$

### 2.5.2. *Spatially adaptive median filter*

To implement a spatially adaptive median filter, we must first calculate a contour image. Depending on the information that we want to preserve, this contour image may be determined based on color differences, color gradients, or some morphological operation such as a chromatic or achromatic top-hat [ANG 07, ROB 08]. Figure 2.4 shows the result of filtering for different methods of detecting the information to be preserved, with a threshold level of 30. The median vector is determined by bit mixing. Depending on the type of information preserved, the results differ. For example, if the achromatic top-hat is used (see Figure 2.4c) then the town name is very well preserved on the filtered image, whereas the colored regions (flags) are degraded.

(a)                                        (b)

(c)                                        (d)

**Figure 2.4.** *Filtered images following detection of information to be preserved using:*
*a) a color difference map in RGB space; b) a color gradient in L\*a\*b\* space;*
*c) an achromatic top-hat in RGB space; and d) a color gradient in HSL space. (For a*
*color version of this figure, see www.iste.co.uk/fernandez/colorimag.zip)*

Figure 2.5 shows images representing the different stages in the spatially adaptive median filter based on bit mixing. The color difference map, with a threshold of 30 (b) is computed from the original image (a).

**Figure 2.5.** *a) Original image; b) color difference map; c) distance map; results for: d) spatially adaptive median filter; e) BMF; f) VMF; g) BVDF; h) DDF*

The Chessboard distance map (c) is then used to determine the half-width of the filtering windows, to give the filtered image (d) using a median filter with bit mixing. The results of the median filter are shown with a fixed-size window with a width of 3 for a bit mixing method (e), a vector median filter $VMF$ (f), a directional median filter $BVDF$ (g) and a directional-distance filter $DDF$ (h).

Figure 2.6 shows the results of the five filters on a zoomed-in image of a church steeple. The degradations induced by the vector filters ($VMF$, $BVDF$, and $DDF$) can be seen around the bell-tower windows and on the textures of the roof and the walls: blur introduced in the case of $VMF$ and $DDF$, and additional erroneous detail introduced in the case of $BVDF$. On the other hand, although the bit mixing filter with a fixed-size window ($BMF$) gives a very blurred result, the filtered image is visually much more acceptable when the spatially adaptive bit mixing filter is used.

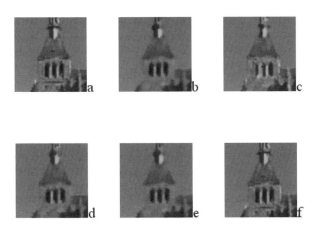

**Figure 2.6.** *Effects of different filters on fine structures: a) original image; b) VMF, c) BVDF; d) DDF; e) BMF; f) spatially adaptive filter. The parameters are a window size of 3 (b, c, d, e) and a threshold value of 30 (f)*

This method can be extended to any filtering method to determine the filtered color using one of the methods described above. This enables the window size to be locally adapted to the context of the current pixel, meaning that the properties of the chosen filter method can then be put to best use on the image.

## 2.6. Performance comparison

The results obtained using these filters can be compared in terms of their MAE (*Mean Absolute Error*), MSE (*Mean Square Error*), NCD (*Normalized Color Difference*), or PSNR (*Peak Signal to Noise Ratio*) [VAR 01, LUK 02, JIN 07]. If the original image $I_{in}$ is of size $N \times M$ then:

$$MAE = \frac{1}{N.M} \sum_{i=1}^{N} \sum_{j=1}^{M} AE_{i,j} \qquad [2.33]$$

$$MSE = \frac{1}{N.M} \sum_{i=1}^{N} \sum_{j=1}^{M} SE_{i,j} \qquad [2.34]$$

where:

$$AE_{i,j} = |I_{in}(i,j) - I_{out}(i,j)| \qquad [2.35]$$

and:

$$SE_{i,j} = (I_{in}(i,j) - I_{out}(i,j))^2 \qquad [2.36]$$

$$PSNR = 10 \log_{10} \frac{255^2}{\frac{h.v}{3} \sum_{i=1}^{N} \sum_{j=1}^{M} \|I_{in}(i,j) - I_{out}(i,j)\|_2^2} \qquad [2.37]$$

For the NCD calculation, a transformation into the color space L*a*b* is required, and we will use $L^I$, $a^I$, and $b^I$ to represent the components of the input image $I_{in}$, and $L^O$, $a^O$, and $b^O$ for the output image $I_{out}$:

$$NCD = \frac{\sum_{i=1}^{N} \sum_{j=1}^{M} \sqrt{[L_{i,j}^I - L_{i,j}^O]^2 + [a_{i,j}^I - a_{i,j}^O]^2 + [b_{i,j}^I - b_{i,j}^O]^2}}{\sum_{i=1}^{N} \sum_{j=1}^{M} \sqrt{[L_{i,j}^O]^2 + [a_{i,j}^O]^2 + [b_{i,j}^O]^2}}$$

$$[2.38]$$

However, since the acquisition conditions for subsequent images are not known, the NCD calculation $NCD$ is not meaningful. For this reason, we will not quote NCD values when evaluating the filters.

In the following subsections, we will compare each of the methods discussed earlier, using a specific image (we will specify which one in each case), to the vector methods described in section 2.3.1.

### 2.6.1. FSVF

Table 2.1 lists the errors that occur when using filters from the FSVF family (see sections 2.4.1.1 and 2.4.4.2), and compares these to the performance of classical vector methods. Three implementations of FSVF are included: using the $L_1$ or $L_2$ norms, and the fuzzy method with $\alpha = 5.5$ and $K = 2^{10}$. It can be seen that the fuzzy method is the one that achieves the best performance.

| Filter | MAE | PSNR |
|--------|------|-------|
| VMF | 6.93 | 25.36 |
| BVDF | 7.81 | 23.81 |
| DDF | 6.67 | 25.70 |
| FSVF $L_1$ | 3.71 | 27.08 |
| FSVF $L_2$ | 3.32 | 27.59 |
| FVF | 3.19 | 27.87 |

**Table 2.1.** *Performance comparison between the fuzzy variant filter and classical vector methods on the "Lena" image following contamination with $30\%$ uniform noise*

### 2.6.2. FRF

Table 2.2 lists the errors that occur when using filters from the $FRF$ family (see section 2.4.4.3), and compares these to the performance of the $VMF$ vector method. Three $FRF$ variants are shown, using different window sizes ($n = 3, 5$ or $7$) and $K = 2^{10}$. It can be seen that the fuzzy method is again the one that achieves the best performance.

| Filter | MAE | PSNR |
|--------|-----|------|
| VMF | 3.38 | 29.89 |
| FRF $n = 3$ | 1.95 | 28.04 |
| FRF $n = 5$ | 1.69 | 30.59 |
| FRF $n = 7$ | 1.82 | 30.21 |

**Table 2.2.** *Performance comparison between the fuzzy FSVF filter and classical vector methods on the "hats" image (from the KODAK test image suite) contaminated with 30% impulse noise*

### 2.6.3. *PGF and FMPGF*

Table 2.3 lists the errors that occur when using filters from the $PGF$ family (see section 2.4.2.1) and $FMPGF$ family (see section 2.4.4.5), and compares these to the performance of vector methods and the arithmetic mean filter ($AMF$). Two variants of PGB and FMPGF are shown, one with $m = 2$ and one with $m = 3$. The larger the value of $m$, the more effective is the filter.

| Filter | MAE | PSNR |
|--------|-----|------|
| AMF | 19.812 | 20.338 |
| VMF | 10.878 | 23.116 |
| DDF | 10.708 | 23.029 |
| BVDF | 11.891 | 22.065 |
| PGF $m = 2$ | 2.678 | 26.931 |
| FMPGF $m = 2$ | 2.163 | 27.738 |
| PGF $m = 3$ | 4.874 | 24.483 |
| FMPGF $m = 3$ | 3.740 | 25.373 |

**Table 2.3.** *Performance comparison between FMPGF and classical vector methods on the "mandrill" image contaminated with 5% impulse noise*

### 2.6.4. *IPGSVF*

Table 2.4 lists the errors that occur when using filters from the $IPGSVF$ family (see section 2.4.2.2), and compares these to the performance of the $VMF$ vector method. Three variants of $IPGSVF$

are shown, using the $M_1$, $M_2$, and $M_{12}$ metrics defined, for each pixel pair $(x_i, x_j)$ with color vectors $c_1$ and $c_2$, by:

1) $M_1(c_i, c_j) = M_{K_1}(c_i, c_j) = \prod_{l=1}^{3} \frac{min\{c_i(l), c_j(l)\} + K_1}{max\{c_i(l), c_j(l)\} + K_1}$

2) $M_2(c_i, c_j) = M_{K_2}(c_i, c_j) = \prod_{l=1}^{3} \frac{min\{c_i(l), c_j(l)\} + K_2}{max\{c_i(l), c_j(l)\} + K_2}$

3) $M_{12}(c_i, c_j) = M_{K_1 K_2}(c_i, c_j) = M_{K_1}(c_i, c_j) . M_{K_2}(c_i, c_j)$

| Filter | MAE | PSNR |
|---|---|---|
| VMF | 15.11 | 20.79 |
| IPGSVF $M_1$ | 5.33 | 24.01 |
| IPGSVF $M_2$ | 4.04 | 25.90 |
| IPGSVF $M_{1}2$ | 4.35 | 25.40 |

**Table 2.4.** *Performance comparison between IPGSVF and classical vector methods on the "mandrill" image contaminated with* 20% *impulse noise*

The values of $K_1$ and $K_2$ were set to 1,024 and 4. All three implementations give very similar results.

### 2.6.5. *Vector filters and spatially adaptive median filter*

Table 2.5 lists the performance of the spatially adaptive median filter (see section 2.5.2) for a range of different methods for determining the contour map. Figure 2.4 shows that a given cartographical method will give better or worse results depending on the nature of the information that needs to be preserved. For example, if the important information is the town name, then it is better not to choose the chromatic top-hat method, since the name is written in black on a white background. Such details can be found in Table 2.5, and this indicates that gradient-based methods give the most consistent results.

Table 2.6 compares the performance of the spatially adaptive median filter with the $VMF$ filter. It can clearly be seen that the $VMF$ degrades the image to a greater extent than the spatially adaptive median filter.

This is consistent with the fact that the $VMF$ does not take into account the context of the pixel being filtered.

| Detection method | MAE | MSE | PSNR |
|---|---|---|---|
| Color difference map | 1.498 | 8.724 | 62.740 |
| Achromatic top-hat | 4.754 | 89.260 | 41.482 |
| Chromatic top-hat | 4.153 | 72.418 | 43.794 |
| Lab gradient | 3.041 | 42.646 | 48.645 |
| LSH gradient | 1.550 | 10.898 | 61.817 |

**Table 2.5.** *Performance comparison between the spatially adaptive median filter, using a range of methods for detecting the regions to be preserved within the Fontainebleau image contaminated with 10% impulse noise*

| % noise | MSE $VMF$ | MAE $VMF$ | MSE $SAMF$ | MAE $SAMF$ |
|---|---|---|---|---|
| 1 | 188.79 | 8.26 | 21.20 | 3.05 |
| 2 | 189.06 | 8.29 | 18.02 | 2.78 |
| 3 | 189.07 | 8.30 | 16.75 | 2.67 |
| 4 | 189.14 | 8.32 | 15.90 | 2.59 |
| 5 | 189.24 | 8.34 | 16.42 | 2.63 |
| 6 | 189.69 | 8.39 | 15.84 | 2.59 |
| 7 | 189.69 | 8.40 | 15.24 | 2.50 |
| 8 | 189.64 | 8.40 | 15.16 | 2.49 |
| 9 | 190.00 | 8.42 | 15.05 | 2.46 |
| 10 | 190.19 | 8.44 | 15.13 | 2.49 |
| 11 | 189.63 | 8.44 | 14.97 | 2.49 |
| 12 | 189.92 | 8.47 | 14.79 | 2.45 |
| 14 | 190.32 | 8.52 | 14.65 | 2.44 |
| 17 | 190.39 | 8.57 | 15.11 | 2.47 |
| 20 | 190.91 | 8.64 | 15.41 | 2.53 |

**Table 2.6.** *Performance comparison between the spatially adaptive median filter ($SAMF$) and the $VMF$ on an image of Mont-St-Michel contaminated with impulse noise*

## 2.7. Conclusion

In this chapter, we have discussed a range of approaches for nonlinear filtering of images, including color images, and have found the median filter to be effective. In the case of color images, implementation of a median filter proves challenging since there is no total ordering relation in the color space.

We have divided such approaches into a number of different families: first, methods that treat all image pixels on an equal footing (see section 2.3), and then methods that incorporate *a priori* information on the nature of a given pixel (see section 2.4), and finally methods that take into account the context of a given pixel to adapt the size of the filtering window (see section 2.5). Each one of these methods has its own advantages and disadvantages. Some of them focus on the modulus of the color vectors, while others focus on the direction of the color vectors. It follows from this that the effects of a given filter will vary widely depending on the type of image being filtered. If the image contains homogeneous regions, then a modulus-based method is to be preferred. If on the other hand, the image contains high-frequency regions, then the angular criterion will be better suited.

However, the more sophisticated methods require higher computation time. Depending on the application and the quality of results required, it will be necessary to find a compromise between computation time and quality of results.

Finally, the generic concept of a spatially adaptive filter opens up the possibility of a wide range of different filters, with each version relying on two main parameters: the nature of the information to be preserved (generally speaking, this is the image contours) and hence the way in which this information is distilled from the image, and the method used to determine the median value. Thus, we can imagine combining this generic method with any one of the fixed-size filtering window methods to produce other filter types, depending on the nature of the pixel and its context. Filters of this type exploit the desirable qualities of a given filter type while adapting the filtering window to the context in which it is applied.

## 2.8. Bibliography

[ABB 99] ABBAS J., DOMANSKI M., "Vector nonlinear recursive filters for color images", *Proceedings of 6th International Workshop on Systems, Signals and Image Processing IWSSIP '99*, p. 30-33, Bratislava, Slovakia, 1999.

[ANG 07] ANGULO J., SERRA J., "Modelling and segmentation of colour images in polar representations", *Image Vision and Computing*, vol. 25, no. 4, p. 475-495, 2007.

[AST 90] ASTOLA J., HAAVISTO P., NEUVO Y., "Vector median filters", *Proceedings of IEEE*, vol. 78, p. 678-689, 1990.

[BAR 76] BARNETT V., "The ordering of multivariate data", *Journal of Royal Statistical Society A*, vol. 139, no. 3, p. 318-354, 1976.

[BOR 86] BORGEFORS G., "Distance transformations in digital images", *CVGIP*, vol. 34, p. 344-371, 1986.

[CAM 08] CAMARENA J.-G., GREGORI V., MORILLAS S., SAPENA A., "Fast detection and removal of impulsive noise using peer groups and fuzzy metrics", *Journal of Visual Communication and Image Representation*, vol. 19, no. 1, p. 20-29, 2008.

[CAM 10] CAMARENA J.-G., GREGORI V., MORILLAS S., SAPENA A., "Two-step fuzzy logic-based method for impulse noise detection in colour images", *Pattern Recognition Letters*, vol. 31, p. 1842-1849, Elsevier Science Inc., 2010.

[CHA 98] CHANUSSOT J., LAMBERT P., "Total ordering based on space filling curves for multivalued morphology", *Proceedings of 4th ISMM*, p. 51-58, 1998.

[CIU 98] CIUC M., RANGAYYAN R., ZAHARIA T., BUZULOIU V., "Adaptive neighbourhood filters for color image filtering", *Proceedings of IXth SPIE Nonlinear Image Processing Conference*, vol. SPIE 3304, p. 277-286, San Jose, USA, 1998.

[DAN 08] DANG D., LUO W., "Color image noise removal algorithm utilizing hybrid vector filtering", *AEU – International Journal of Electronics and Communications*, vol. 62, no. 1, p. 63-67, 2008.

[DIN 07] DINET E., ROBERT-INACIO F., "Color median filtering: a spatially adaptive filter", *Proceedings of Image and Vision Computing New Zealand (IVCNZ '07)*, p. 71-76, Hamilton, 2007.

[FAR 06] FARAJI H., MACLEAN W., "Cod noise removal in digital images", *IEEE Transactions on Image Processing*, vol. 15, p. 227-248, 2006.

[FER 12] FERNANDEZ-MALOIGNE C., ROBERT-INACIO F., MACAIRE L., *Digital Color*, ISTE Ltd, London and John Wiley and Sons, New York, 2012.

[HOD 85] HODGSON R., BAILEY D., NAYLOR M., NG A., MCCNEIL S., "Properties, implementations and applications of rank filters", *Image Vision Computing*, vol. 3, p. 3-14, 1985.

[JIN 07] JIN L., LI D., "A switching vector median filter based on the CIELAB color space for color image restoration", *Signal Processing*, vol. 87, p. 1345-1354, 2007.

[KHR 99] KHRIJI L., GABBOUJ M., "Vector median-rational hybrid filters for multichannel image processing", *IEEE Signal Processing Letters*, vol. 6, no. 7, p. 186-190, 1999.

[KOS 01] KOSCHAN A., ABIDI M., "A comparison of median filter techniques for noise removal in color images", *Proceedings of 7th German Workshop on Color Image Processing*, vol. 34, no. 15, p. 69-79, November, 2001.

[LAM 00] LAMBERT P., MACAIRE L., "Filtering and segmentation: the specificity of color images", *Proceedings of Conference on Color in Graphics and Image Processing*, p. 57-64, Saint-Etienne, France, 2000.

[LUK 02] LUKAC R., "Adaptive vector median filtering", *Pattern Recognition Letters*, vol. 24, p. 1889-1899, 2002.

[LUK 05] LUKAC R., SMOLKA B., MARTIN K., PLATANIOTIS K., VENETSANOPOULOS A., "Vector filtering for color imaging", *IEEE Signal Processing Magazine*, vol. 22, p. 74-86, 2005.

[MA 07] MA Z., WU H., FENG D., "Fuzzy vector partition filtering technique for color image restoration", *Computer Vision and Image Understanding*, vol. 107, no. 1-2, p. 26-37, 2007, Special issue on color image processing.

[MAI 03] MAITRE H., *Le traitement des images*, Hermès Science, 2003.

[MOR 05] MORILLAS S., GREGORI V., PERIS-FAJARNÉS G., LATORRE P., "A fast impulsive noise color image filter using fuzzy metrics", *Real-Time Imaging*, p. 417-428, 2005.

[MOR 08] MORILLAS S., GREGORI V., PERIS-FAJARNÉS G., "Isolating impulsive noise pixels in color images by peer group techniques", *Computer Vision and Image Understanding*, p. 102-116, 2008.

[PIT 90] PITAS I., VENETSANOPOULOS A., *Nonlinear Digital Filters, Principles and Applications*, Kluwer Academic Publ., Norwell, 1990.

[PLA 97] PLATANIOTIS K., ANDROUTSOS D., VENETSANOPOULOS A., "Multichannel filters for image processing", *Signal Processing: Image Communications*, vol. 9, no. 2, p. 143-158, 1997.

[ROB 06] ROBERT-INACIO F., DINET E., "An adaptive median filter for colour image processing", *Proceedings of 3rd International Conference on Colour in Graphics, Imaging and Vision (CGIV '06)*, p. 205-210, Leeds, UK, 2006.

[ROB 08] ROBERT-INACIO F., ANGULO J., DINET E., "Contour and detail detection for spatially adaptive median filtering", *Proceedings of 4th International Conference on Colour in Graphics, Imaging and Vision (CGIV '08)*, p. 388-393, Barcelona-Terrassa, Spain, 2008.

[SMO 02] SMOLKA B., PLATANIOTIS K., CHYDZINSKI A., SZCZEPANSKI M., VENETSANOPOULOS A., WOJCIECHOWSKI K., "Self-adaptive algorithm of impulsive noise reduction in color images", *Pattern Recognition*, vol. 35, p. 1771-1784, 2002.

[TRA 93] TRAHANIAS P., VENETSANOPOULOS A., "Vector directional filters: a new class of multichannel image processing filters", *IEEE Transactions on Image Processing*, vol. 2/4, p. 528-534, 1993.

[TRA 96] TRAHANIAS P., KARAKO D., VENETSANOPOULOS A., "Directional processing of color images: theory and experimental results", *IEEE Transactions on Image Processing*, vol. 5, p. 868-880, 1996.

[TRE 04] TREMEAU A., FERNANDEZ-MALOIGNE C., BONTON P., *Image numérique couleur: de l'acquistion au traitement*, Dunod, Paris, 2004.

[TSA 99] TSAI H.-H., YU P.-T., "Adaptive fuzzy hybrid multichannel filters for removal of impulsive noise from color images", *Signal Processing*, vol. 74, no. 2, p. 127-151, 1999.

[VAR 01] VARDAVOULIA M., ANDREADIS I., TSALIDES P., "A new median filter for colour image processing", *Pattern Recognition Letters*, vol. 22, p. 675-689, 2001.

Chapter 3

# Anisotropic Diffusion PDEs for Regularization of Multichannel Images: Formalisms and Applications

## 3.1. Introduction

One of the primary objectives of image processing has always been to obtain a regularized version of a given noisy image. Regularization serves as a form of *noise removal* for noise present in the data, meaning that it is an element of image pre-processing that is at times indispensable, leading to improved performance of higher-level analysis algorithms, such as ones for the detection of specific characteristics in images (contours, corners, objects, motion, etc.). Regularization can also be used to create *simplified versions* of images, meaning that it plays an important role in the multiscale analysis of the objects contained within the image. Generally speaking, regularization plays a fundamental role in finding consistent solutions to initially *ill-posed* problems in image processing [HAD 23], such as image restoration, image segmentation, registration, and surface reconstruction, to name just a few. This explains the keen interest in this subject that there has always been within the

---

Chapter written by David TSCHUMPERLÉ.

image processing community, and why so many different regularization formalisms have been described in the literature. In their pioneering work at the start of the 1990s, Perona and Malik [PER 90] were the first to consider image regularization in terms of the evolution of anisotropic diffusion PDEs (Partial Differential Equations). Their method, initially applied to images taking scalar values (one single value per pixel), gave rise to a specific interest in PDE formulations, since it was capable of smoothing data in an entirely *nonlinear* manner. This makes it effective at removing noise while at the same time preserving significant discontinuities within images. These discontinuities include contours and corners. It was all the more remarkable that it was later shown that the mathematical formulation they proposed was intrinsically unstable [KIC 97, WEI 97b]. Diffusion PDEs were initially developed to model the local evolution of complex physical systems (liquids, gases), and they are a type of mathematical object that has been heavily studied; the wide selection of theoretical results in this field have had repercussions for data regularization. In the field of image processing, a PDE is an ideal model for describing *local interactions* between pixels, and it can easily be adapted to the case of images corrupted by sources of degradation that are themselves local or semi-local; this is not in the least bit restrictive. Noise, scratches, and compression artifacts are all examples of local degradations that are commonly encountered in digital imagery.

Following the path opened up by Perona and Malik, many authors subsequently developed variants of these diffusion PDEs for image regularization, especially for images consisting of scalar values. The important theoretical contributions in this field revolved around the way in which the classical isotropic diffusion equation (the simplest such equation, the heat transfer equation) can be extended to transform it into a form suitable for anisotropic smoothing [PER 90, SAP 01, WEI 98], the way in which diffusion PDEs can be considered to be gradient descents of a variety of functionals [AUB 06, BLA 95, CHA 97, KIM 00, RUD 92], and the connection between regularization PDEs and the concept of nonlinear scale space [ALV 93, LIN 94, NIE 97]. Extensions of these techniques for handling color images, and more generally multi-dimensional data, appeared subsequently [BLO 98, KIM 00, SAP 01, SAP 96b, TSC 05, WEI 99], leading to expressions that involve one or more coupling terms between the different channels of the images in question. Diffusion equations considering multi-valued *constrained* cases were also proposed, which can be used for example for the regularization of unit vector fields [KIM 02, PER 98, TAN 98], orthonormal matrices [CHE 04], positive-definite matrices [CHE 04, TSC 01], or image data defined over implicit surfaces [BER 01, CHA 00, TAN 00]. In practice, these specific diffusion PDEs contain an additional term for preservation of the constraints, which is added to the regularization term. We will not consider these in the present chapter.

Despite the significant number of PDE formalisms that exist for the regularization of scalar or multi-channel images, we observe that they all rely on the same common principle: a nonlinear regularization PDE $\frac{\partial I}{\partial t} = \mathcal{R}$ acts to *locally smooth* the image $I$ along one or more directions within the plane, chosen differently at each point within the image, and ideally dependent on the local configuration of the neighboring pixels. Typically, the preferred smoothing direction is chosen to be parallel to the contours of structures present within the images, resulting in *anisotropic* regularization that does not destroy these contours. This has an interesting interpretation in terms of *scale space*: as the image data is gradually regularized (according to the time variable $t$ governing the evolution of the PDE), an image sequence $I^{[t]}$ is generated that consists of more and more strongly smoothed images. From this point of view, it seems natural that the regularization algorithms will first remove the least significant image characteristics (ideally noise, but in practice, the data with the least contrast), while the interesting details within the image (the contours) will remain present for longer, until they themselves become negligible with respect to other remaining discontinuities (in other words contours with even more contrast) [ALV 93, LIN 94, NIE 97, PER 90, WIT 83]. From a geometric point of view, regularization PDEs can thus be viewed as iterative and locally adaptive filters that simplify the image bit by bit, by minimizing the variations in pixel level in the neighborhood of a given pixel (see Figure 3.1). It follows from this that most smoothing equations converge to a constant solution (at $t \rightarrow \infty$), which is not an interesting solution, but one that effectively minimizes the *and* pixel levels in the resultant image. To avoid this over-simplification of the regularized images, an evolution speed is sometimes used for the PDE that takes the form $\mathcal{R}' = \mathcal{R} + \alpha\ (I_{\text{noisy}} - I)$, containing an additional *data-driven term* (weighted by a parameter $\alpha \in \mathbb{R}^+$ defined by the user). This ensures that the regularized image is not too different from the original noisy image (and hence all pixel values are not the same). Another possible technique is to stop the pure regularization flow $\frac{\partial I}{\partial t} = \mathcal{R}$ after a finite number of iterations (the time of the cutoff thus becomes a parameter of the method). In this chapter, we will focus purely on the study of regularization terms $\mathcal{R}$. For an advanced study of linear and nonlinear data-driven terms, the reader is referred to [NIK 01].

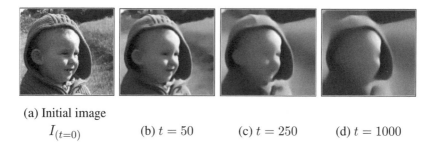

(a) Initial image

$\qquad I_{(t=0)}$ $\qquad$ (b) $t = 50$ $\qquad$ (c) $t = 250$ $\qquad$ (d) $t = 1000$

**Figure 3.1.** *Nonlinear regularization PDE and the concept of anisotropic scale space. (For a color version of this figure, see www.iste.co.uk/fernandez/colorimag.zip)*

A key concept on which the majority of PDE regularization methods are based is therefore the problem of orienting the local smoothing. The problem therefore consists of defining a consistent *local geometry* for scalar or multi-channel images. This must be one of the primary objectives of a good regularization algorithm. It is in pursuit of this goal that the authors of [TSC 05, WEI 98] proposed two different generic formalisms that define regularization processes with a smoothing geometry that can be carefully tailored to the specific application in question. These methods have two main advantages: they unify a large number of different diffusion equations that had previously been proposed in the literature, by giving a local geometric interpretation of the corresponding regularization processes; and they clearly separate the *definition of the smoothing geometry* from the actual process of smoothing. First, the geometry of local image structures is analyzed, and then the appropriate local smoothing geometry is defined by means of a *diffusion tensor field*, which is determined by the earlier analysis phase. Finally, the actual smoothing process is performed by means of one or more iterations of a specific diffusion PDE. This procedure is repeated until a suitably regular image has been obtained.

In this chapter, we will begin by summarizing the possible choices for defining consistent local geometries for multichannel images, giving a state of the art for the field and comparing the variation solutions discussed in the literature [BLO 98, DIZ 86, SAP 96a, WEI 98] (see section 3.3). We will then classify the main techniques for scalar and multi-channel image regularization using PDEs into three different groups. These are: 1) variational formulations, 2) *divergence* diffusion equations, 3) *Laplacian oriented* (or *trace*) expressions. We will focus on the interpretation of these formalisms in terms of local image smoothing, analyzing the advantages and disadvantages of each equation in real-world contexts (see section 3.4). We will then study an alternative regularization proposed more recently in [TSC 06] and formulated as diffusion directed by a tensor field, which takes into account specific constraints on the *curvature of multi-valued contours* within the image (see section 3.5). We will draw a parallel between this formalism and the technique of Line Integral Convolution filtering, originally proposed by Cabral and Leedom [CAB 93] as a solution for the visualization of vector fields. From this analogy, there follows a direct means of numerical implementation, involving explicit evolution of the corresponding PDE through a series of successive integrations over the pixel values along the field lines (see section 3.6). This iterative scheme has two principal advantages compared to the more traditional explicit PDE implementations. Firstly, it is a good solution for preserving fine structures within images, due to its sub-pixel integration resolution (via Runge-Kutta schemes [PRE 92]). Secondly, it converges more rapidly since it is unconditionally stable, even when large time steps are used during its evolution.

To conclude this chapter, we will illustrate the effectiveness of these algorithms in terms of computation time and visual quality, showing application results for denoising and *inpainting* (reconstruction of regions with missing data) within color images. These are just a few examples of applications from among all the possible uses for these regularization techniques, but they give a good illustration of the various remarkable geometric smoothing properties offered by these formalisms (see section 3.7).

### 3.2. Preliminary concepts

We will model a mutli-channel image using a continuous function $\mathbf{I} \colon \Omega \to \mathbb{R}^n$, where $\Omega \subset \mathbb{R}^2$ is the rectangular domain of definition of the image, and $n \in \mathbb{N}^+$ is the number of channels, i.e. the vector dimension of each pixel $\mathbf{I}_{(\mathbf{X})}$ within the image at points $\mathbf{X} = (x \ \ y)^T \in \Omega$. The notation $I_i$ represents the *i*th *channel* of $\mathbf{I}$, i.e. a scalar image $I_i \colon \Omega \to \mathbb{R}$:
$$\forall \mathbf{X} = (x, y) \in \Omega, \mathbf{I}_{(\mathbf{X})} = \left( I_{1(\mathbf{X})} \ \ I_{2(\mathbf{X})} \ \ \cdots \ \ I_{n(\mathbf{X})} \right)^T.$$

For the specific case of color images, we of course have $n = 3$, i.e. three vector components $(R, G, B)$ for each pixel, corresponding to the red ($I_1$), green ($I_2$), and blue ($I_3$) channels of $\mathbf{I}$ (any other choice of color space representation would be equally valid, but is outside the scope of the present discussion).

We will make widespread use of *rank 2 tensors* in the equations used in this chapter. Such a tensor $\mathbf{D}$ can be likened to a $2 \times 2$ symmetric, positive definite matrix having two positive eigenvalues $\lambda_1, \lambda_2$ and two associated orthogonal eigenvectors $\mathbf{u}_1 \perp \mathbf{u}_2 \in S^1$. $\mathbf{D}$ can therefore be written as $\lambda_1 \ \mathbf{u}_1 \mathbf{u}_1^T + \lambda_2 \ \mathbf{u}_2 \mathbf{u}_2^T$ and can be represented in the form of an ellipse whose orientation is defined by the orthonormal basis of the eigenvalues $\mathbf{u}_1 \perp \mathbf{u}_2$ and whose radii are defined by the eigenvalues $\lambda_1$ and $\lambda_2$. When $\lambda_2 \gg \lambda_1$ (elongated ellipse), the tensor $\mathbf{D}$ is said to be *anisotropic* and has $\mathbf{u}_2$ as its principal axis. On the other hand, when $\lambda_1 \approx \lambda_2 \approx \beta$ ("fat" ellipse), the tensor $\mathbf{D}$ is more *isotropic* and is similar to the identity matrix, up to a factor: $\lambda_1 \approx \lambda_2 \approx \beta \implies \mathbf{D} \approx \beta \ \mathbb{I}_d = \begin{pmatrix} \beta & 0 \\ 0 & \beta \end{pmatrix}.$

A purely *isotropic* tensor has no preferred direction, and any vector from $\mathbb{R}^2$ is an eigenvector of $\mathbf{D}$.

We will use $\text{div}(\mathbf{u})$ for the *divergence* of the 2D vector field $\mathbf{u} = (u \ \ v)^T$, i.e. the scalar field $\text{div}(\mathbf{u}) = \frac{\partial u}{\partial x} + \frac{\partial v}{\partial y}$. Finally, we will use $G_\sigma$ to represent the $2D$ normalized Gaussian function, with standard deviation $\sigma$, i.e. $G_\sigma(x, y) = \frac{1}{2\pi\sigma^2} \exp\left(-\frac{x^2 + y^2}{2\sigma^2}\right)$.

## 3.3. Local geometry in multi-channel images

### 3.3.1. *Which geometric characteristics?*

An image regularization process can be considered primarily to consist of the application of a smoothing filter that locally reduces variations between pixel levels. More precisely, we would like to smooth a multi-channel image $\mathbf{I}: \Omega \rightarrow \mathbb{R}^n$ while preserving its contours (signal discontinuities), in other words performing a local adaptive smoothing primarily along the direction of the contours, while avoiding as much as possible any smoothing orthogonal to these directions. An initial approach would be to apply a scalar value regularization filter to every component $I_i$ of a multi-channel image $\mathbf{I}$, performing this operation independently for each channel $i = 1...n$. In this case, any possible correlation that exists between the different components of the image will be ignored. However, this approach will result in significant disparities in the local smoothing behavior for each separate channel: the directions and amplitudes of smoothing may be very different from one component to the next. Such regularization strategies tend to lead to undesirable over-smoothing effects that can rapidly destroy the contour structures that are present.

A multi-channel image regularization method should instead be based on a consistent inter-component smoothing strategy, designed such that the local directions and amplitudes of smoothing are the same for all channels $I_i$. This means that we must first obtain a robust measure of the *multi-valued local image geometry* for the image $\mathbf{I}$. In practice, such a geometry can be defined by the following characteristics, applicable at all points $\mathbf{X} = (x, y)$ within $\mathbf{I}$:

1) two orthogonal directions $\theta_{+(\mathbf{X})}, \theta_{-(\mathbf{X})} \in S^1$, pointing perpendicular and parallel to the contours. They are generally chosen to be the directions of maximum and minimum *and* level within the image at $\mathbf{X}$; $\theta_-$ then corresponds to the *contour direction*, assuming there is one, while $\theta_+$ is naturally associated with the concept of *gradient direction*;

2) a measure of variation $\mathcal{N}_{(\mathbf{X})}$, which quantifies the *local contrast* of a contour. In the case of multi-channel images, this measure extends the concept of the *gradient norm*, as commonly used in the case of scalar images.

To define these characteristics, a range of approaches have been considered in the literature. We will discuss these in the following subsections. For maximum readability, we will omit the suffix $_{(\mathbf{X})}$ in subsequent expressions for functions whose value is evidently to be taken at the point $\mathbf{X} = (x, y)$.

### 3.3.2. Geometry estimated using a scalar characteristic

A very simple method of geometric estimation would involve first reducing a multi-channel image to a scalar image $f(\mathbf{I})$, which would ideally contain all the necessary contour information. The conversion function $f: \mathbb{R}^n \to \mathbb{R}$ could be inspired by mathematical models of human visual perception of image contours, an approach that seems like a reasonable strategy for color images. We could, for example, choose the function $f$ as being the luminosity (perceived response to luminance) as defined in the color space L*a*b* [POY 95]:

$$f = L^* = 116\, g(Y) - 16 \quad \text{where} \quad Y = 0.2125R + 0.7154G + 0.0721B$$

where $g: \mathbb{R} \to \mathbb{R}$ is defined by:

$$\begin{cases} g(s) = \sqrt[3]{s} & \text{if} & s > 0.008856 \\ g(s) = 7.787s + \frac{16}{116} & \text{otherwise} \end{cases} \qquad [3.1]$$

The local color geometry $\{\mathcal{N}, \theta_+, \theta_-\}$ of $\mathbf{I}$ can then be defined as:

$$\begin{cases} \theta_+ = \dfrac{\nabla f(\mathbf{I})}{\|\nabla f(\mathbf{I})\|} \\ \theta_- \perp \theta_+ \end{cases} \quad \text{and} \quad \mathcal{N} = \|\nabla f(\mathbf{I})\| \qquad [3.2]$$

This technique has two major drawbacks. First, it is not always possible to define a function $f$ that is appropriate for any type of multi-channel image (especially when the number of channels exceeds $n > 3$). Moreover, mathematically no scalar function $f(\mathbf{I})$ exists that can detect all multi-valued variations in an image $\mathbf{I}$. For example, the luminosity function defined earlier would not be suitable for detecting *isoluminosity* contours within a color image, as illustrated in Figure 3.2: the contours within the Yin/Yang symbol cannot be detected by $\mathcal{N} = \|\nabla f(\mathbf{I})\|$ since the luminosity $f(\mathbf{I})$ of the two colors was selected to be identical. A smoothing approach based on this geometry would probably have a locally isotropic behavior, or one oriented in an incorrect direction, leading in both cases to over-smoothing (and hence destruction) of the contours.

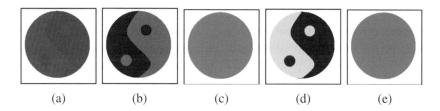

(a)            (b)            (c)            (d)            (e)

**Figure 3.2.** *The use of a scalar function to define a local color geometry can preclude the detection of certain contours: a) color image; b) red component R; c) green component G; d) blue component B; e) scalar luminosity image $L^*$. (For a color version of this figure, see www.iste.co.uk/fernandez/colorimag.zip)*

### 3.3.3. *Di Zenzo multi-valued geometry*

An elegant solution for overcoming this limitation was proposed by Di Zenzo in [DIZ 86]. He considered a multi-channel image $\mathbf{I}: \Omega \rightarrow \mathbb{R}^n$ as a vector field, and focused on the Euclidean norm $\|d\mathbf{I}\|^2$ of the infinitesimal local vector variation $d\mathbf{I}$ at all points $\mathbf{X} \in \Omega$:

$$d\mathbf{I} = \mathbf{I}_x \, dx + \mathbf{I}_y \, dy \quad \text{where} \quad \mathbf{I}_x = \frac{\partial \mathbf{I}}{\partial x} \text{ and } \mathbf{I}_y = \frac{\partial \mathbf{I}}{\partial y} \quad (\in \mathbb{R}^n)$$

and hence, $\|d\mathbf{I}\|^2 = d\mathbf{I}^T \, d\mathbf{I} = \|\mathbf{I}_x\|^2 \, dx^2 + 2 \, \mathbf{I}_x^T \mathbf{I}_y \, dxdy + \|\mathbf{I}_y\|^2 \, dy^2$, in other words:

$$\|d\mathbf{I}\|^2 = d\mathbf{X}^T \, \mathbf{G} \, d\mathbf{X} \quad \text{where} \quad \mathbf{G} = \sum_{i=1}^{n} \nabla I_i \, \nabla I_i^T \quad \text{and}$$

$$d\mathbf{X} = \begin{pmatrix} dx \\ dy \end{pmatrix}, \quad \nabla I_i = \begin{pmatrix} I_{ix} \\ I_{iy} \end{pmatrix}$$

The matrix $\mathbf{G}$ is known as the *structure tensor*. This represents the contributions of the variations in level for each channel $I_i$ of the image $\mathbf{I}$. It is a $2 \times 2$ symmetric and semi positive-definite matrix, whose coefficients are:

$$g_{11} = \sum_{i=1}^{n} I_{i_x}^2, \; g_{12} = g_{21} = \sum_{i=1}^{n} I_{i_x} I_{i_y} \quad \text{and} \quad g_{22} = \sum_{i=1}^{n} I_{i_y}^2$$

Di Zenzo recommended that the $\nabla I_i$ components should be estimated using a Deriche filter [ALV 00]. In the usual case of color images $\mathbf{I} = (R, G, B)$, the structure tensor $\mathbf{G}$ can then be summarized as:

$$\mathbf{G} = \begin{pmatrix} R_x^2 + G_x^2 + B_x^2 & R_x R_y + G_x G_y + B_x B_y \\ R_x R_y + G_x G_y + B_x B_y & R_y^2 + G_y^2 + B_y^2 \end{pmatrix} \quad [3.3]$$

It is interesting to note that the two positive eigenvalues $\lambda_{+/-}$ of $\mathbf{G}$ measure the maximum and minimum values respectively of the *vector variation norm* $\|d\mathbf{I}\|^2$, while the associated orthogonal eigenvectors $\theta_+$ and $\theta_-$ give the corresponding *orientations* of these *extrema*. Analytically, they are defined as:

$$\lambda_{+/-} = \frac{g_{11} + g_{22} \pm \sqrt{\delta}}{2} \quad \text{and} \quad \theta_{+/-} \; /\!/ \begin{pmatrix} 2 \, g_{12} \\ g_{22} - g_{11} \pm \sqrt{\delta} \end{pmatrix} \quad [3.4]$$

where $\delta = (g_{11} - g_{22})^2 + 4 \, g_{12}^2$ . In what follows, we will assume that the vectors $\theta_\pm$ have been normalized to form unit vectors.

Using this simple approach, Di Zenzo opened up a natural path for analyzing the local vector geometry of multi-channel images through the use of the orthonormal orientation basis $\theta_+ \perp \theta_-$ and its associated contrast measures $\lambda_+, \lambda_-$. A slight variation on this tensor structure was proposed by Weickert in [WEI 98]. Here, it was proposed to consider the spectral elements of $\mathbf{G}_{\alpha,\sigma}$, a doubly-smoothed version of the structure tensor $\mathbf{G}$:

$$\mathbf{G}_{\alpha,\sigma} = \sum_{i=1}^{n} \left[ \left( \nabla I_{i_\alpha} \nabla I_{i_\alpha}^T \right) * G_\sigma \right] \quad \text{where} \quad I_{i_\alpha} = I_i * G_\alpha \qquad [3.5]$$

where $G_\alpha$ and $G_\sigma$ are 2D Gaussian kernels with respective standard deviations of $\alpha$ and $\sigma \in \mathbb{R}^+$. Here, the convolutions are applied separately for each coefficient of the raw tensor $\mathbf{G}$. The two parameters $\alpha$ and $\sigma$ can be used to introduce a regularity constraint on the computed structure tensor field, and by extension to constrain the regularity of the local multi-channel geometry of the image in question.

Analysis of the eigenvalues $\lambda_+, \lambda_-$ of $\mathbf{G}_{\alpha,\sigma}$ enables us to distinguish a range of different local geometric configurations within an image:

– when $\lambda_+ \approx \lambda_- \approx 0$, there are very few vector variations around the current point $\mathbf{X}$: the neighborhood is *homogeneous* and probably does not contain any contours or corners (interior of the strips in Figure 3.3a). For this configuration, the variation norm $\mathcal{N}$ as just defined would be very small, or even zero;

– when $\lambda_+ \gg \lambda_-$, there are significant vector variations in the vicinity of the current point, which probably lies on a *contour* or *corner* (contours of the strips in Figure 3.3a). For this configuration, the variation norm $\mathcal{N}$ should ideally be high;

– when $\lambda_+ \approx \lambda_- \gg 0$, the current point lies on a *saddle point* on the vector surface, which represents a specific type of corner structure within the image (intersections between strips in Figure 3.3a). Here, the value of $\mathcal{N}$ should ideally be even higher than for the previously described configurations, since this complex "junction" form is usually difficult to smooth without introducing degradations. The aim should therefore be to suppress smoothing even more strongly here, favoring a very strong measure of variation (meaning that a corner behaves similarly to a highly contrasting contour).

In practice, many of the multi-channel image regularization algorithms proposed in the literature are implicitly or explicitly based on these geometric attributes of Di Zenzo. More specifically, three distinct choices of vector variation norms $\mathcal{N}$ have been considered:

1) $\mathcal{N} = \sqrt{\lambda_+}$, as the most natural extension of the gradient norm in scalar images, considered to be *the value of the maximum local variation* [BLO 98, SAP 96a, SAP 97] (see Figure 3.3b). This norm does not however ascribe particular importance to corner type configurations, as compared to rectilinear contours;

2) $\mathcal{N}_- = \sqrt{\lambda_+ - \lambda_-}$, also known as the *coherence measure* [SAP 96b, WEI 98]. We note that this measure unfortunately does not correctly detect discontinuities, which are saddle points in multi-channel images, seen as "elevations" in the vector surface. This fact is particularly prominent at the intersections of the strips, and in the center and right and left parts of the baby's eye in Figure 3.3c. This is therefore a measure that should be avoided during a regularization process, since regions containing corners will be treated in the same way as homogeneous regions ($\mathcal{N}_-$ will be small in both cases), whereas of course the aim is to treat these two geometric configurations very differently in terms of the geometric smoothing applied to them;

3) $\mathcal{N}_+ = \sqrt{\lambda_+ + \lambda_-}$, sometimes written as $\|\nabla \mathbf{I}\|$, is often chosen [BLO 98, TAN 98, TSC 01], since it can detect both contours and corners in a satisfactory manner, while still being easily calculable. It does not require any spectral decomposition of $\mathbf{G}_{\alpha,\sigma}$, since $\mathcal{N}_+ = \sqrt{\text{trace}(\mathbf{G})} = \sqrt{\sum_{i=1}^n \|\nabla I_i\|^2}$. This measure gives more weight to saddle points in a multi-channel image (see Figure 3.3d), which has the benefit of making it possible to attenuate the smoothing of corner-type structures in the context of image denoising.

Once the local vector geometry has been defined, we can use it to measure any local image configuration encountered in multi-channel image processing, for any type of application (not restricted to regularization). For example, detection of color contours can be performed by detecting the local maxima in the local contrast measure $\mathcal{N}_+$ (see Figures 3.4 and [KOS 95, TSC 02]). In the same way, this local vector geometric analysis introduced by Di Zenzo has been integrated for the measurement of contours in certain PDE-based segmentation techniques for multi-channel images [SAP 96a, SAP 97]. In the context of image regularization, the measure $\mathcal{N}_+ = \sqrt{\lambda_+ + \lambda_-}$ is the one that is the most suited to detecting local contrast variations in multi-channel images.

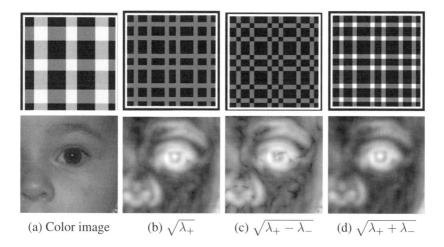

(a) Color image    (b) $\sqrt{\lambda_+}$    (c) $\sqrt{\lambda_+ - \lambda_-}$    (d) $\sqrt{\lambda_+ + \lambda_-}$

**Figure 3.3.** *Comparison of local variation measures $\mathcal{N}$, $\mathcal{N}_-$ and $\mathcal{N}_+$ for two color images (the bright pixels have the highest values)*

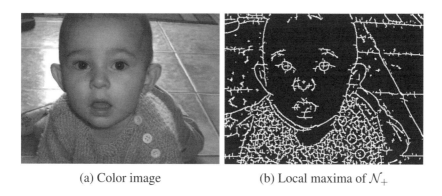

(a) Color image    (b) Local maxima of $\mathcal{N}_+$

**Figure 3.4.** *Calculation of the* extrema *of the measure $\mathcal{N}_+$ for color contour detection*

## 3.4. PDEs for multi-channel image smoothing: overview

We will review the classical methods for smoothing of multi-channel images based on anisotropic diffusion PDEs. We will then classify these methods in three different ways, linked to the distinct levels of interpretation of the regularization process, from the most global to the most local. In each section, we will begin by describing the initial idea, in the context of scalar imaging, and will then extend the concept to multi-channel image data.

### 3.4.1. *Variational methods*

In contrast to the direct formulation of Perona and Malik, a range of methods in the literature have presented a variational view of regularization, treating it as a global energy minimization procedure over the image. The approaches described in particular in [AUB 06, CHA 97, BLA 95, SAP 01, WEI 98] have contributed to the definition of a range of functionals measuring global image variation. Intuitively, minimization of this type of functional can be used to reduce the variations in pixel levels (and hence gradually suppress noise) while taking care to preserve the important variations (in order to avoid destruction of contours). The formulation known as *φ-functionals* encompasses the majority of such approaches under an elegant common formalism.

A noisy *scalar* image $I_{\text{noisy}}$ can be regularized by minimizing the following $\phi$-functional:

$$\min_{I:\Omega \to \mathbb{R}} E(I) = \int_{\Omega} \phi(\|\nabla I\|) \, d\Omega \qquad [3.6]$$

where $\phi: \mathbb{R} \to \mathbb{R}$ is an *increasing function*, with a direct impact on the global behavior of the regularization, penalizing strong gradient norms. This minimization can take the form of a gradient descent, leading to a *diffusion PDE* based around the Euler-Lagrange equations for $E(I)$:

$$\begin{cases} I_{(t=0)} = I_{\text{noisy}} \\[2mm] \dfrac{\partial I}{\partial t} = \text{div} \left( \dfrac{\phi'(\|\nabla I\|)}{\|\nabla I\|} \nabla I \right) \end{cases} \qquad [3.7]$$

Different choices of functions $\phi$ lead to a range of different regularization methods. These include isotropic regularization (equivalent to convolving the image by a Gaussian function), as introduced by Tikhonov [TIK 63], but also the classical Perona-Malik method [PER 90] or the Total Variation method [RUD 92]. Other regularization approaches acting on scalar images can also be expressed within the unifying formalism of $\phi$-functionals (see Figure 3.5).

| Method | $\phi(s)$ | Reference |
|---|---|---|
| Tikhonov | $s^2$ | [TIK 63] |
| Perona-Malik | $1 - \exp(-s^2/K^2)$ | [PER 90] |
| Minimal surfaces | $2\sqrt{1+s^2} - 2$ | [CHA 94] |
| Geman-McClure | $s^2/(1+s^2)$ | [GEM 85] |
| Total variation | $s$ | [RUD 92] |
| Green | $2\log(\cosh(s))$ | [GRE 90] |

**Figure 3.5.** *Different regularization functions for $\phi$-functionals*

A natural extension of $\phi$-functionals for the regularization of a *multi-channel* image $\mathbf{I}$ would then involve minimizing the functional $E(\mathbf{I}) = \int_\Omega \phi(\mathcal{N}(\mathbf{I}))\ d\Omega$, where once again this measures global variation within the image $\mathbf{I}$, where $\mathcal{N}(\mathbf{I})$ could be one of the three measures of local variation as defined in the previous section. But, since a multi-channel image has two distinct measures of variation $\lambda_+, \lambda_-$ (the eigenvalues of the structure tensor $\mathbf{G}$) as opposed to the single measure $\|\nabla I\|$ for scalar images, we may wish to consider minimizing the following more general $\psi$-functional, defined using a function $\psi: \mathbb{R}^2 \to \mathbb{R}$ of two variables, which formulates a more generic extension of $\phi$-functional regularization for multi-channel images:

$$\min_{\mathbf{I}:\Omega\to\mathbb{R}^n} E(\mathbf{I}) = \int_\Omega \psi(\lambda_+, \lambda_-)\ d\Omega \qquad [3.8]$$

The Euler-Lagrange equations in equation [3.8] lead to the following extremely simple form of PDE, a *divergence* PDE, which minimizes $E(\mathbf{I})$:

$$\frac{\partial I_i}{\partial t} = \mathrm{div}\left(\left[\frac{\partial \psi}{\partial \lambda_+}\ \theta_+\theta_+^T + \frac{\partial \psi}{\partial \lambda_-}\ \theta_-\theta_-^T\right]\nabla I_i\right) \quad (i = 1..n) \qquad [3.9]$$

Here again, choice of particular functions $\psi$ can result in familiar variational approaches for scalar or multi-channel regularization, including of course the entire $\phi$-function formalism [BLO 98, TAN 00], with $\psi(\lambda_+, \lambda_-) = \phi\left(\sqrt{\lambda_+}\right)$, or the Beltrami flow formalism [KIM 00, SOC 01b, SOC 98, SOC 01a], with $\psi(\lambda_+, \lambda_-) = \sqrt{(1 + \lambda_+)(1 + \lambda_-)}$. Note that this last functional is proportional to the *area of the image* **I**, viewed as a 2D surface in $(n+2)$D space. This makes it clearer what the role is that is played by such a functional minimization in terms of image smoothing/regularization in this case, causing it to converge toward a surface of minimal area (see Figure 3.6).

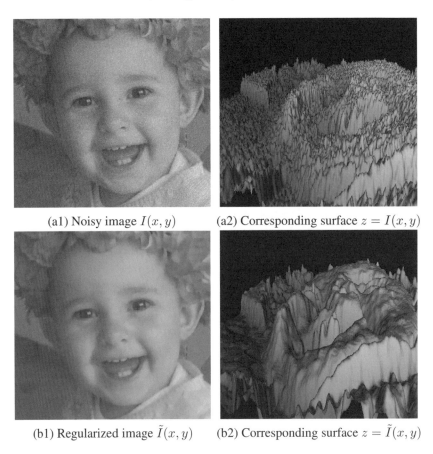

(a1) Noisy image $I(x, y)$      (a2) Corresponding surface $z = I(x, y)$

(b1) Regularized image $\tilde{I}(x, y)$      (b2) Corresponding surface $z = \tilde{I}(x, y)$

**Figure 3.6.** *Image regularization, viewed as minimization of the area of a surface*

In spite of this interesting global geometric interpretation, such variational regularization methods are lacking in flexibility. They are formulated as a global minimization process whereas, in contrast, the geometric smoothing properties that we would like to define are intrinsically local (since the type of degradation that we would like to correct is itself local in nature). The minimizing PDEs, obtained from the Euler-Lagrange equations, cannot be closely adapted to the different local geometric configurations of structures within the image (contours, corners, etc.). Nevertheless, this sort of flexibility in the smoothing behavior is often desirable, particularly when the noise level within an image is considerable.

### 3.4.2. *Divergence PDEs*

The work reported in [ALV 92, AUB 06, KOR 97, SAP 01, WEI 98] led to the development of more generic and locally flexible diffusion PDEs. The idea involves first replacing the scalar diffusivity $\phi'(\|\nabla I\|)/\|\nabla I\|$ that appears in the diffusion PDE [3.7] with an expression that depends on arbitrary local characteristics within the image. Having done this, we start to achieve the local aspect that we would like to see in the smoothing process, accepting that this comes at the expense of the global level of interpretation in the regularization process: generally speaking, these directly-derived PDEs no longer correspond to gradient descents for minimization of a functional.

In historical terms, the authors of [ALV 92] were the first to propose the use of a diffusivity function $g(\|\nabla(I * G_\sigma)\|)$ that no longer depended on the norm of the gradient $\|\nabla I\|$ but on the gradient norm convolved with a Gaussian $\|\nabla(I * G_\sigma)\|$ to measure scalar geometric variation in a way that is more robust in the face of noise:

$$\frac{\partial I}{\partial t} = \text{div}\left(g(\|\nabla(I * G_\sigma)\|) \, \nabla I\right)$$

This technique ensures that the formulations proposed for regularization are well-posed. However, it became clear that this would also enable them to take into account a more consistent local diffusion geometry, by bringing into play information from a more extended neighborhood of the current pixel (through the convolution operation). Subsequently, a significant generalization of these *divergence* type of equations for scalar and multi-channel images was proposed by Weickert in [WEI 97a, WEI 98]. The image pixels are represented as chemical or temperature concentrations subject to physical diffusion laws (Fick's law and continuity equation). Thus Weickert proposed a generic *divergence* equation, parameterized by a field $\mathbf{D}: \Omega \rightarrow \mathcal{P}(2)$ of $2 \times 2$ diffusion tensors:

$$\frac{\partial I_i}{\partial t} = \mathrm{div}\,(\mathbf{D}\nabla I_i) \qquad (i = 1..n) \qquad\qquad [3.10]$$

The tensor field $\mathbf{D}$ defines a *gradient flux* that is intended to give fine control over the local geometric behavior of the diffusion process in equation [3.10]. Note that the formalism of the $\psi$-functionals described in section 3.4.1 becomes a special case of PDE [3.10], with $\mathbf{D}$ defined at all points by $\mathbf{D} = \frac{\partial \psi}{\partial \lambda_+}\,\theta_+\theta_+^T + \frac{\partial \psi}{\partial \lambda_-}\,\theta_-\theta_-^T$.

More specifically, Weickert proposed to define the diffusion tensor at each point $\mathbf{X}$ in the image as $\mathbf{D} = \lambda_1 \mathbf{u}_1 \mathbf{u}_1^T + \lambda_2 \mathbf{u}_2 \mathbf{u}_2^T$, in other words by choosing its two eigenvectors $\mathbf{u}_1, \mathbf{u}_2$ and its eigenvalues $\lambda_1, \lambda_2$ to be functions of the spectral elements of the smoothed structure tensor $\mathbf{G}_{\alpha,\sigma}$, such that:

$$\begin{cases} \mathbf{u}_1 = \theta_+ \\ \mathbf{u}_2 = \theta_- \end{cases} \text{and} \begin{cases} \lambda_1 = \beta \\ \lambda_2 = \begin{cases} \beta & \text{if } \lambda_+ = \lambda_- \\ \beta + (1-\beta)\exp\left(\frac{-C}{(\lambda_+ - \lambda_-)^2}\right) & \text{otherwise} \end{cases} \end{cases}$$

$$[3.11]$$

($C > 0$ and $\beta \in [0, 1]$ are parameters of the method, defined by the user).

In the case of multi-channel images, it can be seen that the same tensor field $\mathbf{D}$ will be used to orient the diffusion over every component $I_i$ of the image, thereby ensuring that the components $I_i$ are smoothed in terms of a consistent multi-valued geometry that takes into account any correlation between the data in every channel of the image (i.e. $\mathbf{D}$ depends on $\mathbf{G}_{\alpha,\sigma}$), in contrast to approaches that treat each component independently.

Thus, in these studies Weickert assumed that the form of the diffusion tensor at each point $\mathbf{X}$ in the field $\mathbf{D}$ is representative of the required smoothing geometry at this point. The choice of the tensor field defined by equation [3.11] then implies that:

– in regions with homogeneous pixel levels, $\lambda_+ \approx \lambda_- \approx 0$ and so we obtain $\lambda_1 \approx \lambda_2 \approx \beta$, i.e. $\mathbf{D} \approx \alpha\, \mathbb{I}_d$ (identity matrix). The tensor $\mathbf{D}$ is then *isotropic* within these regions of small variation, which is consistent since the intention should be to smooth the noise along all axes within this type of region. The PDE in [3.10] becomes locally simplified into a heat equation $\frac{\partial I_i}{\partial t} = \Delta I_i$ for each channel $I_i$, where $\Delta I_i = \frac{\partial^2 I_i}{\partial x^2} + \frac{\partial^2 I_i}{\partial y^2}$ defines the Laplacian of $I_i$;

– along image contours, we instead have $\lambda_+ \gg \lambda_- \gg 0$, and so $\lambda_2 > \lambda_1 > 0$. Here, the diffusion tensor $\mathbf{D}$ is thus fundamentally *anisotropic* (since the value of $\beta$ is small), and is principally oriented along the $\theta_-$ direction of the image contours, which also seems consistent with the aim of avoiding over-smoothing of these contours.

Nevertheless, it is important to note that the actual amplitudes and directions of local smoothing as performed by the PDE [3.10] *are not precisely defined by the spectral elements* (i.e. the shape) of the diffusion tensor $\mathbf{D}$ localized at the point $\mathbf{X}$. It is in fact possible to obtain smoothing behavior that is contradictory to the form of the tensor, as illustrated by the following study example: suppose that we would like to smooth a scalar image $I: \Omega \rightarrow \mathbb{R}$ in a purely anisotropic manner for all pixels along the gradient directions $\frac{\nabla I}{\|\nabla I\|}$ with a constant smoothing magnitude of 1. This is of course not a very interesting case in practice, since in this case we are favoring the smoothing of image discontinuities *orthogonal* to their direction, which will very rapidly lead to over-smoothing of the image. Intuitively, we would then be tempted to define $\mathbf{D}$ at all points $\mathbf{X} \in \Omega$ as:

$$\forall \mathbf{X} \in \Omega, \quad \mathbf{D} = \left( \frac{\nabla I}{\|\nabla I\|} \right) \left( \frac{\nabla I}{\|\nabla I\|} \right)^T$$

i.e. a tensor whose two eigenvalues are 1 and 0, with the associated eigenvectors being respectively $\frac{\nabla I}{\|\nabla I\|}$ and $\frac{\nabla I^\perp}{\|\nabla I\|}$. This would result in equation [3.10] being simplified to:

$$\frac{\partial I}{\partial t} = \mathrm{div}\left(\frac{1}{\|\nabla I\|^2}\,\nabla I \nabla I^T \nabla I\right) = \mathrm{div}\,(\nabla I) = \Delta I$$

However, the evolution of this *heat transfer equation* is known to be similar to the convolution of the image $I$ with an normalized isotropic Gaussian filter $G_\sigma$ with standard deviation $\sigma = \sqrt{2\,t}$ [KOE 84]. Thus, for a specific choice of *purely anisotropic* tensors $\mathbf{D}$ we eventually obtain a purely *isotropic* regularization behavior, without any preferred direction for the smoothing. Note that if we had chosen $\mathbf{D} = \mathbb{I}_{\mathrm{d}}$ (the identity matrix), we would have obtained exactly the same equation: thus different fields $\mathbf{D}$ with very different forms (isotropic and anisotropic) ultimately lead to the same locally isotropic smoothing behavior. In fact, the divergence is a derivative operator. As a consequence, the smoothing defined by equation [3.10] will always depend implicitly on the spatial variation of the tensor field $\mathbf{D}$. From a practical point of view, the *divergence* PDE in equation [3.10] does not offer the possibility of defining a local smoothing behavior that can easily be defined on a point-by-point basis.

### 3.4.3. *Oriented Laplacian PDEs*

2D *Oriented Laplacian* PDEs take the view that a local smoothing process can be decomposed into two 1D heat equations oriented respectively along the two orthogonal directions $\mathbf{u}_1$ and $\mathbf{u}_2$, with each having different associated smoothing magnitudes $c_1$ and $c_2$. The amplitudes and orientations for the smoothing are chosen independently for each point, to adapt to the local geometric configuration of the image (see Figure 3.7). The resultant equation can be written as the sum of two 1D heat transfer equations:

$$\frac{\partial \mathbf{I}}{\partial t} = c_1 \mathbf{I}_{\mathbf{u}_1 \mathbf{u}_1} + c_2 \mathbf{I}_{\mathbf{u}_2 \mathbf{u}_2} \qquad\qquad [3.12]$$

where $\mathbf{u}_1$ and $\mathbf{u}_2$ are orthonormal vectors and $c_1, c_2 \geq 0$. $\mathbf{I}_{\mathbf{u}_1 \mathbf{u}_1}$ and $\mathbf{I}_{\mathbf{u}_2 \mathbf{u}_2}$ represent the second derivatives of $\mathbf{I}$ along the directions $\mathbf{u}_1$ and $\mathbf{u}_2$, and each of their vector components is formally defined as:

$$\forall i = 1..n, \quad I_{i_{\mathbf{u}_1 \mathbf{u}_1}} = \mathbf{u}_1^T \mathbf{H}_i \mathbf{u}_1 \quad \text{and} \quad I_{i_{\mathbf{u}_2 \mathbf{u}_2}} = \mathbf{u}_2^T \mathbf{H}_i \mathbf{u}_2$$

where $\mathbf{H}_i$ is the Hessian matrix of $I_i$, defined for all points $\mathbf{X} \in \Omega$ as:

$$\mathbf{H}_i = \begin{pmatrix} I_{i_{xx}} & I_{i_{xy}} \\ I_{i_{xy}} & I_{i_{yy}} \end{pmatrix} = \begin{pmatrix} \frac{\partial^2 I_i}{\partial x^2} & \frac{\partial^2 I_i}{\partial x \partial y} \\ \frac{\partial^2 I_i}{\partial x \partial y} & \frac{\partial^2 I_i}{\partial y^2} \end{pmatrix} \qquad [3.13]$$

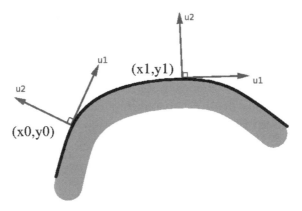

**Figure 3.7.** *Principle of oriented Laplacians: two 1D smoothings performed simultaneously along orthogonal directions*

Here, the diffusion behavior is entirely defined by the supplied smoothing directions $\mathbf{u}_1, \mathbf{u}_2$ and their associated smoothing magnitudes $c_1$ and $c_2$ for each point $\mathbf{X}$ in the image. This very general formulation was first proposed in [KOR 96] for the regularization of a scalar image $I$, with the following choices for the functions $c_1, c_2$ and $\mathbf{u}_1, \mathbf{u}_2$:

$$\begin{cases} \mathbf{u}_1 = \xi = \frac{\nabla I^{\perp}}{\|\nabla I\|} \\ \mathbf{u}_2 = \eta = \frac{\nabla I}{\|\nabla I\|} \end{cases} \text{ and } \begin{cases} c_1 = 1 \\ c_2 = g(\|\nabla I * G_{\sigma}\|) \end{cases} \qquad [3.14]$$

where $g: \mathbb{R} \to \mathbb{R}$ is a function that decreases toward 0 and is chosen to ensure that the smoothing performed orthogonal to discontinuities is attenuated within strong contour regions (i.e. strong gradients). The choice of parameters in equation [3.14] can be used to obtain consistent anisotropic smoothing along the direction of the contours $\xi$, even in regions with very high gradients, since $c_1 = 1$ throughout the image. However, this general formalism of *oriented Laplacians* can also be used to derive many other equations that appear throughout the literature, such as for example the set of $\phi$-functionals, obtained by choosing $c_1 = \phi'(\|\nabla I\|)/\|\nabla I\|$, $c_2 = \phi''(\|\nabla I\|)$, $\mathbf{u}_1 = \xi$ and $\mathbf{v}_2 = \eta$, or the *mean curvature flow* $\frac{\partial I}{\partial t} = I_{\xi\xi}$, with $c_1 = 1$, $c_2 = 0$, $\mathbf{u}_1 = \xi$ and $\mathbf{v}_2 = \eta$ [CAR 98]. Note that this last type of smoothing cannot be formulated in terms of a *divergence* expression.

Ringach and Sapiro [SAP 96b] were the first to propose an extension of mean curvature flow $I_t = I_{\xi\xi}$ to multi-channel images, using an *oriented Laplacian* formulation. Naturally, they based themselves on the geometric attributes of Di Zenzo to incorporate multi-valued geometric information into their diffusion equation:

$$\frac{\partial \mathbf{I}}{\partial t} = g(\lambda_+ - \lambda_-)\, \mathbf{I}_{\theta_-\theta_-} \qquad\qquad [3.15]$$

where $g: \mathbb{R} \to \mathbb{R}$ is a positive increasing function whose role is to avoid over-smoothing in high-gradient regions. Here also, each component $I_i$ is smoothed along *a common direction* $\theta_-$ (that of the vector contours) with *a common amplitude*. In spite of this well-motivated extension to the approach, several drawbacks remain in terms of its application to image regularization:

– the consistency measure $\mathcal{N}_- = \sqrt{\lambda_+ - \lambda_-}$ was used to determine the local multi-valued variation, with the aim of reducing diffusion across image contours. This is not an optimal choice (as noted in section 3.3), since for certain "junction" type structures the measure $\mathcal{N}_-$ becomes small, leading to over-smoothing at such points;

– in locally homogeneous regions (with little variation, where $\mathcal{N}_- \to 0$), the diffusion occurs along a single direction $\theta_-$, which in this case would for the most part be determined randomly by the noise present in the image, since no contrasting geometric structure is present to define a consistent direction. This smoothing, which is one-directional throughout, leads to undesirable texturing effects, especially in the case of multi-channel images where all the components are smoothed in a consistent manner and hence are not allowed to mix. Isotropic smoothing would clearly be preferable for this type of geometric configuration.

### 3.4.4. *Trace PDEs*

A simpler formalization of *oriented Laplacian* PDEs was subsequently proposed in [TSC 05]. The idea was based around the use of a field of diffusion tensors $\mathbf{T}: \Omega \rightarrow \mathcal{P}(2)$ to model the smoothing geometry in equation [3.12], instead of considering the smoothing directions $\mathbf{u}_1$, $\mathbf{u}_2$ and amplitudes $c_1$, $c_2$ separately. The proposed equation is equivalent to the earlier PDE [3.12] rewritten for multi-channel images using the *trace* operator:

$$\forall i = 1, .., n, \qquad \frac{\partial I_i}{\partial t} = \text{trace}\,(\mathbf{TH}_i) \qquad\qquad [3.16]$$

where $\mathbf{H}_i$ represents the Hessian matrix of $I_i$ [3.13] and $\mathbf{T}$ is the diffusion tensor field, calculated as $\mathbf{T}_{(\mathbf{x})} = c_1\ \mathbf{u}_1\mathbf{u}_1^T + c_2\ \mathbf{v}_2\mathbf{v}_2^T$. This re-introduces the coupled aspect of regularization, since each component $I_i$ of $\mathbf{I}$ is smoothed on the basis of the same tensor field $\mathbf{T}$.

Mathematically, equations [3.12] and [3.16] are strictly equivalent, but the latter makes the separation between the smoothing geometry (defined by the tensor field $\mathbf{T}$) and the smoothing process itself more clear. The approach is ultimately very similar to Weickert's approach and to his *divergence* PDE [3.10], with the regularization problem largely consisting of defining a diffusion tensor field appropriate to the specific application in question. However, in the case of *trace* PDEs, the tensor field that defines the local smoothing behavior has the interesting property of *uniqueness*: two *different* tensor fields will necessarily lead to two *distinct* smoothing behaviors (since the *trace* operator is not derivative).

Equation [3.16] in fact has a simple geometric interpretation in terms of *local filtering* by oriented Gaussian kernels. Consider first the case where $\mathbf{T}$ is a constant tensor field. It can then be shown that the formal solution of the PDE [3.16] is:

$$I_i^{[t]} = I_i^{[t=0]} \,*\, G^{(\mathbf{T},t)} \qquad (i = 1..n) \qquad\qquad [3.17]$$

where $*$ defines the convolution operator and $G^{(\mathbf{T},t)}$ is the normalized Gaussian kernel oriented by $\mathbf{T}$:

$$G^{(\mathbf{T},t)}(\mathbf{X}) = \frac{1}{4\pi t} \exp\left(-\frac{\mathbf{X}^T \mathbf{T}^{-1} \mathbf{X}}{4t}\right) \quad \text{where } \mathbf{X} = (x\ y)^T \quad [3.18]$$

Thus, we obtain an anisotropic version of the property demonstrated by Koenderink [KOE 84], relating to the connection between the convolution operator and isotropic diffusion, which we can see here if we select $\mathbf{T} = \mathbb{I}_{\mathrm{d}}$, which then simplifies the PDE [3.16] into the 2D heat transfer equation: $\frac{\partial I_i}{\partial t} = \text{trace}\,(\mathbf{H}_i) = \Delta I_i$.

Figure 3.8 illustrates this geometrical property of the tensor smoothing of the *trace* PDE [3.16], showing three Gaussian kernels $G^{(\mathbf{T},t)}$ that are deformed by isotropic and anisotropic tensors $\mathbf{T}$, and the three resultant evolutions of the corresponding PDE, as applied to a color image. It can be seen that the traces of the Gaussian functions $\mathbf{G}^{(\mathbf{T},t)}$ correctly represent the tensors $\mathbf{T}$ in ellipse form. Conversely, it is clear that the form of the tensors $\mathbf{T}$ does indeed represent the true smoothing geometry performed by the PDE [3.16].

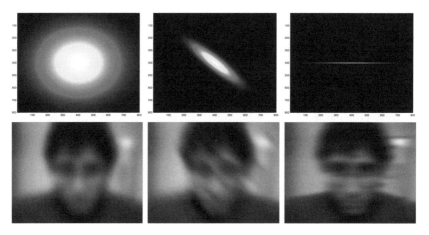

**Figure 3.8.** *Trace PDE viewed as a convolution by oriented kernels*

When $\mathbf{T}$ is not constant (which is generally the case), it then models a field $\Omega \to P(2)$ of diffusion tensors that vary with position.

The PDE [3.16] becomes *nonlinear* but can still be viewed as the application of *local convolution masks* $G^{\mathbf{T},t}(\mathbf{X})$ that vary in space and time over the image $\mathbf{I}$. Figure 3.9 illustrates this property with three distinct examples of non-constant tensor fields $\mathbf{T}$ (represented by fields of ellipses) and the resultant evolutions of the corresponding PDE [3.16]. As before, the form of each tensor $\mathbf{T}$ gives the precise geometry of the local smoothing process performed by the *trace* PDE [3.16] in a pointwise manner. Since the *trace* operator is not derivative, the local interpretation of the smoothing process as a convolution by oriented Gaussian masks over an infinitesimal neighborhood is still valid in this case.

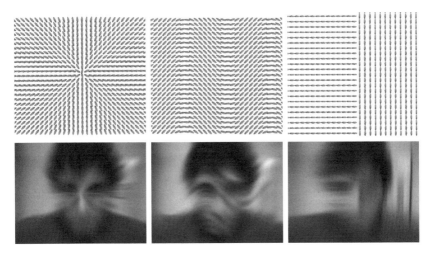

**Figure 3.9.** *Trace PDE using non-constant diffusion tensors*

In the same way that the structure tensors $\mathbf{G}_{\alpha,\sigma}$ measure the principal orientations $\theta_+, \theta_-$ at all points and the local contrasts $\lambda_+ + \lambda_-$ of the contours, the diffusion tensor field $\mathbf{T}$ represents the preferred orientations of local smoothing, along with the amplitudes of the smoothing along these directions again at all points in the image. Intuitively, it would seem sensible to choose $\mathbf{T}$ to be a function of the local geometry of $\mathbf{I}$, which implies that it depends on the spectral elements $\lambda_-, \lambda_+$ and $\theta_-, \theta_+$ of the smoothed structure tensor $\mathbf{G}_{\alpha,\sigma}$. For denoising of multichannel images, the following choice was proposed in [TSC 05]:

$$c_1 = f^-_{(\lambda_+,\lambda_-)} = \frac{1}{(1 + \lambda_+ + \lambda_-)^{p_1}} \quad \text{and}$$

$$c_2 = f^+_{(\lambda_+,\lambda_-)} = \frac{1}{(1 + \lambda_+ + \lambda_-)^{p_2}} \qquad\qquad [3.19]$$

with $\mathbf{u}_1 = \theta_-$ and $\mathbf{u}_2 = \theta_+$.

This choice is a reasonable one, since it satisfies a natural local smoothing behavior for denoising:

– for a point lying on an image contour ($\lambda_+ + \lambda_-$ is large), smoothing mostly occurs along the direction $\theta_-$ of the contour (since $f^+ << f^-$), with an amplitude inversely proportional to the local contrast of the contour;

– for a point lying in a homogeneous region ($\lambda_+ + \lambda_-$ is small), smoothing is performed along all possible orientations in the plane (isotropic smoothing, since $f^+ \approx f^-$) and consequently $\mathbf{T} \approx \mathbb{I}_d$ (identity matrix). Thus the PDE [3.16] behaves locally like a heat transfer equation;

– the two parameters $p_1 < p_2 \in \mathbb{R}$ can be used to define in detail the type of anisotropy of the smoothing as a function of the local geometric configuration, and between these two extremes: If $p_1 \approx p_2$ the smoothing is isotropic almost everywhere, while remaining locally inhibited by strong local contrasts (as is preferred in the case of strong noise). If $p_2 >> p_1$ the smoothing is anisotropic almost everywhere, especially along color contours $\theta_-$, even in relatively homogeneous regions (as is preferred in the case of weak noise).

The *trace* equation [3.16] is an interesting formulation that can be used to separate the smoothing geometry and the smoothing action itself, while offering a geometric interpretation in the form of local filtering by oriented Gaussian kernels used to perform the smoothing. It makes the natural links clearer between diffusion PDEs and other types of local smoothing such as bilateral filtering [BAR 00, TOM 98]. Nevertheless, we may wonder if the local *Gaussian* behavior of the smoothing (whose amplitude and orientation are given by the diffusion tensor $\mathbf{T}$) is the most appropriate for a regularization process.

*A priori*, on highly curved image structures (such as corners) the behavior of this Gaussian smoothing is not optimal. When *the and*, the orientation $\theta_-$ of the contours is significant, a local Gaussian filter will have a tendency to *round off* these contours, even when this smoothing is only performed along their direction $\theta_-$. This is due to the fact that an oriented Gaussian mask such as equation [3.18] *is not itself curved*. This problem is illustrated in Figure 3.10b and Figure 3.11b where many iterations of the PDE [3.16] have been applied to color images (synthetic and real) and where **T** has been defined by equation [3.19]. It can be seen that highly curved structures within the images have been rounded, resulting in undesirable over-smoothing of the corners of the square in Figure 3.10b, or the very fine structure within the fingerprint in Figure 3.11b.

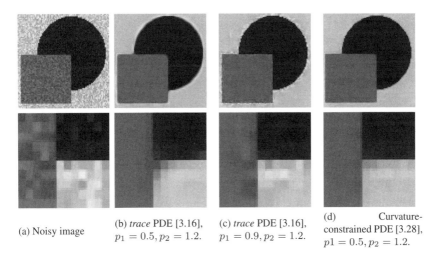

(a) Noisy image

(b) *trace* PDE [3.16], $p_1 = 0.5, p_2 = 1.2.$

(c) *trace* PDE [3.16], $p_1 = 0.9, p_2 = 1.2.$

(d)    Curvature-constrained PDE [3.28], $p1 = 0.5, p_2 = 1.2.$

**Figure 3.10.** *Problems of over- or under-smoothing encountered with the use of a trace PDE on image structures with high curvature (detail on second row). The number of iterations was deliberately exaggerated in order to accentuate the effect*

To prevent this over-smoothing effect, we could imagine halting the evolution of the diffusion PDE at the corners (by setting the tensors **T** to zero in these regions, in other words choosing $f^- = f^+ = 0$). However, this implies a need to explicitly detect highly curved structures in images that are often noisy, something that is in itself an ill-posed problem requiring robust solutions that are difficult or expensive to implement.

The risk is then that the image will be *under-smoothed*, leaving noise present at corners and/or contours. The compromise between good noise suppression and preservation of highly-curved structures is a relatively difficult one to make, when *trace* type PDEs such as [3.16] are used.

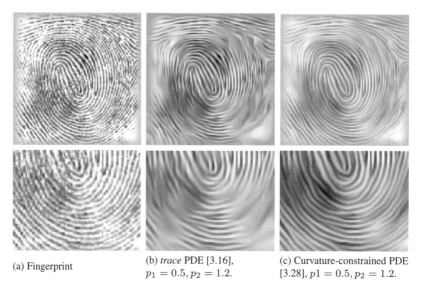

(a) Fingerprint

(b) *trace* PDE [3.16], $p_1 = 0.5, p_2 = 1.2$.

(c) Curvature-constrained PDE [3.28], $p1 = 0.5, p_2 = 1.2$.

**Figure 3.11.** *Comparison of* trace *PDE and curvature-constrained PDE on a real-world image (detail on second row). The number of iterations was deliberately exaggerated to accentuate the effect*

It therefore appears critical that we should take into account the *curvature* of the smoothing directions, and this is what will motivate the rest of our discussion. In what follows, we will define a class of *trace* PDEs that will smooth a multi-channel image **I** based on a tensor geometry **T**, *while implicitly taking into account the curvature of the field lines of* **T**. A comparison of the results of this constrained diffusion equation is shown in Figures 3.10d and 3.11c.

## 3.5. Regularization and curvature preservation

The formalism of *curvature-preserving PDEs* was first introduced in [TSC 06] and defines a specific variation on multi-channel diffusion PDEs. The aim is that they should be both a generic regularization method built around a tensor-based smoothing geometry (like that found with *divergence* or *trace* PDEs), but also focused on the preservation of high-curvature fine structure.

### 3.5.1. *Single smoothing direction*

To illustrate the general idea of these PDEs, we will initially restrict ourselves to the case of image regularization directed not by a tensor field $\mathbf{T}$ but by a *vector field* $\mathbf{w}: \Omega \to \mathbb{R}^2$. The local smoothing is thus performed at each point along a single direction $\frac{\mathbf{w}}{\|\mathbf{w}\|}$, with a smoothing magnitude $\|\mathbf{w}\|$. We will write the two components of $\mathbf{w}$ as $\mathbf{w} = (u \ v)^T$.

The *curvature-preserving* regularization PDE that smooths $\mathbf{I}$ along $\mathbf{w}$ is defined in [TSC 06] as:

$$\forall i = 1, \ldots, n, \qquad \frac{\partial I_i}{\partial t} = \text{trace} \left( \mathbf{w}\mathbf{w}^T \mathbf{H}_i \right) + \nabla I_i^T \mathbf{J}_\mathbf{w} \mathbf{w} \qquad [3.20]$$

where $\mathbf{J}_\mathbf{w}$ is the Jacobian matrix for $\mathbf{w}$, and $\mathbf{H}_i$ is the Hessian matrix for $I_i$:

$$\mathbf{J}_\mathbf{w} = \begin{pmatrix} \frac{\partial u}{\partial x} & \frac{\partial u}{\partial y} \\ \frac{\partial v}{\partial x} & \frac{\partial v}{\partial y} \end{pmatrix} \quad \text{and} \quad \mathbf{H}_i = \begin{pmatrix} \frac{\partial^2 I_i}{\partial x^2} & \frac{\partial^2 I_i}{\partial x \partial y} \\ \frac{\partial^2 I_i}{\partial x \partial y} & \frac{\partial^2 I_i}{\partial y^2} \end{pmatrix}$$

The PDE defined in equation [3.20] is just the same as the *trace* equation we saw earlier, but with an additional term $\nabla I_i^T \mathbf{J}_\mathbf{w} \mathbf{w}$, which in this case smooths the image $\mathbf{I}$ along the $\mathbf{w}$ direction using Gaussian filters with their local orientation defined by $\mathbf{w}$ (see section 3.4.4). This additional term depends on the variation of the vector field $\mathbf{w}$ (and hence implicitly on the curvature of its field lines). Consider now the curve $\mathcal{C}_{(a)}^\mathbf{X}$ defining a *field line* of $\mathbf{w}$, starting from a point $\mathbf{X}$ and parameterized by $a \in \mathbb{R}$ (see Figure 3.12):

$$\begin{cases} \mathcal{C}_{(0)}^\mathbf{X} &= \mathbf{X} \\ \frac{\partial \mathcal{C}_{(a)}^\mathbf{X}}{\partial a} &= \mathbf{w}(\mathcal{C}_{(a)}^\mathbf{X}) \end{cases} \qquad\qquad [3.21]$$

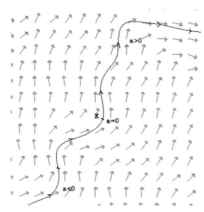

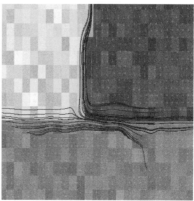

(a) Field line for a vector field **w**.

(b) Example field lines when **w** is chosen as the 2nd eigenvector $\theta_-$ of the smoothed structure tensor $\mathbf{G}_{\alpha,\sigma}$ for a color image **I** (here, a block represents a single pixel).

**Figure 3.12.** *Field lines $\mathcal{C}^{\mathbf{X}}$ for the vector field* **w**: $\Omega \to \mathbb{R}^2$

We will call $\mathcal{F}$ the field line family for **w**.

Taking a 2nd-order Taylor expansion of $\mathcal{C}^{\mathbf{X}}_{(a)}$ around $a = 0$ gives:

$$\mathcal{C}^{\mathbf{X}}_{(h)} = \mathcal{C}^{\mathbf{X}}_{(0)} + h\frac{\partial \mathcal{C}^{\mathbf{X}}_{(a)}}{\partial a}_{|a=0} + \frac{h^2}{2}\frac{\partial^2 \mathcal{C}^{\mathbf{X}}_{(a)}}{\partial a^2}_{|a=0} + O(h^3)$$

$$= \mathbf{X} + h\mathbf{w}_{(\mathbf{X})} + \frac{h^2}{2}\,\mathbf{J}_{\mathbf{w}_{(\mathbf{X})}}\mathbf{w}_{(\mathbf{X})} + O(h^3)$$

where $h \to 0$ and $O(h^n) = h^n\,\epsilon_n$. From this, we can then deduce the 2nd-order Taylor expansion of $I_i(\mathcal{C}^{\mathbf{X}}_{(a)})$ around $a = 0$, which gives information on the variations in the image values in the vicinity of **X** as we move along the field line $\mathcal{C}^{\mathbf{X}}$:

$$I_i(\mathcal{C}^{\mathbf{X}}_{(h)}) = I_i(\mathbf{X}) + h\nabla I^T_{i(\mathbf{X})}\left(\mathbf{w}_{(\mathbf{X})} + \frac{h}{2}\,\mathbf{J}_{\mathbf{w}_{(\mathbf{X})}}\mathbf{w}_{(\mathbf{X})}\right)$$

$$+ \frac{h^2}{2}\mathrm{trace}\left(\mathbf{w}_{(\mathbf{X})}\mathbf{w}^T_{(\mathbf{X})}\mathbf{H}_{i(\mathbf{X})}\right) + O(h^3)$$

Note that trace $\left(\mathbf{w}_{(\mathbf{X})}\mathbf{w}_{(\mathbf{X})}^T\mathbf{H}_{i(\mathbf{X})}\right) = \frac{\partial^2 I_i}{\partial \mathbf{w}^2}$ corresponds to the second directional derivative of $I_i$ along $\mathbf{w}$. The second directional derivative of the function $a \rightarrow I_i(\mathcal{C}_{(a)}^{\mathbf{X}})$ at the point $a = 0$ can then be written as:

$$\frac{\partial^2 I_i(\mathcal{C}_{(a)}^{\mathbf{X}})}{\partial a^2}\bigg|_{a=0} = \lim_{h \to 0} \frac{1}{h^2}\left[I_i(\mathcal{C}_{(h)}^{\mathbf{X}}) + I_i(\mathcal{C}_{(-h)}^{\mathbf{X}}) - 2I_i(\mathcal{C}_{(0)}^{\mathbf{X}})\right]$$

$$= \text{trace}\left(\mathbf{w}_{(\mathbf{X})}\mathbf{w}_{(\mathbf{X})}^T\mathbf{H}_{i(\mathbf{X})}\right) + \nabla I_i^T \mathbf{J}_{\mathbf{w}(\mathbf{X})}\mathbf{w}_{(\mathbf{X})}$$

[3.22]

which turns out to be precisely the velocity term for the curvature-preserving diffusion PDE [3.20]. Now, globally speaking, we can consider the PDE [3.20], for each field line $\mathcal{F}$:

$$\forall \mathcal{C} \in \mathcal{F}, \quad \forall a \in \mathbb{R}, \quad \frac{\partial I_i(\mathcal{C}_{(a)})}{\partial t} = \frac{\partial^2 I_i(\mathcal{C}_{(a)})}{\partial a^2} \qquad [3.23]$$

We now recognize equation [3.23] to be a *1D heat transfer equation along the field line* $\mathcal{C}$, which is thus very different from a heat transfer equation *oriented* by $\mathbf{w}$, as was the case in the formulation $\frac{\partial I_i}{\partial t} = \frac{\partial^2 I_i}{\partial \mathbf{w}^2}$ since in this case, the curvature of the field lines of $\mathbf{w}$ will be implicitly taken into account. In particular, this PDE has the property of being zero when the image values are entirely constant along the field lines $\mathcal{C}$ of $\mathbf{w}$, with this still holding true whatever their curvature. In the context of regularization, by defining a field $\mathbf{w}$, which is at all points tangent to the important structures within the image, we can ensure that these structures are preserved by the smoothing process, *even in cases with high curvature* (such as corners for example). It is not possible to take this curvature into account in such a natural way if *divergence* or *trace* PDEs are used. This property of curvature preservation that is found in equation [3.20] is illustrated in Figures 3.10d and 3.11b. We will also show in the next section that a rapid approximation to the solution of equation [3.20] at time $t$ can be estimated through the use of a well-posed analytical approach.

### 3.5.2. *Analogy with line integral convolutions*

Line integral convolutions (*LIC*) were first proposed in [CAB 93] as a technique for rendering a textured image to represent an arbitrary vector field w: $\Omega \rightarrow \mathbb{R}^2$. The initial idea, expressed in a discrete formulation, involves smoothing a pure noise image $\mathbf{I}_{noisy}$ by averaging the pixel values along the integral curves (in other words the field lines) of $\mathbf{w}$. In its continuous formulation, this averaging is written as:

$$\forall \mathbf{X} \in \Omega, \quad \mathbf{I}^{LIC}_{(\mathbf{X})} = \frac{1}{N} \int_{-\infty}^{+\infty} f(p)\, \mathbf{I}_{noisy}(\mathcal{C}^{\mathbf{X}}_{(p)})\, dp \qquad [3.24]$$

where $f: \mathbb{R} \rightarrow \mathbb{R}$ is an even function (decreasing toward 0 over $\mathbb{R}^+$) and, as before, $\mathcal{C}^{\mathbf{X}}$ defines the *field line* of $\mathbf{w}$ starting from the point $\mathbf{X}$. The normalization factor $N = \int_{-\infty}^{+\infty} f(p)\, dp$ averages the pixel values along $\mathcal{C}^{\mathbf{X}}$.

As noted in the previous section, the curvature-preserving PDE [3.20] can be thought of as a 1D heat transfer equation [3.23] along the field line $\mathcal{C}^{\mathbf{X}} \in \mathcal{F}$. Using the change of variables $\mathbf{L}_{(a)} = \mathbf{I}(\mathcal{C}^{\mathbf{X}}_{(a)})$, equation [3.23] can be rewritten as $\frac{\partial \mathbf{L}}{\partial t}(a) = \mathbf{L}''_{(a)}$. The solution $\mathbf{L}^{[t]}$ for this heat transfer equation at time $t$ is then known to be the 1D convolution of $\mathbf{L}^{[t=0]}$ with the normalized Gaussian kernel $G_{\sqrt{2t}}$ [DER 97, KOE 84], so that:

$$\mathbf{L}^{[t]}_{(a)} = \int_{-\infty}^{+\infty} \mathbf{L}^{[t=0]}_{(p)}\, G_{\sqrt{2t}(a-p)}\, dp \text{ with } G_{\sqrt{2t}(p)} = \frac{1}{\sqrt{4\pi t}} \exp\left(-\frac{p^2}{4t}\right)$$
$$[3.25]$$

Replacing $\mathbf{L}$ with $\mathbf{I}$ in equation [3.25] for $a = 0$, while assuming that $\mathcal{C}^{\mathbf{X}}_{(0)} = \mathbf{X}$ and $G_{t(-p)} = G_{t(p)}$, we find:

$$\forall \mathbf{X} \in \Omega, \quad \mathbf{I}^{[t]}_{(\mathbf{X})} = \int_{-\infty}^{+\infty} \mathbf{I}^{[t=0]}(\mathcal{C}^{\mathbf{X}}_{(p)})\, G_{\sqrt{2t}(p)}\, dp \qquad [3.26]$$

equation [3.26] represents a specific case for the continuous *LIC* equation [3.24], with a Gaussian weighting $f = G_{\sqrt{2t}}$, and a normalization factor $N = \int_{-\infty}^{+\infty} G_{\sqrt{2t}(p)}\, dp = 1$. From the point of view of local filtering, the evolution of the curvature-preserving PDE [3.20] can then be interpreted as the application of infinitesimal local convolutions using local $1D$ Gaussian masks *along the field lines* $\mathcal{C}$ of $\mathbf{w}$. This type of anisotropic smoothing ultimately results in *curved* Gaussian filtering, as opposed to simply *oriented* Gaussian filtering.

The application of this equation to a multi-channel image $\mathbf{I}$, choosing $\mathbf{w}$ to be the vector field of secondary eigenvectors of the smoothed structure tensor $\mathbf{G}_{\alpha,\sigma}$ (i.e. the contour direction), results in anisotropic smoothing of $\mathbf{I}$ with contour preservation, even in the case of highly curved contours. This is illustrated in Figure 3.12b, where a selection of field lines $\mathcal{C}^{\mathbf{X}}$ are shown around a "T-junction" type structure. Note how the field lines curve around the junction with sub-pixel precision. Calculation of the field lines is performed in a robust manner by using classical Runge-Kutta type schemes [PRE 92]. It should, however, be noted that equation [3.26] is only an analytical solution to equation [3.20] when $\mathbf{w}$ is *not time varying*, which is not true in the general case of nonlinear PDEs, since the desired smoothing geometry is re-evaluated at each iteration. This, then, introduces time variation in the smoothing geometry. To make allowances for this, it is therefore necessary to explicitly evaluate several consecutive iterations of the *LIC* scheme [3.26], with the vector field $\mathbf{w}$ being iteratively re-evaluated. This is also what is done with more traditional explicit Euler schemes for solving diffusion PDEs, which assume that the smoothing geometry can be considered to be constant between two successive instants $\mathbf{I}^{[t]}$ and $\mathbf{I}^{[t+dt]}$, as long as $dt$ is sufficiently small.

### 3.5.3. *Extension to multi-directional smoothing*

In [TSC 06], the curvature-preserving one-directional smoothing PDE [3.20] is extended to be driven by a tensor-based smoothing geometry $\mathbf{T} \colon \Omega \to P(2)$ instead of a simple vector-based geometry $\mathbf{w} \colon \Omega \to \mathbb{R}^2$. This extension is useful since a diffusion tensor is capable of describing much more flexible and complex smoothing behaviors than is possible with a single direction: it can simultaneously model *anisotropic* and *isotropic* geometries. The problem is not trivial, however, since the concepts of curvature and field lines for a tensor field $\mathbf{T}$ are not as naturally defined as they are for a vector field $\mathbf{w}$.

To do this, the smoothing process based around a tensor geometry is decomposed as a set of elementary processes based around a single-directional (vector) geometry, along all orientations within the plane. Noting first that:

$$\int_{\alpha=0}^{\pi} a_\alpha a_\alpha^T \, d\alpha = \frac{\pi}{2} \, \mathbb{I}_d \quad \text{where } a_\alpha = \begin{pmatrix} \cos \alpha \\ \\ \sin \alpha \end{pmatrix}$$

we deduce a decomposition of all any tensor $\mathbf{T}$ of 2D in the form:

$$\mathbf{T} = \frac{2}{\pi} \sqrt{\mathbf{T}} \left( \int_{\alpha=0}^{\pi} a_\alpha a_\alpha^T \, d\alpha \right) \sqrt{\mathbf{T}}$$

where $\sqrt{\mathbf{T}} = \sqrt{f^+} \mathbf{u}\mathbf{u}^T + \sqrt{f^-} \mathbf{v}\mathbf{v}^T$ defines the square root (in the matrix sense) of the tensor $\mathbf{T} = f^+ \mathbf{u}\mathbf{u}^T + f^- \mathbf{v}\mathbf{v}^T$. It can be verified that $(\sqrt{\mathbf{T}})^2 = \mathbf{T}$ and $(\sqrt{\mathbf{T}})^T = \sqrt{\mathbf{T}}$. The tensor $\mathbf{T}$ can then be written as:

$$\mathbf{T} = \frac{2}{\pi} \int_{\alpha=0}^{\pi} (\sqrt{\mathbf{T}} a_\alpha)(\sqrt{\mathbf{T}} a_\alpha)^T \, d\alpha \qquad [3.27]$$

Intuitively, the tensor $\mathbf{T}$ has been divided into a sum of *elementary tensors* $(\sqrt{\mathbf{T}} a_\alpha)(\sqrt{\mathbf{T}} a_\alpha)^T$, where each one is purely anisotropic (a single non-zero eigenvalue) and oriented along a single direction $\sqrt{\mathbf{T}} a_\alpha \in \mathbb{R}^2$. Equation [3.27] then suggests that any diffusion PDE based around a tensor geometry can be decomposed into a sum of smoothing processes based around a vector geometry, in such a way as to respect the global tensor geometry $\mathbf{T}$ that we are working with. In particular:

– when $\mathbf{T} = \mathbb{I}_d$ (identity matrix), the tensor is isotropic and $\forall \alpha \in [0, \pi]$, $\sqrt{\mathbf{T}} a_\alpha = a_\alpha$. The resultant smoothing will then be performed correctly in the directions $a_\alpha$ within the plane, with the same smoothing magnitude in all directions;

– if $\mathbf{T} = \mathbf{u}\mathbf{u}^T$ (where $\mathbf{u} \in S^1$ is an arbitrary direction), the tensor is purely anisotropic and $\forall \alpha \in [0, \pi]$, $\sqrt{\mathbf{T}} a_\alpha = (\mathbf{u}^T a_\alpha)\mathbf{u}$. The resultant smoothing will then indeed be performed only along the principal direction $\mathbf{u}$ of the tensor $\mathbf{T}$, with this holding true for any angle $\alpha$.

Furthermore, using the decomposition of equation [3.27] and assuming that each single-direction smoothing operation would ideally be performed by a curvature-preserving approach such as equation [3.20], we derive the following curvature-preserving regularization PDE, acting on a multi-channel image $\mathbf{I}: \Omega \rightarrow \mathbb{R}^n$ and based around a *tensor* smoothing geometry $\mathbf{T}$:

$$\frac{\partial I_i}{\partial t} = \frac{2}{\pi} \int_{\alpha=0}^{\pi} \mathrm{trace}\left((\sqrt{\mathbf{T}}a_\alpha)(\sqrt{\mathbf{T}}a_\alpha)^T \mathbf{H}_i\right) + \nabla I_i^T \mathbf{J}_{\sqrt{\mathbf{T}}a_\alpha} \sqrt{\mathbf{T}}a_\alpha \, d\alpha$$

which can be simplified to:

$$\frac{\partial I_i}{\partial t} = \mathrm{trace}(\mathbf{T}\mathbf{H}_i) + \frac{2}{\pi} \nabla I_i^T \int_{\alpha=0}^{\pi} \mathbf{J}_{\sqrt{\mathbf{T}}a_\alpha} \sqrt{\mathbf{T}}a_\alpha \, d\alpha \qquad [3.28]$$

where $a_\alpha = (\cos\alpha \quad \sin\alpha)^T$ and $\mathbf{J}_{\sqrt{\mathbf{T}}a_\alpha}$ is the Jacobian matrix of the vector field $\Omega \rightarrow \sqrt{\mathbf{T}}a_\alpha$. Here again, as in the one-directional case, we find we have a *trace* type PDE [3.16], but with an additional term that can take into account a specific curvature constraint on the field lines inherent to the tensor geometry $\mathbf{T}$.

## 3.6. Numerical implementation

An efficient implementation of the regularization method based around [3.28] can be developed by drawing inspiration from the geometric interpretation in terms of *LIC*s of the single-direction curvature-preserving PDEs as discussed in section 3.5.2. The PDE [3.28] can be evolved explicitly using the following Euler scheme:

$$\begin{cases} \mathbf{I}^{[t=0]} &= \mathbf{I}_{\mathrm{noisy}} \\ \mathbf{I}^{[t+dt]} &= \mathbf{I}^{[t]} + \frac{2dt}{N}\left(\sum_{k=0}^{N-1} \mathcal{R}(\sqrt{\mathbf{T}}a_\alpha)\right) \end{cases}$$

where $\alpha = k\pi/N$ is an angle discretized over $[0, \pi]$ to cover the half-plane, $dt$ is the standard time step for the temporal discretization of the PDE flow, and $\mathcal{R}(\mathbf{w})$ represents a discretization of the speed of evolution of the PDE [3.20] for the single-direction curvature-preserving smoothing along the vector field $\mathbf{w}$. Rewriting this expression as $\mathbf{I}^{[t+dt]} = \frac{1}{N}\left(\sum_{k=0}^{N-1}\mathbf{I}^{[t]} + 2dt\,\mathcal{R}(\sqrt{\mathbf{T}}a_\alpha)\right)$, we can view it as the averaging of several *LIC* processes, weighted by 1D Gaussian functions, along all the field lines for the vector fields $\sqrt{\mathbf{T}}a_\alpha$:

$$\mathbf{I}^{[t+dt]} = \frac{1}{N}\left(\sum_{k=0}^{N-1}\mathbf{I}^{[t]}_{LIC(\sqrt{\mathbf{T}}a_\alpha)}\right)$$

where the standard deviation of each Gaussian is $\sqrt{2dt}$. The implementation challenge then centers on the calculation of a *LIC*, which requires an integration scheme for the field lines. For this type of task, we find Runge-Kutta numerical integration methods [PRE 92] to be sufficiently robust in our case. It should be noted that more sophisticated and rapid *LIC* implementations have been proposed [STA 95], although these assume the use of top-hat weighting functions, whereas in this case we need to use Gaussian functions for our weighting.

Thus, each iteration of the numerical scheme for time-evolving the curvature-preserving PDE [3.28] can be summarized as:

1) Calculate the smoothed structure tensor field $\mathbf{G}_{\alpha,\sigma}$ from $\mathbf{I}^{[t]}$:

$$\mathbf{G}_{\alpha,\sigma} = G_\alpha * \sum_{i=1}^{n}\left(\begin{array}{cc} \left(\dfrac{\partial I^{[t]}_{i\alpha}}{\partial x}\right)^2 & \left(\dfrac{\partial I^{[t]}_{i\alpha}}{\partial x}\right)\left(\dfrac{\partial I^{[t]}_{i\alpha}}{\partial y}\right) \\ \left(\dfrac{\partial I^{[t]}_{i\alpha}}{\partial x}\right)\left(\dfrac{\partial I^{[t]}_{i\alpha}}{\partial y}\right) & \left(\dfrac{\partial I^{[t]}_{i\alpha}}{\partial y}\right)^2 \end{array}\right)$$

The regularity parameters $\alpha, \sigma$ for the tensor smoothing geometry are generally estimated as a function of the noise level present within the image.

2) Calculate the eigenvalues $\lambda_+, \lambda_-$ and eigenvectors $\theta_+, \theta_-$ of $\mathbf{G}_{\alpha,\sigma}$.

3) Calculate the tensor field $\mathbf{T}$ giving the required smoothing geometry, based on the spectral elements of $\mathbf{G}_{\alpha,\sigma}$, for example:

$$\mathbf{T} = \frac{1}{(1 + \lambda_+ + \lambda_-)^{p_1}} \, \theta_- \theta_-^{\ T} + \frac{1}{(1 + \lambda_+ + \lambda_-)^{p_2}} \, \theta_+ \theta_+^{\ T}$$

4) For every angle $\alpha \in [0, \pi]$, discretized by a fixed angular step $d_\alpha$:

    a) Calculate the vector field $\mathbf{w} = \sqrt{\mathbf{T}} \, a_\alpha$.

    b) Calculate a Line Integral Convolution for $\mathbf{I}^{[t]}$ along the field lines $\mathcal{C} \in \mathcal{F}$ of $\mathbf{w}$.

5) Average all the *LIC* images calculated in step 4.

The main parameters of this algorithm are then $p_1, p_2, \sigma, dt$ and $nb$, the number of PDE iterations to be applied. This implementation scheme is particularly interesting when compared to standard explicit schemes, based on finite differences:

– only the first derivatives need to be estimated (when determining the smoothed structure tensor $\mathbf{G}_{\alpha,\sigma}$), whereas a standard diffusion scheme would require numerical estimation of second derivatives, which would be more sensitive to noisy data;

– very fine image structure is preserved better from a *numerical* point of view: the smoothing is performed along the field lines of $\mathbf{w}$, with *sub-pixel* precision, due to the use of numerical Runge-Kutta integration schemes [PRE 92];

– the time step $dt$ can be considerable, particularly if the smoothing geometry is assumed to be sufficiently regular (in other words its evolution over time is negligible). From this point of view, the proposed scheme is always stable, since the parameter $dt$ only features in the standard deviation of the Gaussian weighting within the convolution along the field lines $\mathcal{C} \in \mathcal{F}$;

– an immediate consequence of this is the fact that this smoothing algorithm can be executed very rapidly, since very few iterations (sometimes only one) are in practice required to obtain a sufficiently regularized result, in spite of the fact that each iteration is itself more complex to calculate than with a classical explicit scheme. This, of course, gives a coarser approximation to the exact solution to the PDE [3.28], since the time variation of the smoothing geometry is ignored, instead focusing on its spatial variation. However, in reality, this assumption does often hold, particularly when processing images with low noise levels.

The choice of the parameter $d_\alpha$ giving the angular discretization step is a relatively sensitive part of the method, since the smoothing is in practice calculated as the average of multiple *LICs* oriented along all angles $\alpha$ in the 2D plane. In regions where the smoothing should be performed in a largely anisotropic manner, only a few values of $\alpha$ may be enough, since in this case the smoothing will be performed along a single unique direction irrespective of the value of $\alpha$. In homogeneous regions on the other hand, where isotropic smoothing is required, the results will be improved if smaller values of $d_\alpha$ are used, especially if the inter-iteration time step $dt$ is large. In practice, $d_\alpha = 30^o$ is found to give satisfactory precision for isotropic smoothing.

Figure 3.13 illustrates the *numerical* effectiveness of this scheme, comparing it to the results that can be obtained with a more traditional explicit implementation based around the calculation of first and second derivatives of the image using finite differences. Both results were obtained from applying the same anisotropic diffusion PDE [3.28], with the following parameters: $p_1 = 0.01$ and $p_2 = 100$ (highly anisotropic smoothing, purely along the color contours $\theta_-$, with the smoothing magnitude equal to 1 throughout). The *LIC*-based scheme (see Figure 3.13c) is clearly more effective at preserving the fine structures, after a large number of iterations. The advantage of the sub-pixel precision in the calculation of the underlying *LICs* is clearly reflected in these results.

## 3.7. Some applications

We will illustrate some classical problems in color image processing that can be efficiently tackled through the use of the regularization PDEs that we have discussed throughout this chapter. We have opted for the curvature-preserving regularization method described in section 3.5, since it consistently produces the best visual results.

1) *Denoising of color images and artifact suppression.* Image denoising is one of the most direct applications of regularization methods. Sensor measurement errors, digital quantization, or compression artifacts are all sources of noise that can have local effects on a digital image. These artifacts generally manifest themselves in the form of small variations that are added to what is assumed to be the "perfect" value of the image pixels. Figure 3.14 illustrates some results from the application of the curvature-preserving PDE formalism [3.28], which can correct such artifacts while preserving the important structures, in even the finest detail, within the source images. The common parameters $p_1 = 0.5$ and $p_2 = 0.7$ were used throughout.

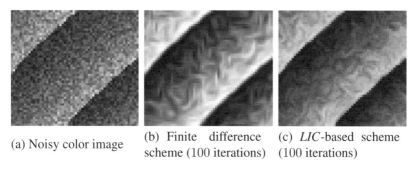

(a) Noisy color image   (b) Finite difference scheme (100 iterations)   (c) *LIC*-based scheme (100 iterations)

**Figure 3.13.** *Comparison between explicit schemes based on finite differences and based on LICs*

2) *Inpainting of color images.* This type of problem has only recently been considered in the literature. The challenge is to fill entire regions whose pixel values are not known. The values for these pixels must be reconstructed in such a way that the reconstructed image looks as natural as possible. In practice, the user provides a color image $I: \Omega \rightarrow \mathbb{R}^3$, and a *mask* image $M: \Omega \rightarrow \{0, 1\}$. The *inpainting* algorithm must then fill in the regions where $M_{(\mathbf{x})} = 1$, using intelligent interpolation techniques. Such techniques can be used for example to remove undesirable structures within images (scratches, logos, or entire objects). Historically speaking this *inpainting* problem was proposed and studied by Masnou and Morel [MAS 98], and their work was followed by a number of authors who proposed a range of solutions based on diffusion or transport PDEs [BER 00, TSC 05]. Other effective

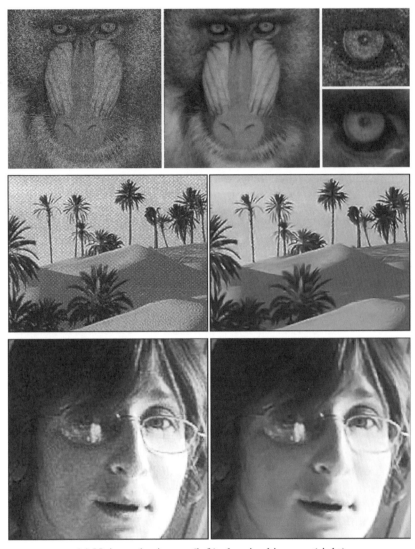

(a) Noisy color image (left), denoised images (right)

**Figure 3.14.** *Denoising of color images using curvature-preserving smoothing PDEs. (For a color version of this figure, see www.iste.co.uk/fernandez/colorimag.zip)*

techniques such as patch cloning methods also exist outside the PDE formalism [CRI 03, JIA 03]. Here, we tackle the *inpainting* problem through direct application of curvature-preserving regularization

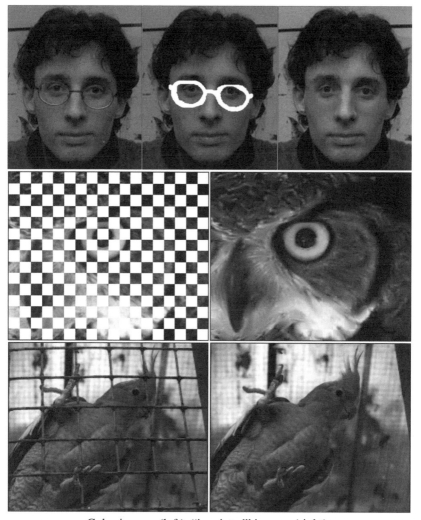

Color images (left), "inpainted" images (right).

**Figure 3.15.** *Object suppression in color images using* inpainting

PDEs [3.28], performing the evolution *only over the pixels within the region to be reconstructed*, which has the effect of causing the values of pixels bordering these regions to diffuse in to the interior of these unknown regions. This results in a natural and nonlinear completion of data along structure contours, thanks to the anisotropic aspect of the diffusion process. This is one possible way of reconstructing the missing parts of an image while best preserving the global geometry therein. Figure 3.15 illustrates some results obtained using equation [3.28] for a range of applications of *inpainting* (object suppression and reconstruction of pre-defined blocks). The parameters $p_1 = 0$ and $p_2 = 1.2$ are used throughout (anisotropic smoothing at all points).

This curvature-preserving regularization technique is available for free in the open source C++ image processing library *CImg* [TSC 00].

## 3.8. Conclusion

Multi-channel image regularization is a fundamental stage in image processing, and it is essential that this process be controlled as closely as possible to ensure it is flexible and adaptive to the required application. In this chapter, we have attacked this problem by using local geometric interpretations of the most well-established PDE-based regularization techniques in the literature, as applied to scalar or multi-channel images. Curvature-preserving PDEs are one of the most promising of these formalisms. Not only do they have the property of preserving fine details and curved structures within the images, but they also enable fast, elegant and efficient implementations. This is due to the fact that the associated numerical schemes can operate on sub-pixel scales with a reduced computation time (with this last point probably being one of the major drawbacks of iterative image regularization methods). We have illustrated all these properties through a range of applications of denoising and *inpainting* of color images. Of course, this only represents a limited selection of applications, and many other problems in color image processing can benefit from the use of PDE-based regularization techniques of the sort we have discussed in this chapter.

## 3.9. Bibliography

[ALV 92]  ALVAREZ L., LIONS P.-L., MOREL J.-M., "Image selective smoothing and edge detection by nonlinear diffusion. II", *SIAM Journal on Numerical Analysis*, vol. 29, no. 3, p. 845-866, 1992.

[ALV 93]  ALVAREZ L., GUICHARD F., LIONS P.-L., MOREL J.-M., "Axioms and fundamental equations of image processing", *Archive for Rational Mechanics and Analysis*, vol. 123, p. 199-257, September 1993.

[ALV 00]  ALVAREZ L., DERICHE R., SANTANA F., "Recursivity and PDE's in image processing", *Proceeding of International Conference on Pattern Recognition*, p. 242-248, 2000.

[AUB 06]  AUBERT G., KORNPROBST P., "Mathematical problems in image processing: partial differential equations and the calculus of variations (second edition)", *Applied Mathematical Sciences*, vol. 147, Springer-Verlag, 2006.

[BAR 00]  BARASH D., "Bilateral filtering and anisotropic diffusion: towards a unified viewpoint", In *Third International Conference on ScaleSpace and Morphology*, p. 273-280, 2000.

[BER 00]  BERTALMIO M., SAPIRO G., "Image inpainting", *Proceedings of the SIGGRAPH*, p. 417-424, 2000.

[BER 01]  BERTALMIO M., CHENG L.-T., OSHER S., SAPIRO G., "Variational problems and partial differential equations on implicit surfaces", *Computing and Visualization in Science*, vol. 174, no. 2, p. 759-780, 2001.

[BLA 95]  BLANC-FERAUD L., CHARBONNIER P., AUBERT G., BARLAUD M., "Nonlinear image processing: modeling and fast algorithm for regularization with edge detection", *Proceedings of the International Conference on Image Processing (ICIP)*, Washington, USA, p. 474-477, 1995.

[BLO 98]  BLOMGREN P., CHAN T., "Color tv: total variation methods for restoration of vector-valued images", *IEEE Transactions on Image Processing*, vol. 7, no. 3, p. 304-309, 1998.

[CAB 93]  CABRAL B., LEEDOM L., "Imaging vector fields using line integral convolution", *SIGGRAPH '93, in Computer Graphics*, vol. 27, p. 263-272, 1993.

[CAR 98]  CARMONA R., ZHONG S., "Adaptive smoothing respecting feature directions", *IEEE Transactions on Image Processing*, vol. 7, no. 3, p. 353-358, 1998.

[CHA 94]  CHARBONNIER P., AUBERT G., BLANC-FÉRAUD M., BARLAUD M., "Two deterministic half-quadratic regularization algorithms for computed imaging", *Proceedings of the International Conference on Image Processing (ICIP)*, vol. 2, p. 168-172, 1994.

[CHA 97]  CHAMBOLLE A., LIONS P., "Image recovery via total variation minimization and related problems", *Nümerische Mathematik*, vol. 76, no. 2, p. 167-188, 1997.

[CHA 00]  CHAN T., SHEN J., "Variational restoration of non-flat image features: models and algorithms", *SIAM Journal of Applied Mathematics*, vol. 61, no. 4, p. 1338-1361, 2000.

[CHE 04] CHEFD'HOTEL C., TSCHUMPERLÉ D., DERICHE R., FAUGERAS O., "Regularizing flows for constrained matrix-valued images", *Journal of Mathematical Imaging and Vision*, vol. 20, no. 4, p. 147-162, 2004.

[CRI 03] CRIMINISI A., PEREZ P., TOYAMA K., "Object removal by exemplar-based inpainting", *IEEE Conference on Computer Vision and Pattern Recognition (CVPR)*, vol. 2, p. 721-728, 2003.

[DER 97] DERICHE R., FAUGERAS O., "Les EDP en traitement des images et vision par ordinateur", *Traitement du Signal*, vol. 13, no. 6, 1997.

[DIZ 86] DIZENZO S., "A note on the gradient of a multi-image", *Computer Vision, Graphics and Image Processing*, vol. 33, p. 116-125, 1986.

[GEM 85] GEMAN S., MCCLURE D., "Bayesian image analysis: an application to single photon emission tomography", *Proceedings of the Statistical Computing Section*, p. 12-18, 1985.

[GRE 90] GREEN P., "Bayesian reconstruction from emission tomography data using a modified em algorithm", *IEEE Transactions on Medical Imaging*, vol. 9, no. 1, p. 84-93, 1990.

[HAD 23] HADAMARD J., *Lectures on the Cauchy Problem in Linear Partial Differential Equations*, Yale University Press, 1923.

[JIA 03] JIA J., TANG C., "Image repairing: robust image synthesis by adaptive $N$D tensor voting", *IEEE Conference on Computer Vision and Pattern Recognition (CVPR)*, vol. 1, p. 643-650, 2003.

[KIC 97] KICHENASSAMY S., "The perona-malik paradox", *SIAM Journal of Applied Mathematics*, vol. 57, no. 5, p. 1328-1342, 1997.

[KIM 00] KIMMEL R., MALLADI R., SOCHEN N., "Images as embedded maps and minimal surfaces: movies, color, texture, and volumetric medical images", *International Journal of Computer Vision (IJCV)*, vol. 39, no. 2, p. 111-129, 2000.

[KIM 02] KIMMEL R., SOCHEN N., "Orientation diffusion or how to comb a porcupine", *Journal of Visual Communication and Image Representation*, vol. 13, p. 238-248, 2002.

[KOE 84] KOENDERINK J., "The structure of images", *Biological Cybernetics*, vol. 50, p. 363-370, 1984.

[KOR 96] KORNPROBST P., DERICHE R., AUBERT G., "Image restoration via PDE's", *First Annual Symposium on Enabling Technologies for Law Enforcement and Security - SPIE Conference*, 1996.

[KOR 97] KORNPROBST P., DERICHE R., AUBERT G., "Nonlinear operators in image restoration", *Proceedings of the IEEE International Conference on Computer Vision and Pattern Recognition (CVPR)*, p. 325-331, 1997.

[KOS 95]  KOSCHAN A., "A comparative study on color edge detection", *Proceedings of the 2nd Asian Conference on Computer Vision (ACCV)*, p. 574-578, 95.

[LIN 94]  LINDEBERG T., *Scale-Space Theory in Computer Vision*, Kluwer Academic Publishers, 1994.

[MAS 98]  MASNOU S., MOREL J.-M., "Level lines based disocclusion", *IEEE International Conference on Image Processing (ICIP)*, vol. 3, p. 259-263, 1998.

[NIE 97]  NIELSEN M., FLORACK L., DERICHE R., "Regularization, scale-space and edge detection filters", *Journal of Mathematical Imaging and Vision (JMIV)*, vol. 7, no. 4, p. 291-308, 1997.

[NIK 01]  NIKOLOVA M., "Image restoration by minimizing objective functions with nonsmooth data-fidelity terms", *IEEE Workshop on Variational and Level Set Methods (VLSM)*, p. 11-19, 2001.

[PER 90]  PERONA P., MALIK J., "Scale-space and edge detection using anisotropic diffusion", *IEEE Transactions on Pattern Analysis and Machine Intelligence (PAMI)*, vol. 12, no. 7, p. 629-639, 1990.

[PER 98]  PERONA P., "Orientation diffusion", *IEEE Transactions on Image Processing*, vol. 7, no. 3, p. 457-467, 1998.

[POY 95]  POYNTON C., "Poynton's colour FAQ", www.inforamp.net/ poynton, 1995.

[PRE 92]  PRESS W., FLANNERY B., TEUKOLSKY S., VETTERLING W., *Numerical recipes in FORTRAN: the art of scientific computing*, p. 704-716, Cambridge University Press, 1992.

[RUD 92]  RUDIN L., OSHER S., FATEMI E., "Nonlinear total variation based noise removal algorithms", *Physica D*, vol. 60, p. 259-268, 1992.

[SAP 96a]  SAPIRO G., "Vector-valued active contours", *Proceedings of the IEEE International Conference on Computer Vision and Pattern Recognition (CVPR)*, p. 680-685, 1996.

[SAP 96b]  SAPIRO G., RINGACH D., "Anisotropic diffusion of multivalued images with applications to color filtering", *IEEE Transactions on Image Processing*, vol. 5, no. 11, p. 1582-1585, 1996.

[SAP 97]  SAPIRO G., "Color snakes", *Computer Vision and Image Understanding*, vol. 68, no. 2, 1997.

[SAP 01]  SAPIRO G., *Geometric Partial Differential Equations and Image Analysis*, Cambridge University Press, 2001.

[SOC 98]  SOCHEN N., KIMMEL R., MALLADI R., "A geometrical framework for low level vision", *IEEE Transaction on Image Processing, Special Issue on PDE based Image Processing*, vol. 7, no. 3, p. 310-318, 1998.

[SOC 01a]  SOCHEN N., "On affine invariance in the Beltrami framework for vision", *IEEE Workshop on Variational and Level Set Methods (VLSM)*, p. 51-56, 2001.

[SOC 01b] SOCHEN N., KIMMEL R., BRUCKSTEIN A., "Diffusions and confusions in signal and image processing", *Journal of Mathematical Imaging and Vision (JMIV)*, vol. 14, no. 3, p. 195-209, 2001.

[STA 95] STALLING D., HEGE H., "Fast and resolution independent line integral convolution", *ACM SIGGRAPH, 22nd Annual Conference on Computer Graphics and Interactive Technique*, p. 249-256, 1995.

[TAN 98] TANG B., SAPIRO G., CASELLES. V., "Direction diffusion", *International Conference on Computer Vision (ICCV)*, 1998.

[TAN 00] TANG B., SAPIRO G., CASELLES V., "Diffusion of general data on non-flat manifolds via harmonic maps theory: the direction diffusion case", *International Journal of Computer Vision (IJCV)*, vol. 36, no. 2, p. 149-161, 2000.

[TIK 63] TIKHONOV A., "Regularization of incorrectly posed problems", *Soviet Mathematics – Doklady*, vol. 4, p. 1624-1627, 1963.

[TOM 98] TOMASI C., MANDUCHI R., "Bilateral filtering for gray and color images", *Proceedings of the IEEE International Conference on Computer Vision (ICCV)*, p. 839-846, 1998.

[TSC 00] TSCHUMPERLÉ D., "The CImg library: http://cimg.sourceforge.net", The C++ Template Image Processing Library, 2000.

[TSC 01] TSCHUMPERLÉ D., DERICHE R., "Diffusion tensor regularization with constraints preservation", *IEEE Computer Society Conference on Computer Vision and Pattern Recognition (CVPR)*, 2001.

[TSC 02] TSCHUMPERLÉ D., DERICHE R., "Diffusion PDE's on vector-valued images: local approach and geometric viewpoint", *IEEE Signal Processing Magazine*, vol. 19, no. 5, p. 16-25, 2002.

[TSC 05] TSCHUMPERLÉ D., DERICHE R., "Vector-valued image regularization with PDE's: a common framework for different applications", *IEEE Transactions on Pattern Analysis and Machine Intelligence (PAMI)*, vol. 27, no. 4, 2005.

[TSC 06] TSCHUMPERLÉ D., "Fast anisotropic smoothing of multi-valued images using curvature-preserving PDE's", *International Journal of Computer Vision (IJCV)*, vol. 68, no. 1, p. 65-82, 2006.

[WEI 97a] WEICKERT J., "A review of nonlinear diffusion filtering", SPRINGER B. (ed.), *Scale-Space Theory in Computer Vision, Lecture Notes in Computer Science*, vol. 1252, p. 3-28, 1997.

[WEI 97b] WEICKERT J., BENHAMOUDA B., Why the perona-malik filter works, Technical Report 97/22, Department of Computer Science, University of Copenhagen, 1997.

[WEI 98] WEICKERT J., *Anisotropic Diffusion in Image Processing*, Teubner-Verlag, 1998.

[WEI 99]  WEICKERT J., "Coherence-enhancing diffusion of colour images", *Image and Vision Computing*, vol. 17, p. 199-210, 1999.

[WIT 83]  WITKIN A., "Scale-space filtering", *International Joint Conference on Artificial Intelligence*, p. 1019-1021, 1983.

Chapter 4

# Linear Prediction in Spaces with Separate Achromatic and Chromatic Information

## 4.1. Introduction

Spectral analysis of a stationary zone[1] within an image in the red green blue (RGB) color space is possible using multi-channel 2D linear prediction (see section 4.2) [ELS 87]. However, a criticism of this approach is that the three RGB channels are often strongly correlated, and spectral analysis reveals not only three power spectral densities (PSD) associated with the three 2D autocorrelation functions, but also three PSDs associated with the three cross-correlation functions between pairs of color planes. If we now consider color spaces with a separation between achromatic and chromatic information, we can perform a spectral analysis over a real plane (intensity or achromatic part) and a complex plane (chromatic part). This approach was proposed in

Chapter written by Olivier ALATA, Imtnan QAZI, Jean-Christophe BURIE and Christine FERNANDEZ-MALOIGNE.

1 A stationary zone within an image is spatially invariant in terms of its statistical and probabilistic properties. For example, the colors of individual pixels are assumed to be realizations of the same probability distribution (stationarity in the strict sense). These aspects will be discussed in depth later in this chapter.

[QAZ 10a, QAZ 10b, QAZ 11b] where complex vector 2D linear prediction was used, for this particular case. Spectral analysis of a colored region is then performed with the help of two PSDs associated with two autocorrelation functions, and a PSD associated with the cross-correlation function. Thus, the spectral analysis is simplified. This approach is also interesting from the point of view of characterization [QAZ 10a] because the transformation of RGB coding to such color spaces is intended to separate the information contained in the three initial channels. Chapter 6 presents some results for color texture classification using the approach developed in the present chapter, and compares these results to other tools for color texture description. For more information on 2D linear prediction and color textures, you may refer to a state-of-the-art publication: section 6.4.

In this chapter, we will begin by defining complex vector 2D linear prediction, and discuss its use with Hue-Saturation-Intensity (HSI) color spaces and spaces containing an achromatic component and two chromatic components such as the CIE space L*a*b* [CIE 86]. We will then give some spectral analysis results. We will also explain the use of this approach for the segmentation of textured color images [QAZ 09, QAZ 11a].

## 4.2. Complex vector 2D linear prediction

In this chapter, we will adopt the same notation as used in Chapters 1 and 6. Consequently, we will write the discrete support of the image as $E \subset \mathbb{Z}^2$, and represent a point or pixel as a pair of integers $\mathbf{x} = (x_1, x_2) \in E$. A color image can therefore be either a mapping $\boldsymbol{f}: E \mapsto V^{rgb}$ where $\boldsymbol{f}(\mathbf{x}) = (f_R(\mathbf{x}), f_V(\mathbf{x}), f_B(\mathbf{x}))$, or a mapping $\boldsymbol{f}: E \mapsto V^{hsl}$ where $\boldsymbol{f}(\mathbf{x}) = (f_H(\mathbf{x}), f_S(\mathbf{x}), f_L(\mathbf{x}))$, or a mapping $\boldsymbol{f}: E \mapsto V^{lc_1c_2}$ where $\boldsymbol{f}(\mathbf{x}) = (f_L(\mathbf{x}), f_{C_1}(\mathbf{x}), f_{C_2}(\mathbf{x}))$, respectively for the RGB and HSI color spaces, and a color space with an achromatic and two chromatic components such as L*a*b*. Let us remark that the achromatic component can be called "Intensity" like in HSI or "Luminance" like in L*a*b* or like in Improved Hue Luminance Saturation (IHLS) color space [HAN 03]. In our mathematical notations, "L" will stand for the achromatic component.

If we now consider the possibility of describing the values of the chromatic component using complex numbers, a color image in an HSI type color space can be represented in the form of two components, a real component for intensity (or achromatic information) and a complex component for the chromatic information [PAL 02]:

$$f(\mathbf{x}) = \begin{bmatrix} f_1(\mathbf{x}) = l \\ f_2(\mathbf{x}) = se^{ih} \end{bmatrix} \qquad [4.1]$$

where $h$, is the hue expressed in radians. In color spaces with an achromatic component and two chromatic components, we can write:

$$f(\mathbf{x}) = \begin{bmatrix} f_1(\mathbf{x}) = l \\ f_2(\mathbf{x}) = c_1 + i \times c_2 \end{bmatrix} \qquad [4.2]$$

The description of a region of a color image in terms of a model obtained from linear prediction implies the assumption that the observed colors are the realization of random variables. Thus, the color image is considered to be the realization $f$ of a random field $\mathbf{F} = \{\mathbf{F}(\mathbf{x})\}_{\mathbf{x} \in E}$, where the $\mathbf{F}(\mathbf{x})$ are random vectors of dimension $p = 2$, with a mean value $\mathbf{m} = \mathrm{E}\{\mathbf{F}(\mathbf{x})\}, \forall \mathbf{x} \in E$, where $\mathrm{E}\{.\}$ is the mathematical expectation operator. Even though the first coordinate is *a priori* real, we will assume that the realization space for each component is the set of complex numbers $\mathbb{C}$.

The complex vector 2D linear prediction models that we will use in this section are defined in the following manner:

$$\mathbf{F}(\mathbf{x}) = \hat{\mathbf{F}}(\mathbf{x}) + \mathbf{m} + \mathbf{E}_F(\mathbf{x}) \qquad [4.3]$$

where $\hat{\mathbf{F}}(\mathbf{x}) = -\sum_{\mathbf{y} \in D} \mathbf{A}_\mathbf{y} (\mathbf{F}(\mathbf{x} - \mathbf{y}) - \mathbf{m})$ is the linear prediction of $\mathbf{F}(\mathbf{x})$ with the help of the finite prediction support $D \subset \mathbb{Z}^2$ and the set of matrices $\{\mathbf{A}_\mathbf{y}\}_{\mathbf{y} \in D}$ (with complex coefficients). The random field $\mathbf{E}_F = \{\mathbf{E}_F(\mathbf{x})\}_{\mathbf{x} \in E}$ is the excitation or the linear prediction error (LPE) of the model, the nature of which may vary depending on the choice of prediction support, as we will see later on. The prediction supports traditionally used in the literature are causal supports, quarter-plane (QP), or non-symmetric half-plane (NSHP) of order

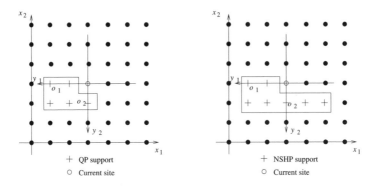

**Figure 4.1.** *Supports of order* $(o_1, o_2) = (2, 1)$*: first quadrant quarter-plane (QP1) support and non-symmetric half-plane (NSHP) support*

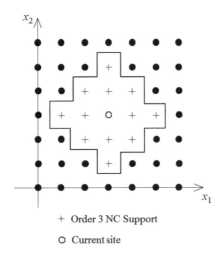

+  Order 3 NC Support

○  Current site

**Figure 4.2.** *Non-causal (NC) support of order* $o = 3$

$\mathbf{o} = (o_1, o_2) \in \mathbb{N}^2$ (see Figure 4.1), or the non-causal support (NC) of order $o \in \mathbb{N}$ (see Figure 4.2):

$$D_{\mathbf{o}}^{QP1} = \{\mathbf{y} \in \mathbb{Z}^2, 0 \le y_1 \le o_1, 0 \le y_2 \le o_2, \mathbf{y} \ne (0,0)\} \quad [4.4]$$

$$D_{\mathbf{o}}^{NSHP} = \{\mathbf{y} \in \mathbb{Z}^2, 0 < y_1 \le o_1 \text{ for } y_2 = 0$$
$$-o_1 < y_1 \le o_1 \text{ for } 0 < y_2 \le o_2\} \quad [4.5]$$

$$D_1 = \left\{ \mathbf{y} \in \mathbb{Z}^2, \underset{\mathbf{y}}{\arg\min} \|\mathbf{y}\|_2, \mathbf{y} \neq (0,0) \right\}$$

$$D_k = \left\{ \mathbf{y} \in \mathbb{Z}^2, \underset{\mathbf{y} \notin \underset{1 \leq l \leq k-1}{\bigcup} D_l}{\arg\min} \|\mathbf{y}\|_2, \mathbf{y} \neq (0,0) \right\}, k > 1 \quad [4.6]$$

$$D_o^{NC} = \underset{1 \leq k \leq o}{\bigcup} D_k$$

These models can be used for multidimensional spectral analysis of a color process since the PSD of the process can be expressed in terms of the PSD of $\mathbf{E}_F$ and complex coefficient matrices:

$$\mathbf{S}_F(\nu) = \mathbf{A}(\nu)^{-1}\mathbf{S}_{E_F}(\nu)\mathbf{A}^H(\nu)^{-1} = \begin{bmatrix} S_{LL}(\nu) & S_{LC}(\nu) \\ S_{CL}(\nu) & S_{CC}(\nu) \end{bmatrix} \quad [4.7]$$

where $\nu = \{\nu_1, \nu_2\} \in \mathbb{R}^2$, the 2D normalized spatial frequency[2], $\mathbf{S}_{E_F}(\nu)$ is the matrix PSD of the excitation, $\mathbf{A}^H(\nu)$ is the Hermitian conjugate of $\mathbf{A}(\nu)$, which can be written as:

$$\mathbf{A}(\nu) = 1 + \sum_{\mathbf{y} \in D} \mathbf{A}_{\mathbf{y}} \exp\left(-i2\pi \langle \nu, \mathbf{y} \rangle\right) \quad [4.8]$$

In equation [4.7], $S_{LL}(\nu)$ is the PSD of the "achromatic" channel, $S_{CC}(\nu)$ is the PSD of the "chromatic" channel, and $S_{LC}(\nu) = S_{CL}^*(\nu)$ is the inter-channel spectrum of the two channels. We note that in the RGB space, where the image has three real components, $\mathbf{f}(\mathbf{x}) = (f_R(\mathbf{x})f_G(\mathbf{x})f_B(\mathbf{x}))$, the matrix takes the following form:

$$\mathbf{S}_F(\nu) = \begin{bmatrix} S_{RR}(\nu) & S_{RG}(\nu) & S_{RB}(\nu) \\ S_{GR}(\nu) & S_{GG}(\nu) & S_{GB}(\nu) \\ S_{BR}(\nu) & S_{BG}(\nu) & S_{BB}(\nu) \end{bmatrix} \quad [4.9]$$

Recall that these PSDs are all periodic, with period 1 along both axes. For this reason, a representation for $\nu \in [-0.5, 0.5]^2$ can be used to visualize all the information contained within them (see Figure 4.4).

---

2 The normalized spatial frequency along a given axis is the spatial frequency (the inverse of a spatial period) divided by the spatial sampling frequency along that same axis.

Under the assumption that the support is causal (QP and NSHP supports), we have an AutoRegressive (AR) model. Its excitation is assumed to be a white noise and its PSD is constant and equal to the variance-covariance matrix of $\boldsymbol{E_F}$: $\mathbf{S}_{\boldsymbol{E_F}}(\nu) = \Sigma_{\boldsymbol{E_F}}$ and $\mathbf{S}_F(\nu) = \mathbf{A}(\nu)^{-1}\Sigma_{\boldsymbol{E_F}}\mathbf{A}^H(\nu)^{-1}$. In the case of the AR QP1 model, the resultant PSD exhibits an anisotropy, which can be corrected with the use of an estimator constructed from the harmonic mean (HM) of the PSDs obtained for the AR QP1 and AR QP2 models of order $\mathbf{o} = (o_1, o_2) \in \mathbb{N}^2$ [CAR 01]:

$$\mathbf{S}_F^{HM}(\nu) = 2 \left( \mathbf{S}_F^{QP1}(\nu)^{-1} + \mathbf{S}_F^{QP2}(\nu)^{-1} \right)^{-1} \qquad [4.10]$$

where:

$$\mathbf{D}_{\mathbf{o}}^{QP2} = \left\{ \mathbf{y} \in \mathbb{Z}^2, -o_1 \leq y_1 \leq 0, 0 \leq y_2 \leq o_2, \mathbf{y} \neq (0,0) \right\} \quad [4.11]$$

The other model that is traditionally used is the Gauss-Markov Random Field (GMRF) [GUY 95], which makes use of the definition of the non-causal prediction support (see equation [4.6] and Figure 4.2).

In the case of the GMRF, the orthogonality condition for square-summable random variables [REL 02] between the components of a random vector $\boldsymbol{E_F}(\mathbf{x})$ and the components of the random vectors $F(\mathbf{y})$, $\mathbf{y} \in E \backslash \{\mathbf{x}\}$, means that the PSD of $\boldsymbol{E_F}$ can be written as:

$$\mathbf{S}_{\boldsymbol{E_F}}(\nu) = \mathbf{A}(\nu)\Sigma_{\boldsymbol{E_F}} \qquad [4.12]$$

which leads to:

$$\mathbf{S}_F^{GMRF}(\nu) = \Sigma_{\boldsymbol{E_F}}\mathbf{A}^H(\nu)^{-1} \qquad [4.13]$$

To obtain estimates of the PSD using the harmonic mean method (which we will refer to henceforth as the PSD_HM method), the AR non-symmetric half-plane model (PSD_NSHP method) and the Gauss-Markov random field model (PSD_GMRF model), we must first estimate the matrices of coefficients. A number of methods exist for carrying out this estimation, making use of the least squares minimization

(Yule-Walker method or normal equations) or the maximum likelihood (ML) criterion [REL 02]. For causal methods using the Gaussian hypothesis for the excitation, the minimization in the least-squares sense involves making an estimation in the ML sense.

In the next section, we will compare the various methods of spectral analysis, which we will refer to as PSD_HM, PSD_NSHP and PSD_GMRF, using a HSI type space, the IHLS space [HAN 03] and the L*a*b* space. We will then perform a spectral analysis experiment to compare the interference that occurs between the achromatic part and the chromatic part for these two color spaces.

## 4.3. Spectral analysis in the IHLS and L*a*b* color spaces

To compare the performance of different PSD estimation methods, as has previously been done for grayscale images [CAR 01], we generated synthetic images containing noisy sinusoids. In [QAZ 10a], this comparison was performed for the IHLS and L*a*b* color spaces, with $c_1 = a^*$ and $c_2 = b^*$ (see equation [4.2])[3].

To begin with, the IHLS space, with its structure consisting of an achromatic axis and a perpendicular chromatic plane, seemed to be the most appropriate space to work in for the vector approach we had in mind. This is the reason why only the IHLS space was considered in [QAZ 10b]. Other HSI-type color spaces could also be used.

### 4.3.1. *Comparison of PSD estimation methods*

The noisy sinusoids consist of a simulated 2D real sinusoid for the achromatic component and a 2D complex sinusoid for the chromatic component, to which was added the realization of a multivariate Gaussian white noise:

---

3 We could have chosen $c_1 = b^*$ and $c_2 = a^*$.

$$f(\mathbf{x}) = \left[ \begin{array}{c} A_l \cos\left(2\pi \left\langle \mathbf{x}, \nu_l \right\rangle + \phi_l\right) \\ A_c \times \exp\left(j(2\pi \left\langle \mathbf{x}, \nu_c \right\rangle + \phi_c)\right) \end{array} \right] + \boldsymbol{b}(\mathbf{x}) \qquad [4.14]$$

where $A_i$, $i = l$ or $c$, are the amplitudes, $Phi_i$, the phases and $nu_i$ the normalized 2D frequencies of the sinusoids in each channel. Figure 4.3 shows a chromatic sinusoid (constant intensity and white noise with a null variance-covariance matrix in equation [4.14]) generated in the IHLS color space. The function follows a circular trajectory in the plane perpendicular to the achromatic axis, along the direction of the wavefront. For this reason, all the colors appear at a fixed saturation level (equal to $A_c$) and produce a wave whose orientation and variations depend on the value of $\nu_c$ ($\nu_c = (0.05, 0.05)$ in Figure 4.3a and $\nu_c = (-0.3, 0.3)$ in Figure 4.3b[4]).

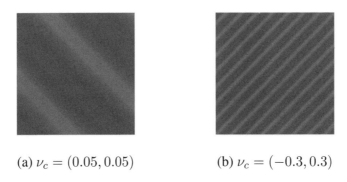

(a) $\nu_c = (0.05, 0.05)$             (b) $\nu_c = (-0.3, 0.3)$

**Figure 4.3.** *Chromatic sinusoids computed in IHLS space and shown here in RGB space. (For a color version of this figure, see www.iste.co.uk/fernandez/colorimag.zip)*

Figure 4.4 shows examples of spectral estimations using the PSD_HM method on noisy "two-channel" sinusoids, $\nu_l = (0.3, 0.1)$ and $\nu_c = (0.03, -0.03)$ for the IHLS and L*a*b* color spaces. Note that both symmetric lobes in $S_{LL}^{HM}$ are well localized (aside from the estimation errors) around $\nu_l$ and $-\nu_l$ (see Figures 4.4a and 4.4c) and that the lobe in $S_{CC}^{HM}$ is well localized around $\nu_c$ (see Figures 4.4b and 4.4d).

---

4 A normalized frequency close to 0.5 in absolute value is a "high" frequency whereas a normalized frequency close to 0 is a "low" frequency.

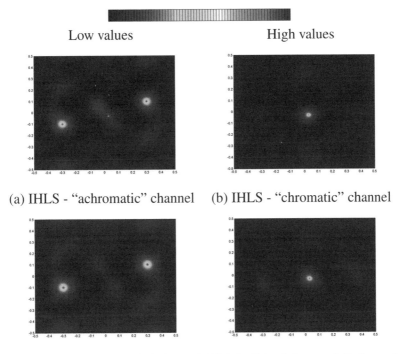

(a) IHLS - "achromatic" channel    (b) IHLS - "chromatic" channel

(c) L*a*b* - "achromatic" channel (d) L*a*b* - "chromatic" channel

**Figure 4.4.** *Spectral estimations ($\nu \in [-0.5, 0.5]^2$) calculated using the PSD_HM method for the IHLS and L*a*b* color spaces. The images have undergone a double transformation to study the information separation abilities of each color space: from IHLS or L*a*b* to RGB and then from RGB back to IHLS or L*a*b**

To obtain precise information on the performance of these methods in terms of spectral analysis, we computed the estimation bias (or accuracy) and the estimation variance (or precision) for several frequencies ($\nu_l = (0.3, 0.3)$ and $\nu_c = (0.05, 0.05)$ - $\nu_l = (0.05, 0.3)$ and $\nu_c = (-0.3, 0.3)$), several realizations of white noise, with a SNR = 0 dB, varying the image size from $24 \times 24$ sites to $64 \times 64$ sites. Figure 4.5 shows the estimation precision of the frequency of the sinusoid contained in the achromatic component. Figure 4.6 presents the same information for the chromatic component. Equivalent prediction supports have been used for all three methods. Overall, we obtained the same result as for grayscale images:

the PSD_HM method has the best performance in terms of accuracy and precision, and better isotropy (the reader is referred to [QAZ 10a, QAZ 10b] for more details and more extensive results). For the different color spaces, no significant difference can be seen in the curves of the estimation precision of the different frequencies.

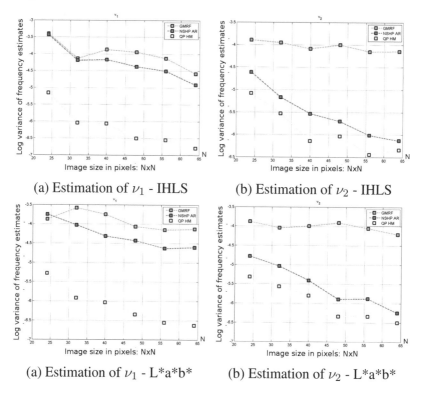

(a) Estimation of $\nu_1$ - IHLS        (b) Estimation of $\nu_2$ - IHLS

(a) Estimation of $\nu_1$ - L\*a\*b\*        (b) Estimation of $\nu_2$ - L\*a\*b\*

**Figure 4.5.** *Comparison of precision of spectral analysis methods in IHLS and L\*a\*b\* spaces for achromatic information, based on the log variance of the estimated frequencies, as a function of image size*

### 4.3.2. Study of inter-channel interference associated with color space changing transformations

In [QAZ 10a, QAZ 11b], we described an experiment that can be used to study interference between the achromatic channel and the chromatic channels, interference associated with transformations giving color space changes between RGB and IHLS or L*a*b*. This experiment involves generating a noisy sinusoid (see equation [4.14]) in the color space considered. The transformations from this space to RGB and from RGB back to this space are then applied successively. Spectral analysis using complex vector 2D linear prediction techniques then reveals lobes associated with the interference created by these successive transformations. Observation of $S_{LL}^{HM}$ as obtained from a spectral analysis in IHLS (see Figure 4.4a) then reveals the existence of a spurious lobe localized at the frequency of the chromatic sinusoid. This parasitic lobe cannot

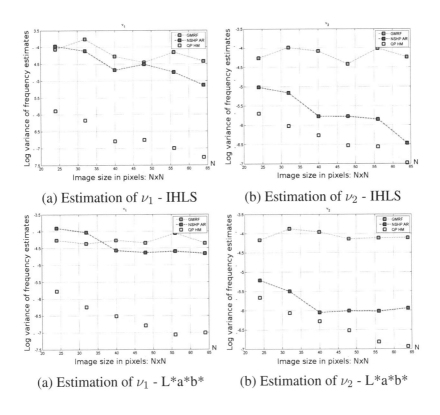

(a) Estimation of $\nu_1$ - IHLS

(b) Estimation of $\nu_2$ - IHLS

(a) Estimation of $\nu_1$ - L*a*b*

(b) Estimation of $\nu_2$ - L*a*b*

**Figure 4.6.** *Comparison of precision of spectral analysis methods in IHLS and L*a*b* spaces for chromatic information, based on the log variance of the estimated frequencies, as a function of image size*

however be observed in the result for $S_{LL}^{HM}$ obtained from spectral analysis in L*a*b* (see Figure 4.4c). Conversely, since frequency interference from the "achromatic" channel within the "chromatic" channel is less pronounced, this is not visible in $S_{CC}^{HM}$ for either color space (see Figures 4.4b and 4.4d).

To measure the level of this interference, we generated twenty $n \times n$ images for each color space (IHLS and L*a*b*), for $n \in \{64, 96, 128, 160, 192, 224, 256\}$ and containing sinusoids with similar amplitudes and phases ($A_l = 0.25$, $A_c = 0.25$, $\phi_l = 30°$, and $\phi_c = 30°$), and three sets of different frequencies. $\nu_l$ always had the same value, $\nu_l = (0.3, 0.3)$, whereas the frequency of the sinusoid in the "chromatic" channel could take one of three different values, $\nu_c \in \{(-0.3, 0.3), (0.3, -0.3), or (-0.3, -0.3)\}$. The mean vectors for the images were set to zero. In [QAZ 10a], the PSDs were computed for three different SNR levels, SNR $\in \{-3, 0, 3\}$ dB. Here, we will only present the results obtained for SNR = 0 dB. The PSDs were only estimated using the harmonic mean (PSD_HM) using AR QP models of order $(2, 2)$.

The level of interference from the chromatic channel within the achromatic channel is measured using the ratio $IR_{CL}$, defined as follows:

$$IR_{CL} = \frac{A_{cl}}{A_l} \qquad [4.15]$$

where $A_{cr}$, is the mean value (over 20 images, of size $n$ and for a given frequency pair $(\nu_l, \nu_c)$) of the height of the lobe associated with the sinusoid originally in the chromatic channel but appearing in the achromatic channel. In the same way, we measured the level of interference from the achromatic channel within the chromatic channel using the ratio $IR_{LC}$:

$$IR_{LC} = \frac{A_{lc}}{A_c} \qquad [4.16]$$

where $A_{rc}$, is the mean value (over 20 images, of size $n$, and for a given frequency pair $(\nu_l, \nu_c)$) of the height of the lobe associated with

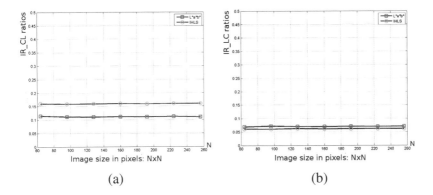

(a)                                    (b)

**Figure 4.7.** *Comparison of levels of interference between the achromatic and chromatic channels for the IHLS and CIE L\*a\*b\* spaces:* a) $IR_{CL}$ *(left) and b)* $IR_{LC}$ *(right)*

the sinusoid originally in the achromatic channel but appearing in the chromatic channel.

Figure 4.7 shows graphical representations of these ratios for different image sizes, for the IHLS and L\*a\*b\* color spaces. These ratios were calculated for the frequency pair $\{(0.3, 0.3), (0.3, -0.3)\}$ and an SNR of 0 dB. These curves were given for similar $y$ axis values to aid their visual comparison. Consideration of all these results leads to the following observations:

– the values of the ratios obtained from the calculation of the interference of achromatic information in the chromatic PSD, $IR_{LC}$, are around half the values of the ratios obtained from the calculation of the interference of chromatic information in the achromatic PSD, $IR_{CL}$, as can be seen from Figure 4.7;

– the values of $IR_{LC}$ are similar for both color spaces;

– the values of $IR_{CL}$ are larger for the IHLS color space than for the L\*a\*b\* color space.

These results, obtained using a heuristic approach, would benefit from more detailed study. Nevertheless, they lead us to form the hypothesis that the transformation associated with the L\*a\*b\* color space offers a better separation of achromatic information and chromatic information than is offered by the IHLS color space. It would also be worth measuring this interference for other color spaces.

In section 6.4, we describe how spectral analysis exploiting the separation of the "achromatic" and "chromatic" components can be used to characterize the spatial structure of color textures. Figure 4.8 gives an example of this, showing the spectral analysis of a brick-based color texture. The PSD for both channels, as obtained using the three different models, can be compared with the moduli of the discrete Fourier transforms associated with each channel. The inter-spectra show the presence of correlations between the two channels. We will now show how complex vector 2D linear prediction over the IHLS and L*a*b* spaces can be used in the context of supervised segmentation of textured color images.

## 4.4. Application to segmentation of textured color images

In a supervised context, it is possible to use a training sample for each texture present in the image to determine all the parameters for its model (see equation [4.3]), $\theta = \left\{ \mathbf{m}, \{\mathbf{A_y}\}_{\mathbf{y} \in D}, \Sigma_{E_F} \right\}$. These parameters can be used to calculate the linear prediction error (LPE) $e = \{e(\mathbf{x})\}_{\mathbf{x} \in E}$ associated with each texture over the entire image. To make use of Bayesian segmentation approaches (see equation [4.22]), we can use parametric models to describe the distributions associated with the LPEs.

### 4.4.1. Prediction error distribution

Classically, the distribution of each prediction error can be approximated by a Gaussian distribution (see [BOU 91, ALA 05] for the case of grayscale textures). In the present context, this distribution must necessarily be multidimensional:

$$ p(e(\mathbf{x})|\theta) = \frac{(2\pi)^{-\omega/2}}{\sqrt{det(\Sigma_{E_F})}} \exp \left[ -\frac{e(\mathbf{x})^T (\Sigma_{E_F})^{-1} e(\mathbf{x})}{2} \right] \qquad [4.17] $$

where $e(\mathbf{x}) = (\boldsymbol{f}(\mathbf{x}) - \mathbf{m}) - \hat{\boldsymbol{f}}(\mathbf{x}), \mathbf{x} \in E$ and $\omega$ is the dimension of the vectors $e(\mathbf{x})$. In the case of an LPE associated with two complex channels defined by equation [4.1] or [4.2], the imaginary component is almost zero for the LEP obtained in the "achromatic" channel. For this reason, we have $\omega = 3$, representing the real part of the "achromatic"

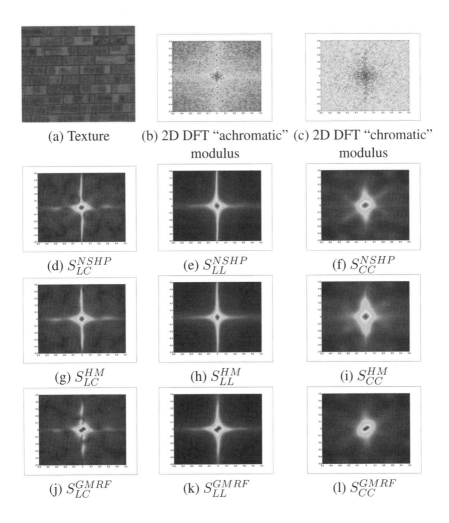

(a) Texture

(b) 2D DFT "achromatic" modulus

(c) 2D DFT "chromatic" modulus

(d) $S_{LC}^{NSHP}$

(e) $S_{LL}^{NSHP}$

(f) $S_{CC}^{NSHP}$

(g) $S_{LC}^{HM}$

(h) $S_{LL}^{HM}$

(i) $S_{CC}^{HM}$

(j) $S_{LC}^{GMRF}$

(k) $S_{LL}^{GMRF}$

(l) $S_{CC}^{GMRF}$

**Figure 4.8.** *Spectral analysis of a color texture. DFT stands for Discrete Fourier Transform. The false-color scale used to represent the power spectral densities in each plot is given in Figure 4.4*

channel and the real and imaginary parts of the "chromatic" channel. Of course $\omega$ is also equal to three for the RGB color space.

Although this approximation is simple and easily exploitable, it may appear insufficient in terms of the variety of distributions that can be observed, since these may be neither Gaussian nor unimodal. In [QAZ 11a], we investigated two alternative approaches for describing LPE distributions:

    – the Wishart distribution;

    – multivariate Gaussian mixture models (MGMM).

The Wishart distribution is a multidimensional generalization of the $\chi^2$ distribution. We chose this probability distribution since this particular model takes into account multiple observations to define the probability of a given observation, instead of using a single observation ($e(\mathbf{x})$ in our case), which makes the evaluation calculated from its density more robust. Thus, the LPE vectors from a finite neighborhood are used along with the LPE vector of the current pixel when determining the probability density of the LPE for this particular pixel.

Let $\mathbf{J}(\mathbf{x}), \mathbf{x} \in E$ be a matrix of $\alpha$ LPE vectors of dimension $\omega$ that are taken into account in the definition of the probability density for $e(\mathbf{x})$. We propose to replace $p\left(e(\mathbf{x})\right)$ with $p\left(\mathbf{J}(\mathbf{x})\right)$, where $\alpha \geq \omega$. The Wishart distribution is then defined as follows:

$$p(\mathbf{J}(\mathbf{x})|\theta) = \frac{|\mathbf{M}|^{\frac{1}{2}(\alpha-\omega-1)} \exp\left(-\frac{1}{2}\mathrm{Tr}\left(\Sigma_{E_F}^{-1}\mathbf{M}\right)\right)}{2^{\alpha(\omega/2)} \pi^{\omega(\omega-1)/4} |\Sigma_{E_F}|^{\alpha/2} \prod_{i=1}^{\omega} \Gamma\left(\frac{1}{2}(\alpha+1-i)\right)} \qquad [4.18]$$

where $\mathbf{S}$ is a matrix of $\alpha$ LEP vectors of dimension $\omega$, $\mathbf{M} = \mathbf{SS}^T$ is a positive semi-definite $\omega \times \omega$ matrix and $\Gamma$ is the gamma function. Here, we will consider a first-order spatial neighborhood. As a result, $\alpha$ is equal to 5 and $\mathbf{S}$ is given by:

$$\mathbf{S} = [e(\mathbf{x} - \mathbf{1}_v), e(\mathbf{x} - \mathbf{1}_h), e(\mathbf{x}), e(\mathbf{x} + \mathbf{1}_v), e(\mathbf{x} + \mathbf{1}_h)] \qquad [4.19]$$

where $\mathbf{1}_h = [1, \emptyset]$ and $\mathbf{1}_v = [\emptyset, 1]$.

The multichannel LPE distribution associated with a color image can also be approximated using an MGMM, a parametric model of multimodal multivariate density that has the following general form:

$$p\left(e(\mathbf{x})|\theta\right) = \sum_{k=1}^{K} \alpha_k p\left(e(\mathbf{x})|\theta_k\right)$$
[4.20]

where $\alpha_1, \ldots, \alpha_K$ are the *a priori* probabilities of each Gaussian component within the mixture, and $K \geq 1$ is the number of components in the MGMM. For $K = 1$, the MGMM corresponds to a multidimensional Gaussian distribution. Each $\theta_k = \{\mathbf{m}_{e,k}, \Sigma_{e,k}\}$ is the set of parameters for the model characterizing the $k$th component of the mixture model. These parameters are estimated using the EM (expectation-maximization) algorithm [QAZ 09, QAZ 11a]. The *a priori* probability values must satisfy $\alpha_k > 0, k = 1, \ldots, K$ and $\sum_{k=1}^{K} \alpha_k = 1$. In what follows, $K$ will be equal to 5, but note that this value can also be estimated [ALA 09].

### 4.4.2. *Label field estimation*

The first step in the segmentation of color textures involves applying a site classification without performing any spatial regularization. The labels $l = \{l(\mathbf{x})\}_{\mathbf{x} \in E}$ are applied using the maximum likelihood criterion, which maximizes the product of the probabilities, assuming the LPEs are mutually independent:

$$\hat{l}(\mathbf{x}) = \arg\max_{c=1,\ldots,C} \left(p\left(e(\mathbf{x})|\hat{\theta}_c\right)\right)$$
[4.21]

where $C$ is the total number of classes in the textured color image and the sets of parameters used in equation [4.21] are estimated using various approximations to the LPE distribution. During the second step, a maximum *a posteriori* estimate (MAP) is used to determine the final classification of each pixel [ALA 05]. A Markov hypothesis is made over $P(l|f)$, describing it in terms of a Gibbs distribution:

$$P\left(l|f\right) \propto \exp(-U_D\left(f, l\right) - U_i\left(l\right))$$
[4.22]

in which $U_D$ is an energy that is a function of the given observation field $\mathbf{f}$ and the label field $l$, while $U_i$ is an energy that is a function of the label field alone, which is used for spatial regularization of that label field. $U_D$ is calculated as follows:

$$U_D\left(\mathbf{f}, l\right) = \sum_{\mathbf{x}} \left(-\log\left(p\left(\mathbf{e}(\mathbf{x})|\theta_{l(\mathbf{x})}\right)\right)\right) \qquad [4.23]$$

where $p\left(\mathbf{e}(\mathbf{x})|\theta_{l(\mathbf{x})}\right)$ is the conditional probability of the LPE given the texture class at $\mathbf{x}$, in other words $l(\mathbf{x})$.

We propose to use an internal energy for the label field that consists of two terms: $U_i\left(l\right) = U_{i,1}\left(l\right) + U_{i,2}\left(l\right)$. $U_{i,1}\left(l\right)$ corresponds to the Gibbs energy term associated with Potts model [ALA 05]:

$$U_{i,1}\left(l\right) = \beta \left(\sum_{\langle\mathbf{x},\mathbf{y}\rangle_1} 1_{(l(\mathbf{x})\neq l(\mathbf{y}))} + \frac{1}{\sqrt{2}} \sum_{\langle\mathbf{x},\mathbf{y}\rangle_2} 1_{(l(\mathbf{x})\neq l(\mathbf{y}))}\right) \qquad [4.24]$$

where $\beta$ is the weighting term, or hyper parameter, of the Potts model, and $\langle\mathbf{x},\mathbf{y}\rangle_p$, $p = 1,\ 2$, represents $\|\mathbf{x} - \mathbf{y}\|_2 = \sqrt{p}$, $(\mathbf{x},\mathbf{y}) \in E^2$, $\mathbf{x} \neq \mathbf{y}$. To determine $U_{i,2}\left(l\right)$, we use an energy term that depends on the size of the region consisting purely of connected pixels that have been assigned the same class label. The size of the region is written as $|R_i|$, $i = 1,\ldots,n_R$, with $n_R$ the total number of regions in the label field. The $|R_i|$ values are assumed to follow a distribution that encourages the formation of large regions [TU 02]. The associated energy term is then defined as follows:

$$U_{i,2}\left(l\right) = \gamma \left(\sum_{i=1}^{n_R} |R_i|^{\kappa}\right) \qquad [4.25]$$

where $\kappa$ is a constant introduced in [TU 02]. $\gamma$ is also a hyper parameter. Its value will be given in the following section.

### 4.4.3. *Experiments and results*

The "ground truth" associated with natural images is difficult to obtain. Attempts to define this are strongly influenced by subjectivity in the human operator. Thus, we have evaluated our proposed texture segmentation algorithm both on natural textured images and on synthetic images whose underlying structure is perfectly known. The test images are drawn from the color texture collection used in [ILE 08]. This collection was constructed using textures obtained from the VisTex and Photoshop databases. During the first segmentation step, a single $32 \times 32$ pixel sample was used as a training example for each class. The parameters of the image observation model and the multichannel prediction error were computed for each model and for each image. These parameters were then used to calculate the initial classes of the label fields for each of the ten textured color images shown in Figure 4.9. Examples of these segmentations prior to spatial regularization, for images 3 and 10, are shown in the second row of Figures 4.10 and 4.11. In the second step of the algorithm, the region classification is refined using a spatial regularization based on the Potts model and the energy calculated from the size of each region. An iterative method (ICM, *Iterated Conditional Modes*) was used to obtain the label fields. In this method, $\beta$, the hyper parameter of the Potts model, is used as a parameter whose value is gradually varied. Over the course of the regularization, the segmentation result obtained for a given value of $\beta$ is used as the initial field for the next

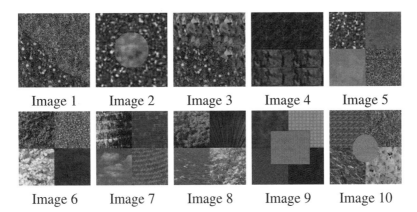

Image 1    Image 2    Image 3    Image 4    Image 5

Image 6    Image 7    Image 8    Image 9    Image 10

**Figure 4.9.** *Textured color images used in our experiments are numbered from left to right and then top to bottom*

next value of $\beta$. The value of the $\beta$ hyper parameter is varied from 0.1 to 4.0 in an exponential increase. For the energy term associated with each region, the $\gamma$ hyper parameter was fixed at 2 and the $\kappa$ coefficient at 0.9 as given in [TU 02]. The third rows in Figures 4.10 and 4.11 show the results after spatial regularization for the two textured color images.

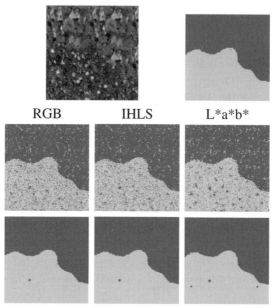

RGB          IHLS          L*a*b*

**Figure 4.10.** *Segmentation results in the absence of spatial regularization ($\beta = \gamma = 0$, 2nd row) and with spatial regularization (3rd row) for textured color image number 3 (1st row, left). These results have been obtained with the 2D QP AR model and the MGMM using RGB, IHLS, and L\*a\*b\* color spaces. The "ground truth" is shown on the 1st row, to the right of the original image*

The mean percentage pixel classification error without spatial regularization ($\beta = \gamma = 0$) and with spatial regularization are shown in Table 4.1 and plots as a function of $\beta$ are shown in Figure 4.12. The improvement of both these parametric models over the classical Gaussian approximation can clearly be seen in Table 4.1. This result confirms the hypothesis that the multichannel LPE distribution cannot be perfectly approximated using a simple multidimensional Gaussian distribution. It is clear that the MGMM approximation of the multichannel LPE distribution gives better results than the two rival approaches in terms

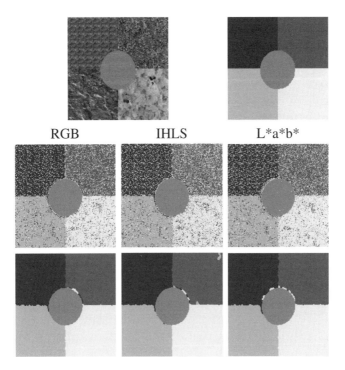

RGB                    IHLS                    L*a*b*

**Figure 4.11.** *Segmentation results without spatial regularization ($\beta = \gamma = 0$, 2nd row) and with spatial regularization (3rd row) for textured color image number 10 (1st row, left). These results have been obtained with the 2D QP AR model and the MGMM using RGB, IHLS, and L\*a\*b\* color spaces. The "ground truth" is shown on the 1st row, to the right of the original image*

| | without regularization | | | with regularization | | |
|---|---|---|---|---|---|---|
| | RGB | IHLS | L*a*b* | RGB | IHLS | L*a*b* |
| Gaussian distribution | 12.98 | 18.41 | 14.97 | 1.62 | 1.85 | 1.68 |
| MGMM | 12.47 | 16.83 | 13.67 | **1.41** | **1.58** | **1.52** |
| Wishart distribution | **6.04** | **8.14** | **6.35** | 3.15 | 3.37 | 3.09 |

**Table 4.1.** *Mean percentage pixel classification error for the 10 textured color images (see Figure 4.9) with and without spatial regularization. The best results are highlighted in bold*

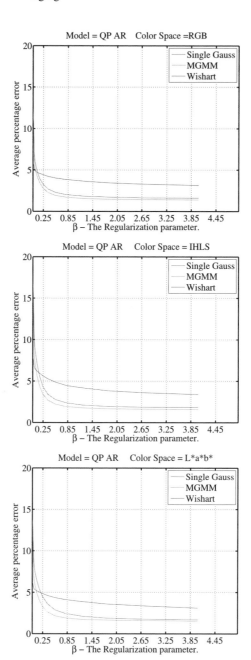

**Figure 4.12.** *Comparison of segmentation results obtained using three different parametric models of the LPE distribution. (For a color version of this figure, see www.iste.co.uk/fernandez/colorimag.zip)*

of the mean percentage error calculated after spatial regularization, for the 10 color textures used in our experiments. However, if we consider the same criterion *without* spatial regularization, the Wishart distribution shows better performance. This result can be explained by the fact that the latter uses multiple LPE vectors, thereby allowing more robust pixel classification in the absence of spatial regularization.

In contrast to the results we obtained for classification of color texture databases (see [QAZ 10a] and Chapter 6), these segmentation results for the 10 color images used in the study in the present chapter are not improved by the use of color spaces that separate achromatic and chromatic information (IHLS or L*a*b*), when compared to those obtained using the RGB color space. The main reason for this finding stems from the approach used, in which the model and the LPE probability distribution (a joint distribution) takes into account the dependencies that may be present between the different color planes. Nevertheless, more comprehensive results given in [QAZ 10a, QAZ 11a], in particular using the simulated annealing algorithm and satellite images, reveal the advantages of using the L*a*b* color space as opposed to the two alternative spaces, IHLS and RGB. This result is therefore in accordance with those obtained for classification of color texture databases.

## 4.5. Conclusion

Complex vector 2D linear prediction on color spaces with separate achromatic and chromatic information provides the characterization of the second order statistics simultaneously for the achromatic and chromatic channels, along with any correlation that may be present between these two channels. Through the use of manipulations involving transformations from the IHLS or L*a*b* color space to the RGB color space and then back again, we have been able to compare the level of interference between each channel introduced by these transformations. This comparison shows that the IHLS color space produces more interference of chromatic information inside the achromatic information than the L*a*b* space does.

In the PhD thesis written by Imtnan Qazi [QAZ 10a], these parametric models are applied to the classification of color texture databases (see Chapter 6) and to the segmentation of textured color images. Overall, we obtained the best results with the 2D auto-regressive model with quarter-plane support, bearing in mind that we did not optimize the use of GMRF, and with the L*a*b* color space. Other color spaces may merit investigation in future.

One of the main potential areas for future work is the coupling of linear prediction models with methods involving decomposition in a functional basis adapted to the particular color space. Such an approach could be used to characterize color textures based on their deterministic and random parts. As well as being a highly effective tool of analysis, this would offer the further possibility of color texture synthesis.

## 4.6. Bibliography

[ALA 05] ALATA O., RAMANANJARASOA C., "Unsupervised textured image segmentation using 2-D quarter plane autoregressive model with four prediction supports", *Pattern Recognition Letters*, vol. 26, p. 1069-1081, 2005.

[ALA 09] ALATA O., QUINTARD L., "Is there a best color space for color image characterization or representation based on multivariate gaussian mixture model?", *Computer Vision and Image Understanding*, vol. 113, no. 8, p. 867-877, August 2009.

[BOU 91] BOUMAN C., LIU B., "Multiple resolutions segmentation of textured images", *IEEE Transactions on Pattern Analysis and Machine Intelligence*, vol. 13, no. 2, p. 99-113, 1991.

[CAR 01] CARIOU C., ROUQUETTE S., ALATA O., "2-D spectral analysis", in *Two-Dimensional Signal Analysis*, GARELLO R. (ed.), p. 115-174, ISTE Ltd, London and John Wiley and Sons, New York, 2001.

[CIE 86] International Commission on Illumination, Colorimetry, Report no. CIE 15.2, 1986.

[ELS 87] EL-SHAER H.T.M., Multichannel 2-D Power Spectral Estimation and Applications, PhD thesis, Naval Postgraduate School, Monterey, California, USA, 1987.

[GUY 95] GUYON X., *Random Fields on a Network: Modeling, Statistics, and Applications*, Probability and Its Applications, Springer, 1995.

[HAN 03] HANBURY A., SERRA J., A 3D-polar coordinate colour representation suitable for image analysis, Technical Report no. PRIP-TR-77, Institute of Computer Aided Automation, Vienna University of Technology, Vienna, Austria, 2003.

[ILE 08]  ILEA D.E., WHELAN P.F., "CTex an adaptive unsupervised segmentation algorithm based on color-texture coherence", *IEEE Transactions on Image Processing*, vol. 10, no. 17, p. 1926-1939, 2008.

[PAL 02]  PALM C., LEHMANN T., "Classification of color textures by Gabor filtering", *Machine Graphics & Vision International Journal*, vol. 11, no. 2, p. 195-219, 2002.

[QAZ 09]  QAZI I.-U.-H., GHAZI F., ALATA O., BURIE J.-C., FERNANDEZ-MALOIGNE C., "A multivariate gaussian mixture model of linear prediction error for colour texture segmentation", *Proceedings of EUSIPCO*, p. 1537-1541, 2009.

[QAZ 10a]  QAZI I.-U.-H., Luminance-Chrominance Linear Prediction Models for Color Textures: An Application to Satellite Image Segmentation, PhD thesis, University of Poitiers, 2010.

[QAZ 10b]  QAZI I.-U.-H., ALATA O., BURIE J.-C., FERNANDEZ-MALOIGNE C., "Colour spectral analysis for spatial structure characterization of textures in IHLS colour space", *Pattern Recognition*, vol. 43, no. 3, p. 663-675, March 2010.

[QAZ 11a]  QAZI I.-U.-H., ALATA O., BURIE J.-C., ABADI M., MOUSSA A., FERNANDEZ-MALOIGNE C., "Parametric models of linear prediction error distribution for color texture and satellite image segmentation", *Computer Vision and Image Understanding*, vol. 115, no. 8, p. 1245-1262, 2011.

[QAZ 11b]  QAZI I.-U.-H., ALATA O., BURIE J.-C., MOUSSA A., FERNANDEZ-MALOIGNE C., "Choice of a pertinent color space for color texture characterization using parametric spectral analysis", *Pattern Recognition*, vol. 44, no. 1, p. 16-31, 2011.

[REL 02]  RELLIER G., DESCOMBES X., FALZON F., ZERUBIA J., "Texture feature analysis using a Gauss-Markov model in hyperspectral image classification", *IEEE Transactions on Geoscience and Remote Sensing*, vol. 42, no. 7, p. 1543-1551, 2004.

[TU 02]  TU Z., ZHU S.-C., "Image segmentation by data-driven Markov chain Monte Carlo", *IEEE Transactions on Pattern Analysis and Machine Intelligence*, vol. 24, p. 657-673, 2002.

# Chapter 5

# Region Segmentation

## 5.1. Introduction

Region segmentation is an intermediate stage in image processing, involving the reconstruction of regions corresponding to objects present in the image, based on the original image or a filtered image. Segmentation transforms the color image into an image where each pixel is represented by a label indicating the region that it belongs to. Having reconstructed these regions, the analysis stage generally aims to describe them with the help of attributes that enable objects contained within the image to be recognized.

In the specific case of color images, it is generally assumed that the different colors present in the image broadly correspond to different orientations and reflective properties of the surfaces of the observed objects and the presence of shadows. Segmentation methods analyze these colors to distinguish the different objects that make up a scene being observed by a color camera. The differences between the colors present in the image can be more or less prominent depending on the color representation system being used [VAN 03].

---

Chapter written by Alain CLÉMENT, Laurent BUSIN, Olivier LEZORAY and Ludovic MACAIRE.

The segmentation methods for color images that we will describe in this chapter assume that a region consists of connected pixels that share similar colorimetric properties or form a specific color texture. Methods based on this approach, referred to as a region-based approach, look within the image for subsets of connected pixels consisting of homogeneous colors or those that form a consistent texture together.

We will not attempt to give an exhaustive list of all segmentation methods for color images. The reader can find a complete review of segmentation techniques in [CHE 01, PAL 07]. We will instead try and demonstrate the concepts inherent to the most contemporary segmentation methods.

Since color information is multi-dimensional, analysis of color images requires the manipulation of data structures such as histograms, which can be demanding in terms of memory requirements. Scanning of such structures may also require a significant number of operations. In the part 1 of this chapter, we will describe an original implementation of the color histogram, known as the compact histogram, which can be used to reduce the memory requirements as well as the algorithmic complexity of its use.

Region construction techniques are based on the joint analysis of the color distribution within the color space and over the image plane. The second part of this chapter describes spatio-colorimetric classification techniques that are tailored toward color space analysis, while the third part discusses graph analysis techniques used to model the interaction between pixels within the image plane.

Finally, the question of how to evaluate the segmentation quality remains an open problem. The final part describes one such approach, preferred by a large proportion of the community, which compares automatic segmentation and a range of partitions performed by human observers.

## 5.2. Compact histograms

The histogram of an image is the representation of a discrete function, which for each pixel value, lists the number of pixels in the image that have this particular value. It can be thought of as the probability density of a random variable, with the image being a set of realizations of this distribution. When the pixel values are 3D vectors, as is the case for color images, this is referred to as a multi-dimensional histogram.

### 5.2.1. *Classical multi-dimensional histogram*

In its classical representation, the histogram $H^c$ of an $N$ pixel image, with each pixel having $P$ components in a color space $c$, each encoded using $Q$ bits, takes the form of a $P$-dimensional table consisting of $2^{P.Q}$ entries. When this table is filled out, each entry must be able to contain a positive integer number with a maximum value of $N$, which therefore requires storage of $E$ bits, where:

$$E > \log_2(N) \tag{5.1}$$

Note that digital encoding of numbers normally involves multiples of 8 bits. The multi-dimensional histogram thus occupies $2^{P.Q}E$ bits. In the case of a color image ($P = 3$) consisting of $512 \times 512$ pixels, with each component encoded over 256 levels ($Q = 8$), this value represents a minimum of 36 Mb. For a multi-component image with 10 components of the same resolution, the multi-dimensional histogram would require more than $2.5 \times 10^{18}$ Mb.

Faced with the challenge of manipulating such a vast volume of data, there are currently two strategies available:

– the first involves projecting the multi-dimensional histogram onto a reduced number of axes $p$ ($p < P$). In a marginal approach ($p = 1$), the $P$ 1D histograms will then only occupy a minimum of $2^Q.P. \log_2(N)$ bits. The drawback of this strategy is that some or all of the correlation between the different image components is lost, with the risk that certain significant modes (high-density regions) in the original multi-dimensional space will not be distinguishable;

– the second involves resampling each component over $q$ bits ($q < Q$), which is equivalent to performing a *a priori* classification of the image.

The consequences of this pre-segmentation cannot be predicted, and run counter to the efforts made to use high-resolution colorimetric or spectral cameras.

### 5.2.2. Compact multi-dimensional histogram

Let $C$ be the number of cells occupied in the multi-dimensional image histogram for an image with $P$ components, each encoded using $Q$ bits, in other words, the number of $P$-*tuplets* (or colors) in the image. In practice, the number $C$ is always much smaller than $2^{P.Q}$, the number of available cells. For a fixed number of pixels, the number of empty cells increases with the number $P$ of image components. The principle of the compact multi-dimensional histogram involves only encoding the $C$ cells that are effectively occupied, by sorting these cells in lexicographical order over the $P$ components of the image. This encoding uses two tables, one with dimensions $C \times P$ to store the colorimetric $P$-*tuplets*, and the other with dimensions $C \times 1$ for the corresponding pixel counts. Table 5.1 illustrates this concept, showing an extract from the compact histogram of a color image.

| R | G | B | count |
|---|---|---|---|
| 0 | 0 | 5 | 13 |
| 0 | 0 | 23 | 5 |
| ... | ... | ... | ... |
| 255 | 10 | 0 | 21 |
| 255 | 251 | 254 | 3 |

**Table 5.1.** *Extract from the compact histogram of a color RGB image with 8 bits per component*

For $E$ bits per entry, as defined in equation [5.1], the amount of memory occupied by the compact histogram is $C.E + C.P.Q$ bits, which represents a compression of the classical encoding scheme by a factor of:

$$\frac{2^{P.Q}}{C.(\frac{P.Q}{E} + 1)} \qquad [5.2]$$

The most unfavorable situation for the compact histogram would be if each image pixel had a different value $(C = N)$. In this worst case scenario, for a $512 \times 512$ color image with 24 bits of resolution, the compression factor is greater than 27:1.

To illustrate the reduction in memory requirements through the use of the compact histogram, Table 5.2 lists some comparative results obtained with Matlab©, using the *Double* (64 bit) and *Uint8* (8 bit) data types to encode the counts and the colorimetric values.

| Image ($Q = 8$ bits) | Histogram | Memory (Mb) classical histogram | Memory (Mb) compact histogram |
|---|---|---|---|
| RGB, 6 pure colors | | 128 | $6.29 \times 10^{-5}$ |
| Synthetic RGB | | 128 | 0.07 |
| Natural RGB | | 128 | 0.32 |

**Table 5.2.** *Comparison of memory requirements for classical and compact multi-dimensional histograms. (For a color version of this figure, see www.iste.co.uk/fernandez/colorimag.zip)*

### 5.2.2.1. *Algorithm*

The processing of the compact histogram is based on lexicographical sorting of the levels of the $N$ pixels in the image, structured using $P$ sub-keys into an ordering relation defined by the ordering of the $P$ image components. We recommend the quicksort algorithm, which is faster than any iterative method for $N > 20$, and a factor of 1.5 to 2 faster than the Heapsort algorithm for $N > 1000$ [PRE 92]. Our aim here is not to discuss the detail of a specific sorting algorithm, the implementation of which presents no particular challenges. For more details on this algorithm and its complexity, the reader is referred to [CLE 03].

### 5.2.2.2. *Properties*

The main advantage of the compact histogram is that it reduces the memory volume occupied by a multi-dimensional histogram, without any loss of information. The gain in memory space is higher for larger numbers of colorimetric components. Due to their different designs, the compact histogram and the classical histogram have structural differences that lead to differences in the algorithmic costs of accessing the data contained within them.

### 5.2.2.2.1. Complete histogram scan

A complete scan of the classical histogram requires $P$ nested loops of size $2^Q$, which entails a total of $2^{P.Q}$ comparisons, to identify the $C$ non-zero counts. A full scan of the compact histogram requires only $C$ iterations, reading $P + 1$ values. The compact histogram can therefore result in a non-negligible reduction in the algorithmic complexity of any operation that requires all the different values within an image to be listed and counted. Examples of this include plotting the histogram, statistical calculations or the construction of a color palette.

### 5.2.2.2.2. Searching for specific colors

The classical histogram is a set that is directly indexed by its colorimetric coordinates. A specific $P$-*tuplet* can be accessed directly, and a single comparison is all that is required to check whether its count is non-zero. The compact histogram is sorted in lexicographical order, and searching for a specific $P$-*tuplet* is analogous to searching for a specific word in a dictionary. The same strategies established for searching for an element in a sorted list can also be applied here: linear search, binary search, random search, etc. The compact histogram will therefore be less efficient than the classical histogram for this type of operation.

### 5.2.2.2.3. Searching for specific counts

The counts are not directly addressable in either type of histogram. Searching for a specific count therefore requires a complete scan, meaning that the compact histogram is favored.

### 5.2.2.3. *Labeling-connected components*

Labeling-connected components of a multi-dimensional histogram involve performing a scan of all the *P-tuplets* with non-zero counts to apply a single consistent label to those *P-tuplets* that are connected in color space. This stage is essential for many pixel classification methods based on histogram analysis [PAL 07]. The compact histogram is a sorted sequential structure in which an iterative displacement is not linearly related to a displacement in the geometric space formed by the colorimetric components. This means that classical labeling methods are not directly applicable. Here, we will present the compact labeling algorithm developed by Ouattara and Clément.

As in the classical case, labeling of a compact histogram is performed with a single scan, with the help of a label equivalence table. In this case, only the preceding neighbors of a *P-tuplet* need to be considered (see Table 5.3).

| (i-1, j-1) | (i-1, j) | (i-1, j+1) |
|:---:|:---:|:---:|
| (i, j-1) | **(i, j)** | |
| | | |

**Table 5.3.** *2D neighbors of the point with coordinates (i, j) in lexographical scan order for the components IJ*

The sequential scan of the $C$ *P-tuplets* takes place in lexicographical order for the components. A particular feature of the compact histogram is that the positions of the neighbors of the *P-tuplet* are not known in advance (see section 5.2.2.2.2). As illustrated in Table 5.4, these positions will nevertheless always precede the *P-tuplet* in question in the scan order, and as a result they will already have been labeled. For $P$ components, the theoretical number of predecessors of a *P-tuplet* is $(3^P - 1)/2$. In practice, the true number of predecessors is limited by the number of *P-tuplets* present in the image.

| Component I | Component J |
|:-----------:|:-----------:|
| 0 | 0 |
| ... | ... |
| i-1 | j-1 |
| i-1 | j |
| i-1 | j+1 |
| ... | ... |
| i | j-1 |
| **i** | **j** |
| ... | ... |
| $2^Q - 1$ | $2^Q - 1$ |

**Table 5.4.** *2D coordinates of the theoretical neighbors of the point (i, j) in the compact histogram IJ of an image encoded with Q bits per component*

The labeling of connected components of the compact histogram makes it possible for pixel classification methods to operate without re-quantification or sub-sampling of the multi-dimensional image space. We will describe an implementation example in the following section. The reader is also referred to [TOR 10] for an example of the use of compact multi-dimensional histograms for spatio-colorimetric classification of color images as discussed in the rest of this chapter.

### 5.2.3. *Pixel classification through compact histogram analysis*

Ouattara and Clément developed a non-supervised process of pixel classification based on the analysis of compact multi-dimensional histograms. This process delivers as output a labeled image where each pixel has an associated label representing the class it has been assigned to. Connected pixels, assigned to the same class, are then combined into a single region using a connected component analysis of the labeled image.

First introduced in [CLE 03], the principle of histogram mode analysis involves hierarchical decomposition of the multi-dimensional image histogram by constructing a tree of modes representative of the different classes. The algorithm scans the different values of pixels counts from the compact histogram sorted in ascending order. At each stage, connected components within the histogram are labeled. The histogram modes identified by connected components are then recursively decomposed into sub-modes with minimal dispersion. A mode will be considered significant if it has a total count that is greater than a population threshold $S$, the choice of which ultimately determines the number of classes that will be present. Once the tree of modes has been constructed, the colorimetric values that have not been assigned to significant modes (class kernels) are classified by minimizing the colorimetric distance to the centers of mass of these various modes. The regions of the segmented image thus consist of regions of connected pixels whose colors belong to the same class. The small memory footprint of compact histograms means that the segmentation method can treat an arbitrary number of colorimetric components ($P$) in a vector manner, without rebinning or sub-sampling. An example of this classification strategy is given in Figure 5.1 for a natural color image. The authors show that the method is able to distinguish classes that are colorimetrically very close to one another, identified in the histogram by low-dispersion modes. The drawback in the case of textured images or images containing only a few regions of homogeneous colors is a tendency to over-segment the image. The distributions of the two vertical regions in Figure 5.1a (the blue component is set to 0) are so close together in the RG chromatic plane that they cannot be distinguished by analysis of the color histogram shown in Figure 5.1b. Figure 5.2 shows that analysis of the color distribution alone cannot be used to recover the two regions. This example illustrates the need for a joint analysis of both the color distribution in the color space and the spatial distribution of the colors within the image plane.

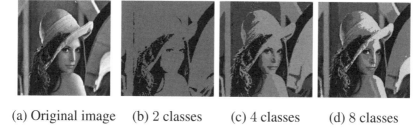

(a) Original image    (b) 2 classes    (c) 4 classes    (d) 8 classes

**Figure 5.1.** *Pixel classification in the "Lena" image for different numbers of classes. The results are presented in the form of label images representing the mean colors of each class*

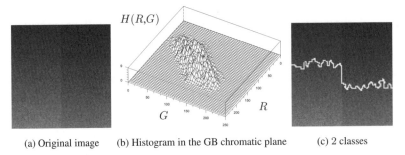

(a) Original image    (b) Histogram in the GB chromatic plane    (c) 2 classes

**Figure 5.2.** *Pixel classification for the synthetic Figure 5.2a through histogram analysis. The results are shown in the form of region contours based on the false color label image. (For a color version of this figure, see www.iste.co.uk/ fernandez/colorimag.zip)*

## 5.3. Spatio-colorimetric classification

### 5.3.1. *Introduction*

By taking into account both the spatial arrangement of colors in the image plane and the distribution of colors in the color space, it is possible to partition the color space in such a way that the pixel classes effectively correspond to regions within the image. We will divide such methods, referred to as "spatio-colorimetric methods" into two groups based on whether they perform a joint or a sequential analysis of the spatial and colorimetric information representing the image.

### 5.3.2. *Joint analysis*

This analysis associates the pixels at two points, described in terms of their spatial coordinates and their color components and hence projected into a 5D space. Here, we will describe the *mean shift* method, which is based on an estimation of the probability density of these two points in this feature space. We will also discuss the degree of spatio-colorimetric compactness, which couples a measurement of the color dispersion in color space with a measure of pixel connectivity in the spatial image plane.

#### 5.3.2.1. *Mean shift*

Comaniciu and Meer constructed a spatio-colorimetric function describing the image and proposed to determine the different modes by considering jointly the spatial distribution and the color distribution. To segment the image, they applied the *mean shift* algorithm in this spatio-colorimetric space [COM 02]. The *mean shift* technique is based on a kernel used by the Parzen density estimator, along with a second kernel involving its derivative. At each point in the combined color and pixel coordinate feature space, the *mean shift* is calculated as the difference between the weighted mean of the neighboring observations and the center of the kernel. For a set of points, the procedure converges to the underlying density *maxima* without actually having to estimate that density. In addition, the translation of the kernel in this feature space is automatically adapted to the local point density. Low densities lead to a significant displacement distance for the *mean shift*.

A color image can be represented by $N$ 5D $\mathbf{x}_i$ representing the $N$ image pixels in the spatial domain ($\mathbf{x}_i^s$: spatial coordinates) and the color domain ($\mathbf{x}_i^c$: color point in the color space $c$).

The initial phase sets $j$ to 1 and $\mathbf{x}_i$ to $\mathbf{y}_{i,1}$. The algorithm then repeats the calculation of $\mathbf{y}_{i,j+1}$ until convergence, using the following equation:

$$\mathbf{y}_{i,j+1} = \frac{\sum_{k=1}^{N} \mathbf{y}_{k,j} \cdot \frac{\delta}{h_s^2 . h_c^3} g\left(\left\|\frac{\mathbf{y}_{k,j}^s - \mathbf{y}_{i,j}^s}{h_s}\right\|_2^2\right) g\left(\left\|\frac{\mathbf{y}_{k,j}^c - \mathbf{y}_{i,j}^c}{h_c}\right\|_2^2\right)}{\sum_{k=1}^{N} \frac{\delta}{h_s^2 . h_c^3} g\left(\left\|\frac{\mathbf{y}_{k,j}^s - \mathbf{y}_{i,j}^s}{h_s}\right\|_2^2\right) g\left(\left\|\frac{\mathbf{y}_{k,j}^c - \mathbf{y}_{i,j}^c}{h_c}\right\|_2^2\right)} \qquad [5.3]$$

where $\|.\|_2$ is the $\mathcal{L}_2$ norm, $g$ is a Gaussian kernel function, $\delta$ a normalization factor, and $h_s$ and $h_c$ define the size of the spatial and color domains used during estimation of the probability densities. Let the points $\hat{\mathbf{y}}_i$ represent the pixels after convergence. The label image then consists of the points $\mathbf{z}_i = (\mathbf{x}_i^s, \hat{\mathbf{y}}_i^c)$. Those points $\mathbf{z}_i$ whose distance in the image plane is less than $h_s$, and whose distance in the color space is less than $h_c$, are combined to form a region. Each region whose area is less than a threshold value is fused with the adjacent region whose mean color is the closest to that of the current region.

Losson *et al.* showed that this method tends to result in over-segmentation, especially when the objects in the observed scene are not illuminated in a uniform manner [LOS 08]. This phenomenon is illustrated by Figure 5.4a, showing the segmentation resulting from a *mean shift* procedure[1] applied to the synthetic Figure 5.2a. In this image, the contours of the reconstructed regions are shown in white. The results are generally highly sensitive to adjustments in the $h_s$ and $h_c$ parameters and lead to over-segmentation of the image. This is why we need to fuse adjacent regions with similar mean colors.

A number of additional segmentation methods have been inspired by the *mean shift* method, such as that of Paris *et al.* who suggested simplifying the *mean shift* method by detecting region seeds through a simple search for local *maxima* in the estimated probability density [PAR 07]. Since the number of resultant regions reconstructed by the *mean shift* method is excessive, they are fused using an iterative analysis of the region adjacency graph, leading to a hierarchical segmentation of the image. Another method is that of Shapira *et al.* who suggested replacing the weighted mean of the neighboring observations, used to calculate the difference from the center of the kernel, with the median value of the observations [SHA 09]. As with median color filtering, the difficulty then lies in defining an ordering relation between these multi-dimensional observations.

The *mean shift* method juxtaposes spatial and colorimetric information in a common 5D feature space. In view of the heterogeneity of these different types of information, it is necessary to adjust the size $h_s$ of the spatial domain separately from the size $h_c$ of the color domain as used when estimating the probability density. It is nevertheless difficult to define thresholds for a distance computed in this space, which combines attributes that are heterogeneous in nature. For this reason, Macaire *et al.* proposed the use of a degree of color compactness, which measures separately the color distribution in color space and their spatial distribution over the image plane, when constructing the pixel classes [LOS 08, MAC 06, BUS 05].

---

1 This image was obtained using the executable available at the address http://www.caip.rutgers.edu/riul/research/code/EDISON/.

### 5.3.2.2. *Analysis of degrees of spatio-colorimetric compactness*

Working in the RGB color space, let $\mathcal{D}_l(\mathbf{x}_i^c)$ be a cube centered on $\mathbf{x}_i^c = [x_i^R, x_i^G, x_i^B]^T$ with sides of length $l$ (an odd number) parallel to the axes of this space. The cube $\mathcal{D}_l(\mathbf{x}_i^c)$ contains all the colors $\mathbf{c}' = [c'^R, c'^G, c'^B]^T$ adjacent to $\mathbf{x}_i^c$, such that $x_i^k - \frac{l-1}{2} \leq c'^k \leq x_i^k + \frac{l-1}{2}$, $k = R, G, B$. Let $\mathcal{S}_l(\mathbf{x}_i^c)$ be the subset consisting of all pixels $\mathbf{x}_j$ whose color $\mathbf{x}_j^c$ lies in the color cube $\mathcal{D}_l(\mathbf{x}_i^c)$.

The degree of connectivity $DC_l(\mathbf{x}_i^c)$ is defined as the mean number of neighbors of each pixel in $\mathcal{S}_l(\mathbf{x}_i^c)$ that also belong to $\mathcal{S}_l(\mathbf{x}_i^c)$ [BUS 05]. When the subset $\mathcal{S}_l(\mathbf{x}_i^c)$ is empty, $DC_l(\mathbf{x}_i^c)$ is set to 0. If this is not the case, for a spatial neighborhood of $nb \times nb$ pixels ($nb$ being an odd number that we will take to be three here), $DC_l(\mathbf{x}_i^c)$ is defined as:

$$DC_l(\mathbf{x}_i^c) = \frac{\sum\limits_{\mathbf{x}_j \in \mathcal{S}_l(\mathbf{x}_i^c)} \mathrm{Card}\{N\,[\mathcal{S}_l(\mathbf{x}_i^c)]\,(\mathbf{x}_j)\}}{(nb^2 - 1) \cdot \mathrm{Card}\{\mathcal{S}_l(\mathbf{x}_i^c)\}} \qquad [5.4]$$

where $N\,[\mathcal{S}_l(\mathbf{x}_i^c)]\,(\mathbf{x}_j)$ represents those neighbors of pixel $\mathbf{x}_j \in \mathcal{S}_l(\mathbf{x}_i^c)$, of its $(nb^2 - 1)$ neighbors in total that also belong to $\mathcal{S}_l(\mathbf{x}_i^c)$. This degree $DC_l(\mathbf{x}_i^c)$ can vary from 0 to 1; a value close to 0 means that the pixels of $\mathcal{S}_l(\mathbf{x}_i^c)$ are scattered within the image plane, whereas a value close to 1 indicates that most of the pixels in this subset are connected within the image.

The degree of homogeneity $DH_l(\mathbf{x}_i^c)$ is defined as the ratio between the mean local dispersion of colors in the neighborhood of each pixel belonging to $\mathcal{S}_l(\mathbf{x}_i^c)$ and the global color dispersion of the pixels of $\mathcal{S}_l(\mathbf{x}_i^c)$ [MAC 06]:

$$DH_l(\mathbf{x}_i^c) = \frac{\sigma_{local}(\mathcal{S}_l(\mathbf{x}_i^c))}{\sigma(\mathcal{S}_l(\mathbf{x}_i^c))} \qquad [5.5]$$

where:

$$\sigma(\mathcal{S}) = \frac{1}{\mathrm{Card}\{\mathcal{S}\}} \cdot \sqrt{\sum_{\mathbf{x}_j \in \mathcal{S}} \left\| \mathbf{x}_j^c - \mathbf{m}_\mathcal{S}^c \right\|_2^2} \qquad [5.6]$$

and:

$$\sigma_{local}(\mathcal{S}) = \frac{1}{\text{Card}\{\mathcal{S}\}} \cdot \sum_{x_j \in \mathcal{S}} \sigma\left(N\left[\mathcal{S}\right](x_j)\right) \qquad [5.7]$$

where $\mathbf{m}_{\mathcal{S}}^c$ is the center of mass of the colors representing the pixels that belong to $\mathcal{S}$.

When the colors of the pixels belonging to $S_l(\mathbf{x}_i^c)$ result in a compact cluster in color space, the degree of homogeneity estimated at $\mathbf{x}_i^c$ is close to 1. Conversely, when the colors form several distinct clusters, then the degree of homogeneity is close to 0.

The spatio-colorimetric compactness function $sccf_l$ is a function whose value for each color $\mathbf{x}_i^c$ is defined as the product of the degree of connectivity and the degree of homogeneity [LOS 08]:

$$sccf_l(\mathbf{x}_i^c) = DC_l(\mathbf{x}_i^c) \cdot DH_l(\mathbf{x}_i^c) \qquad [5.8]$$

A high value for $sccf_l(\mathbf{x}_i^c)$ indicates that the pixels of the subset $S_l(\mathbf{x}_i^c)$ are strongly connected within the image ($DC_l(\mathbf{x}_i^c)$ close to 1) and that their colors are concentrated in the color space ($DH_l(\mathbf{x}_i^c)$ close to 1). Conversely, a small value of $sccf_l(\mathbf{x}_i^c)$ indicates that the pixels belonging to $S_l(\mathbf{x}_i^c)$ are scattered within the image ($DC_l(\mathbf{x}_i^c)$ is close to 0) and/or their colors do not form a compact cluster in the color space ($DH_l(\mathbf{x}_i^c)$ is close to 0). The length $l$ of the color cube must be selected with care by the user based on the content of the image. The algorithmic complexity of the construction of $sccf_l$ is $N.l^3.C$, where $C$ is the number of different colors present in the image, which consists of $N$ pixels.

Figure 5.3a shows the $sccf_7$ function for Figure 5.2a, showing two regions whose color distributions are mixed in the RG chromatic plane. The length $l$ is set to 7 to ensure that the pixel subsets $S_l(\mathbf{x}_i^c)$ are sufficiently well populated. Let us examine the three different colors $c_1$, $c_2$, and $c_3$ as indicated by the color symbols in the figure. It can be seen that the values of $sccf_7$ are high for colors $c_1$ and $c_3$, since the majority of the pixels in subsets $S_7(c_1)$ and $S_7(c_3)$ are connected in the image, and their colors are similar to one another (see Figures 5.3b and 5.3d). Note that these two colors lie on modes that should be detected. On the other hand, the value of $sccf_7$ is low for the color $c_2$, which lies in a valley in the histogram since the pixels of subset $S_7(c_2)$ are scattered throughout the image (see Figure 5.3c). This example illustrates that the degree of spatio-colorimetric compactness reveals two modes that would not have been distinguishable by a simple analysis of the color distribution (see Figure 5.2).

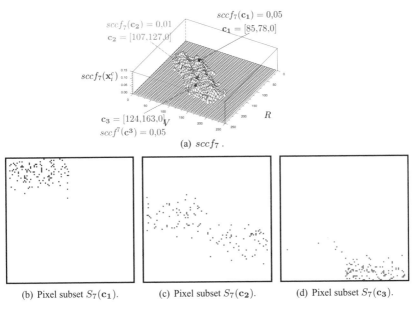

(a) $sccf_7$ .

(b) Pixel subset $S_7(c_1)$.      (c) Pixel subset $S_7(c_2)$.      (d) Pixel subset $S_7(c_3)$.

**Figure 5.3.** *Spatio-colorimetric compactness function for Figure 5.2a using three colors, along with their corresponding pixel subsets*

As is the case with the compact histogram, we still need to detect the modes of the spatio-colorimetric compactness function to partition the color space into different classes. The connected pixels, whose colors belong to the same mode, form the regions that are generated in the segmented image. Figure 5.4b shows an example of segmentation of synthetic Figure 5.2a following detection of the modes using fuzzy morphological tools as described in [LOS 08]. This image demonstrates that this analysis of the degree of spatio-colorimetric compactness is for the most part effective at recovering the two regions whose color distributions are mixed.

The segmentation quality depends strongly on the function used for the joint representation of the color distribution within the color space and its spatial distribution across the image plane. The *mean shift* method, along with analysis of the degrees of spatio-colorimetric compactness, assumes that the modes of this function correspond to the regions to be recovered from the image. These approaches reach their limits when the observed scene is so complex that it is difficult to associate distinct modes to the regions that are to be recovered. For this reason, certain authors prefer successive analysis in color space and in the image plane.

### 5.3.3. *Successive analysis*

JSEG is one of the most widely-known segmentation methods. It involves a classification stage in color space followed by spatial analysis [DEN 01]. The first stage quantifies the colors present in the image in a non-uniform manner into $N_c$ colors, yielding an image known as the *class-map*, where each pixel represented by the 2D point $\mathbf{x}_i^s$ is assigned a scalar label $\mathbf{x}_i^l$, $\mathbf{x}_i^l = 1, ..., N_c$. Let $\omega_k$ be the subset of pixels $\mathbf{x}_i$ whose label $\mathbf{x}_i^l$ is equal to $k$.

Let us assume that the image is partitioned into $n^{\mathcal{A}}$ regions $\mathcal{R}_n^{\mathcal{A}}$, ($n = 1, 2, ..., n^{\mathcal{A}}$). For each region $\mathcal{R}_n^{\mathcal{A}}$, we evaluate the criterion $J_n$:

$$J_n = \frac{\sum_{\mathbf{x}_i^s \in \mathcal{R}_n^{\mathcal{A}}} \sum_{k=1}^{N_c} \left\| \mathbf{x}_i^s - \mathbf{m}_{k,n}^s \right\|_2^2}{\sum_{\mathbf{x}_i^s \in \mathcal{R}_n^{\mathcal{A}}} \left\| \mathbf{x}_i^s - \mathbf{m}_n^s \right\|_2^2} \qquad [5.9]$$

where:

$$\mathbf{m}_{k,n}^s = \frac{1}{\mathrm{Card}\{\mathcal{R}_n^{\mathcal{A}} \cap \omega_k\}} \cdot \sum_{\mathbf{x}_i^s \in \mathcal{R}_n^{\mathcal{A}} \cap \omega_k} \mathbf{x}_i^s \qquad [5.10]$$

and:

$$\mathbf{m}_n^s = \frac{1}{\mathrm{Card}\{\mathcal{R}_n^{\mathcal{A}}\}} \cdot \sum_{\mathbf{x}_i^s \in \mathcal{R}_n^{\mathcal{A}}} \mathbf{x}_i^s \qquad [5.11]$$

The $J_n$ criterion measures the ratio between the spatial dispersion of the pixels of $\mathcal{R}_n^\mathcal{A}$ assigned to a given label and the spatial dispersion of the pixels throughout the entire region. Deng *et al.* showed through various examples that the lower this ratio, the better the connectivity between the pixels assigned identical labels within the region [DEN 01].

A global measure $\overline{J}$ over the entire image describes the full set of regions as follows:

$$\overline{J} = \frac{1}{n^\mathcal{A}} \sum_{n=1}^{n^\mathcal{A}} \text{Card}\{\mathcal{R}_n^\mathcal{A}\} J_n \qquad\qquad [5.12]$$

By minimizing this criterion, it is possible to obtain a partition where the pixels assigned to the same label within each region are as highly connected as possible. Using the $\overline{J}$ criterion, a region growing procedure is applied to the *class-map*, followed by a region fusion stage to avoid over-segmentation.

Wang *et al.* showed that the coarse classification provided by the color quantification stage degrades the flexibility of the JSEG criterion [WAN 06b]. Thus, there will be a tendency to separate neighboring regions with gradual color transitions into several distinct classes. This phenomenon is illustrated by Figure 5.4c, which was generated by an implementation of the JSEG algorithm that is available on the Internet[2], which was configured using its default parameter values.

Wang *et al.* showed using a simple example that the $\overline{J}$ criterion applied to the *class-map* cannot be used to obtain information on the level of color transitions between two regions [WAN 06c]. As a result, it is not possible to distinguish between regions with similar textures but whose color distribution is different. JSEG therefore has a tendency to over-segment images in the presence of non-uniform illumination. This probably stems from the fact that the color and spatial information are taken into account separately. Wang *et al.* therefore proposed combining the $\overline{J}$ criterion

2 http://vision.ece.ucsb.edu/segmentation/jseg/.

based on a local measure of texture homogeneity with $H$, a measure of color discontinuity used by the HSEG method [JIN 03].

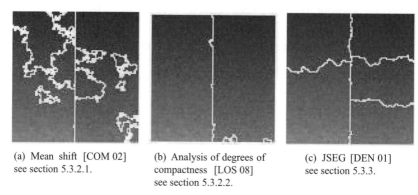

(a) Mean shift [COM 02]
see section 5.3.2.1.

(b) Analysis of degrees of compactness [LOS 08]
see section 5.3.2.2.

(c) JSEG [DEN 01]
see section 5.3.3.

**Figure 5.4.** *Results for segmentation of Figure 5.2a using different methods of spatio-colorimetric classification. The results are shown in the form of the contours of the reconstructed regions*

### 5.3.4. Conclusion

To conclude this section, we propose to investigate the computation time required to segment a 1,000 × 100 pixel image using the three approaches described earlier. These were implemented on a PC with a 2 GHz microprocessor. The time required for the *mean shift* algorithm is the smallest at 5s, followed by the JSEG algorithm at 8s. The time required to calculate the degree of spatio-colorimetric compactness was significantly higher at around 60s. This increase can be reduced by an implementation similar to that of the compact histogram. The results obtained from these three methods will be presented and compared at the end of this chapter.

The methods referred to as spatio-colorimetric classification are generally well suited to images containing regions of homogeneous colors, with spatial analysis being most suited to distinguishing regions whose color distributions are close together or even mixed in the color space. They yield an initial segmentation that must be followed up by using graph analysis to formalize the spatial relationships between adjacent pixels, as discussed in the next section.

## 5.4. Segmentation by graph analysis

A graph is a structure that is ideally suited for representing data contained within images, since it models the adjacency relationships in the data. In this section, we will discuss how to formalize an image in the form of a graph, and the operations that must be applied to this graph to segment a color image. We will first describe the structure of a graph and the operations that can be applied to it, and we will then discuss their use for what is known as semi-supervised segmentation. This is segmentation starting from markers provided by the user. The edges of a graph may be weighted based on the similarity between adjacent data. We will see later that these similarities can be combined in the form of a matrix, spectral analysis of which can be used to divide up the graph to classify the image data.

### 5.4.1. *Graphs and color images*

#### 5.4.1.1. *Introduction to graphs*

In image processing, it is common to treat the support of the image as a grid, with the spatial connectivity relationships between each pixel determining the neighborhood that will be considered. Thus, on a 2D grid, the neighborhood graph associated with an image corresponds, for example, to the use of four- or eight-way connectivity for each pixel (see Figures 5.5a and 5.5b). This is known as a grid graph, with the vertices representing pixels and the edges representing the connectivity relationships between pixels. A grid is a regular tessellation of square elements, but other polygonal tessellations exist, the most well known of which is the Voronoï tessellation. This tessellation also has an associated neighborhood graph known as the Delaunay graph. Figure 5.5c shows a Voronoï partition, with its Delaunay graph superimposed. More specifically, when an image is segmented into regions, a neighborhood graph known as the region adjacency graph can be associated with this partitioning, where each vertex represents a region and each edge represents a neighborhood relationship between these regions. Figure 5.5d shows an image partitioned into regions, with its region graph superimposed. Finally, a graph may be associated with any arbitrary representation of image data just as long as some measure of distance or similarity is available. In this context, analysis of image data involves analysis of graphs, with the properties associated with the vertices and edges depending on the problem under consideration.

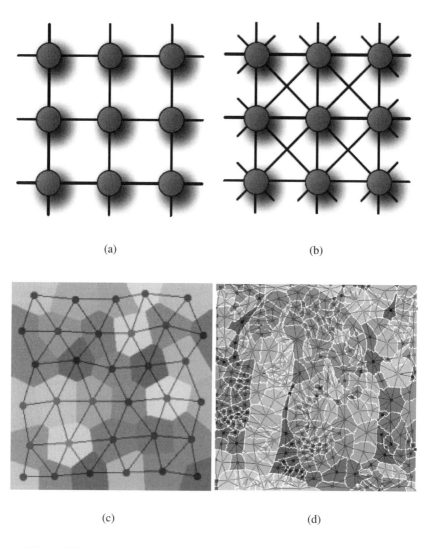

(a)                                    (b)

(c)                                    (d)

**Figure 5.5.** *Examples of grid type graphs a) with four-way connectivity; b) with eight-way connectivity; c) Delaunay graph; d) region adjacency*

## 5.4.1.2. *Graphs: basic concepts*

A graph is a data structure used to describe a set of objects and the relationships between them. The objects are the *vertices* of the graph and the relationships between them are the *edges*. A weighted graph $G = (\mathcal{V}, \mathcal{E}, w)$ consists of a set $\mathcal{V} = \{v_1, \ldots, v_N\}$ of $N$ vertices and a set $\mathcal{E} \subset \mathcal{V} \times \mathcal{V}$ of weighted edges. A graph $G$ is assumed to be undirected, and without loops or multiple edges [DIE 05]. Let $(i, j)$ be an edge of $\mathcal{E}$ that connects two vertices $i$ and $j$ belonging to $\mathcal{V}$. Its weight, written $w(i, j)$, represents the similarity between these two nodes. These similarities are obtained through the use of a positive, symmetric function $w \colon \mathcal{V} \times \mathcal{V} \to \mathbb{R}_+$ satisfying $w(i, j) = 0$ for $(i, j) \notin \mathcal{E}$.

Associated with a graph $G$ are the function spaces over its edges and vertices. Let $\mathcal{H}(\mathcal{V})$ be the Hilbert space of real-valued functions defined over the vertices of a graph $G = (\mathcal{V}, \mathcal{E}, w)$. A function $f \colon \mathcal{V} \to \mathbb{R}^3$ of $\mathcal{H}(\mathcal{V})$ assigns a color $f(j) = \mathbf{x}_j^c = (f_k(j))_{k=1,2,3}^T$ to each vertex $j \in \mathcal{V}$. The space $\mathcal{H}(\mathcal{V})$ is equipped with the standard scalar product $\langle f, h \rangle_{\mathcal{H}(\mathcal{V})} = \sum_{j \in \mathcal{V}} f(j) h(j)$, where $f, h \colon \mathcal{V} \to \mathbb{R}^3$. Similarly, let $\mathcal{H}(\mathcal{E})$ be the Hilbert space of real-valued functions defined over the edges of $G$. This is also equipped with the scalar product $\langle F, H \rangle_{\mathcal{H}(\mathcal{E})} = \sum_{i \in \mathcal{V}} \sum_{j \sim i} F(i, j) H(i, j)$, where $F, H \colon \mathcal{E} \to \mathbb{R}^3$ are two functions of $\mathcal{H}(\mathcal{E})$. We will write $i \sim j$ to represent the fact that two vertices $i$ and $j$ are adjacent. Finally, it is standard for a weighted graph to assume the following weightings: $w(i, j) = \exp(-\|f(i) - f(j)\|_2^2 / 2\sigma^2)$ where $\sigma$ is a scale parameter and $\|.\|_2$ is the $\mathcal{L}_2$ norm. The set of weights can be expressed in the form of an $N \times N$ similarity matrix $w$.

## 5.4.1.3. *Difference operators on graphs*

Here, we will present a formalism based on partial differential equations acting on graphs for color image segmentation[3]. A set of weighted difference operators on graphs was introduced in [ELM 08b, ELM 08a, LEZ 07, TA 09]. Let $G = (\mathcal{V}, \mathcal{E}, w)$ be a weighted graph, and let $f \colon \mathcal{V} \to \mathbb{R}^3$ be a function of $\mathcal{H}(\mathcal{V})$. The *difference*

---

3 In collaboration with Abderrahim Elmoataz and Vinh-Thong Ta.

*operator* for $f$, written $d\colon \mathcal{H}(\mathcal{V}) \to \mathcal{H}(\mathcal{E})$, is defined for a vertex $(i,j) \in \mathcal{E}$ as:

$$(df)(i,j) = \sqrt{w(i,j)}(f(j) - f(i)) \qquad [5.13]$$

The adjoint operator $d^*\colon \mathcal{H}(\mathcal{E}) \to \mathcal{H}(\mathcal{V})$ for the difference operator is defined, for all functions $f \in \mathcal{H}(\mathcal{V})$ and $H \in \mathcal{H}(\mathcal{E})$, as:

$$\langle df, H \rangle_{\mathcal{H}(\mathcal{E})} = \langle f, d^*H \rangle_{\mathcal{H}(\mathcal{V})} \qquad [5.14]$$

Using the definitions of scalar products, the expression for the adjoint operator of a function $H \in \mathcal{H}(\mathcal{E})$ can be expressed for a vertex $i \in \mathcal{V}$ as:

$$(d^*H)(i) = \sum_{j \sim i} \sqrt{w(i,j)}(H(j,i) - H(i,j)) \qquad [5.15]$$

The *divergence operator* for a function $H \in \mathcal{H}(\mathcal{E})$ is defined as $-d^*$. The *weighted gradient operator* $\nabla_w\colon \mathcal{H}(\mathcal{V}) \to \mathbb{R}^{3 \times \mathrm{Card}\{\mathcal{E}\}}$ for a function $f \in \mathcal{H}(\mathcal{V})$ at a vertex $i \in \mathcal{V}$ is the matrix of all the differences for the set of vertices of $\mathcal{E}$ and for every color component: $\nabla_w f(i) = [(df)(i,j)]^T_{(i,j) \in \mathcal{E}}$. The $\mathcal{L}_2$ norm of this vector represents the *local variation* of the function $f$ at a given vertex of the graph, and is defined as:

$$\|\nabla_w f(i)\|_2 = \sqrt{\sum_{j \sim i}((df)(i,j))^2} \overset{(5.13)}{=} \sqrt{\sum_{k=1}^{3} \sum_{j \sim i} w(i,j)(f_k(j) - f_k(i))^2}$$

$$[5.16]$$

The *weighted p-Laplacian* $p \in \mathbb{R}^+$ of a function $f \in \mathcal{H}(\mathcal{V})$, written $\Delta_w^p\colon \mathcal{H}(\mathcal{V}) \to \mathcal{H}(\mathcal{V})$, is defined as:

$$\Delta_w^p f(i) = \tfrac{1}{2} d^*(\|\nabla_w f(i)\|_2^{p-2} df(i,j))(i) \qquad [5.17]$$

The weighted $p$-Laplacian of $f \in \mathcal{H}(\mathcal{V})$, at a vertex $i \in \mathcal{V}$, can be obtained as follows:

$$\Delta_w^p f(i) = \tfrac{1}{2} \sum_{j \sim i} \gamma_w^f(i,j)(f(i) - f(j)) \qquad [5.18]$$

where:

$$\gamma_w^f(i,j) = w(i,j)(\|\nabla_w f(j)\|_2^{p-2} + \|\nabla_w f(i)\|_2^{p-2}) \qquad [5.19]$$

The weighted $p$-Laplacian is a nonlinear operator except in the case of $p = 2$ (in which case it corresponds to the classical Laplacian [CHU 97]). In practice to avoid a division by zero in equation [5.19] when $p \leq 1$, the local variation in equation [5.16] is replaced by a regularized version: $\|\nabla_w f(j)\|_2 \approx \sqrt{\|\nabla_w f(j)\|_2^2 + \epsilon^2}$, where $\epsilon \to 0$ is a small constant value [CHA 01].

### 5.4.1.4. *Discrete regularization on graphs*

Let $f^0 \colon \mathcal{V} \to \mathbb{R}^3$ be a function defined on the vertices of a weighted graph $G = (\mathcal{V}, \mathcal{E}, w)$. We will assume that the function $f^0$ represents a measure of an initial function $g \colon \mathcal{V} \to \mathbb{R}^3$ that has been corrupted by additive noise $n$ (with a mean of zero and a variance of $\sigma^2$) such that $f^0 = g + n$. The standard method used to recover the original function $g$ involves finding a function $f \colon \mathcal{V} \to \mathbb{R}^3$ that is sufficiently regular over $G$ but is also close to $f^0$. This inverse problem can be formalized in terms of the minimization of a function containing a regularization term and an approximation term. This can be expressed in the form of the following variational problem:

$$g \approx \min_{f:\mathcal{V} \to \mathbb{R}^3} \left\{ E_w^p(f, f^0, \lambda) = R_w^p(f) + \tfrac{\lambda}{2} \|f - f^0\|_2^2 \right\} \qquad [5.20]$$

where the regularization functional $R_w^p \colon \mathcal{H}(\mathcal{V}) \to \mathbb{R}$ is the discrete $p$-Dirichlet form of the function $f \in \mathcal{H}(\mathcal{V})$:

$$R_w^p(f) = \frac{1}{p} \sum_{i \in \mathcal{V}} \|\nabla_w f(i)\|_2^p \overset{(5.16)}{=} \frac{1}{p} \sum_{i \in \mathcal{V}} \left( \sum_{k=1}^{3} \sum_{j \sim i} w(i,j)(f_k(j) - f_k(i))^2 \right)^{\frac{p}{2}}$$

[5.21]

The second data-driven term is weighted by a fidelity parameter $\lambda \geq 0$ expressing the compromise between the regularization and approximation terms. The two terms of $E_w^p(f, f^0, \lambda)$ in equation [5.20] are strictly convex functions [CHA 01]. This optimization problem has a unique solution for $p = 1$ and $p = 2$, which for all $i \in \mathcal{V}$ satisfies:

$$\frac{\partial}{\partial f(i)} E_w^p(f, f^0, \lambda) = \Delta_w^p f(i) + \lambda(f(i) - f^0(i)) = 0 \qquad [5.22]$$

making use of the fact that $\frac{\partial R_w^p(f)}{\partial f(i)} = 2\Delta_w^p f(i), \ \forall i \in \mathcal{V}$ (see [ELM 08a] for proof) equation [5.22] can be interpreted as a graph-based discrete analog of the Euler-Lagrange equation. Using the $p$-Laplacian formulation of equation [5.18] in equation [5.22], the solution to the optimization problem is also the solution to the following equation system. For all $i \in \mathcal{V}$:

$$\left( \lambda + \sum_{j \sim i} \gamma_w^f(i,j) \right) f(i) - \sum_{j \sim i} \gamma_w^f(i,j) f(j) = \lambda f^0(i) \qquad [5.23]$$

To approximate the solution minimizing equation [5.20], the equation system is linearized using the Gauss-Jacobi method to obtain the following iterative algorithm for each component [ELM 08b, ELM 08a, LEZ 07]:

$$\begin{cases} f_k^{(0)} = f_k^0 \\ f_k^{(t+1)}(i) = \dfrac{\lambda f_k^0(i) + \sum_{j \sim i} \gamma_w^{f_k^{(t)}}(i,j) f_k^{(t)}(j)}{\lambda + \sum_{j \sim i} \gamma_w^{f_k^{(t)}}(i,j)}, \ \forall i \in \mathcal{V} \end{cases} \qquad [5.24]$$

where $\gamma_w^{f_k^{(t)}}(i,j)$ is the $\gamma$ function (in equation [5.19]). In this process, the regularizations are performed separately over each component. This is not ideal for the processing of color images, and the local geometry must take into account vector information [TSC 05]. To overcome this issue, the norm of the gradient operator as defined for color vectors can be used to couple these regularizations and take into account the vector aspect of the color information (when $p = 1$). When $p = 2$, the color gradient is not involved, but the weighting function $w$ also acts as a coupling term, once again making it possible to take the vector aspect of the data being processed into account. Finally, this formalism can be used directly for denoising and simplifying color images, with the advantage that it naturally permits the integration of non-local information that exploits the patch structure [BUA 05] (the interested reader is also referred to the following references: [ELM 08b, ELM 08a, LEZ 07]).

### 5.4.2. Semi-supervised classification using graphs

A range of automatic segmentation schemes have been proposed in the literature [COM 02, DEN 01, MAC 06]. There has recently been a resurgence of interest in semi-automatic approaches. These reformulate the segmentation problem into a semi-supervised learning problem [ZHO 05, BEL 06] based on label propagation strategies [WAN 06a, GRA 06, SIN 07]. The graph regularization formalism discussed earlier can be adapted to the segmentation of color images as a semi-supervised classification method. To make this adaptation, the problem must be rewritten as [TA 09]:

– let $\mathcal{V} = \{v_1, \dots, v_N\}$ be a set of vertices with associated color vectors;

– let $G = (\mathcal{V}, \mathcal{E}, w)$ be a weighted graph formed from the vertices of $\mathcal{V}$, connected by the edges of $\mathcal{E}$.

The semi-supervised classification of $\mathcal{V}$ involves grouping the set $\mathcal{V}$ into $N_\omega$ classes, where the number of classes is assumed to be known in advance. The aim is then to estimate the labels for the unlabeled data based on the labeled data.

Let $\Omega = \{\omega_m\}_{m=1,\dots,N_\omega}$ be the initial set of labeled nodes and let $\mathcal{V} \backslash \Omega$ be the initial set of unlabeled nodes. The mapping of a node to a class is modeled by $N_\omega$ initial label functions (one per class) $f_m^0 \colon V \to \mathbb{R}$; where $m = 1, \ldots, N_\omega$. For a given vertex $i \in V$, if $i$ is initially labeled then:

$$f_m^0(i) = \begin{cases} +1, & \text{if } i \in \omega_m \\ -1, & \text{otherwise} \end{cases} \qquad [5.25]$$

If $i$ is initially unlabeled (in other words $i \in V \backslash \Omega$) then $f_m^0(i) = 0$. The semi-supervised classification is obtained by performing $N_\omega$ regularization processes in parallel to estimate the functions $f_m \colon V \to \mathbb{R}$ for each class $\omega_m$. Using the above discrete regularization formalism, we can formalize this as follows:

$$\min_{f_m \in \mathcal{H}(V)} \left\{ R_w^p(f_i) + \tfrac{\lambda}{2} \| f_m(i) - f_m^0(i) \|_2^2 \right\} \qquad [5.26]$$

where the $R_w^p(f_m)$ term is the regularization term defined in equation [5.21]. The discrete diffusion process described by equation [5.24] is used for each minimization. At the end of the process, the probabilities of belonging to each class can be estimated, and the final classification can be obtained for a vertex $i \in V$ as:

$$\arg \max_{m \in 1, \ldots, N_\omega} \left\{ f_m(i) / \sum_m f_m(i) \right\} \qquad [5.27]$$

The method of image segmentation by semi-supervised classification is based in the image plane as represented in the graph form. The overall objective is to first obtain a coarse segmentation and then to refine it by the introduction of new markers. In addition to the initial markers provided by the user, four parameters are required for this method: the graph topology, the edge weighting function $w$, the fidelity parameter $\lambda$ and the value of $p$. Three parameters are generally fixed: $p$ is chosen to be equal to 2 except in the case of images with large numbers of contours, $\lambda = 1$ to avoid modifying the initial labels, and the edge weighting function is traditionally a Gaussian kernel. A simple graph topology (a grid graph with four-way connectivity) is sufficient for simple images, but in the case of textured images, a wider topology is necessary, in addition to taking into account the texture through the use of *patches*. The size of these patches is fixed by the user and depends on the textures present in the image. The robustness of the method therefore depends on three main factors: the initial seeds, the topology, and the weighting of the graph. For a graph consisting of $|\mathcal{V}|$ edges, the associated complexity is $O(nk|\mathcal{V}|)$, where $n$ is the number of iterations and $k$ the number of neighbors for each node. Figure 5.6 shows the results for Figure 5.2a when the user sets the initial seeds in the very center of each of the two regions. If this figure is compared to Figure 5.4 it can be seen that this semi-supervised technique gives persuasive results even when the color distributions within each region are mixed in color space.

| Initial markers | Partition | Segmentation |
|---|---|---|

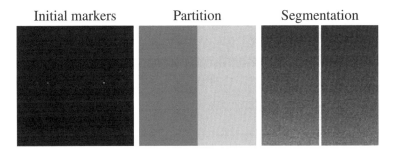

**Figure 5.6.** *Segmentation of Figure 5.2a using semi-supervised classification over a four-way adjacent grid graph. The edges are weighted using a Gaussian kernel ($\sigma = 5$), $\lambda = 1$ and $p = 2$. The distance between two edges is calculated based on the pixel colors*

Another example showing the use of the semi-supervised segmentation method is shown in Figure 5.7 for segmentation into three classes of an image of biological cells (background, nuclei, and cytoplasm). Figure 5.7a shows the initial image along with three initial markers (one per class). The semi-supervised segmentation then operates on the complete graph of an initial partition of the original color image (see Figure 5.7b), meaning that all regions are connected by an edge. The edge weighting function uses the mean region color. We can draw two useful conclusions from the final result (see Figure 5.7c). Firstly, only a small number of markers are required to obtain complete segmentation of non-connected objects, making the semi-automatic method less cumbersome for the user. Secondly, rapid convergence of the algorithm and a reduction in execution time are both obtained thanks to the reduction in the amount of data to be processed (following the initial partitioning, the number of vertices to be processed was reduced by more than 90% relative to the number of pixels in the image). The use of the complete graph is not practical if the graph vertices are associated with individual image pixels, but in the case where an initial partition map is considered instead of the pixel lattices, the number of vertices in the graph is reduced enormously.

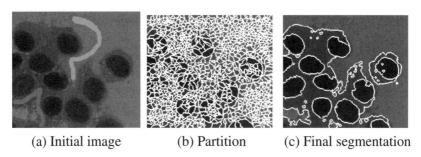

(a) Initial image        (b) Partition        (c) Final segmentation

**Figure 5.7.** *Semi-supervised label diffusion segmentation*

### 5.4.3. *Spectral classification applied to color image segmentation*

#### 5.4.3.1. *Introduction*

Rather than iteratively regularizing the functions describing each vertex on a graph, spectral classification methods make direct use of the weightings of the edges between vertices to combine the vertices into classes or regions. The data classification problem for similarity graphs can be redefined in the following manner: how can we partition a graph in such a way that the weights of all edges between vertices belonging to different sub-graphs are low, while the edges within a given sub-graph are weighted highly? To achieve this, the weights are combined into an *affinity* or *similarity* matrix, upon which a spectral analysis (in the sense of an eigenvalue decomposition) is performed. Although a wide range of different spectral classification algorithms exist, many of them are based around the following scheme:

– construct a similarity graph between the data, which is formalized in the form of an affinity matrix built from the data to be analyzed.

The similarity within the data is generally calculated through the use of Gaussian type kernels;

– spectrally analyze the data projected onto a new basis formed by the eigenvectors of this affinity matrix;

– apply a classification method (generally a simple *k-means*) to the data to be analyzed in this new basis.

Let $G = (\mathcal{V}, \mathcal{E}, w)$ be an undirected weighted graph where $\mathcal{V} = \{v_1, \ldots, v_N\}$ represents the set of vertices that make up the graph. The weighting between two vertices $v_i$ and $v_j$ is $w(i, j)$ and the similarity matrix $w$ is a square $N \times N$ symmetric matrix, since the graph is undirected. The degree $d_i = \sum_{j=1}^{N} w(i, j)$ of a vertex $v_i$ represents the sum of the weights associated with the vertices that are connected to it by an edge. The matrix $D$ of the degrees is a diagonal matrix where the degrees $d_i$ lie on the $i$th row and $i$th column of the matrix.

The matrices $D$ and $w$ are used to construct the affinity matrix $L$, also known as the Laplacian matrix. Several different Laplacian matrices are used in the literature, with the main ones being the non-normalized Laplacian matrix, defined as $L = D - w$ and the normalized Laplacian matrix $L_{sym} = D^{-1/2}LD^{-1/2}$. One matrix or the other can be used to solve different graph subdivision problems, and the choice of which one to use depends on the exact task at hand [LUX 07]. General derivations of how to solve this problem, depending on the Laplacian matrix that is to be used, can be found in [LUX 07], while Shi and Malik [SHI 00] solve this problem for the $L_{sym}$ matrix applied to image segmentation.

Spectral classification methods can be applied either in the image plane (see section 5.4.3.2) or in the color space (see section 5.4.3.3).

### 5.4.3.2. *Segmentation by spectral classification in the image plane*

Shi and Malik [SHI 00] introduced a method of spectral classification applicable to segmentation based on image plane analysis. Each image pixel has a corresponding vertex on the graph, and these vertices are linked by edges whose weights $w(i, j)$ are defined as:

$$w(i, j) = \exp^{-\left(\frac{\|\mathbf{x}_i^c - \mathbf{x}_j^c\|_2}{\sigma^c}\right)^2} \cdot \begin{cases} \exp^{-\left(\frac{\|\mathbf{x}_i^s - \mathbf{x}_j^s\|_2}{\sigma^s}\right)^2} & \text{if} \|\mathbf{x}_i^s - \mathbf{x}_j^s\|_2 < r \\ 0 & \text{otherwise} \end{cases}$$

[5.28]

where $\mathbf{x}_i^s$ represents the spatial coordinates of the pixel and hence of vertex $i$, and $\mathbf{x}_i^c$ is a characteristic vector calculated from measurements of intensity, color, and texture. Note that equation [5.28] requires the neighborhood size $r$ and the Gaussian kernel parameters $\sigma^c$, $\sigma^s$ to be set by the user.

Having created the graph representing the image to be segmented, the proposed method involves iteratively extracting regions from the image $I$ one by one, by splitting the graph into two. This algorithm, known as the "Ncut" algorithm, measures the dissimilarity between two sub-graphs as well as the similarity within a given sub-graph [SHI 00]. It uses the Laplacian matrix $L_{sym}$ so as to take into account the population of each of the sub-graphs. In this way, it is possible to avoid a partition into sub-graphs consisting purely of isolated pixels. The proposed image segmentation method can be divided into four stages:

1) construct an undirected weighted graph $G = (\mathcal{V}, E, w)$ using a similarity measure between pairs of vertices;

2) solve for the eigenvectors of $L_{sym}x = \lambda x$ that have the smallest eigenvalues;

3) use the eigenvector with the second smallest eigenvalue (known as the Fielder vector) to partition the graph;

4) decide whether the current partition should be further segmented or not.

Yu and Shi [YU 03] observed that calculation of the eigenvalues and eigenvectors may be unstable when the Laplacian matrices are not block diagonal, in other words when the graph cuts required to partition it into subgraphs are not clear. They proposed instead to divide the graph into several subgraphs instead of doing this iteratively. This approach also offers the ability to directly partition the image into regions using a single iteration, thus reducing the processing time required.

Spectral classification methods require the adjustment of certain parameters such as the standard deviation of the Gaussian kernels used to determine the similarity between two vertices, as well as the number of classes. For this reason Zelnik-Manor and Perona proposed automatic adjustment of these parameters [ZEL 04] to give a non-supervised method.

Segmentation methods within the image plane consider each image pixel as the vertex of a graph that is to be subdivided. To process an $N$-pixel image, an affinity matrix must be constructed with $N^2$ elements, and this may lead to memory allocation issues. This therefore limits its applicability to small images or sub-resolution images.

To limit the memory space required for the affinity matrix, Cour *et al.* proposed a multiscale classification algorithm that replaces the neighborhood parameter $r$ with an empirically determined scale parameter [COU 05]. The authors also emphasized the significance of the kernel function in the quality of the segmentation result. They constructed an undirected weighted graph $G = (\mathcal{V}, \mathcal{E}, w)$ based on the following similarity measure $w(i, j)$ between two vertices:

$$w(i,j) = \sqrt{w^I(i,j) \times w^e(i,j)} + \alpha w^e(i,j) \qquad [5.29]$$

Since the measure $w^I(i,j)$ cannot discriminate between textured regions, based as it is on individual pixel intensities, it is coupled with the measure $w^e(i,j)$ which analyzes the magnitude of the contours detected within the image. The intensity measure is calculated as follows: $w^I(i,j) = \exp^{-\frac{\|x_i^s - x_j^s\|_2^2}{2\sigma^{s2}} - \frac{\|x_i^c - x_j^c\|_2^2}{2\sigma^{c2}}}$. The contour-based measure is calculated as follows: $w^e(i,j) = \exp^{-\frac{max_{\mathbf{x} \in line(i,j)}\|Edge(\mathbf{x})\|_2^2}{2\sigma^{e2}}}$, where $line(i,j)$ is a straight line linking pixel $i$ with pixel $j$, $Edge(\mathbf{x})$ is the gradient magnitude at pixel $\mathbf{x}$, and $\sigma^e$ is the parameter for a Gaussian kernel.

Experiments performed on $481 \times 321$ pixel images required significant computation time, in the order of a minute using a computer with a 2.4 GHz microprocessor.

### 5.4.3.3. *Segmentation by spectral classification in color space*

If spectral classification is to be performed in the image plane, this requires the construction of a very large affinity matrix. To reduce the size of this matrix, it may be useful to instead apply the spectral classification in the color space, since the number of colors present within the image is *a priori* smaller than the pixel count. Color image segmentation methods based on classification of color points aim to determine the point clusters in the color space that represent the different regions within the image. Whereas classical classification methods look for specific shapes, like the *k-means* algorithm, which seeks globular clusters, spectral classification methods can be used to overcome this restriction on the shape of the point clusters representing image regions in the color space. The key problem lies in the definition of similarity between vertices $i$ and $j$ representing the colors present within the input image. The image colors are first subdivided into $N_C$ colors to reduce the size of the similarity matrix as much as possible, while still maintaining the structure of the image.

Busin *et al.* considered several different color spaces in which to perform the segmentation operation [BUS 09]. For each color space that they examined, a graph consisting of $N_C$ vertices was constructed, and the weightings between these vertices were:

$$w^c(i,j) = min\{H^c(\mathbf{x}_i^c), H^c(\mathbf{x}_j^c)\} \exp^{-\frac{\left\| \mathbf{x}_i^c - \mathbf{x}_j^c \right\|_2^2}{2\sigma^{c2}}} \qquad [5.30]$$

where $H^c(\mathbf{x}_i^c)$ is the number of occurrences of the color $\mathbf{x}_i^c$ in color space $c$, and $\sigma^c$ is the standard deviation of the Gaussian kernel selected by the user. Another weighting based on the spatio-colorimetric compactness function (see equation [5.8]) was proposed by Hébert *et al.* [HÉB 08]. The graph was then divided into sub-graphs using the "Ncut" algorithm, and the quality of the results obtained for each candidate color space was evaluated using a criterion based on the difference between two successive eigenvalues [LUX 07]. The candidate space with the greatest difference between eigenvalues was then used to partition the colors.

Regions consisting of connected pixels whose colors were assigned to the same class are iteratively divided using this same algorithm until a halting criterion was satisfied.

A reduction in $C$, the number of colors in the input image, to $1024$ can reduce the computation time to around 15 s for $481 \times 321$ pixel images on a computer with a 2.4 GHz microprocessor. Note that the computation time for this method varies as a function of the number of dominant colors chosen to quantify the image, rather than as a function of the image size.

In conclusion, the algorithm of Zelnik-Manor and Perona [ZEL 04] is the simplest algorithm to use, since it does not require any parameters to be selected by the user. However, the large memory requirements of this algorithm mean that it can only be used for small images, and this considerably limits its practical applications. The algorithms of Cour *et al.* [COU 05] and Busin *et al.* [BUS 09] can be used to overcome this limitation. However, these algorithms require the user to fix in advance the number of regions to be recovered from the image (in the first case), or the number of pixel classes (in the second case). Thus, the choice of one of these algorithms must be made based on whether the user wishes to segment using a region-based approach or an approach based on color classification.

## 5.5. Evaluation of segmentation methods against a "ground truth"

Procedures for evaluating segmentation quality can be loosely divided into two groups: those that do not make use of a ground truth, for which the reader can find a detailed discussion in [PHI 06], and those that do make use of a ground truth. The aim of the present section is not to compare the performance of the different segmentation methods discussed over the course of this chapter, but rather to show how the segmentation quality can be evaluated using a range of ground truths. Measuring the quality of segmentation can be useful when comparing the performances of different methods, but it can also be useful for optimal adjustment of the values of the parameters that a given method requires.

With this in mind, Martin *et al.* constructed a database of natural images segmented by human observers [MAR 01][4]. Each observer delineated the objects that in their view were the most important in the image, such that each segmented image contained between 2 and 30 closed contours. This ground truth is entirely relative, since the partition was performed once by each observer. To judge the quality of segmentation output from a procedure, the authors proposed comparing this automatic partition with each of the partitions provided by an observer [MAR 04].

A range of evaluation criteria has been proposed, the most recent of which is the NPR-index [UNN 07]. Nevertheless, the Jaccard index remains one of the most widely-used criteria [GE 06] for measuring the correspondence of the regions from each human segmentation $\mathbf{S}^{\mathcal{H}}$ (consisting of $n^{\mathcal{H}}$ regions $\mathcal{R}_i^{\mathcal{H}}, i = 1, 2, ..., n^{\mathcal{H}}$) with the automatic segmentation $\mathbf{S}^{\mathcal{A}}$ (consisting of $n^{\mathcal{A}}$ regions $\mathcal{R}_j^{\mathcal{A}}, j = 1, 2, ..., n^{\mathcal{A}}$), where the human partition is considered to be the ground truth. For two regions, $\mathcal{R}_i^{\mathcal{H}}$ and $\mathcal{R}_j^{\mathcal{A}}$, the Jaccard index is defined as:

$$J(\mathcal{R}_i^{\mathcal{H}}, \mathcal{R}_j^{\mathcal{A}}) = \frac{\mathrm{Card}\{\mathcal{R}_i^{\mathcal{H}} \cap \mathcal{R}_j^{\mathcal{A}}\}}{\mathrm{Card}\{\mathcal{R}_i^{\mathcal{H}} \cup \mathcal{R}_j^{\mathcal{A}}\}} \qquad [5.31]$$

The numerator in equation [5.31] measures the degree to which the region $\mathcal{R}_j^{\mathcal{A}}$, resulting from the automatic segmentation, coincides with the region $\mathcal{R}_i^{\mathcal{H}}$ from the ground truth. The denominator normalizes the Jaccard index such that it lies in the range $[0, 1]$.

For each pair of human and automatic segmentations, a pairwise comparison of all their respective regions is performed using the Jaccard index. The resultant similarity measure is:

$$Sim(\mathbf{S}^{\mathcal{H}}, \mathbf{S}^{\mathcal{A}}) = \frac{1}{\max(n^{\mathcal{H}}, n^{\mathcal{A}})} \sum_{i=1}^{n^{\mathcal{H}}} \sum_{j=1}^{n^{\mathcal{A}}} J(\mathcal{R}_i^{\mathcal{H}}, \mathcal{R}_j^{\mathcal{A}}) \qquad [5.32]$$

---

4 http://www.eecs.berkeley.edu/Research/Projects/CS/vision/bsds/.

This measure varies from 0, indicating that the human and automatic segmentations are completely different, to 1, indicating that the segmentations are identical.

To give a practical demonstration, we propose to segment reference images (#15088 and #37073) from the Berkeley Dataset [MAR 01], which can be seen in Figures 5.8a and 5.9a, referred to as the *Boat* and *Plane* images. Each of these images shows one of the five available human partition maps. Since these images contain objects that can be extracted without ambiguity, the five human partitions are all mutually consistent.

For the purpose of performance comparisons, we used three spatio-colorimetric methods: the *mean shift* method, analysis degree of compactness, and the JSEG method. We also used three graph analyses, spectral pixel classification, spectral color classification, and semi-supervised label diffusion segmentation. The first five methods use unsupervised learning (the number of classes or regions may however need to be supplied), whereas the final method requires the user to define initial markers within the image (see Figures 5.8g and 5.9g). The automatic results shown in Figures 5.8 and 5.9 are compared with each of the five human segmentations, using the similarity measure. Low values of the Jaccard index (maximum value 0.2) reveal that these segmentation methods struggle to reproduce the partition supplied by human observers. These figures also clearly show that the Jaccard index is relatively effective at evaluating the segmentation quality as judged by visual comparison between the human and automatic partitioning results.

For the case of the *Boat* image in Figure 5.8, it can be seen that analysis of the degree of spatio-colorimetric compactness and the semi-supervised segmentation do a fairly good job of distinguishing the region representing the water from the boat, and for this reason the resultant Jaccard indices are greater than those obtained from the alternative methods. In the case of the *Plane* image in Figure 5.9, only the spectral classification approaches are able to partly reproduce the human partitioning of the image background into several regions. Since the JSEG method is effective at distinguishing the different elements

(a) Human segmentation

(b) *Mean shift* [COM 02]. *Jaccard index* = 0.02

(c) Analysis of degree of compactness [LOS 08]. *Jaccard index* = 0.14

(d) JSEG [DEN 01]. *Jaccard index* = 0.10

(e) Spectral pixel classification [COU 05]. 6 regions must be recovered. *Jaccard index* = 0.05

(f) Spectral color classification [BUS 09]. 2 classes must be recovered. *Jaccard index* = 0.02

(g) Initial markers for semi-supervised label diffusion segmentation

(h) Semi-supervised label diffusion segmentation based on the image markers in 5.8(g). *Jaccard index* = 0.20

**Figure 5.8.** *Segmentation of the Boat image*

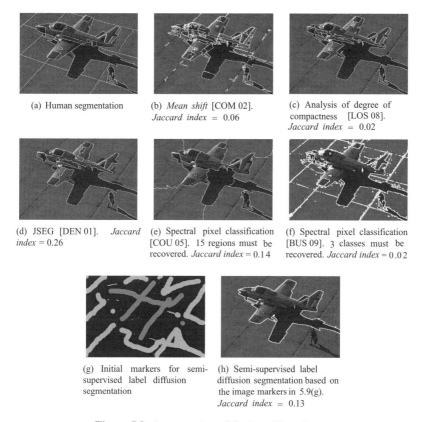

(a) Human segmentation

(b) *Mean shift* [COM 02]. *Jaccard index* = 0.06

(c) Analysis of degree of compactness    [LOS 08]. *Jaccard index* = 0.02

(d) JSEG [DEN 01].    *Jaccard index* = 0.26

(e) Spectral pixel classification [COU 05]. 15 regions must be recovered. *Jaccard index* = 0.14

(f) Spectral pixel classification [BUS 09]. 3 classes must be recovered. *Jaccard index* = 0.02

(g) Initial markers for semi-supervised label diffusion segmentation

(h) Semi-supervised label diffusion segmentation based on the image markers in 5.9(g). *Jaccard index* = 0.13

**Figure 5.9.** *Segmentation of the Boat Plane image*

of the airplane as revealed in the human partitioning, it receives the highest Jaccard index, which is very sensitive to over-segmentation. Since the initial markers did not entirely respect the detail of the human partitioning, the Jaccard index obtained for the semi-supervised segmentation is lower than that obtained by the JSEG method. This shows that detailed partitioning by semi-supervised segmentation requires the placement of multiple markers representing different classes, which may prove cumbersome for the user.

These results are in accordance with those shown in earlier sections, in that spatio-colorimetric classification methods, which analyze a function representing both the color distribution and their distribution throughout the image (see section 5.3.2), give coarse segmentation results that would benefit from refinement using further spatial analysis. This is the approach taken by the JSEG method (see section 5.3.3), and this leads to satisfactory results at the cost of an increase in computation time due to the use of two successive stages. This requires careful adjustment of the parameters involved.

These figures also show the advantage of using *a priori* knowledge in the form of the markers described in section 5.4.2 used by semi-supervised segmentation algorithms. The final partition remains largely consistent with the *a priori* information supplied by way of the markers, which ensures that the segmentation pattern desired by the user is respected.

## 5.6. Conclusion

Without attempting to provide an exhaustive list of possible approaches, we have presented the most well-known methods. These are spatio-colorimetric classification methods and graph analysis methods. The reader can find additional discussion on color segmentation in Chapter 1, which focuses on color segmentation using morphological tools, and in Chapter 4, which focuses on the segmentation of images containing color textures.

It should be noted that we have not discussed methods of detection of color contours, since very little study has actually been devoted to this area, due in particular to the requirement to obtain closed contours for subsequent object recognition.

Spatio-colorimetric classification methods, which jointly analyze the color distribution in the color space and their spatial distribution within the image plane, often call for the use of data structures that are cumbersome to manipulate. The compact histogram, discussed at the beginning of this chapter, offers a promising solution that makes it possible to reduce the required computation time and storage space. Spatio-colorimetric classification methods are based on strong assumptions of color homogeneity within the regions to be recovered.

They do not require any *a priori* information on the image, and give satisfactory results for images that are consistent with this assumption. Methods based on this assumption, which tends not to hold for complex natural scenes, often produce over-segmentation; this must be compensated for by subsequent region fusion. These methods based on the analysis of color distribution also turn out to be sensitive to the choice of color space used in the segmentation analysis. The search for segmentation methods whose parameters can be adapted to a wide range of color image families remains an open problem, as does the determination of color spaces that will give satisfactory segmentation, with both these problems depending heavily on the application in question.

These classification methods provide an initial segmentation, which may be complemented by graph analysis formalizing the spatial relationships between adjacent regions. Among other uses, the formalization of the elements of an image in the form of a graph makes it possible to express expert *a priori* knowledge in the form of initial markers. These easy-to-implement markers are useful for guiding the segmentation process, which in this case is said to be semi-supervised.

Only a small number of markers are required to obtain good segmentation, meaning that the semi-supervised method is not overly cumbersome for the user. The result is a rapid convergence of the algorithm and a reduction in execution time, due to the initial partitioning provided by this classification. Finally, since analysis of a complete graph over all the image pixels is not practical, the graph vertices may be associated with the colors present within an image in order to classify them.

## 5.7. Bibliography

[BEL 06]  BELKIN M., NIYOGI P., SINDHWANI V., BARTLETT P., "Manifold regularization: a geometric framework for learning from labeled and unlabeled examples", *Journal of Machine Learning Research*, vol. 7, p. 2399-2434, 2006.

[BUA 05]  BUADES A., COLL B., MOREL J.-M., "A review of image denoising algorithms, with a new one", *Multiscale Modeling and Simulation*, vol. 4, no. 2, p. 490-530, 2005.

[BUS 05]  BUSIN L., VANDENBROUCKE N., MACAIRE L., POSTAIRE J.-G., "Colour space selection for unsupervised colour image segmentation by analysis of connectedness properties", *International Journal of Robotics and Automation*, vol. 20, no. 2, p. 70-77, 2005.

[BUS 09]  BUSIN L., SHI J., VANDENBROUCKE N., MACAIRE L., "Color space selection for color image segmentation by spectral clustering", *IEEE International Conference on Signal and Image Processing Applications*, p. 262-267, Kuala Lumpur, Malaysia, 2009.

[CHA 01]  CHAN T., OSHER S., SHEN J., "The digital TV filter and nonlinear denoising", *IEEE Transactions on Image Processing*, vol. 10, no. 2, p. 231-241, 2001.

[CHE 01]  CHENG H.D., JIANG X.H., SUN Y., WANG J., "Color image segmentation: advances and projects", *Pattern Recognition*, vol. 34, no. 12, p. 2259-2281, 2001.

[CHU 97]  CHUNG F.R., "Spectral graph theory", *CBMS Regional Conference Series in Mathematics*, vol. 92, p. 1-212, American Mathematical Society, 1997.

[CLE 03]  CLEMENT A., VIGOUROUX B., "Unsupervised segmentation of scenes containing vegetation (Forsythia) and soil by hierarchical analysis of bi-dimensional histograms", *Pattern Recognition Letters*, vol. 24, no. 12, p. 1951-1957, 2003.

[COM 02]  COMANICIU D., MEER P., "Mean shift: a robust approach toward feature space analysis", *IEEE Transactions on Pattern Analysis and Machine Intelligence*, vol. 24, no. 5, p. 603-619, 2002.

[COU 05]  COUR T., BENEZIT F., SHI J., "Spectral segmentation with multiscale graph decomposition", *IEEE Computer Society Conference on Computer Vision and Pattern Recognition (CVPR '05)*, vol. 2, Washington, USA, IEEE Computer Society, p. 1124-1131, 2005.

[DEN 01]  DENG Y., MANJUNATH B.S., "Unsupervised segmentation of color-texture regions in images and video", *IEEE Transactions on Pattern Analysis and Machine Intelligence*, vol. 23, no. 8, p. 800-810, 2001.

[DIE 05]  DIESTEL R., *Graph Theory, Graduate Texts in Mathematics*, vol. 173, Springer-Verlag, 2005.

[ELM 08a]  ELMOATAZ A., LÉZORAY O., BOUGLEUX S., "Nonlocal discrete regularization an weighted graphs: a framework for image and manifolds processing", *IEEE transactions on Image Processing*, vol. 17, no. 7, p. 1047-1060, 2008.

[ELM 08b]  ELMOATAZ A., LEZORAY O., BOUGLEUX S., TA V., "Unifying local and nonlocal processing with partial difference operators on weighted graphs", *International Workshop on Local and Non-Local Approximation in Image Processing (LNLA)*, p. 11-26, 2008.

[GE 06]  GE F., WANG S., LIU T., "A new benchmark for image-segmentation evaluation", *Journal of Electronic Imaging*, vol. 16, no. 3, p. 033011-033027, 2006.

[GRA 06]  GRADY L., "Random walks for image segmentation", *IEEE Transactions on Pattern Analysis and Machine Intelligence*, vol. 28, no. 11, p. 1768-1783, 2006.

[HÉB 08]  HÉBERT P.-A., MACAIRE L., "Spatial-color pixel classification by spectral clustering for color image segmentation", *3rd International Conference on Information and Communication Technologies: from Theory to Applications*, p. 1-5, 2008.

[JIN 03]  JING F., LI M., ZHANG H.-J., ZHANG B., "Unsupervised image segmentation using local homogeneity analysis", *Proceedings of the 2003 International Symposium on Circuits and Systems (ISCAS '03)*, vol. 2, p. 456-459, Bangkok, Thailand, 2003.

[LEZ 07]  LEZORAY O., ELMOATAZ A., BOUGLEUX S., "Graph regularization for color image processing", *Computer Vision and Image Understanding (CVIU)*, vol. 107, no. 1-2, p. 38-55, 2007.

[LOS 08]  LOSSON O., BOTTE-LECOCQ C., MACAIRE L., "Fuzzy mode enhancement and detection for color image segmentation", *EURASIP Journal on Image and Video Processing*, Special issue: Color in Image and Video processing, p. 1-19, 2008.

[LUX 07]  VON LUXBURG U., "A tutorial on spectral clustering", *Statistics and Computing*, vol. 17, no. 4, p. 395-416, Kluwer Academic Publishers, 2007.

[MAC 06]  MACAIRE L., VANDENBROUCKE N., POSTAIRE J.-G., "Color image segmentation by analysis of subset connectedness and color homogeneity properties", *Computer Vision and Image Understanding*, vol. 102, no. 1, p. 105-116, 2006.

[MAR 01]  MARTIN D., FOWLKES C., TAL D., MALIK J., "A database of human segmented natural images and its application to evaluating segmentation algorithms and measuring ecological statistics", *Proceedings of the 8th International Conference on Computer Vision (ICCV '01)*, vol. 2, p. 416-423, Vancouver, BC, Canada, July 2001.

[MAR 04]  MARTIN D.R., FOWLKES C., MALIK J., "Learning to detect natural image boundaries using local brightness, color, and texture cues", *IEEE Transactions on Pattern Analysis and Machine Intelligence*, vol. 26, no. 5, p. 530-549, IEEE Computer Society, 2004.

[PAL 07]  PALUS H., "Color image segmentation: selected techniques" *Color Image Processing: Methods and Applications*, LUKAC R., PLATANIOTIS K.N. (eds), p. 103-128, CRC Press, 2007.

[PAR 07]  PARIS S., DURAND F., "A topological approach to hierarchical segmentation using mean shift", *IEEE Conference on Computer Vision and Pattern Recognition (CVPR '07)*, Minneapolis, p. 1-8, 2007.

[PHI 06]  PHILIPP-FOLIGUET S., GUIGUES L., "Evaluation de la segmentation: état de l'art, nouveaux indices et comparaison", *Traitement du Signal*, vol. 23, no. 2, p. 109-125, 2006.

[PRE 92] PRESS W., TEUKOLSKY S., VETTERLING W., FLANNERY B., *Numerical Recipes in C. The Art of Scientific Computing*, Second Edition, Cambridge University Press, 1992.

[SHA 09] SHAPIRA L., AVIDAN S., SHAMIR A., "Mode-detection via median-shift", *Computer Vision, 2009 IEEE 12th International Conference on*, p. 1909-1916, 2009.

[SHI 00] SHI J., MALIK J., "Normalized cuts and image segmentation", *IEEE Transactions on Pattern Analysis and Machine Intelligence*, vol. 22, no. 8, p. 888-905, 2000.

[SIN 07] SINOP A. K., GRADY L., "A seeded image segmentation framework unifying graph cuts and random walker which yields a new algorithm", *International Conference on Computer Vision*, p. 1-8, 2007.

[TA 09] TA V.-T., LEZORAY O., ELMOATAZ A., SCHÜPP S., "Graph-based tools for microscopic cellular image segmentation", *Pattern Recognition*, vol. 42, no. 6, p. 1113-1125, 2009.

[TOR 10] TORRES C., CLEMENT A., "Unsupervised hierarchical spatio-colorimetric classification for color image segmentation", *Fifth European Conference on Color in Graphics, Image and Vision*, Joensuu, Finland, p. 235-239, 2010.

[TSC 05] TSCHUMPERLÉ D., DERICHE R., "Vector-valued image regularization with PDEs: a common framework for different applications", *IEEE Transactions on Pattern Analysis and Machine Intelligence*, vol. 17, no. 4, p. 506-517, 2005.

[UNN 07] UNNIKRISHNAN R., PANTOFARU C., HEBERT M., "Toward objective evaluation of image segmentation algorithms", *IEEE Transactions on Pattern Analysis and Machine Intelligence*, vol. 29, no. 6, p. 929-944, 2007.

[VAN 03] VANDENBROUCKE N., MACAIRE L., POSTAIRE J.-G., "Color image segmentation by pixel classification in an adapted hybrid color space, application to soccer image analysis", *Computer Vision and Image Understanding*, vol. 90, no. 2, p. 190-216, 2003.

[WAN 06a] WANG F., WANG J., ZHANG C., SHEN H. C., "Semi-supervised classification using linear neighborhood propagation", *IEEE Computer Society Conference on Computer Vision and Pattern Recognition - (CVPR '06)*, vol. 1, p. 160-167, 2006.

[WAN 06b] WANG Y., YANG J., PENG N., "Unsupervised color-texture segmentation based on soft criterion with adaptive mean-shift clustering", *Pattern Recognition Letters*, vol. 27, no. 5, p. 386-392, 2006.

[WAN 06c] WANG Y.-G., YANG J., CHANG Y.-C., "Color-texture image segmentation by integrating directional operators into JSEG method", *Pattern Recognition Letters*, vol. 27, no. 16, p. 1983-1990, 2006.

[YU 03] YU S., SHI J., "Multiclass spectral clustering", *International Conference on Computer Vision*, p. 313-319, 2003.

[ZEL 04]  ZELNIK-MANOR L., PERONA P., "Self-tuning spectral clustering", *Advances in Neural Information Processing Systems 17*, MIT Press, p. 1601-1608, 2004.

[ZHO 05]  ZHOU D., SCHÖLKOPF B., "Regularization on discrete spaces", *LNCS 3663, Proceedings of the 27th DAGM Symposium*, Springer-Verlag, p. 361-368, 2005.

Chapter 6

# Color Texture Attributes

## 6.1. Introduction

In image processing, the 3D nature of a colored object can be perceived as the form of a "texture". Thus the concept of a texture involves the visual perception of what can be intrinsically 3D information, but projected onto a plane. Texture analysis based around image processing and machine vision techniques has been the subject of a huge range of scientific publications over the last 40 years [PET 06]. Although initially applied to gray level images, texture analysis methods have seen a growing interest from the scientific community in terms of their extension to color images.

Texture analysis methods aim to extract pertinent attributes for a specific application from a color image, a window, a region or a pixel neighborhood, in order to characterize or discriminate the textures that are present. These attributes provide *color texture features* representing texture and color information. They can be divided into several different categories: statistical features, spatio-frequential features and

Chapter written by Nicolas VANDENBROUCKE, Olivier ALATA, Christèle LECOMTE, Alice POREBSKI and Imtnan QAZI.

features based on models. They are particularly used in classification, segmentation, object recognition and object tracking applications.

In the first part of this chapter, we will begin by introducing the concept of color textures and the details of color texture features. In this part, we will then discuss the most widely used color texture image databases and list the main applications of color texture characterization. In the subsequent parts we will describe color texture features, beginning with statistical features, followed by spatio-frequential features and finally features based on stochastic modeling. In the last part of this chapter we will consider the problems of feature selection and color space choice, discussed through comparison of color texture classification results.

### 6.1.1. *Concept of color texture*

In a natural landscape scene, the eye can easily discriminate and recognize the different textures present within the image (such as: grass, sand, wood, water, asphalt, etc.). The human visual system is extremely effective at characterizing textures using adjectives such as smooth or rough, fine or coarse, granular or fibrous, isotropic or with preferred directions, regular or irregular, contrasting, etc. The study of textures is a very difficult problem in image analysis since there is no universal definition of a texture that would be universally recognised and accepted. Haralick defines a texture by describing an elementary pattern known as the *primitive*, along with the spatial organization of these primitives [HAR 79]. Unser describes textures in terms of their properties of spatial homogeneity and translational invariance [UNS 86]. Tuceryan *et al.* define a texture as being a function of the spatial variation of pixel colors within the image that contains it [TUC 98]. In practice there are two main observational scales on which a texture can be defined, corresponding to two levels of perception [HAR 92]: *microscopic* and *macroscopic*.

*Microscopic* observation reveals an *irregular* or *disordered* structure of pixel colors within the image. The texture is considered on the reduced neighborhood of a given pixel. It is then defined using a *probabilistic* or *statistical* approach. The fine structure within block paving illustrated in Figure 6.1a corresponds to a microscopic texture.

*Macroscopic* observation involves the concept of either an elementary pattern or a privileged direction. In the presence of an elementary pattern, also known as texton [JUL 81], the macroscopic texture is viewed as a repetitive or periodic spatial distribution of this pattern. This is illustrated by the image in Figure 6.1b, which shows the same block paving, in which the elementary pattern is a block that is repeated in a structured manner. The macroscopic texture is then defined using a *deterministic* or *structural* approach, so that the elementary patterns are repeated in a *regular* or *ordered* manner within the image, following precise rules of direction and placement.

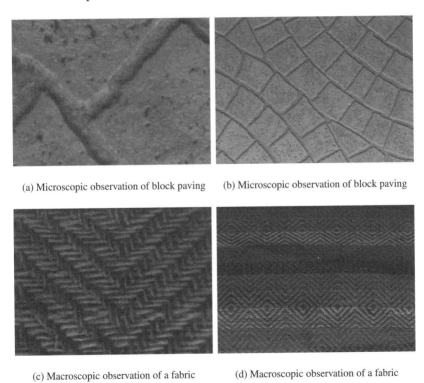

(a) Microscopic observation of block paving    (b) Microscopic observation of block paving

(c) Macroscopic observation of a fabric    (d) Macroscopic observation of a fabric

**Figure 6.1.** *Observations of textures (746 × 538 pixel images obtained from the Outex database). (For a color version of this figure, see www.iste.co.uk/fernandez/colorimag.zip)*

With the concept of a privileged direction, a macroscopic texture can be essentially characterized by particular dominant orientations, without truly regular or random repetition of an elementary pattern. It is defined as an *oriented texture* or *directional texture* [HAN 01, HAN 02, MAV 01, MAV 04].

However, a texture definition draws elements from both these approaches. Gagalowicz defines a texture as "a two-level hierarchical structure" involving both the microscopic and the macroscopic, noting that there is a random aspect within each primitive [GAG 85].

Generally speaking, it is accepted that a texture consists of one or more primitives depending on the scale of observation of the texture. The further away that a texture is viewed from (pattern shrinkage), the larger the extent of the observed surface; for this reason several small primitives may be combined to form a single primitive. Similarly, as the texture is approached more closely (pattern magnification) a larger number of primitives become evident, each one having a random arrangement since they are associated with the appearance of detail within the texture. Microscopic observation of the repeated pattern included in the fabric image of Figure 6.1d reveals a new pattern that can be seen in the image of Figure 6.1c.

Both the microscopic and macroscopic levels of perception may determine the choice of features to be used to describe the texture information. An irregular texture will be better characterized by statistical features, whereas a regular texture will be well described in terms of frequency-based and geometric features. For example, Zheng *et al.* proposed a set of specific geometrical features for color textures that are sensitive to the regular texture of meat [ZHE 07]. Thus texture information can depend on both the levels of perception described earlier.

We still need to determine how we can take color information into account in color texture features. This color information depends on the color representation space that is used. The default color space considered for encoding the color of an image pixel is the RGB space, based on the three primary colors red, green and blue, as obtained as the output of digital sensors (video camera, still camera or scanner). A digital color image, written as $f$, acquired by a camera is a matrix of pixels whose color is defined by the three components red ($R$), green ($G$) and blue ($B$). In this way, color information is expressed in a representation space consisting of three discrete variables whose values generally vary from 0 to 255, each stored in a single byte. For the purposes of color analysis, the color may also be represented in other color spaces [BUS 08].

In the general case, the color $\mathbf{c} = (c_1, c_2, c_3)$ of a pixel $\mathbf{x}$ of an image $f$ is represented in a space $C_1 C_2 C_3$ where $C_1$, $C_2$ and $C_3$ are the three color components in this space[1]. From a color image encoded in an arbitrary color space $C_1 C_2 C_3$, we can extract three *component images* which we will write as $f_{C_1}$, $f_{C_2}$ and $f_{C_3}$, where each pixel represents the level $c_w$ of the corresponding color component $C_w$ ($w \in \{1, 2, 3\}$ in the general case and $C_w \in \{R, G, B\}$ in the specific case of the RGB space, for example).

Having introduced the concept of color texture, we will now discuss color texture feature specificities.

### 6.1.2. *Color texture feature specificities*

#### 6.1.2.1. *Modification of observation and acquisition conditions*

The majority of texture analysis methods assume that texture images are acquired under identical observation conditions. When the conditions are not controlled, images may involve different textures. The images in Figures 6.2a and 6.2b represent changes in orientation and illumination of the texture in Figure 6.1b. Figure 6.3 shows the texture in Figure 6.1d observed with different orientations and under different lighting conditions.

For this reason, an important criterion in the choice of color texture features for certain applications is *transformational invariance* associated with the scale of observation (homothety), changes in illumination (intensity, color, lighting, geometry) [MUN 05, CUL 05], observation direction or changes in orientation (rotation) and

---

1 For reasons of consistency, the mathematical notation used throughout this chapter will be the same as that defined in Chapter 1.

translation [OJA 00, VAR 05]. An inventory of methods for analyzing texture invariants is given by Zhang *et al.* [ZHA 02].

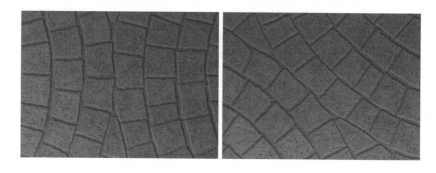

(a) Change in orientation                    (b) Change in illumination

**Figure 6.2.** *Changes in observation and acquisition conditions (746 × 538 images from the Outex database)*

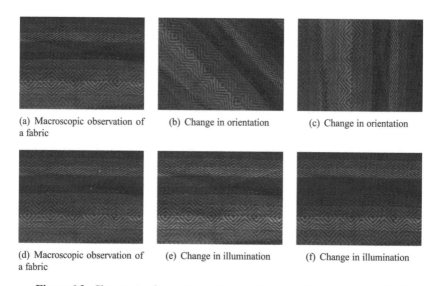

(a) Macroscopic observation of a fabric

(b) Change in orientation

(c) Change in orientation

(d) Macroscopic observation of a fabric

(e) Change in illumination

(f) Change in illumination

**Figure 6.3.** *Changes in observation and acquisition condition under controlled conditions (746 × 538 images from the Outex database). (For a color version of this figure, see www.iste.co.uk/fernandez/colorimag.zip)*

Changes in illumination are particularly relevant to outdoor images. When attempting to characterize and classify regions in the images, we come up against problems of time variation due to the motion of the sun over the course of a day, the shadows that are cast, the weather conditions (sunny, cloudy, alternately cloudy and sunny, rain, snow, fog), and reflections, all of which will alter the perception of the object as observed by the camera. In order to overcome this problem, it is recommended to make the correct choice of color space [PAS 00, MUN 05]. Other solutions have been proposed, such as a kernel method tested by Klein and shown to be effective in his work, based on weighted color co-occurrence matrices [KLE 10]. The invariance of these texture features as a function of image resolution makes it possible to perceive textures from a moving vehicle, while reducing the influence of perspective effects.

### 6.1.2.2. *Limitations introduced by real time constraints*

For solutions to industrial problems, methods using fast algorithms are preferred. In this framework, Paschos proposed a color texture recognition method based on chromatic moments that have made it possible to achieve excellent classification results on granite and marble images [PAS 00]. In applications with real time constraints, it is often necessary to choose color texture features with low computational complexity. Thus features extracted from histograms of sums and differences have been used for the classification of marble slabs [MAR 05], and color local binary patterns (LBP) were chosen for quality control of flooring [MÄE 03]. Features extracted from chromatic co-occurrence matrices have also been applied to the quality control of colored glass [POR 09]. With the correct choice of a compact color texture attribute, it is possible to rapidly segment outdoor images [BLA 08]. Real time systems come from parallel processing and optimized color texture analysis methods, or methods combined with other characteristics such as shape. In transport and remote sensing applications, the RGB space is often preferred as a first choice, since it avoids the time required to change to a different color space [HER 05].

### 6.1.3. *Image databases*

The creation of a range of color texture databases shows the growing interest in color texture analysis within the scientific community. It also highlights the need to have common reference databases available that can be used to test different texture analysis algorithms and compare their performance, in the same way that the Brodatz database drawn from the Brodatz album [BRO 66] has become the reference database for gray level textures. The need to work on images acquired under natural conditions or under varying lighting conditions has led to the creation of new color texture image databases. Here we will list those databases that are regularly used in the literature.

The VisTex database is a collection of color texture images representative of those that can be encountered in the real world [PIC 95]. Acquired without resorting to controlled conditions, this reference database consists of 168 images of color textures divided into 19 categories, and these images are available in different sizes. However, for each category of texture there are only a few samples available. The number of images per category varies from 2 to 20 depending on the category.

The BarkTek database consists of 6 classes of tree bark, with 68 images in each class, giving a total of 408 images, available in two different sizes [LAK 98]. This database is much more complex that the VisTex database since every image in this database, acquired under natural lighting conditions, represents the same type of object: tree bark. This means that visual discrimination between different classes of tree bark is sometimes difficult.

The Outex database was created more recently with the aim of providing a large selection of textures for image processing applications [OJA 02]. As with the VisTex database, the Outex database contains a large number of different objects, divided into 29 categories of color texture. The number of images in each category varies from 1 to 47 depending on the category. One of the special features of the Outex database is that it offers $768 \times 538$ pixel images acquired under different lighting conditions, in several different observation directions and with different fields of view. In total there are three different light sources, six spatial resolutions (100, 120, 300, 360, 500 and 600 dpi) and nine angles of rotation (0°, 5°, 10°, 15°, 30°, 45°, 60°, 75° and 90°). The acquired images are both gray level and color ones.

The CUReT database was created to aid the recognition of color textures acquired in different orientations [DAN 99]. It contains 14,000 images of color textures divided into 70 classes of around 200 images each. Each class represents a given texture viewed from different observation directions but with fixed illumination.

### 6.1.4. *Applications involving color texture characterization*

These applications include the most important problems in color texture image analysis and synthesis.

*Classification* is the division of images into texture classes. This has a wide range of applications in quality control, fault detection [KHO 06, HAN 01, HAN 02], document analysis, facial recognition and satellite imaging [QAZ 11a].

*Segmentation* involves dividing the image into regions with different textures [HOA 05, PER 06, SHI 07]. It can also be used as a low level processing in order to track a moving object [OZY 02].

*Object recognition* is used when picking up objects [ZHA 05], for tracking vehicles on a highway [KLE 10], for robotic visual navigation [MAT 05] and for driverless navigation [RAS 02].

*Indexing* involves searching through all the images in a database and identifying the closest match to a reference image.

*Texture synthesis* is used to give a realistic rendering of a surface. It is widely used in driving simulations and video games [KOK 02].

Following this chapter introduction, we will discuss the first type of color texture feature: statistical features.

### 6.2. Statistical features

Statistical features can be used to characterize any type of texture. For this type of feature a texture is defined in terms of its color variation, and it is the relationship between a pixel and its neighbors that is examined.

A large range of statistical attributes are used for color texture classification. These include image statistics, image histograms, local binary patterns, chromatic co-occurrence matrices, sum and difference histograms, and run length matrices.

These different attributes can be grouped into a number of categories based on their *order*, where the order of the attribute depends on the type of spatial interaction between the pixels in question. For image histograms, pixels are considered independently of its neighbors and so this attribute belongs to the category of first order statistical attributes. In contrast co-occurrence matrices, for example, consider pairs of pixels, which means that they are second order attributes.

### 6.2.1. *Statistical features describing color distribution*

Image histograms are an example of first order statistical attributes. They describe the distribution of color component levels in the input image. This type of attribute has been used by Mäenpää, Pietikäinen *et al.* in the context of color texture classification [MÄE 04, PIE 02]. Additional features such as the median, mode or interquartile interval are often extracted from these histograms to discriminate the different classes that are present [VAN 00].

Many different statistics can also be directly extracted from an image for the purposes of characterizing the color textures that they contain [HAR 92]. The most widely-used statistics are the mean, the variance, the skewness and the kurtosis [VAN 00].

The statistical features discussed in this section serve purely to describe the color distribution. They do not provide any information on the spatial relationships that may exist between the colors associated with individual image pixels. In the rest of this section we will discuss statistical features that can be used to characterize not only the color distribution within the color space, but also their spatial distribution.

## 6.2.2. Second-order statistical features

### 6.2.2.1. Color local binary patterns

Color local binary patterns have been used repeatedly by Mäenpää, Pietikäinen *et al.* in their studies of the joint use of texture and color for image classification purposes [MÄE 04, PIE 02].

LBPs require each pixel $\mathbf{x}$ of the input textured image $f$ to be assigned a value that depends on the color components $C_1$, $C_2$ and $C_3$ describing the local pattern around this pixel. These values are calculated by comparing the levels of color components of each pixel to the levels of the color components of its neighboring pixels: if we consider two color components $C_w$ and $C_{w'}$ ($w$, $w' \in \{1, 2, 3\}$), the level $f_{C_w}(\mathbf{x})$ of color component $C_w$ for each pixel $\mathbf{x}$ is treated as a value that can be used to threshold the levels of color component $C_{w'}$ for its neighboring pixels.

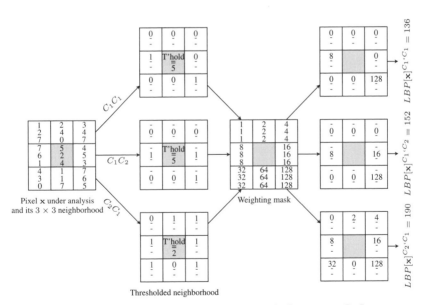

**Figure 6.4.** *Demonstration calculation of $LBP[\mathbf{x}]^{C_1,C_1}$, $LBP[\mathbf{x}]^{C_1,C_2}$, and $LBP[\mathbf{x}]^{C_2,C_1}$ for a color pixel $\mathbf{x}$ encoded in the color space $C_1 C_2 C_3$ where $C = 8$*

Note that the comparison of the color component levels of each pixel $\mathbf{x}$ with the color component levels of its neighboring pixels can also be performed using the color vector, which requires the definition of an ordering relation between the different colors [POR 08].

The binary comparison result performed for each neighboring pixel is then encoded using a weighting mask. We will write the color LBP feature characterizing the spatial interactions between the color components $C_w$ and $C_{w'}$ of the pixels lying in the neighborhood of pixel $\mathbf{x}$ as $LBP[\mathbf{x}]^{C_w, C_{w'}}$. Figure 6.4 illustrates the calculation of $LBP[\mathbf{x}]^{C_1, C_1}$, $LBP[\mathbf{x}]^{C_1, C_2}$ and $LBP[\mathbf{x}]^{C_2, C_1}$ for a pixel $\mathbf{x}$ whose color is encoded in a color space $C_1 C_2 C_3$ with $C = 8$ quantization levels (the color of pixel $\mathbf{x}$ is represented by the element $\begin{vmatrix} f_{C_1}(\mathbf{x}) \\ f_{C_2}(\mathbf{x}) \\ f_{C_3}(\mathbf{x}) \end{vmatrix}$). In this example a $3 \times 3$ neighborhood is used.

For the calculation of $LBP[\mathbf{x}]^{C_1, C_1}$ at a target pixel $\mathbf{x}$ (the central pixel), the components $C_1$ of the pixels in its $3 \times 3$ neighborhood are compared to the value $f_{C_1}(\mathbf{x}) = 5$ of the target pixel $\mathbf{x}$. The label 0 is assigned to all pixels in the neighborhood whose component $C_1$ is less than $f_{C_1}(\mathbf{x})$, and the label 1 is assigned to all pixels in the neighborhood whose component $C_1$ is greater than or equal to $f_{C_1}(\mathbf{x})$. A weighting mask, used to encode the neighborhood in terms of larger or smaller weightings, is then applied to the resultant labels, and these values are finally added together to obtain the value of $LBP[\mathbf{x}]^{C_1, C_1}$ for the target pixel (here, $LBP[\mathbf{x}]^{C_1, C_1} = 8 + 128 = 136$).

For the calculation of $LBP[\mathbf{x}]^{C_1, C_2}$, the $C_2$ component of the pixels contained in the $3 \times 3$ neighborhood of the central pixel that are compared to the $f_{C_1}(\mathbf{x}) = 5$ component.

Finally, when calculating $LBP[\mathbf{x}]^{C_2, C_1}$, the comparison threshold corresponds to the $f_{C_2}(\mathbf{x}) = 2$ component of the central pixel $\mathbf{x}$ and it is the $C_1$ components of the pixels contained in the $3 \times 3$ neighborhood of the central pixel that are thresholded.

This operation is performed for each pair of components $C_w$ and $C_{w'}$ ($w, w' \in \{1, 2, 3\}$) and for each pixel in the image $f$, yielding nine LBP images. The distributions associated with the nine LBPs are then expressed in the form of nine separate histograms. Three of these histograms represent the *within-component* spatial relationships, while the six others represent the *between-component* spatial relationships. These nine histograms are then concatenated to form a single histogram with a size of $9 \times C$ (where $C$ is the number of levels for a given color component) [PIE 02]. For the classification of color textures, Mäenpää *et al.* suggested the maximum likelihood method for subsequent comparison of these histograms [MÄE 04].

These color texture attributes are particularly well suited to real time quality control applications since they are both fast and easy to implement [MÄE 03]. Other statistical attributes can also be used to characterize color textures. This is particularly true of the chromatic co-occurrence matrices that we will discuss in the following section.

### 6.2.2.2. *Chromatic co-occurrence matrices*

Co-occurrence matrices, introduced by Haralick *et al.* in 1973, were initially implemented for gray level images [HAR 73]. Since the use of color can improve texture classification results, Palm proposed to extend the concept of co-occurrence matrices to color images, starting from the definition of multichannel co-occurrence matrices proposed by Rosenfeld [ROS 82]. These were used to define chromatic co-occurrence matrices [PAL 04].

For each pair of color components $C_w$ and $C_{w'}$ ($w, w' \in \{1, 2, 3\}$), the chromatic co-occurrence matrix $M^{C_w, C_{w'}}[f](v, \theta)$ measures the spatial interaction between the $C_w$ and $C_{w'}$ components of the pixels of an image $f$ that lie at a spatial infinity norm distance $v$ from each other along the direction (or directions) $\theta$. The content of cell $M^{C_w, C_{w'}}[f]((v, \theta), (i, j))$ of this matrix represents the number of times that a pixel $\mathbf{x}$ of the image $f$, whose color component level $f_{C_w}(\mathbf{x})$ is equal to $i$, has a pixel $\mathbf{x}'$ that lies at a distance $v$ from $\mathbf{x}$ in the direction(s) $\theta$ and has a value of $j$ for component level $f_{C_{w'}}(\mathbf{x}')$.

It is most common to consider four different directions $\theta$ when calculating the co-occurrence matrices (see Figure 6.5).

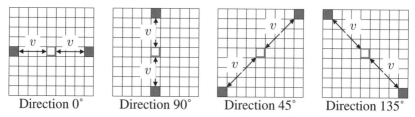

| Direction 0° | Direction 90° | Direction 45° | Direction 135° |

**Figure 6.5.** *Neighborhoods used for calculating co-occurrence matrices. v is an infinity norm distance. (For a color version of this figure, see www.iste.co.uk/ fernandez/colorimag.zip)*

The case where these four directions are considered together, and $v$ is equal to 1, is referred to as the isotropic neighborhood, and the within-component co-occurrence matrix represents the color correlogram [VAD 07].

Figure 6.6 illustrates the calculation of $M^{C_1,C_2}[f](1, 0°)$ and $M^{C_1,C_2}[f](1, 45°)$ for an image $f$ whose pixel colors are encoded in a space $C_1 C_2 C_3$ with $C = 4$ quantization levels (the color of pixel $\mathbf{x}$ is represented by the matrix element $\begin{bmatrix} f_{C_1}(\mathbf{x}) \\ f_{C_2}(\mathbf{x}) \\ f_{C_3}(\mathbf{x}) \end{bmatrix}$).

For example, to determine the content of the cell lying on the third row and first column of the matrix $M^{C_1,C_2}[f](1, 0°)$ in Figure 6.6 (in other words the content of cell $M^{C_1,C_2}[f]((1, 0°), (0, 2)))$, we examine the "horizontal" neighborhood of the image where $f_{C_1}(\mathbf{x}) = 0$ (outlined with a red box – see www.iste.co.uk/fernandez/colorimag.zip for the figure in color) and count the number of times that pixels in this neighborhood are found that lie at a distance $v = 1$ and whose color component $C_2$ is equal to 2 (circled in red). The first pixel where $f_{C_1}(\mathbf{x}) = 0$ (top left) has a neighboring pixel whose component $C_2$ is equal to 2 (to its right) and the second pixel where $f_{C_1}(\mathbf{x}) = 0$ (top right) also has a neighboring pixel whose $C_2$ component is equal to 2 (to its left), making a total of two occurrences.

To determine the content of the $M^{C_1,C_2}[f]((1, 45°), (0, 2))$ cell in Figure 6.6, we examine the neighborhood consisting of pixels lying on the first diagonal, and count the number of times that pixels are found in this neighborhood lying at a distance $v = 1$ and whose $C_1$ and $C_2$ components are equal to 0 and 2 respectively. There is no pixel where

$f_{C_1}(\mathbf{x}) = 0$ has a neighboring pixel whose $C_2$ component is equal to 2. The content of the $M^{C_1,C_2}[f]((1, 45°), (0, 2))$ cell is therefore 0.

For a given direction and distance, there are therefore six chromatic co-occurrence matrices, since the $M^{C_w,C_{w'}}[f](v, \theta)$ and $M^{C_{w'},C_w}[f](v, \theta)$ are symmetric. Three of these matrices represent the within-component spatial relationships, while the three others represent the between-component relationships.

| 0 | 3 | 0 |
|---|---|---|
| 1 | (2) | 0 |
| 0 | 1 | 0 |
| 1 | 2 | 1 |
| (2) | 0 | 1 |
| 1 | 1 | 3 |
| 2 | 1 | 3 |
| 0 | 0 | 2 |
| 0 | 0 | 3 |

Color image represented in $C_1C_2C_3$ space

| $C_2$ \ $C_1$ | 0 | 1 | 2 | 3 |
|---|---|---|---|---|
| 0 | 0 | 3 | 1 | 2 |
| 1 | 0 | 0 | 1 | 1 |
| (2) | 2 | 1 | 1 | 0 |
| 3 | 0 | 0 | 0 | 0 |

Associated $M^{C_1,C_2}[f](1,0°)$ matrix

| $C_2$ \ $C_1$ | 0 | 1 | 2 | 3 |
|---|---|---|---|---|
| 0 | 1 | 1 | 3 | 1 |
| 1 | 0 | 1 | 0 | 0 |
| (2) | 0 | 1 | 1 | 0 |
| 3 | 0 | 0 | 0 | 0 |

Associated $M^{C_1,C_2}[f](1,45°)$ matrix

**Figure 6.6.** *Color image f and associated co-occurrence matrices $M^{C_1,C_2}[f](1, 0°)$ and $M^{C_1,C_2}[f](1, 45°)$ for $(C = 4)$. (For a color version of this figure, see www.iste.co.uk/fernandez/colorimag.zip)*

Many authors have used chromatic co-occurrence matrices to characterize color textures [PAL 04, ARV 04, AKH 08]. However, these matrices have seen little direct use for classifying color texture images, since they can be highly demanding in terms of their memory requirements and computation time, depending on the number of quantization levels used. As a result, users therefore prefer to use only specific features from these matrices, in order to reduce the amount of information contained within the matrices while still retaining their relevance.

### 6.2.2.3. Haralick features extracted from co-occurrence matrices

Haralick *et al.* listed fourteen texture features that represent statistical information drawn from co-occurrence matrices [HAR 73]: angular second-moment (or energy), contrast, correlation, variance (or inertia), inverse difference moment (or homogeneity), sum average, sum variance, sum entropy, entropy, difference variance, difference entropy, two information measures of correlation, maximum correlation coefficient.

A number of authors such as Anys *et al.* have also proposed additional co-occurrence features [ANY 95].

The Haralick features obtained from the chromatic co-occurrence matrices have been used by authors such as Pydipati *et al.* Drimbarean *et al.* and Palm in the context of color texture classification [PYD 06, DRI 01, PAL 04].

### 6.2.2.4. Sum and difference histograms

Sum and difference histograms have an almost identical discrimination ability to the chromatic co-occurrence matrix, with the advantage that their calculations are much less demanding in terms of memory requirements [MUN 02, MAR 05].

For each pair of color components $C_w$ and $C_{w'}$ ($w, w' \in \{1, 2, 3\}$), the sum and difference histograms $H_S^{C_w, C_{w'}}[f](v, \theta)$ and $H_D^{C_w, C_{w'}}[f](v, \theta)$ measure the spatial interaction between the $C_w$ and $C_{w'}$ components of those pixels of an image $f$ that lie at a distance $v$ from each other in the direction $\theta$. The content of matrix element $H_S^{C_w, C_{w'}}[f]((v, \theta), (i))$ (or $H_D^{C_w, C_{w'}}[f]((v, \theta), (j))$) represents the number of times that the sum (or difference) of the levels of the color components $f_{C_w}(\mathbf{x})$ and $f_{C_{w'}}(\mathbf{x'})$ of two pixels $\mathbf{x}$ and $\mathbf{x'}$ in the image $f$, lying at a distance $v$ from one another in the $\theta$ direction, is equal to $i$, $i \in [0, 2 \times (C - 1)]$ (or equal to $j$, $j \in [-(C - 1), C - 1])$.

Figure 6.7 (where the color of each pixel $\mathbf{x}$ in the image is represented by a matrix element $\begin{vmatrix} f_{C_1}(\mathbf{x}) \\ f_{C_2}(\mathbf{x}) \\ f_{C_3}(\mathbf{x}) \end{vmatrix}$ and where the color components are encoded using $C = 4$ quantization levels) illustrates the calculation of these histograms.

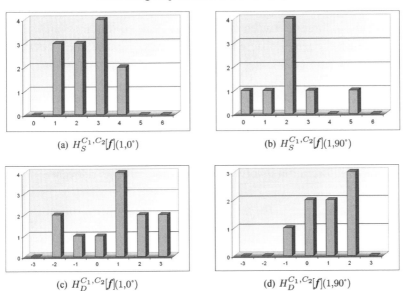

Color image represented in $C_1 C_2 C_3$ space

(a) $H_S^{C_1, C_2}[f](1, 0°)$

(b) $H_S^{C_1, C_2}[f](1, 90°)$

(c) $H_D^{C_1, C_2}[f](1, 0°)$

(d) $H_D^{C_1, C_2}[f](1, 90°)$

**Figure 6.7.** *Color image f and its associated sum and difference histograms ($C = 4$). (For a color version of this figure, see www.iste.co.uk/fernandez/colorimag.zip)*

For example, to determine the content of matrix cell $H_S^{C_1,C_2}[f]((1,0°)(3))$ in the sum histogram $H_S^{C_1,C_2}[f](1,0°)$ associated with the color image $f$ in Figure 6.7, we count the number of times that the sum of the color component levels $f_{C_1}(\mathbf{x})$ and $f_{C_2}(\mathbf{x'})$ of two pixels $\mathbf{x}$ and $\mathbf{x'}$ in the image $f$, lying at a distance $v = 1$ from one another in the 0°direction, is equal to 3. In this example the content of matrix cell $H_S^{C_1,C_2}[f]((1,0°)(3))$ is equal to 4 (see the spatial interactions between the pixels circled in blue – see www.iste.co.uk/fernandez/colorimag.zip for a color version of this figure).

Similarly for the matrix cell $H_D^{C_1,C_2}[f]((1,45°)(-1))$ in the difference histogram $H_D^{C_1,C_2}[f](1,45°)$ associated with the color image $f$ in Figure 6.7, we count the number of times that the difference between the color component levels $f_{C_1}(\mathbf{x})$ and $f_{C_2}(\mathbf{x'})$ of two pixels $\mathbf{x}$ and $\mathbf{x'}$ in the image $f$, lying at a distance $v = 1$ from one another in a 45°direction, is equal to $-1$. In this example $H_D^{C_1,C_2}[f]((1,45°)(-1)) = 1$ (see the spatial interactions between the pixels circled in red).

For a given direction and distance, there are therefore three within-component sum histograms, three within-component difference histograms, three between-component sum histograms and three between-component difference histograms, since the between-component histograms $H_S^{C_w,C_{w'}}[f](v,\theta)$ and $H_S^{C_{w'},C_w}[f](v,\theta)$ (and $H_D^{C_w,C_{w'}}[f](v,\theta)$ and $H_D^{C_{w'},C_w}[f](v,\theta)$) are symmetric.

As with the co-occurrence matrices, histograms are rarely used directly for color texture image classification. Users tend to prefer to extract texture features from these histograms in order to reduce the volume of information involved, while maintaining its relevance.

### 6.2.2.5. Features extracted from sum and difference histograms

Unser listed sixteen texture features drawn from sum and difference histograms to describe textures present in gray level textures [UNS 86]. This feature set was subsequently extended to color, and was applied by Münzenmayer et al. in the context of color texture image classification [MUN 02]. These include features that are drawn from sum and difference histograms such as the gravity center, mean, variance and entropy, as well as features drawn from both histograms together, such as energy, contrast, correlation or homogeneity.

In addition to Münzenmayer *et al.* Martinez-Alajarin *et al.* also made use of features drawn from sum and difference histograms to characterize color textures in the context of image classification [MAR 05, MUN 02]. Münzenmayer *et al.* also proposed a new set of features that are invariant under changes in illumination [MUN 05].

### 6.2.3. *Higher-order statistical features*

Statistical attributes of orders greater than two, such as run length matrices, can also be used in texture characterization.

#### 6.2.3.1. *Run length matrices*

While texture analysis based on chromatic co-occurrence matrices is carried out by studying the color component levels of pairs of pixels, run length matrices can be used to analyze images by looking for sets of pixels with the same color component level along a given direction [ZHE 07]. A run length is a set of consecutive and adjacent pixels which all have the same component level.

For each color component $C_w$ ($w \in \{1, 2, 3\}$) and each direction $\theta$, the run length matrix $\mathscr{P}^{C_w}[f](\theta)$ analyzes the relationships between pixels along the $\theta$ direction. It consists of $C$ rows, where $C$ is the number of levels for the color component $C_w$, and $M$ columns, where $M$ is the maximum image size in the chosen direction. The matrix cell $\mathscr{P}^{C_w}[f](i, j, \theta)$ represents the number of times that a run of $j$ consecutive and adjacent pixels can be found in the $\theta$ direction with a level of $i$ for color component $C_w$.

Figure 6.8 (where the color of each image pixel $\mathbf{x}$ is represented by the matrix element $\begin{vmatrix} f_{C_1}(\mathbf{x}) \\ f_{C_2}(\mathbf{x}) \\ f_{C_3}(\mathbf{x}) \end{vmatrix}$ and where the color components are encoded with $C = 4$ quantization levels) illustrates this concept.

For example, to determine the content of the matrix element in the second column of the third row of the matrix $\mathscr{P}^{C_1}[f](0°)$ in Figure 6.8 (in other words the content of the matrix cell $\mathscr{P}^{C_1}[f](2, 2, 0°)$ ), we examine the image pixels where $f_{C_1}(\mathbf{x}) = 2$, and count the number of times that there is a run of two consecutive and adjacent pixels in the horizontal direction. In this example we have two runs where two and only two contiguous pixels have $f_{C_1}(\mathbf{x}) = 2$.

| 0 0 0 | 0 1 3 | 0 3 3 | 1 1 2 | 2 3 3 |
|---|---|---|---|---|
| 1 3 3 | 1 3 3 | 1 3 3 | 1 3 3 | 1 3 3 |
| 3 3 3 | 0 3 3 | 0 0 3 | 2 0 3 | 2 3 3 |
| 1 3 3 | 1 0 2 | 1 0 2 | 2 2 2 | 2 2 2 |
| 2 3 3 | 3 3 0 | 1 3 0 | 1 3 0 | 2 3 0 |

Color image $f$ represented in $C_1 C_2 C_3$ space

|   | 1 | 2 | 3 | 4 | 5 |
|---|---|---|---|---|---|
| 0 | 0 | 1 | 1 | 0 | 0 |
| 1 | 1 | 1 | 1 | 0 | 1 |
| 2 | 3 | 2 | 0 | 0 | 0 |
| 3 | 2 | 0 | 0 | 0 | 0 |

Associated $\mathscr{P}^{C_1}[f](0°)$ matrix

|   | 1 | 2 | 3 | 4 | 5 |
|---|---|---|---|---|---|
| 0 | 5 | 0 | 0 | 0 | 0 |
| 1 | 9 | 1 | 0 | 0 | 0 |
| 2 | 5 | 1 | 0 | 0 | 0 |
| 3 | 2 | 0 | 0 | 0 | 0 |

Associated $\mathscr{P}^{C_1}[f](45°)$ matrix

**Figure 6.8.** *Color image $f$ and associated run length matrices $\mathscr{P}^{C_1}[f](0°)$ and $\mathscr{P}^{C_1}[f](45°)$ (for $C = 4$)*

To determine the content of the matrix element in the second column of the second row of the matrix $\mathscr{P}^{C_1}[f](45°)$ in Figure 6.8 (in other words the content of the matrix cell $\mathscr{P}^{C_1}[f](1, 2, 45°)$), we examine the image pixels where $f_{C_1}(\mathbf{x}) = 1$, and count the number of times that there is a run of two consecutive and adjacent pixels in a 45°direction. Here we have just one run where two and only two pixels that are 45°neighbors have $f_{C_1}(\mathbf{x}) = 1$.

As with co-occurrence matrices, run length matrices require a significant amount of space to store in memory. In order to reduce the amount of information, while retaining their pertinent features, five texture features are extracted from these matrices and used.

### 6.2.3.2. *Texture features extracted from run length matrices*

Galloway listed five main features to be extracted from run length matrices [GAL 75]: short run emphasis, long run emphasis, color component level non-uniformity, run length non-uniformity and run percentage.

These features have seen recent use by Zheng *et al.* in the context of color texture image classification [ZHE 07]. It is however worth noting that only the within-component relationships are described by run length matrices.

### **6.2.4. *Conclusion***

We have described the main statistical features used in the context of color texture classification. Other less well known features can also be used to characterize color textures. These include for example the color autocorrelation function [PAS 98], chromatic moments [PAS 00], the color covariance model [LAK 02] and fractals [SHE 94]. The following section focuses on another category of color texture features: spatio-frequential features.

### **6.3. Spatio-frequential features**

The set of spatio-frequential features can be divided into three domains, which we will describe below.

*Spatial domain*: for features based in the spatial domain, the aim is to characterize the texture in terms of the number of transitions per unit area: detailed textures tend to have a high transition density per unit area, in contrast to coarser textures. Cumani, Laplace and Sobel filters are all examples of filters widely used for the detection of color edges [KOS 95]. However this type of feature has never yet been applied to the classification of color texture images.

*Frequency domain*: other attributes such as the *Fourier transform* or *discrete cosine transform* give an alternative texture representation that is purely based in the frequency domain. These attributes are particularly well suited to the case of images containing coarse textures, where there is considerable continuity between the levels of each pixel color component. Since high frequencies are restricted to local changes in pixel color components, it is possible to express all the information present in the image using just a small number of coefficients, corresponding to low frequencies. Drimbarean *et al.* used the gray level discrete cosine transform and its color extension to characterize textures in the VisTex database [DRI 01]. They used this to compare the classification results obtained either by assuming textures to be defined with gray levels or by considering their color equivalents. In this study they also compared different texture features (features obtained from the color Gabor transform, Haralick features obtained from chromatic co-occurrence matrices and features obtained from the color discrete cosine transform). They concluded that the discrete cosine transform gives the best classification performance for color texture images, whether applied to gray level characterization or color texture features. They also noted that this attribute is the least costly in terms of computation time.

*Spatio-frequential domain*: finally, other features exist that are of particular interest due to the way they combine the two different representations discussed so far: spatio-frequential features. Some of the features that are most widely used in color texture classification include features drawn from the *Gabor transform* and the *wavelet transform*. These will be discussed in the next sections.

### 6.3.1. *Gabor transform*

The Fourier transform of an image can be used to reveal regularities within a texture by viewing it in the frequency domain. The problem posed by this operation, which acts globally on the image, is that it has no concept of spatial locality.

One solution to this problem is to use an alternative transform known as the moving window Fourier transform, which involves applying the Fourier transform over an observation window that is moved around the image. The choice of window size and displacement step depends on the spatial characteristics of the textures under analysis.

Different observation windows can be used: a triangular window, a Hamming window, a Hanning window or a Gaussian window [HAR 78]. When a Gaussian window is used, this transform is known as the Gabor transform.

A bank of different Gabor filters are used when classifying color texture images, with each one sensitive to a specific frequency. The chosen frequencies can be used to describe the entire frequency domain [PAL 02]. Each one of these filters is applied separately to each of the sliding windows over the component images of the input color image, with the output being the Gabor coefficients. In order to study the relationships between the individual component images, it is also possible to filter the difference between each pair of component images [MÄE 04].

Since the number of Gabor coefficients is considerable, they are not used directly as texture features. Traditionally the energy of the coefficients obtained for each filter is calculated [DRI 01]. In [PAL 02], where a polar representation of the frequency domain was used, it is shown how to build rotation-invariant attributes by calculating the mean and variance of the energies associated with frequencies that have the same modulus but different angles. They also study local phase changes by considering the differentials of the real and imaginary parts of the coefficients.

Following on from the work of Drimbarean *et al.* Palm *et al.* investigated the use of Gabor filters on color images [DRI 01, PAL 02]. They again showed that the consideration of color texture features could improve classification results for images in the VisTex database over those obtained through the use of gray level features [PAL 02, PAL 00].

The features extracted from the Gabor transform are some of the most popular features in the field of color texture image classification, since they are effective for the analysis of both *macrotextures* and *microtextures*. In addition to this, physiological studies have shown that parallels can be drawn between the behavior of certain neurons in the visual cortex and this type of filter [CAS 04].

The main disadvantage of this method is the need to set parameters for the filters. Moreover, in order to characterize certain textures it is necessary to have a relatively large analysis window, which will require a relatively long computation time.

### 6.3.2. *Wavelet transform*

The Gabor representation is based on a fixed-size observation window, which is a significant handicap when processing data whose spatial variations may span several orders of magnitude. One way of overcoming this limitation is to use the wavelet transform, which is based around a multiscale analysis of the image, in the sense that analysis windows of several different sizes are used [CAR 08].

The energy of filtered images remains the most popular feature for texture characterization. An example of this is the work of Sengur, who used these energies to classify textures in the Outex database, demonstrating that the use of color information improves the characterization of color texture images [OJA 02, SEN 08].

Other statistical features or co-occurrence features (*Wavelet Statistical Features* and *Wavelet Co-occurrence Features* (WSF and WCF)) can be extracted from color wavelet transforms of an image [ARI 05, VAN 99, KAR 03]. Arivazhagan *et al.* used these color texture features to classify images in the VisTex database [ARI 05].

Other authors such as van de Wouwer *et al.* Xu *et al.* and Hiremath *et al.* also studied problem of color texture classification through the use of the wavelet transform [VAN 99, XU 05, HIR 06]. The advantage of this transform is that it can give a multiscale characterization of a texture by considering both global and local information content within the image. As with the other spatio-frequential features described earlier, wavelet-based features again have parallels with the process of human vision, which performs a systematic frequency decomposition of the images falling onto the retina.

However, in spite of the many advantages of this transform, the features obtained from wavelets are not always the most suitable for texture characterization, as revealed by the work of Iakovidis *et al.* [IAK 05]. They in fact showed that color LBPs gave better classification results for the VisTex and Outex databases, compared to those obtained by analysis of features obtained from the wavelet transform.

## 6.4. Stochastic modeling

Studies of color texture characterization by stochastic modeling are mostly extensions of works previously reported for gray level textures [ALA 05]. The main advantage of this approach is that it can be used to obtain features that can be used for texture classification [HER 05, KHO 06], as we will see later in this section, as well as to segment color texture images [HAI 06] and for texture synthesis [KOK 02]. It should be noted that a number of authors have reported work involving stochastic modeling of color textures (classification and/or segmentation), but using texture descriptions calculated purely using luminance information, with the color information only being computed from the color distribution [KAT 06, PER 06]. We will begin, though, with the basics of this approach, which involves two main directions:

– describing spatial dependencies from a probabilistic point of view, traditionally through the use of a Markov field. This can be extended without difficulty (from a theoretical point of view) to other types of multispectral or hyperspectral images [REL 04];

– developing multichannel spectral analysis methods [QAZ 10] (see Chapter 4), with the help of linear prediction models (a "signal-based" approach[2]) [CAR 08].

As we will see later, both these approaches merge when the spatial dependencies are expressed in the form of a linear relationship between random vectors[3] used to represent the process, which is assumed to be Gaussian. The Markov field associated with such a process is known as an L-Markov field or *Gauss Markov Random Field* (GMRF).

We should emphasize another important point, which is that work involving GMRF and linear prediction models for color textures are often based in RGB space – see for example [HER 05]. Nevertheless, there have been recent works where different color spaces have been used, such as the work of Kokaram [KOK 02] (YUV space), Chindaro *et al.* [CHI 05], where in this case each channel was modeled separately, followed by a subsequent fusion process, and Qazi *et al.* [QAZ 10, QAZ 11b], who studied the advantages of using color spaces with separation between the intensity and the chrominance parts, such as IHLS (see Chapter 4) and L*a*b* instead of RGB.

### 6.4.1. *Markov fields*

#### 6.4.1.1. *General definition*

The two main properties of a Markov field, associated with a symmetric and reflexive graph [GUY 95, REL 04] built using a neighborhood relationship (we will write $V(\mathbf{x})$ for the set of neighboring sites of $\mathbf{x}$, $\mathbf{x} \notin V(\mathbf{x})$), are as follows:

– the local conditional probability (at all sites $\mathbf{x}$ in $E$) with respect to the other values within the image only depends on the realization of its neighboring sites:

---

2 The origin of this approach is the spectral analysis of signals with the help of linear prediction, such as for example with voice signals [MAR 76].

3 Since the color image is considered to be the realization $f$ of the random field $\boldsymbol{F} = \{\boldsymbol{F}(\mathbf{x})\}_{\mathbf{x} \in E}$, where $\boldsymbol{F}(\mathbf{x})$ are random vectors of size $p$ (see Chapter 4).

$$p\left(f(\mathbf{x}) \,|\, \{f(\mathbf{y})\}_{\mathbf{y} \in E \setminus \{\mathbf{x}\}}\right) = p\left(f(\mathbf{x}) \,|\, \{f(\mathbf{y})\}_{\mathbf{y} \in V(\mathbf{x})}\right) \qquad [6.1]$$

– if $p(f) > 0$, $\forall f \in \Omega_f$, where $\Omega_f$ represents the sample space of $F$, the joint probability can be expressed in the form of a Gibbs distribution (Hammersley-Clifford theorem):

$$p(f) \propto \exp\left(-U(f)\right) = \exp\left(-\sum_{c \in Cl} f_c(f)\right) \qquad [6.2]$$

where "$\propto$" indicates that the probability is defined up to some normalization constant. $Cl$ is the set of cliques[4] constructed from a neighborhood system, $U(f)$ is the energy of a realization $f$, and $f_c$ is a potential whose value only depends on the realization of the sites in the clique $c$ that it is associated with.

One of the main advantages of this model is the fact that a range of different potentials can be used depending on the properties of interest within the image or the label field [WIN 03]. It is this aspect that makes Markov fields very attractive for image segmentation, with the energy appearing as the sum of a data-driven term (usually containing the color and/or texture information) and an "internal" energy used to model the label field. The segmentation is obtained by optimizing what is often a Bayesian criterion such as the maximum *a posteriori* (MAP) criterion [KAT 06, KAT 08], which means that it takes the form of a specific realization of the region field, chosen as the minimum energy solution.

### 6.4.1.2. *Multivariate Gauss-Markov random fields (MGMRF)*

Here we will assume that the random vectors are centered. For this model, the general formula given in equation [6.1] takes the following particular form:

---

4 A clique contains pairs of neighboring sites or is a *singleton* containing just one site.

$$p\left(f(\mathbf{x}) \,\middle|\, \{f(\mathbf{y})\}_{\mathbf{y} \in V(\mathbf{x})}\right) \propto \exp\left\{-\frac{1}{2} \left\|e_f(\mathbf{x})\right\|_{\Sigma_{E_F}}^2\right\} \qquad [6.3]$$

with $e_f(\mathbf{x}) = f(\mathbf{x}) + \sum\limits_{\mathbf{y} \in V(\mathbf{x})} \mathbf{A}_{\mathbf{y}-\mathbf{x}} f(\mathbf{y})$ and $\left\|e_f(\mathbf{x})\right\|_{\Sigma_{E_F}}^2 = e_f(\mathbf{x})^T \Sigma_{E_F} e_f(\mathbf{x})$,

where $\Sigma_{E_F}$ is the conditional variance matrix associated with the random vectors $\boldsymbol{E}_F = \{\boldsymbol{E}_F(\mathbf{x})\}_{\mathbf{x} \in E}$. It should be noted that the sequence $\boldsymbol{E}_F$ is correlated (see section 4.2). According to equation [6.3], the conditional distribution is a Gaussian distribution with constant covariance over all sites, and with a mean that varies depending on its neighborhood (= $-\sum\limits_{\mathbf{y} \in V(\mathbf{x})} \mathbf{A}_{\mathbf{y}-\mathbf{x}} f(\mathbf{y})$).

Equation [6.3] can also be used to write down the following equation which defines the model for all $\mathbf{x} \in E$:

$$\boldsymbol{F}(\mathbf{x}) = -\sum_{\mathbf{y} \in V(\mathbf{x})} \mathbf{A}_{\mathbf{y}-\mathbf{x}} \boldsymbol{F}(\mathbf{y}) + \boldsymbol{E}_F(\mathbf{x}) = -\sum_{\mathbf{y} \in D} \mathbf{A}_{\mathbf{y}} \boldsymbol{F}(\mathbf{x}-\mathbf{y}) + \boldsymbol{E}_F(\mathbf{x}) \quad [6.4]$$

where $D$ is the support of the neighborhood used around each site[5]. $D$ is a non-causal support of finite order $o$ (see equation [4.6] and Figure 4.2). The set of model parameters is $\Theta_{MGMRF} = \left\{ \{\mathbf{A}_{\mathbf{y}}\}_{\mathbf{y} \in D_2}, \Sigma_{E_F} \right\}$, with $D_2$ being half of the support $D$, bearing in mind that $\mathbf{A}_{\mathbf{y}} = \mathbf{A}_{-\mathbf{y}}$ when the vectors consist of real values. $\mathbf{A}_{\mathbf{y}}, \mathbf{y} \in D$ are known as the transformation matrices, and these contain the matrix interaction parameters. These can be used as color texture attributes to represent the interactions that are present between different color planes (see for example [HER 05]). This is also the case for the other color models we will discuss.

For details of how to estimate these model parameters, the reader is referred to the work of Rellier *et al.* [REL 04], where the main algorithms are described: maximum likelihood estimation (ML), maximum pseudo-likelihood estimation[6] and estimation by minimizing the mean quadratic error (MMSE or *Minimum Mean Square Error* estimator).

---

5 This is also referred to as the linear prediction support in section 4.2.

6 The aim in this case is to find the parameters that maximize the probability $\prod\limits_{\mathbf{x} \in E} p\left(f(\mathbf{x}) \,\middle|\, \{f(\mathbf{y})\}_{\mathbf{y} \in V(\mathbf{x})}\right)$ in view of the fact that the different $\boldsymbol{F}(\mathbf{x})$ are not mutually independent.

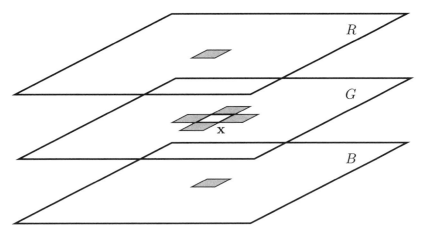

**Figure 6.9.** *3D neighborhood associated with the nearest neighbors,*
*for the model associated with the "G" channel in RGB space*

### 6.4.1.3. *3D Gaussian Markov field*

Rather than looking to define a 2D vector model of the image, it may be preferable to use a 3D scalar model for each plane $i = 1, 2, 3$:

$$p\left( f_i(\mathbf{x}) \middle| \{f_j(\mathbf{y})\}_{\mathbf{y} \in V_{i,j}(\mathbf{x})}, j = 1, 2, 3 \right) \propto \exp \left\{ -\frac{1}{2\sigma_{e_{f,i}}^2} e_{f,i}(\mathbf{x})^2 \right\}$$

[6.5]

where $e_{f,i}(\mathbf{x}) = f_i(\mathbf{x}) + \sum\limits_{j=1,2,3} \sum\limits_{\mathbf{y} \in V_{i,j}(\mathbf{x})} a_{i,j}(\mathbf{y} - \mathbf{x}) f_j(\mathbf{y})$ and $\sigma_{e_{f,i}}^2$ is the conditional variance associated with the random variables $E_{f,i} = \{E_{f,i}(\mathbf{x})\}$. Thus the main difference from MGMRF is the possibility of having a different definition of the support from one plane to another. Figure 6.9 shows an example of a 3D neighborhood system that uses a three-plane nearest neighbor model. The associated ML estimation method is given in [REL 04].

### 6.4.2. *Linear prediction models*

Just as with Markov fields, both 2D vector models and 3D scalar models, one per plane, can be found in the literature.

### 6.4.2.1. *Multichannel or vector case*

Multichannel linear prediction was discussed in section 4.2 in its most general context, which is the case of complex random vectors. Whatever color space is used to separate the intensity from the chromatic part, the data for the chromatic part can be expressed in the form of a complex number respectively. Section 4.3 introduced this approach for the IHLS color space, taking the hue and saturation to be the modulus and phase of a complex number. In [QAZ 11b], the L*a*b* color space was used, based on the following definitions:

$$f(\mathbf{x}) = \left[ \begin{array}{l} f_1(\mathbf{x}) = l \\ f_2(\mathbf{x}) = a + i \times b \end{array} \right] \qquad [6.6]$$

It is also important to remember that although in many papers these are the parameters of the model that are directly used to describe textures, these parameters can also be used to obtain an estimation of the Power Spectral Density (PSD) (see equations [4.7] and [4.9]), which is a PSD matrix. These PSDs can serve as a form of characteristic signature for a particular texture (see Figure 4.8). They were used for texture classification in [QAZ 10, QAZ 11b].

### 6.4.2.2. *MSAR model*

The MSAR model (*Multispectral Simultaneous AutoRegressive*) [HER 05, HAI 06] is defined in a similar way to the 3D Gauss-Markov random field, except that the error sequences are assumed to be white noise. The MMSE estimation method is summarized in [HER 05, KHO 06].

Stochastic models can be used to describe textures whose content varies spatially [SUE 99]. From a theoretical point of view, this is relatively simple: all that is required allows the model parameters to vary spatially. However, in practical terms things are not so simple, and to our knowledge there have been relatively few studies on this subject, in contrast to the field of signal processing[7]. There still remains a huge amount of work to be done on this subject.

---

7 See studies into techniques such as *Time-Varying* AR (TVAR).

## 6.5. Color texture classification

Color texture classification involves partitioning a set of images or regions into groups or classes, based around their similarity [JAI 00]. The main distinction is between approaches that make use of supervised learning (supervised classification) from those that use non-supervised learning (unsupervised classification, automatic classification or *clustering*). In a supervised approach, characterization and discrimination of different classes is entirely based on *prototypes*, which are observations of known classes. In contrast to this, in an unsupervised approach the classes to which the available observations belong are not known in advance.

The process of color texture classification can therefore be divided into two successive stages:

1) The *learning* stage aims to construct color texture classes from a set of prototypes (also known as a learning set or learning sample). This involves describing the color textures present within the prototype images using a set of *attributes* or *features*. Each of these textures is described in the form of an *feature vector* in a *feature space*. A *classifier*[8] is then designed in order to determine the class that a given texture belongs to, based on its characteristics.

2) The *classification* stage involves applying the decision rules, determined during the learning phase, to classify the input texture by assigning a label to it. A wide number of classification methods exist for multidimensional data, which can then be applied to color textures. These include for example neural networks, support vector machines (SVM), the $k$ nearest neighbors ($k$-NN), *k-means*, etc. In some approaches, several classifiers are combined to assign an input texture to a particular class [WU 07].

In the preceding sections, we have discussed several feature families used for color texture characterization. Although this list is not exhaustive, it covers the color texture features most commonly encountered in the literature.

---

8 We will use the term "classifier" to refer to a classification method associated with a given parameter set.

We have seen that the concept of *color texture* content in an image involves two types of information: color information, generally available for each pixel in the form of a triplet of values that depend on the color space being used, and texture information representing the spatial structure of these colors in the neighborhood of each pixel. It is for this reason that we distinguish two different types of approach for describing the color texture, where these two different types of information are considered either separately or jointly [MÄE 04].

A number questions then naturally arise as to how we can make best use of these features in the context of a color texture classification application: which features or what feature family should be chosen for different intended applications, each of which will come with its own specific requirements? In what color space are these features best represented? Should features be used that can describe both color and texture jointly, or features that deal with these two types of information separately? What classifier should be used in conjunction with the chosen features?

A wide range of studies have been carried out, and indeed are still being carried out to this day, with the aim of answering these questions [MÄE 04, ARV 04, VAN 04, DRI 01]. In this section we will give some possible answers in the form of various investigations carried out on this theme.

We will begin by focusing more specifically on approaches designed to take into account simultaneously the color and texture information present in color textures. The subsequent section will consider the choice of color space and the selection of color texture features. A third section will then present some classification results obtained using different features applied to a particular reference color texture database that is widely used in the literature, following which we will draw our final conclusions.

### 6.5.1. *Color and texture approaches*

Two different types of approach can be identified from among the approaches proposed for combining both texture information and color information content within color texture images [MÄE 04].

The first approach involves considering color and texture information separately [PER 06]. In this type of approach, texture features representing the spatial structure of the image are extracted from the luminance image and these are used in conjunction with other features describing the color distribution in a given representation space. In the context of color texture classification, different strategies are then used to combine these two different types of information, which are treated as independent:

– texture features and color features are fused into a single feature vector by simple concatenation. This feature vector is then the input to a classifier which gives as its output the class to which this particular color texture belongs to;

– the color is first used to segment or quantify the color image in such a way that each pixel is assigned to a label. Texture features are then directly evaluated over this label image in order to generate the feature vector that will be used by the classifier;

– a texture feature vector and a color feature vector are evaluated separately. For each of these feature vectors, a similarity measure can be calculated between two color textures to be compared. These two measures are finally combined to estimate a global similarity measure that is used by the classifier;

– the final strategy involves using each of the two feature vectors defined earlier as input to a different set of one or more classifiers. The classification results obtained by each of these classifiers are then combined to determine the class that this particular color texture belongs to.

The second approach involves considering the color texture to consist of joint information on its spatial structure and color distribution [PAL 04]. Two different strategies then exist for evaluating the corresponding features:

– evaluate the features independently for each color component of an image, without considering spatial interactions between the levels of two separate color components. In most cases, then, this is just an extension of luminance features to each of the color components independently;

– consider the spatial color distribution both within each separate color component of a given color space (within-component relationships) and also between these different color components (between-component relationships). In this case, therefore, interactions between different color components are taken into account.

An original approach proposed by Qazi *et al.* involves estimating the power spectral density (PSD) of a color texture consisting of an *achromatic* channel ("luminance" component) and a *chromatic* channel [QAZ 10]. This chromatic channel is obtained using a complex number representation of the "chrominance" components of the color space in question. The authors then showed the benefits of evaluating color texture attributes using the chromatic channel and combining the results with those evaluated over the achromatic channel. By associating these texture attributes with color attributes, they also showed the benefit of fusing these two different types of information [QAZ 11b].

### 6.5.2. *Color texture and choice of color space*

A range of studies have shown the relevance of color to texture classification problems [PAL 04, DRI 01, IAK 05]. It is widely acknowledged that classification results depend on the color space used to encode the texture images. For this reason, the choice of color space is an important stage in developing a successful application of color texture classification.

However, a wide range of color spaces exist, all with different properties: this means it is difficult to make broad statements about which is best.

A number of papers have attempted to compare color texture classification performance when the texture images are encoded in different color spaces. Table 6.1 lists some such studies carried out on the VisTex and Outex databases, in which several different color spaces were compared in order to determine which was the most suitable for a given color texture classification application. The first column in this table gives a reference to the study. The second column states which image database was used. The color texture attributes used in the study are listed in the third column. The forth column lists the color spaces that were used and the final column states which of these color spaces was ultimately chosen by the study.

| Reference | Database | Attribute | Color spaces used | Best space |
|---|---|---|---|---|
| Van de Wouwer et al. [VAN 99] | VisTex | Wavelet Correlation Signatures | RGB, YIQ, UVW, I1I2I3 | I1I2I3 |
| Drimbarean et al. [DRI 01] | VisTex | Discrete cosine transform | RGB, XYZ, YIQ, L*a*b*, ISH | YIQ |
| Singh et al. [SIN 02] | VisTex | Color correlogram | RGB, sRGB, XYZ, YIQ, YCC, L*a*b*, L*u*v*, I1I2I3 | L*a*b* |
| Van Den Broek et al. [VAN 04] | VisTex | Color correlogram | RGB, XYZ, YIQ, YUV, L*u*v*, HSV | HSV |
| Mäenpää et al. [MÄE 04] | VisTex | 3D color histogram | RGB, rgb, L*a*b*, HSV, I1I2I3 | I1I2I3 |
| Mäenpää et al. [MÄE 04] | VisTex | LBP | RGB, rgb, L*a*b*, HSV, I1I2I3 | L*a*b* |
| Chindaro et al. [CHI 05] | VisTex | Gaussian Markov fields | RGB, rgb, YIQ, YUV, L*a*b*, HSV | HSV |
| Iakovidis et al. [IAK 05] | VisTex | Color Wavelet Covariance | RGB, L*a*b*, HSV, I1I2I3 | I1I2I3 |
| Hiremath et al. [HIR 06] | VisTex | Wavelets | RGB, YCbCr, HSV | RGB |
| Qazi et al. [QAZ 11b] | VisTex | Color spectral analysis | RGB, L*a*b*, IHLS | L*a*b* |
| Mäenpää et al. [MÄE 04] | Outex | 3D color histogram | RGB, rgb, L*a*b*, HSV, I1I2I3 | HSV |
| Mäenpää et al. [MÄE 04] | Outex | LBP | RGB, rgb, L*a*b*, HSV, I1I2I3 | RGB |
| Iakovidis et al. [IAK 05] | Outex | Color Wavelet Covariance | RGB, L*a*b*, HSV, I1I2I3 | L*a*b* |
| Aptoula et al. [APT 07] | Outex | Morphological covariance | RGB, YUV, L*a*b* | L*a*b* |
| Qazi et al. [QAZ 11b] | Outex | Color spectral analysis | RGB, L*a*b*, IHLS | L*a*b* |

**Table 6.1.** *Comparison of color spaces*

Although not intended to be exhaustive, Table 6.1 shows that no color space is an ideal solution for all types of application in the field of color texture classification. It should nevertheless be noted that this table confirms the view that the RGB space is not generally to be recommended. In contrast, perceptual color spaces and perceptually uniform color spaces seem to be preferred [PAS 01, QAZ 11b].

For example, the work of Mäenpää *et al.* reveals that the best choice of color space depends on the image database being used, and hence the application being considered [MÄE 04]. They used the same method and the same features to classify the color textures in the VisTex and Outex databases, and showed that the best results were obtained using different color spaces for each of these two databases. Iakovidis *et al.* reached the same conclusions [IAK 05]. The choice of color space also depends on the type of features and classification method to be used. Mäenpää *et al.* showed that, for a given image database, the color space that yields the best results may be different depending on which features are used [MÄE 04].

In view of the fact that it is difficult to determine *a priori* the best color space, an alternative approach makes use of the properties of several different color spaces simultaneously. In this approach the color images are first encoded in several different color spaces. Two different approaches can then be used to combine the information present in these different color spaces, in the context of color texture classification:

1) The first involves evaluating the texture features over these different image representations and choosing the features that give the best discrimination using a feature selection procedure during supervised learning:

    - for example, Porebski proposed a multispace approach that could be used to automatically select the Haralick features giving the best discrimination, based on reduced-size chromatic co-occurrence matrices calculated for image encoded in 28 different color spaces [POR 09]. A discriminating feature space is determined using a sequential feature selection procedure known as SFS (*Sequential Forward Selection*) during the supervised learning process,

    - in the course of their work developing a biometric identification system, Nanni *et al.* proposed to convert images of eyes used for identity verification into 13 different color spaces in order to calculate frequency-space features based on the Gabor transform [NAN 09]. The SFFS

(*Sequential Floating Forward Selection*) feature selection process was then used to select the features that give the best discrimination;

2) The second strategy involves fusing the results from several classifiers, each one operating in a different color space. For example, in order to take into account information from each of seven different color spaces, Chindaro *et al.* suggested fusing the information obtained from the seven different classifiers applied to images encoded in each of these seven different spaces [CHI 05]. In [NAN 09], the color components giving rise to features that were the best at discriminating were used to define several classifiers, the outputs from which were then fused.

### 6.5.3. *Experimental results*

The various different benchmark color texture image databases are rarely used in the way described in section 6.1. In order to have access to a large number of observations, most authors who use these image databases tend to divide the images into subimages or regions of interest (ROI). For example, one decomposition of the Outex database that is often used in the literature involves constructing 68 classes of color texture by first extracting 68 different images of size $746 \times 538$ pixels from the 29 categories in this database. Each of the 68 images is then divided into a set of 20 separate images of size $128 \times 128$ pixels to construct each class, which means that a total of 1,360 images are available. Figure 6.10 illustrates each of these different classes with a single image per class. This set of images drawn from the Outex database is available on the Internet[9] under the name Outex_TC_00013.

We require both a set of training images and a set of test images, so for this reason the Outex_TC_00013 database is divided into two databases each containing 680 images, 10 for each texture class. Similar decompositions have also been performed for the VisTex database[10] and the BarkTex database [MUN 02], with alternative decompositions also existing for these three databases.

---

9 http://www.outex.oulu.fi/index.php?page=classification#Outex_TC_00013.
10 http://www.outex.oulu.fi/index.php?page=contributed#Contrib_TC_00006.

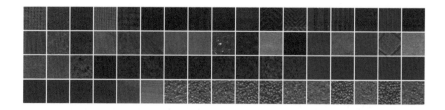

**Figure 6.10.** *Examples of color textures in the Outex_TC_00013 database: each image represents a class of color texture. (For a color version of this figure, see www.iste.co.uk/fernandez/colorimag.zip)*

Table 6.2 lists some color texture classification results for the Outex_TC_00013 database. The first column lists the features used to perform the classification, along with the corresponding reference. The color space in which the images are encoded is listed in the second column. The third column gives the size of the feature vector. Finally, the classifier used and the rate of correct classification achieved with these parameters are listed in the fourth and fifth columns respectively. In this table, $C$ represents the level of quantization of each color component.

Table 6.2 shows that the multispace approach proposed by Porebski *et al.* can be used to exploit the different properties of several different color spaces, leading to improved classification results compared either to approaches that only make use of "luminance" information or to approaches that use the properties of just one single color space [POR 10]. The performance they obtained using the Outex_TC_00013 database is in fact similar to that obtained by Mäenpää *et al.* who used 3D color histograms in HSV space, and the performance is higher to that obtained using only the HSV space to evaluate the Haralick features using reduced-size chromatic co-occurrence matrices.

Since these are features that consider both the within- and between-component spatial relationships that are present within a color space, this table also highlights the advantage of using this type of feature to describe color textures. This conclusion is consistent with the results presented by Iakovidis *et al.* and Arvis *et al.* [IAK 05, ARV 04].

| Features | Space | Dim. | Class. | Score |
|---|---|---|---|---|
| 3D color histogram ($C = 16$) [PIE 02] | RGB | 4096 | 3-nn | 94.7% |
| 3D color histogram ($C = 16$) [MÄE 04] | HSV | 4096 | 1-nn | 95.4% |
| Haralick features ($C = 32$) [ARV 04] | RGB | 30 | 5-nn | 94.9% |
| between- and within-component LBP histograms [IAK 05] | HSV | 2304 | SVM | 93.4% |
| Wavelet-Domain Hidden Markov Model [XU 05] | RGB | 5 | 7-nn | 85.2% |
| Morphological covariance [APT 07] | L*a*b* | 300 | 1-nn | 80.13% |
| Haralick features ($C = 16$) [POR 10] | Multi-space | 38 | 1-nn | 95.4% |
| Haralick features ($C = 16$) [POR 10] | HSV | 20 | 1-nn | 91.9% |
| Haralick features ($C = 16$) [POR 10] | RGB | 45 | 1-nn | 88.1% |
| Haralick features ($C = 16$) [POR 10] | "L" | 13 | 1-nn | 72.9% |
| DSP "L" [QAZ 11b] | L*a*b* | – | 1-nn | 79.4% |
| DSP "C" [QAZ 11b] | L*a*b* | – | 1-nn | 78.5% |
| DSP "L" + DSP "C" [QAZ 11b] | L*a*b* | – | 1-nn | 88.0% |
| 3D color histogram ($C = 16$) [QAZ 11b] | IHLS | – | 1-nn | 94.5% |
| DSP "L" + DSP "C" + 3D color histogram ($C = 16$) [QAZ 11b] | IHLS | – | 1-nn | 88.9% |

**Table 6.2.** *A selection of classification results obtained for the Outex_TC_00013 database*

The methodology proposed by Porebski finds a concrete application in the context of quality control of decorative drinking glasses, where it is important to identify aspect flaws present in the color surfaces, while also meeting the constraints of an industrial process in terms of the quality of results and computation time required [POR 09].

In a different context, Qazi *et al.* reported that fusion of texture features evaluated both on the chromatic channel ("C" feature) and also on the achromatic channel ("L" feature) offered a significant improvement on results obtained by using either of these two types of feature on its own. For best texture classification, the authors then appended features obtained from the color distribution to features that can be used to characterize the spatial structure [QAZ 11b]. Thus a color texture is characterized in terms of its color histogram ("H" feature), its PSD associated with the achromatic channel, and its PSD associated with the chromatic channel. In order to measure the similarity between two color textures, the authors proposed the use of a symmetrized Kullback divergence for each of these three types of feature, with these various different sources of information then being fused together. The conclusions drawn by Qazi *et al.* are consistent with those reported by Mäenpää *et al.* [MÄE 04].

Finally, Table 6.2 also reveals that the classifier used to evaluate classification performance using the Outex_TC_00013 database is generally the $k$-nn (nearest neighbor with $k = 1$), which is known for its robustness and ease of implementation. It is however important to note that, although the Outex_TC_00013 database is one of the most popular databases used in the literature, attributes that only consider the color distribution are able to obtain excellent results with this database when they are used in the context of a $k$-nn algorithm, since the color textures in the test database and in the learning database have their origins in the same individual image [MÄE 04, QAZ 11b]. In spite of the fact that this database seems relevant for comparing different color spaces or different classifiers within the field of color texture classification, it is of questionable value for evaluating the performance of texture attributes.

## 6.6. Conclusion

This chapter began by defining the concept of color textures, before discussing various color texture attributes reported in recent years in the literature. We divided these into three main families: statistical features, spatio-frequential features, and features based on stochastic modeling. An example application for color texture classification was then described.

Although this list is not exhaustive, the diversity and number of these attributes show that color texture classification remains a problem that is open to new approaches.

Faced with such a wide range of options, it can seem challenging to choose a set of features that are appropriate for a given application. Nevertheless, we have shown over the course of this chapter that this choice can be based on:

– invariance under different observation and acquisition conditions (illumination, scale, resolution, orientation, etc.);

– computation time;

– parameter setup;

– the approach used to combine color and texture information;

– the type of texture to be analyzed (microscopic, macroscopic, etc.);

– the type of application (segmentation, classification, recognition, indexing, etc.);

– the application field (industry, medical, transport, multimedia, biometrics, etc.).

It appears that the scientific research community has come to recognize the advantage of making simultaneous use of color and texture information in order to improve performance in image analysis applications, and increasing numbers of research papers are choosing to adopt this approach.

## 6.7. Bibliography

[AKH 08]  AKHLOUFI M.A., MALDAGUE X., LARBI W.B., "A new color-texture approach for industrial products inspection", *Journal of Multimedia*, vol. 3, no. 3, p. 44-50, 2008.

[ALA 05]  ALATA O., RAMANANJARASOA C., "Unsupervised textured image segmentation using 2-D quarter plane autoregressive model with four prediction supports", *Pattern Recognition Letters*, vol. 26, no. 8, p. 1069-1081, 2005.

[ANY 95]  ANYS H., HE D.C., "Evaluation of textural and multipolarization radar features for crop classification", *IEEE Transactions on Geoscience and Remote Sensing*, vol. 23, no. 5, p. 1170-1181, 1995.

[APT 07]  APTOULA E., LEFÈVRE S., "A comparative study on multivariate mathematical morphology", *Pattern Recognition*, vol. 40, no. 11, p. 2914-2929, 2007.

[ARI 05]  ARIVAZHAGAN S., GANESAN L., ANGAYARKANNI V., "Color texture classification using wavelet transform", *Sixth International Conference on Computational Intelligence and Multimedia Applications*, p. 315-320, Las Vegas, USA, 2005.

[ARV 04]  ARVIS V., DEBAIN C., BERDUCAT M., BENASSI A., "Generalization of the cooccurrence matrix for colour images: application to colour texture classification", *Image Analysis and Stereology*, vol. 23, p. 63-72, 2004.

[BLA 08]  BLAS R., AGRAWAL M., SUNDARESAN A., KONOLIGE K., "Fast color/texture segmentation for outdoor robots", *IEEE/RSJ International Conference on Intelligent Robots and Systems*, vol. 1, p. 4078-4085, Nice, France, 2008.

[BRO 66]  BRODATZ P., *Textures: A Photographic Album for Artists and Designers*, Dover Publications, New York, 1966.

[BUS 08]  BUSIN L., VANDENBROUCKE N., MACAIRE L., "Color spaces and image segmentation", *Advances in Imaging and Electron Physics*, p. 65-168, Elsevier, 2008.

[CAR 08]  CARIOU C., ROUQUETTE S., ALATA O., "2-D spectral analysis" *Two-dimensional Signal Analysis*, GARELLO R. (ed.), p. 115-174, ISTE Ltd, London and John Wiley and sons, New York 2008.

[CAS 04]  CASTELLANOS-SÁNCHEZ C., GIRAU B., ALEXANDRE F., "A connectionist approach for visual perception of motion", *Brain Inspired Cognitive Systems - BICS 2004*, p. BIS3-1 1-7, University of Stirling, Scotland, UK, 2004.

[CHI 05]  CHINDARO S., SIRLANTZIS K., DERAVI F., "Texture classification system using colour space fusion", *Electronics letters*, vol. 41, no. 10, p. 589-590, 2005.

[CUL 05]  CULA O.G., DANA K.J., MURPHY F.P., RAO B.K., "Skin texture modeling", *International Journal of Computer Vision*, vol. 62, no. 1-2, p. 97-119, 2005.

[DAN 99]  DANA K.J., VAN-GINNEKEN B., NAYAR S.K., KOENDERINK J.J., "Reflectance and texture of real world surfaces", *ACM Transactions on Graphics (TOG)*, vol. 18, no. 1, p. 1-34, http://www.cs.colombia.edu/CAVE/curet/, 1999.

[DRI 01]  DRIMBAREAN A., WHELAN P.F., "Experiments in colour texture analysis", *Pattern Recognition Letters*, vol. 22, no. 10, p. 1161-1167, 2001.

[GAG 85]  GAGALOWICZ A., MA S.D., "Sequential synthesis of natural textures", *Computer Vision, Graphics, and Image Processing*, vol. 30, no. 3, p. 289-315, 1985.

[GAL 75]  GALLOWAY M.M., "Texture analysis using gray level run lengths", *Computer Graphics and Image Processing*, vol. 4, no. 2, p. 172-179, 1975.

[GUY 95]  GUYON X., *Random Fields on a Network: Modeling, Statistics, and Applications, Probability and its Applications*, Springer, 1995.

[HAI 06]  HAINDL M., MIKES S., "Unsupervised texture segmentation using multispectral modelling approach", *International Conference on Pattern Recognition*, vol. 2, p. 203-206, Hong Kong, 2006.

[HAN 01]  HANBURY A., SERRA J., "Morphological operators on the unit circle", *IEEE Transactions on Image Processing*, vol. 10, no. 12, p. 1842-1850, 2001.

[HAN 02]  HANBURY A., SERRA J., "Analysis of oriented textures using mathematical morphology", *Annual Workshop of the Austrian Association for Pattern Recognition*, p. 201-208, Graz, Austria, 2002.

[HAR 73]  HARALICK R.M., SHANMUGAM K., DINSTEIN I., "Textural features for image classification", *IEEE Transactions on Systems, Man, and Cybernetics*, vol. 3, no. 6, p. 610-621, 1973.

[HAR 79]  HARALICK R.M., "Statistical and structural approaches to texture", *Proceedings of the IEEE*, vol. 67, no. 5, p. 786-804, 1979.

[HAR 92]  HARALICK R.M., SHAPIRO G.L., "Computer and robot vision", *Research in Computer and Robot Vision*, vol. 1, Addison-Wesley Publishing Company, 1992.

[HAR 78]  HARRIS F.J., "On the use of windows for harmonic analysis with the discrete fourier transform", *Proceedings of the IEEE*, vol. 66, no. 1, p. 51-83, 1978.

[HER 05]  HERNANDEZ O.J., COOK J., GRIFFIN M., RAMA C.D., MCGOVERN M., "Classification of color textures with random field models and neural networks", *Journal of Computer Science & Technology*, vol. 5, no. 3, p. 150-157, 2005.

[HIR 06]  HIREMATH P.S., SHIVASHANKAR S., PUJARI J., "Wavelet based features for color texture classification with application to CBIR", *International Journal of Computer Science and Network Security (IJCSNS)*, vol. 6, no. 9, p. 124-133, 2006.

[HOA 05]  HOANG M.A., GEUSEBROEK J.-M., SMEULDERS A.W.M., "Color texture measurement and segmentation", *Signal Processing*, vol. 85, no. 2, p. 265-275, 2005.

[IAK 05]  IAKOVIDIS D., MAROULIS D., KARKANIS S., "A comparative study of color-texture image features", *International Workshop on Systems, Signals & Image Processing*, Chalkida, Greece, p. 203-207, 2005.

[JAI 00]  JAIN A.K., DUIN R.P.W., MAO J., "Statistical pattern recognition: a review", *IEEE Transactions on Pattern Analysis and Machine Intelligence*, vol. 22, no. 1, p. 4-37, 2000.

[JUL 81]  JULESZ B., "Textons, the elements of texture perception and their interactions", *Nature*, vol. 290, p. 91-97, 1981.

[KAR 03]  KARKANIS S.A., IAKOVIDIS D.K., MAROULIS D.E., KARRAS D.A., TZIVRAS M., "Computer-aided tumor detection in endoscopic video using color wavelet features", *IEEE Transactions on Information Technology in Biomedicine*, vol. 7, no. 3, p. 141-152, 2003.

[KAT 06]  KATO Z., PONG T.-C., "A markov random field image segmentation model for color textured images", *Image and Vision Computing*, vol. 24, no. 10, p. 1103-1114, 2006.

[KAT 08]  KATO Z., "Segmentation of color images via reversible jump MCMC sampling", *Image and Vision Computing*, vol. 26, no. 3, p. 361-371, 2008.

[KHO 06]  KHOTANZAD A., HERNANDEZ O.J., "A classification methodology for color textures using multispectral random field mathematical models", *Mathematical and Computational Applications*, vol. 11, no. 2, p. 111-120, 2006.

[KLE 10]  KLEIN J., LECOMTE C., MICHÉ P., "Hierarchical and conditional combination of belief functions induced by visual tracking", *International Journal of Approximate Reasoning*, vol. 51, no. 4, p. 410-428, 2010.

[KOK 02]  KOKARAM A., "Parametric texture synthesis for filling holes in pictures", *IEEE International Conference on Image Processing*, vol. 1, p. 325-328, Rochester, USA, 2002.

[KOS 95]  KOSCHAN A., "A comparative study on color edge detection", *2nd Asian Conference on Computer Vision*, vol. 3, p. 574-578, Singapore, 1995.

[LAK 98]  LAKMANN R., Bark texture, Koblenz University, Germany, ftp://www. uni-koblenz.de/outgoing/vision/Lakmann/BarkTex, 1998.

[LAK 02]  LAKMANN R., "Textural features in multi-channel color images", *5th Asian Conference on Computer Vision*, p. 199-204, Melbourne, Australia, 2002.

[MÄE 03]  MÄENPÄÄ T., VIERTOLA J., PIETIKÄINEN M., "Optimising colour and texture features for real-time visual inspection", *Pattern Analysis and Applications*, vol. 6, no. 3, p. 169-175, 2003.

[MÄE 04]  MÄENPÄÄ T., PIETIKÄINEN M., "Classification with color and texture: jointly or separately?", *Pattern Recognition*, vol. 37, no. 8, p. 1629-1640, 2004.

[MAR 76]  MARKEL J.D., GRAY JR. A.H., *Linear Prediction of Speech*, Communication and Cybernetics Series, Springer-Verlag, 1976.

[MAR 05]  MARTINEZ-ALAJARIN J., LUIS-DELGADO J.D., TOMAS-BALIBREA L.M., "Automatic system for quality-based classification of marble textures", *IEEE Transactions on Systems, Man and Cybernetics - Part C*, vol. 35, no. 4, p. 488-497, 2005.

[MAT 05]  MATEUS D., CERVANTES J.G.A., DEVY M., "Robot visual navigation in semi-structured outdoor environments", *IEEE International Conference on Robotic and Automation*, p. 4691-4696, 2005.

[MAV 01]  MAVROMATIS S., BOI J.-M., SEQUEIRA J., "Medical image segmentation using texture directional features", *23rd Annual International Conference of the IEEE Engineering in Medicine and Biology Society*, vol. 3, p. 2673-2676, Istanbul, Turkey, October 2001.

[MAV 04]  MAVROMATIS S., BOI J.-M., BULOT R., SEQUEIRA J., "Texture analysis using directional local extrema", *Machine Graphics and Vision International Journal*, vol. 13, no. 3, p. 289-302, 2004.

[MUN 02]  MUNZENMAYER C., VOLK H., KÜBLBECK C., SPINNLER K., WITTENBERG T., "Multispectral texture analysis using interplane sum- and difference-histograms", *Lecture Notes in Computer Science*, vol. 2449, p. 42-49, 2002.

[MUN 05]  MUNZENMAYER C., WILHARM S., HORNEGGER J., WITTENBERG T., "Illumination invariant color texture analysis based on sum- and difference-histograms", *Lecture Notes in Computer Science*, vol. 3663, p. 17-24, 2005.

[NAN 09]  NANNI L., LUMINI A., "Fusion of color spaces for ear authentication", *Pattern Recognition*, vol. 42, no. 9, p. 1906-1913, 2009.

[OJA 00]  OJALA T., PIETIKÄINEN M., MÄENPÄÄ T., "Gray scale and rotation invariant texture classification with local binary patterns", *Lecture Notes in Computer Science*, vol. 1842, p. 404-420, 2000.

[OJA 02]  OJALA T., MÄENPÄÄ T., PIETIKÄINEN M., VIERTOLA J., KYLLÖNEN J., HUOVINEN S., "Outex new framework for empirical evaluation of texture analysis algorithms", *Proceedings of the 16th International Conference on Pattern Recognition*, vol. 1, p. 701-706, http://www.outex.oulu.fi/, 2002.

[OZY 02]  OZYILDIZ E., KRAHNSTOEVER N., SHARMA R., "Adaptive texture and color segmentation for tracking moving objects", *Pattern Recognition*, vol. 35, no. 10, p. 2013-2029, 2002.

[PAL 00]  PALM C., KEYSERS D., LEHMANN T.M., SPITZER K., "Gabor filtering of complex hue saturation images for color texture classification", *Proceedings of the 5th Joint Conference on Information Science*, p. 45-49, Atlantic City, USA, February 2000.

[PAL 02]  PALM C., LEHMANN T.M., "Classification of color textures by gabor filtering", *Machine Graphics and Vision International Journal*, vol. 11, no. 2, p. 195-219, 2002.

[PAL 04]  PALM C., "Color texture classification by integrative co-occurrence matrices", *Pattern Recognition Letters*, vol. 37, no. 5, p. 965-976, 2004.

[PAS 98]  PASCHOS G., "Chromatic correlation features for texture recognition", *Pattern Recognition Letters*, vol. 19, no. 8, p. 643-650, 1998.

[PAS 00]  PASCHOS G., "Fast color texture recognition using chromaticity moments", *Pattern Recognition Letters*, vol. 21, no. 9, p. 837-841, 2000.

[PAS 01]  PASCHOS G., "Perceptually uniform color spaces for color texture analysis: an empirical evaluation", *IEEE Transactions on Image Processing*, vol. 10, no. 6, p. 932-936, 2001.

[PER 06]  PERMUTER H., FRANCOS J., JERMYN I., "A study of Gaussian mixture models of color and texture features for image classification and segmentation", *Pattern Recognition*, vol. 39, no. 4, p. 695-706, 2006.

[PET 06]  PETROU M., *Image Processing: Dealing with Texture*, Wiley, 2006.

[PIC 95]  PICARD R., GRACZYK C., MANN S., WACHMAN J., PICARD L., CAMPBELL L., Vision texture database, Media Laboratory, Massachusetts Institute of Technology (MIT), Cambridge, http://vismod.media.mit.edu/pub/VisTex/VisTex.tar.gz, 1995.

[PIE 02]  PIETIKÄINEN M., MÄENPÄÄ T., VIERTOLA J., "Color texture classification with color histograms and local binary patterns", *International Workshop on Texture Analysis and Synthesis*, p. 109-112, Copenhagen, Denmark, 2002.

[POR 08] POREBSKI A., VANDENBROUCKE N., MACAIRE L., "Haralick feature extraction from LBP images for color texture classification", *First International Workshops on Image Processing Theory, Tools and Applications*, p. 1-8, Sousse, Tunisia, 2008.

[POR 09] POREBSKI A., VANDENBROUCKE N., MACAIRE L., "Selection of color texture features from reduced size chromatic co-occurrence matrices", *IEEE International Conference on Signal and Image Processing Applications*, Kuala Lumpur, Malaysia, 2009.

[POR 10] POREBSKI A., VANDENBROUCKE N., MACAIRE L., "A multi color space approach for texture classification: experiments with outex, vistex and barktex image databases", *5th European Conference on Colour in Graphics, Imaging, and Vision*, Joensuu, Finland, 2010.

[PYD 06] PYDIPATI R., BURKS T.F., LEE W.S., "Identification of citrus disease using color texture features and discriminant analysis", *Computers and Electronics in Agriculture*, vol. 52, no. 1-2, p. 49-59, 2006.

[QAZ 10] QAZI I.-U.-H., ALATA O., BURIE J.-C., FERNANDEZ-MALOIGNE C., "Color spectral analysis for spatial structure characterization of textures in IHLS color space", *Pattern Recognition*, vol. 43, no. 3, p. 663-675, 2010.

[QAZ 11a] QAZI I.-U.-H., ALATA O., BURIE J.-C., ABADI M., MOUSSA A., FERNANDEZ-MALOIGNE C., "Parametric models of linear prediction error distribution for color texture and satellite image segmentation", *Computer Vision and Image Understanding*, vol. 115, no. 8, p. 1245-1262, 2011.

[QAZ 11b] QAZI I.-U.-H., ALATA O., BURIE J.-C., MOUSSA A., FERNANDEZ-MALOIGNE C., "Choice of a pertinent color space for color texture characterization using parametric spectral analysis", *Pattern Recognition*, vol. 44, no. 1, p. 16-31, 2011.

[RAS 02] RASMUSSEN C., "Combining laser range, color, and texture cues for autonomous road following", *IEEE International Conference on Robotics and Automation*, vol. 4, p. 4320-4325, Washington DC, USA, 2002.

[REL 04] RELLIER G., DESCOMBES X., FALZON F., ZERUBIA J., "Texture feature analysis using a gauss-markov model in hyperspectral image classification", *IEEE Transactions on Geoscience and Remote Sensing*, vol. 42, no. 7, p. 1543-1551, 2004.

[ROS 82] ROSENFELD A., "Multispectral texture", *IEEE Transactions on Systems, Man and Cybernetics*, vol. 12, no. 1, p. 79-84, 1982.

[SEN 08] SENGUR A., "Wavelet transform and adaptive neuro-fuzzy inference system for color texture classification", *Expert Systems with Applications*, vol. 34, no. 3, p. 2120-2128, 2008.

[SHE 94] SHE A.C., HUANG T.S., "Segmentation of road scenes using color and fractal-based texture classification", *IEEE International Conference on Image Processing*, vol. 3, p. 1026-1030, Austin, USA, 1994.

[SHI 07]  SHI L., FUNT B., "Quaternion color texture segmentation", *Computer Vision and Image Understanding*, vol. 107, no. 1-2, p. 88-96, 2007.

[SIN 02]  SINGH M., MARKOU M., SINGH S., "Colour image texture analysis: dependence on colour spaces", *IAPR International Conference on Pattern Recognition*, vol. 1, p. 672-675, Quebec, Canada, 2002.

[SUE 99]  SUEN P.-H., HEALEY G., "Modeling and classifying color textures using random fields in a random environment", *Pattern Recognition*, vol. 32, no. 6, p. 1009-1017, 1999.

[TUC 98]  TUCERYAN M., JAIN A.K., "Texture analysis" *Handbook of Pattern Recognition and Computer Vision*, p. 207-248, World Scientific Publishing Company, 1998.

[UNS 86]  UNSER M., "Sum and difference histograms for texture classification", *IEEE Transactions on Pattern Analysis and Machine Intelligence*, vol. 8, no. 1, p. 118-125, 1986.

[VAD 07]  VADIVEL A., SURAL S., MAJUMDAR A.K., "An integrated color and intensity co-occurrence matrix", *Pattern Recognition Letters*, vol. 28, no. 8, p. 974-983, 2007.

[VAN 99]  VANDEWOUWER G., SCHEUNDERS P., LIVENS S., VAN DYCK D., "Wavelet correlation signatures for color texture characterization", *Pattern Recognition*, vol. 32, no. 3, p. 443-451, 1999.

[VAN 00]  VANDENBROUCKE N., MACAIRE L., POSTAIRE J.-G., "Color image segmentation by supervised pixel classification in a color texture feature space. Application to soccer image segmentation", *IAPR International Conference on Pattern Recognition*, vol. 3, p. 625-628, Barcelona, Spain, 2000.

[VAN 04]  VANDENBROEK E.L., VAN RIKXOORT E.M., "Evaluation of color representation for texture analysis", *16th Belgian-Dutch Conference on Artificial Intelligence*, p. 35-42, 2004.

[VAR 05]  VARMA M., ZISSERMAN A., "A statistical approach to texture classification from single images", *International Journal of Computer Vision*, vol. 62, no. 1-2, p. 61-81, 2005.

[WIN 03]  WINKLER G., *Image Analysis, Random Fields and Markov Chain Monte Carlo Methods - A Mathematical Introduction, Stochastic Modelling and Applied Probability*, Springer, 2003.

[WU 07]  WU Y., LI M., LIAO G., "Multiple features data fusion method in color texture analysis", *Applied Mathematics and Computation*, vol. 185, no. 2, p. 784-797, 2007.

[XU 05]  XU Q., YANG J., DING S., "Color texture analysis using the wavelet-based hidden Markov model", *Pattern Recognition Letters*, vol. 26, no. 11, p. 1710-1719, 2005.

[ZHA 02]  ZHANG J., TAN T., "Brief review of invariant texture analysis methods", *Pattern Recognition*, vol. 35, no. 3, p. 735-747, 2002.

[ZHA 05]  Zhao J., Tow J., Katupitiya J., "On-tree fruit recognition using texture properties and color data", *IEEE/RSJ International Conference on Intelligent Robots and Systems*, vol. 1, p. 3993-3998, Edmonton, Canada, 2005.

[ZHE 07]  Zheng C., Sun D.W., Zheng L., "A new region-primitive method for classification of colour meat image texture based on size, orientation and contrast", *Meat Science*, vol. 76, no. 4, p. 620-627, 2007.

Chapter 7

# Photometric Color Invariants for Object Recognition

## 7.1. Introduction

### 7.1.1. *Object recognition*

Object recognition is a specific problem that is encountered in applications such as image retrieval. It involves searching among all the candidate images in a database that contains the same object as that depicted in a source image.

In the majority of object recognition applications, the conditions under which the images are acquired are not controlled (see Figure 7.1). For example, in two different acquisitions of images representing the same object:

– the objects may have undergone a rotation and/or translation in space;

– the acquisition sensors may be different;

– the scene illumination may be different.

Chapter written by Damien MUSELET.

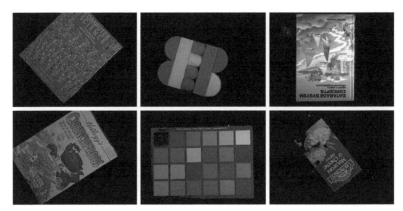

Examples of candidate images

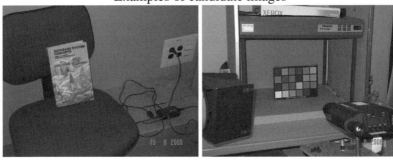

Examples of source images

**Figure 7.1.** *These images have been extracted from the Simon Fraser University database [BAR 02]. The candidate images can be accessed at the address http://www.cs.sfu.ca/~colour/data. (For a color version of this figure, see www.iste.co.uk/fernandez/colorimag.zip)*

In addition, an image may contain several different objects (which may or may not be partially occluded) on a non-uniform background. Having said that, in certain object recognition applications, the candidate images will contain just one single isolated object on a uniform background, to make extraction easier.

Since a global approach has been found to be inadequate under these conditions (multiple objects, occlusions, changes in viewpoint), the classical solution involves describing the content of an image in terms of a set of local descriptors extracted from particular key points. The procedure for searching for candidate images that contain an object similar to the one shown in the source image requires analysis of each pair $(\mathbf{I}_{src}, \mathbf{I}_{cand})$ consisting of the source image $\mathbf{I}_{src}$ and one of the candidate images $\mathbf{I}_{cand}$. The algorithm used to compare the source and candidate images can be broken down into three stages:

– extraction of key points in the two images $\mathbf{I}_{src}$ and $\mathbf{I}_{cand}$;

– description of local regions around these key points to construct a set of descriptors for the source and candidate images;

– comparison between the sets of local descriptors for the source and candidate images to determine a similarity measure between the two images.

The candidate images are then sorted in decreasing order of the similarity measures between their descriptor sets and that of the source image, to identify which images are most similar to the source image. The wide range of existing object recognition systems can therefore be distinguished in terms of the key point detection algorithms that they use, the descriptors that they extract from around these points, and finally the procedure used for comparing sets of local descriptors. The choice made for each of these different stages will have an influence on the recognition results achieved by the system, and careful thought must therefore be put into this choice.

Although the majority of image acquisition systems provide color images, many object recognition systems only consider gray level information. Nevertheless, the use of color information has two major advantages. Firstly, two different surfaces may be characterized by the same gray level but by very different colors [SWA 91]. Secondly, the extraction of discriminating characteristics that are insensitive to variations in scene acquisition conditions is made easier if the size of the representation space is increased, as is the case when three color components are used to characterize the surface, as opposed to the case with gray level images where just one single component is available [WEI 06]. Thus, color information can increase the discriminating power of the system, while at the same time rendering it invariant to certain photometric and radiometric variations. A precise analysis of the invariance requirements must be carried out with respect to the intended application, so that the system will not be "too invariant" in such a way that the discriminating power of the system is reduced.

## 7.1.2. *Compromise between discriminating power and invariance*

Of the three stages in comparing a pair of images, the aim of the two first stages (detection and description) is to provide the "best" set of local descriptors for a given image, in the context of the specific application. A range of criteria can be used to judge the quality of a descriptor. In this chapter and the following one, we will focus on their discriminating power without worrying about other characteristics such as their memory requirements or the algorithmic complexity involved in their extraction. For a given image database, the sets of local descriptors that are extracted from the images are good discriminators if a threshold can be applied to the measure of similarity between the source image and a candidate image to determine whether the candidate image represents one of the objects present in the source image or whether none of the objects in the source image is present in the candidate image.

The discriminating power of a set of local descriptors is a strong function of the application, i.e. the image database that is being used, and no descriptor is ideal for all situations. Here, we will consider different applications in terms of the variations that can exist between acquisitions of two images of the same object: variations in intensity, color and/or direction of illumination, variation in observation angle of the object (or point of view) and variation in "ambient lighting", as well as photometric effects that may or may not be present in images, such as reflections and shadows. The term "ambient lighting" was used by Shafer to represent a range of different effects such as the influence of reflections from surface elements around the surface being observed, the sensor response to infra-red waves or lens diffraction [SHA 85].

A range of interest point detectors and local descriptors have been defined in the literature for grayscale images, and these have subsequently been extended to color images. These detectors and descriptors must be sensitive only to the radiometric and photometric variations that may be present in the image database in question. For example, if the database only includes images of objects consisting of matte surfaces, there is no point using detectors that are invariant to the presence of reflections, since any unnecessary invariance reduces the discriminating power of the system. It is therefore vital to understand the manner in which color is formed in the images, and to understand the impact of radiometric or photometric variation within the images, to define or select detectors and descriptors that are best suited to the given application.

### 7.1.3. *Content of this chapter*

As we have stated, the aim of this chapter is to reveal the impact that photometric and radiometric variations can have on pixel colors and to discuss the way in which color characteristics that are insensitive to these variations can be extracted. The next chapter will give a state of the art of detectors and descriptors in the literature, whereas the present chapter will focus more on the preprocessing steps to be applied to images before this extraction phase. This chapter will not however consider how to define the method used to compare sets of local descriptors, since this is independent of the choice of detectors and descriptors, and whether or not color information is used. This question is nevertheless a pivotal aspect of defining an object recognition system.

To define color invariant characteristics, we require models of photometric and radiometric variations, which describe the consequent changes in color by means of a mathematical function. To better understand how such a model of photometric and radiometric variation works, consider two color images: a source image $\mathbf{I}_{\mathbf{src}}$ and a candidate image $\mathbf{I}_{\mathbf{cand}}$, both representing the same object. Let $P_{src}$ and $P_{cand}$ be two pixels belonging to $\mathbf{I}_{\mathbf{src}}$ and $\mathbf{I}_{\mathbf{cand}}$, respectively, such that the same surface element of the object represented by both images is projected onto these pixels. This surface element was illuminated and observed differently during the acquisition of the source and candidate images. Thus, pixel $P_{src}$ is described by the color $\mathbf{C}(P_{src})$ in image $\mathbf{I}_{\mathbf{src}}$ and pixel $P_{cand}$ is described by the color $\mathbf{C}(P_{cand})$ in image $\mathbf{I}_{\mathbf{cand}}$. A model of photometric and radiometric variations must define the transformation $\mathbf{F}_{\mathrm{ill}}$ between the colors associated with these two pixels:

$$\mathbf{C}(P_{cand}) = \mathbf{F}_{ill}(\mathbf{C}(P_{src})) \qquad\qquad [7.1]$$

It should be noted that such a function does not exist because of the effect of metamerism, where two surfaces that appear identically colored under particular lighting conditions would appear as two different colors under a different set of lighting conditions. However, models of photometric and radiometric variation attempt to approximate this relationship using a function that makes a number of assumptions. In the second part of this chapter, we will describe the main hypotheses that are used to develop models of photometric and radiometric variation. In Part 3, we will give a state-of-the-art of the main color invariant characteristics that are built around these assumptions.

## 7.2. Basic assumptions

Models of photometric and radiometric variation are based on assumptions of how color formation occurs, the reflective properties of surface elements, the camera sensor response, the illumination used to light the scene, and assumptions inherent to the photometric and radiometric model itself. We will discuss the range of hypotheses on which models of photometric and radiometric variation are typically built.

### 7.2.1. Hypotheses on color formation

The majority of color formation models are based on the assumption that a color stimulus incident on a material is partially reflected immediately by the surface (specular reflection) and the other part of the stimulus that penetrates the material, is reflected in a random manner by the pigments making up the material. This is then emitted by the material in a direction that is also itself random (diffuse reflection). This is the reason why specular reflection is not perceived in the same way for all positions of the observer or detector. In both cases, the spectrum of the original stimulus is modified before being transmitted.

The reflected color stimulus is then transmitted to the acquisition sensors, the spectral responses of which we will write as $k(\lambda)$,

$k = \{R, G, B\}$. If we represent the color stimulus reflected by a surface element as $C(\mathbf{x}, \lambda)$, we recall that we can obtain the color components of pixel $P$ which is "observing" this surface element by integrating the product of the response of each sensor with the spectrum of the stimulus over the response interval of each sensor:

$$\begin{cases} C^R(P) = \int_\lambda R(\lambda)C(\mathbf{x}, \lambda)d\lambda \\ C^G(P) = \int_\lambda G(\lambda)C(\mathbf{x}, \lambda)d\lambda \\ C^B(P) = \int_\lambda B(\lambda)C(\mathbf{x}, \lambda)d\lambda \end{cases} \qquad [7.2]$$

The three most widely used models for color formation are the Kubelka-Munk model, Shafer's model, and Lambert's model.

### 7.2.1.1. Hypothesis 1: Kubelka-Munk model of color formation

Let us consider a material whose spectral reflectance at a position $\mathbf{x}$ in space is $\beta(\mathbf{x}, \lambda)$ and whose specular (or Fresnel) reflectance at the same position is $F_{spec}(\mathbf{x}, \lambda)$.

The Kubelka-Munk model [KUB 48] assumes that the color stimulus $C_{Kub-Munk}(\mathbf{x}, \lambda)$ reflected by this surface element, lit by illumination with a spectral power distribution $E(\mathbf{x}, \lambda)$, can be expressed as:

$$C_{Kub-Munk}(\mathbf{x}, \lambda) = (1 - F_{spec}(\mathbf{x}, \lambda))^2.\beta(\mathbf{x}, \lambda).E(\mathbf{x}, \lambda)$$
$$+ F_{spec}(\mathbf{x}, \lambda).E(\mathbf{x}, \lambda) \qquad [7.3]$$

### 7.2.1.2. Hypothesis 2: Shafer's model of color formation

According to Shafer's dichromatic model [SHA 85], the color stimulus $C_{Shafer}(\mathbf{x}, \lambda)$ reflected by this same surface element, lit by illumination with a spectral power distribution $E(\mathbf{x}, \lambda)$ can be expressed as:

$$C_{Shafer}(\mathbf{x}, \lambda) = m_{diff}(\theta).\beta(\mathbf{x}, \lambda).E(\mathbf{x}, \lambda)$$
$$+ m_{spec}(\theta, \alpha).F_{spec}(\mathbf{x}, \lambda).E(\mathbf{x}, \lambda) \qquad [7.4]$$

where $m_{diff}$ and $m_{spec}$ represent the dependence on the illumination direction $\theta$ and observation direction $\alpha$.

Shafer's model and Kubelka-Munk's model are similar in that they decompose the reflection into a specular reflection and a diffuse reflection. This type of decomposition of a color stimulus into two terms corresponding to two different physical phenomena has been validated by Beckmann [BEC 87].

However, both these models assume that the light "projected" onto a pixel is only emitted by a point source (the surface element x in question). In his article [SHA 85] Shafer described the extended dichromatic model, in which an ambient lighting term $L_a(\lambda)$ is added. This is the same for all surfaces of an observed scene, and therefore does not depend on the position x. As we stated earlier, this term can be used to take into account a range of phenomena such as the effects of reflections from surface elements on the surface being observed, the sensor response to infrared wavelengths, or lens diffraction [SHA 85]. The full reflected color stimulus then becomes:

$$C_{extended-Shafer}(\mathbf{x}, \lambda) = m_{diff}(\theta).\beta(\mathbf{x}, \lambda).E(\mathbf{x}, \lambda)$$
$$+ m_{spec}(\theta, \alpha).F_{spec}(\mathbf{x}, \lambda).E(\mathbf{x}, \lambda) + L_a(\lambda)$$
$$[7.5]$$

### 7.2.1.3. Hypothesis 3: Lambert's model of color formation

When a matte surface is being observed, specular reflection can be ignored. In this specific case, Lambert's model estimates the color stimulus $C_{Lambert}(\mathbf{x}, \lambda)$ reflected by the surface element in question, illuminated by a light source with spectral distribution $E(\mathbf{x}, \lambda)$ in the following way:

$$C_{Lambert}(\mathbf{x}, \lambda) = \beta(\mathbf{x}, \lambda).E(\mathbf{x}, \lambda) \qquad [7.6]$$

### 7.2.2. Assumptions on the reflective properties of surface elements

### 7.2.2.1. Hypothesis 4: neutral specular reflection

Analysis of the specular reflectance spectra of a wide range of materials has revealed that they show very little variation over the visible wavelength band [SHA 85], in other words, their spectrum is virtually flat. This is referred to as neutral specular reflection, where it is assumed that the specular reflectance of the surface element being observed is wavelength-independent:

$$F_{spec}(\mathbf{x}, \lambda) = F_{spec}(\mathbf{x}) \qquad [7.7]$$

This hypothesis is widely adopted since most models assume that chromatic information is only conveyed by the diffuse reflection (and not by the specular reflection).

### 7.2.2.2. Hypothesis 5: matte surface

In the case of a matte surface, it is common to use Lambert's model of color formation, but certain authors prefer to begin with a more complex model (Shafer or Kubelka-Munk) and then assume that the surface is matte. This is simply a case of setting specular reflectivity to zero in the model:

$$F_{spec}(\mathbf{x}, \lambda) = 0 \qquad [7.8]$$

### 7.2.3. Assumptions on camera sensor responses

#### 7.2.3.1. Hypothesis 6: normalized spectral response curves

This hypothesis assumes that the spectral responses $k(\lambda)$, $k = R, G, B$ of camera sensors are all normalized in such a way that the integrals of each such curve over the visible spectrum will be equal to a single constant, written $i_{RGB}$:

$$\int_{380nm}^{780nm} R(\lambda)d\lambda = \int_{380nm}^{780nm} G(\lambda)d\lambda = \int_{380nm}^{780nm} B(\lambda)d\lambda = i_{RGB} \quad [7.9]$$

#### 7.2.3.2. Hypothesis 7: sensor bandwidths

According to this assumption, the bandwidths of the spectral responses $k(\lambda)$, $k = R, G, B$ of the sensors are so narrow that each sensor associated with the response $k(\lambda)$ is only sensitive to a single wavelength, which we will denote $\lambda_k$ [FUN 95]:

$$\int_{\lambda} k(\lambda)d\lambda = k(\lambda_k), \quad k = R, G, B \qquad [7.10]$$

This assumption, although widely used, is rarely true in practice. Finlayson *et al.* therefore suggested artificially narrowing the sensor bandwidth by applying an affine transformation to the $RGB$ components output of the camera [FIN 94a].

### 7.2.3.3. *Hypothesis 8: from RGB sensor responses to the CIE 1964 XYZ components*

To obtain the invariant characteristics listed by Geusebroek *et al.* [GEU 01], we must work in the CIE 1964 XYZ color space. Geusebroek *et al.* assumed that if neither the characteristics of the camera sensors nor the lighting are known, the affine transformation proposed by the ITU [ITU 90] can be used to obtain a fairly good approximation of the XYZ components from the RGB components provided by the camera:

$$\begin{bmatrix} C^X(P) \\ C^Y(P) \\ C^Z(P) \end{bmatrix} = \begin{pmatrix} 0.62 & 0.11 & 0.19 \\ 0.3 & 0.56 & 0.05 \\ -0.01 & 0.03 & 1.11 \end{pmatrix} \begin{bmatrix} C^R(P) \\ C^G(P) \\ C^B(P) \end{bmatrix} \qquad [7.11]$$

If the spectral responses of the sensors are known, this approximation can be further refined.

### 7.2.4. *Assumptions on the characteristics of the illumination*

### 7.2.4.1. *Hypothesis 9: Planck equation*

Finlayson proposed an illumination model based on the Planck model [FIN 01a]. This model describes the relative spectral distribution of the energy of the illumination reaching the surface element at position **x** as:

$$E(\mathbf{x}, \lambda) = \frac{e(\mathbf{x})c_1}{\lambda^5 \left( exp(\frac{c2}{T(\mathbf{x})\lambda}) - 1 \right)} \qquad [7.12]$$

where:

$$\begin{cases} e(\mathbf{x}): \text{ illumination intensity at } \mathbf{x} \\ T(\mathbf{x}): \text{ temperature in Kelvins of the illumination at } \mathbf{x} \\ c_1 = 3.74183 \times 10^{-16} \, Wm^2 \\ c_2 = 1.4388 \times 10^{-2} \, mK \end{cases} \qquad [7.13]$$

In addition, since $\lambda \in [10^{-7}; 10^{-6}]$ in the visible and $T(\mathbf{x}) \in [10^3; 10^4]$, Finlayson set $exp(\frac{c2}{T(\mathbf{x})\lambda}) \gg 1$.

In this way, he obtained the following illumination model:

$$E(\mathbf{x}, \lambda) = \frac{e(\mathbf{x})c_1}{\lambda^5 exp(\frac{c2}{T(\mathbf{x})\lambda})} \qquad [7.14]$$

### 7.2.4.2. Hypothesis 10: illumination color is locally constant

Gevers *et al.* [GEV 99] made the assumption that the illumination $E(\mathbf{x}, \lambda)$ can be written in the form of a product of two separate terms. One, written $e(\mathbf{x})$, depends on the position $\mathbf{x}$ of the surface element and will affect the intensity of the illumination. The other is the spectral curve $E(\lambda)$, which is identical for every surface element observed by pixels in a given neighborhood:

$$E(\mathbf{x}, \lambda) = e(\mathbf{x}).E(\lambda) \qquad [7.15]$$

This hypothesis therefore involves the assumption that the color of the illumination is locally constant, and only the intensity will vary as a function of position.

### 7.2.4.3. Hypothesis 11: locally constant illumination

Funt *et al.* [FUN 95] assumed that two surface elements observed by neighboring pixels in an image are illuminated in the same way. Thus, if the surface element at position $\mathbf{x}$, projected onto pixel $P$, is lit by illumination with a spectral power distribution (SPD) $E(\mathbf{x}, \lambda)$, then the surface elements projected onto the pixels $P_{neighbor}$ that lie in the neighborhood of $P$ will be lit with illumination of the same relative spectral energy distribution. The illumination is therefore independent of position:

$$E(\mathbf{x}, \lambda) = E(\lambda) \qquad [7.16]$$

There is no restriction for the extent of the neighborhood under consideration, but the larger is this neighborhood, the less is the validity of this hypothesis. A $3 \times 3$ neighborhood is often used, but in the context of object recognition based on local description, it is not unusual to assume that the illumination is constant over the entire local region extracted from the interest point.

If we assume locally constant illumination, this implies that the illumination spectrum reaching two neighboring surface elements is constant, and that the orientation of these surfaces with respect to incident rays is the same. In order for this assumption to be valid, the illumination must be uniform and the object locally planar.

### 7.2.4.4. *Hypothesis 12: white illumination*

This hypothesis assumes that the SPD $E(\mathbf{x}, \lambda)$ of the illumination hitting the surface element at a position $\mathbf{x}$ is constant for all wavelengths, although the intensity of this illumination is not necessarily fixed from one surface element to the next. This is what is defined as white illumination, where the SPD is independent of wavelength:

$$E(\mathbf{x}, \lambda) = E(\mathbf{x}) \qquad [7.17]$$

This hypothesis, which may seem very restrictive, is closer to being satisfied if correct white balancing has been performed for the lighting illuminating the scene, even if the lighting is not completely white.

### 7.2.4.5. *Hypothesis 13: known illumination color*

When defining the color invariant characteristics of shadows and reflections, it may sometimes be necessary to know the color of the illumination [WEI 06]. In this chapter, we are considering object recognition where the acquisition conditions are not controlled, and so the illumination color is not known in advance. A number of methods can, however, be used to estimate this color [FIN 01b, FUN 99]. For the purposes of our discussion of this hypothesis, we will assume that the color of the lighting used to illuminate the scene is known.

### **7.2.5. *Hypotheses of the photometric and radiometric variation model***

Some hypotheses are based more on experimental results than on theoretical analyses of color formation. This is the case for most of the hypotheses we will discuss in this section, which are based directly on models of photometric and radiometric variation. We will see that some of the models discussed here can be justified theoretically since they are a natural progression from hypotheses discussed in earlier sections.

We will therefore discuss various models of photometric and radiometric variation here, i.e. different formula for the function $F_{ill}$ in equation [7.1]. Recall that this function models the impact of a photometric or radiometric variation, since it can be used to convert from the color of a pixel $P_{src}$ in the source image $\mathbf{I_{src}}$ to the color of a pixel $P_{cand}$ in the candidate image $\mathbf{I_{cand}}$. Both images $\mathbf{I_{src}}$ and $\mathbf{I_{cand}}$ represent the same object, but were acquired under different conditions. The pixels $P_{src}$ and $P_{cand}$ represent the same surface element of this object.

### 7.2.5.1. *Hypothesis 14: diagonal model*

A diagonal model assumes that the color $\mathbf{C}(P_{cand}) = (C^R(P_{cand}), C^G(P_{cand}), C^B(P_{cand}))$ of the pixel $P_{cand}$ can be determined from the color $\mathbf{C}(P_{src}) = (C^R(P_{src}), C^G(P_{src}), C^B(P_{src}))$ of the pixel $P_{src}$ through a transformation $F_{ill}$ that is defined by a diagonal matrix [FIN 94b, KRI 70]:

$$\mathbf{C}(P_{cand}) = \begin{pmatrix} a_R & 0 & 0 \\ 0 & a_G & 0 \\ 0 & 0 & a_B \end{pmatrix} \mathbf{C}(P_{src}) \qquad [7.18]$$

All models of photometric and radiometric variations resulting from a transformation defined by a single diagonal matrix are known as diagonal models [FIN 94b]. They differ only in terms of the values and dependencies of the elements of this diagonal matrix [GEV 99, FUN 95]. The diagonal model can be justified, for example, by assuming that the surface is matte and the acquisition sensors have very narrow spectral bandwidths [FUN 95]. When $a_R = a_G = a_B$, the variation is limited to a change in illumination intensity.

### 7.2.5.2. *Hypothesis 15: diagonal-offset model*

It can be seen that diagonal models are based on rather restrictive models of color formation. Finlayson *et al.* [FIN 05] also proposed to lift some of these constraints by adding an offset in color space. The transformation $F_{ill}$ is then defined in terms of two matrices: a $3 \times 3$ diagonal matrix and a $3 \times 1$ matrix:

$$\mathbf{C}(P_{cand}) = \begin{pmatrix} a_R & 0 & 0 \\ 0 & a_G & 0 \\ 0 & 0 & a_B \end{pmatrix} \mathbf{C}(P_{src}) + \begin{pmatrix} b_R \\ b_G \\ b_B \end{pmatrix} \qquad [7.19]$$

The diagonal-offset model can be justified, for example, by assuming that the surface is matte, the spectral bandwidths of the acquisition sensors are very narrow, and by adding the ambient lighting term proposed by Shafer [SHA 85] (the $L_a(\lambda)$ term introduced in equation [7.5]).

### 7.2.5.3. Hypothesis 16: linear transformation

A number of authors assume that the photometric and radiometric variations can be modeled by the following transformation [LEN 99]:

$$\mathbf{C}(P_{cand}) = \begin{pmatrix} a & b & c \\ d & e & f \\ g & h & i \end{pmatrix} \mathbf{C}(P_{src}) \qquad [7.20]$$

This equation assumes that a component $C^k(P_{cand})$ depends on all three components of pixel $P_{src}$, and not just on the $C^k(P_{src})$ component.

### 7.2.5.4. Hypothesis 17: affine transformation

When an ambient term is added to the previous model, photometric and radiometric variations can be modeled by the following transformation [MIN 04]:

$$\mathbf{C}(P_{cand}) = \begin{pmatrix} a & b & c \\ d & e & f \\ g & h & i \end{pmatrix} \mathbf{C}(P_{src}) + \begin{pmatrix} j \\ k \\ l \end{pmatrix} \qquad [7.21]$$

### 7.2.5.5. Hypothesis 18: monotonically increasing functions

Finlayson [FIN 05] considered each color component independently and assumed that the level $C^k(P_{cand})$, $k = R, G, B$ of a pixel $P_{cand}$

can be deduced from the level $C^k(P_{src})$ of the corresponding pixel $P_{src}$ using a strictly increasing function $f^k$:

$$C^k(P_{cand}) = f^k(C^k(P_{src})), k = R, G, B \qquad [7.22]$$

We recall that a function $f^k$ is strictly increasing if $a > b \Rightarrow f^k(a) > f^k(b)$. The three monotonically increasing functions $f^k$, $k = R, G, B$, are not necessarily linear functions, as would be the case for a diagonal model.

These five models can be used to express a photometric or radiometric variation in terms of the application of a function to the colors of each pixel. The more degrees of freedom that are added (from the diagonal model to the affine model) the closer to reality the model will be. However, in the context of object recognition, these models are used to normalize images. As a result, the more degrees of freedom that are added, the less suitable the resultant descriptor will be as a discriminator, since this increases the range of variability in the colors of the object as the acquisition conditions change. A compromise is therefore necessary between the precision of the model and the discriminating power of the final descriptor.

All these hypotheses form the basis of the main color invariant characteristics that we will discuss in the next section.

## 7.3. Color invariant characteristics

We will describe the main color invariant characteristics that are used in the context of object recognition. Our aim is not to give an exhaustive discussion of color invariant characteristics, but rather to understand how these are built upon the choice of base hypotheses. We will divide them into three categories. The first consists of invariant characteristics that are obtained by taking the ratio between different color components of a given pixel or between color components of neighboring pixels. The second category consists of invariant characteristics that make use of the color distribution of pixels within the local region being characterized. The third category of invariant characteristics consists of those that consider the spectral and/or spatial derivatives of the original color components.

### 7.3.1. *Inter- and intra-component color ratios*

7.3.1.1. *Ratios between neighboring pixel components*

  - *Funt et al. approach [FUN 95]*

Funt *et al.* suggested using a diagonal model for lighting conditions, based on the following three hypotheses:

  – Lambert's model of color formation (see equation [7.6]): $C_{Lambert}(\mathbf{x}, \lambda) = \beta(\mathbf{x}, \lambda)E(\mathbf{x}, \lambda)$;

  – narrow spectral bandwidth of detectors (see equation [7.10]): $\int_\lambda k(\lambda)d\lambda = k(\lambda_k)$;

  – constant illumination over a $3 \times 3$ neighborhood, equal to $E(V_{3X3}(P), \lambda)$: see equation [7.16].

Thus, using the same notation as in the previous section, the color components $C^k(P)$, $k = R, G, B$, of a pixel $P$, which is observing the surface element at coordinate $\mathbf{x}$ can be estimated as:

$$C^k(P) = \int_\lambda \beta(\mathbf{x}, \lambda).E(V_{3X3}(P), \lambda).k(\lambda)d\lambda$$

$$= \beta(\mathbf{x}, \lambda_k).E(V_{3X3}(P), \lambda_k).k(\lambda_k) \qquad [7.23]$$

In the same way, the components $C^k(P_{neighbor})$, $k = R, G, B$, of a pixel $P_{neighbor}$ belonging to the $3 \times 3$ neighborhood of the pixel $P$, which is observing the surface element at coordinate $\mathbf{x_{neighbor}}$, can be estimated as:

$$C^k(P_{neighbor}) = \beta(\mathbf{x_{neighbor}}, \lambda_k).E(V_{3X3}(P_{neighbor}), \lambda_k).k(\lambda_k)$$

$$[7.24]$$

We can deduce from equations [7.23] and [7.24] that the following ratio:

$$\frac{C^k(P)}{C^k(P_{neighbor})} = \frac{\beta(\mathbf{x}, \lambda_k).E(V_{3X3}(P), \lambda_k).k(\lambda_k)}{\beta(\mathbf{x_{neighbor}}, \lambda_k).E(V_{3X3}(P_{neighbor}), \lambda_k).k(\lambda_k)}$$

$$= \frac{\beta(\mathbf{x}, \lambda_k)}{\beta(\mathbf{x_{neighbor}}, \lambda_k)}$$

[7.25]

is a function only of the spectral reflectances of the surface elements being observed and of the spectral responses of the detectors in the form of their dominant wavelengths $\lambda_k$.

Thus, for the case of a matte surface, with narrow spectral bandwidths for the detectors and with locally uniform illumination, Funt *et al.* showed that if the level of one pixel is divided by the level of a neighboring pixel, this ratio will be invariant to the color of the illumination, the intensity of the illumination, and the angle of observation (an inherent consequence of the assumption of a Lambertian surface).

Funt *et al.* [FUN 95] therefore proposed to express the color invariant characteristics $(X^1(P), X^2(P), X^3(P))$ for pixel $P$ as follows:

$$\begin{cases} X^1(P) = log(C^R(P_{neighbor})) - log(C^R(P)) \\ X^2(P) = log(C^G(P_{neighbor})) - log(C^G(P)) \\ X^3(P) = log(C^B(P_{neighbor})) - log(C^B(P)) \end{cases}$$

[7.26]

where $P_{neighbor}$ is one of the pixels in the neighborhood of $P$ in the image in question.

Based on an equivalent model, Nayar *et al.* [NAY 96] and Koubaroulis *et al.* [KOU 00] also suggested using the ratios between color component levels for neighboring pixels.

If the hypotheses of Funt *et al.* are broadened to extend the assumption of uniform illumination to the entire region extracted from around a point of interest, other approaches are also possible. Inspired by the work of Gershon *et al.* [GER 88], we can divide the level of a given pixel by the mean of the levels of particular pixels in the extracted region, an operation referred to as "gray-world normalization" [MUS 07]. Similarly, based on the same hypotheses, certain authors prefer to normalize the pixel levels not by the mean level in the neighborhood but by the maximum level that is found among all the pixels in this neighborhood [LAN 77, CIO 01]. Finlayson *et al.* [FIN 04b] also proposed a generalization of these normalizations to use statistical measures, and showed that such normalizations are just specific cases of a normalization based on Minkowski norms of order between 1 and infinity. In the specific case of illumination estimation, they showed that the 6th order gives the best results. In the case of object recognition using local descriptors, these normalizations have not been tested, but are based on the same assumptions as those defined earlier, and should therefore be applicable.

Still based on the same hypotheses, and assuming that the illumination is uniform over the entire region extracted from around the key point, Finlayson considered an $N_{pix}$-dimensional space containing 3 vectors **VEC$^R$**, **VEC$^G$**, and **VEC$^B$**, each associated with a color component $R$, $G$, and $B$. $N_{pix}$ represents the number of pixels in the region under consideration. The coordinates $VEC_1^k, VEC_2^k, ..., VEC_{N_{pix}}^k$ of the **VEC$^k$** vectors, for $k = R, G, B$, are the levels of component $C^k(P)$ of the pixels $P$ in the region. The pixels are considered in the same order for all three components, in such a way that the values $VEC_j^R$, $VEC_j^G$, and $VEC_j^B$, $j = 1...N_{pix}$, correspond to the coordinates of the $j^{th}$ pixel considered in the region. Finlayson observed that if the hypotheses given earlier are respected, the angles $angle^{kk'}$, $k, k' = R, G, B$ formed by the vectors **VEC$^k$** and **VEC$^{k'}$** will be insensitive to changes in illumination [FIN 95]. Thus, under these hypotheses, a change in illumination leads to a multiplication of every pixel by the same constant. This leads to a modification of the norm of each vector **VEC$^k$** associated with each color component $k$, but no change in its direction. Finlayson therefore proposed to treat the three values representing the angles between the three color vectors as color invariant characteristics.

- *The $m_1, m_2, m_3$ characteristics of Gevers et al. [GEV 99]*

Gevers *et al.* introduced, among others, invariant characteristics written $\{m_1, m_2, m_3\}$, based on the four following hypotheses [GEV 99]:

– Shafer's dichromatic model (see equation [7.4]): $C_{Shafer}(\mathbf{x}, \lambda) = m_{diff}(\theta).\beta(\mathbf{x}, \lambda).E(\mathbf{x}, \lambda) + m_{spec}(\theta, \alpha).F_{spec}(\mathbf{x}, \lambda).E(\mathbf{x}, \lambda)$;

– matte surface (see equation [7.8]): $F_{spec}(\mathbf{x}, \lambda) = 0$;

– narrow spectral bandwidth sensors (see equation [7.10]): $\int_{\lambda} k(\lambda)d\lambda = k(\lambda_k)$;

– locally constant illumination color (see equation [7.15]): $E(\mathbf{x}, \lambda) = e(\mathbf{x}).E(\lambda)$.

Thus, the $C^k(P)$ color components, for $k = R, G, B$, of the pixel $P$, which is observing the surface element at position $\mathbf{x}$ can be estimated to be:

$$C^k(P) = m_{diff}(\theta).\beta(\mathbf{x}, \lambda_k).e(\mathbf{x}).E(\lambda_k).k(\lambda_k) \qquad [7.27]$$

Similarly, the $C^k(P_{neighbor})$ components, for $k = R, G, B$, of a pixel $P_{neighbor}$ lying within the $3 \times 3$ neighborhood of pixel $P$, observing the surface element at position $\mathbf{x_{neighbor}}$ can be estimated to be:

$$C^k(P_{neighbor}) = m_{diff}(\theta_{neighbor}).\beta(\mathbf{x_{neighbor}}P, \lambda_k)$$
$$.e(\mathbf{x_{neighbor}}).E(\lambda_k).k(\lambda_k) \qquad [7.28]$$

where $\theta_{neighbor}$ represents the direction of illumination relative to the surface normal at $\mathbf{x_{neighbor}}$. This direction may be different from $\theta$, the direction of the illumination relative to the surface normal at $\mathbf{x}$. This parameter can be used to take into account variations in surface orientation.

If we consider another color component $k' \neq k$, we can calculate the color components of pixels $P$ and $P_{neighbor}$:

$$C^{k'}(P) = m_{diff}(\theta).\beta(\mathbf{x}, \lambda'_k).e(\mathbf{x}).E(\lambda'_k).k'(\lambda'_k) \qquad [7.29]$$

and:

$$C^{k'}(P_{neighbor}) = m_{diff}(\theta_{neighbor}).\beta(\mathbf{x_{neighbor}}, \lambda'_k)$$
$$.e(\mathbf{x_{neighbor}}).E(\lambda'_k).k'(\lambda'_k) \qquad [7.30]$$

Reviewing these last four equations, it is easy to show that the following ratio depends only on the spectral reflectances of the surface elements in question, and on the spectral responses of the sensors (in the form of their dominant wavelengths $\lambda_k$):

$$\frac{C^k(P)C^{k'}(P_{neighbor})}{C^k(P_{neighbor})C^{k'}(P)} = \frac{\beta(\mathbf{x}, \lambda_k)\beta(\mathbf{x}(P_{neighbor}, \lambda_k')}{\beta(\mathbf{x}(P_{neighbor}, \lambda_k)\beta(\mathbf{x}, \lambda_k')} \qquad [7.31]$$

Thus for a matte surface, when the spectral bandwidth of the acquisition sensors is very narrow and the color of the illumination is locally constant, Gevers *et al.* showed that the cross-ratio between the levels of two neighboring pixels for two different color components was insensitive to the color, intensity and direction of illumination, as well as the observation angle.

Gevers *et al.* therefore suggested expressing the color invariant characteristics $(X^1(P), X^2(P), X^3(P))$ of pixel $P$ in the following way [GEV 99]:

$$\begin{cases} X^1(P) = \frac{C^R(P)C^G(P_{neighbor})}{C^R(P_{neighbor})C^G(P)} \\ X^2(P) = \frac{C^R(P)C^B(P_{neighbor})}{C^R(P_{neighbor})C^B(P)} \\ X^3(P) = \frac{C^G(P)C^B(P_{neighbor})}{C^G(P_{neighbor})C^B(P)} \end{cases} \qquad [7.32]$$

where $P_{neighbor}$ is one of the pixels from the neighborhood of $P$ in the image in question.

### 7.3.1.2. Ratios between components of a single pixel

- *The $l_1, l_2, l_3$ characteristics of Gevers et al. [GEV 99]*

Gevers *et al.* then proposed further invariant characteristics $\{l_1, l_2, l_3\}$ based on the four following hypotheses:

– Shafer's model of color formation (see equation [7.4]): $C_{Shafer}(\mathbf{x}, \lambda) = m_{diff}(\theta).\beta(\mathbf{x}, \lambda).E(\mathbf{x}, \lambda) + m_{spec}(\theta, \alpha).F_{spec}(\mathbf{x}, \lambda).E(\mathbf{x}, \lambda)$;

– neutral specular reflection (see equation [7.7]): $F_{spec}(\mathbf{x}, \lambda) = F_{spec}(\mathbf{x})$;

– identical integrated sensor spectral response curves (see equation [7.9]): $\int_{380nm}^{780nm} R(\lambda)d\lambda = \int_{380nm}^{780nm} G(\lambda)d\lambda = \int_{380nm}^{780nm} B(\lambda)d\lambda = i_{RGB}$;
– white illumination (see equation [7.17]): $E(\mathbf{x}, \lambda) = E(\mathbf{x})$.

Thus, the color components $C^k(P)$ and $k = R, G, B$ of a pixel $P$ observing the surface element at position $\mathbf{x}$ can be estimated as:

$$C^k(P) = m_{diff}(\theta).E(\mathbf{x}) \int_\lambda \beta(\mathbf{x}, \lambda).k(\lambda)d\lambda$$
$$+ m_{spec}(\theta, \alpha).F_{spec}(\mathbf{x}).E(\mathbf{x})i_{RGB}$$

[7.33]

In the same way, considering the three different components $k$, $k'$, and $k''$, the following ratio of differences will depend only on the spectral reflectance of the surface element under consideration, as well as the detector response:

$$\frac{C^k(P) - C^{k'}(P)}{C^k(P) - C^{k''}(P)} = \frac{\int_\lambda \beta(\mathbf{x}, \lambda).k(\lambda)d\lambda - \int_\lambda \beta(\mathbf{x}, \lambda).k'(\lambda)d\lambda}{\int_\lambda \beta(\mathbf{x}, \lambda).k(\lambda)d\lambda - \int_\lambda \beta(\mathbf{x}, \lambda).k''(\lambda)d\lambda}$$

[7.34]

Thus, in the case of neutral specular reflection, when the detector integrals are identical and white-light illumination is used, Gevers *et al.* showed that for a given pixel, the ratio between the differences in levels of the different components was insensitive to the illumination intensity, the direction of illumination, the angle of observation, and specular reflections.

Gevers *et al.* [GEV 99] therefore proposed to express the color invariant characteristics $(X^1(P), X^2(P), X^3(P))$ of a pixel $P$ as follows:

$$\begin{cases} X^1(P) = \frac{(C^R(P) - C^G(P))^2}{(C^R(P) - C^G(P))^2 + (C^R(P) - C^B(P))^2 + (C^G(P) - C^B(P))^2} \\ X^2(P) = \frac{(C^R(P) - C^B(P))^2}{(C^R(P) - C^G(P))^2 + (C^R(P) - C^B(P))^2 + (C^G(P) - C^B(P))^2} \\ X^3(P) = \frac{(C^G(P) - C^B(P))^2}{(C^R(P) - C^G(P))^2 + (C^R(P) - C^B(P))^2 + (C^G(P) - C^B(P))^2} \end{cases}$$

[7.35]

This proof can be applied to all color characteristics based on the ratio between differences in the levels of different components of the same pixel. This is the case for example for the hue $H$, defined as $H(P) = arctan(\frac{\sqrt{3}(C^G(P)-C^B(P))}{(C^R(P)-C^G(P))+(C^R(P)-C^B(P))})$.

- *The $c_1, c_2, c_3$ components of Gevers et al. [GEV 99]*

Finally, Gevers *et al.* proposed invariant characteristics $\{c_1, c_2, c_3\}$, based on the three following hypotheses:

– Shafer's dichromatic model (see equation [7.4]): $C_{Shafer}(\mathbf{x}, \lambda) = m_{diff}(\theta).\beta(\mathbf{x}, \lambda).E(\mathbf{x}, \lambda) + m_{spec}(\theta, \alpha).F_{spec}(\mathbf{x}, \lambda).E(\mathbf{x}, \lambda)$;

– matte surface (see equation [7.8]): $F_{spec}(\mathbf{x}, \lambda) = 0$;

– white illumination (see equation [7.17]): $E(\mathbf{x}, \lambda) = E(\mathbf{x})$.

Thus, the color components $C^k(P)$, $k = R, G, B$, of a pixel $P$ observing the surface element at position $\mathbf{x}$ can be estimated as:

$$C^k(P) = \int_\lambda m_{diff}(\theta).\beta(\mathbf{x}, \lambda).E(\mathbf{x}, \lambda).k(\lambda)d\lambda$$

$$= m_{diff}(\theta).E(\mathbf{x}). \int_\lambda \beta(\mathbf{x}, \lambda).k(\lambda)d\lambda \qquad [7.36]$$

In the same way, if we consider the color component $C^{k'}$, for $k' \neq k$, we find:

$$C^{k'}(P) = m_{diff}(\theta).E(\mathbf{x}). \int_\lambda \beta(\mathbf{x}, \lambda).k'(\lambda)d\lambda \qquad [7.37]$$

The ratio between these two color components therefore depends only on the spectral reflectance of the surface element and on the detector response:

$$\frac{C^k(P)}{C^{k'}(P)} = \frac{\int_\lambda \beta(\mathbf{x}, \lambda).k(\lambda)d\lambda}{\int_\lambda \beta(\mathbf{x}, \lambda).k'(\lambda)d\lambda} \qquad [7.38]$$

Thus, Gevers *et al.* showed that when the surface is matte and white-light illumination is used, the ratio for a given pixel between the level of one component and the level of another component was insensitive to the intensity of illumination, the direction of illumination, and the observation angle.

Gevers *et al.* therefore proposed to express the color invariant characteristics $(X^1(P), X^2(P), X^3(P))$ of a pixel $P$ as follows [GEV 99]:

$$\begin{cases} X^1(P) = arctan(\frac{C^R(P)}{max(C^G(P),C^B(P))}) \\ X^2(P) = arctan(\frac{C^G(P)}{max(C^R(P),C^B(P))}) \\ X^3(P) = arctan(\frac{C^B(P)}{max(C^R(P),C^G(P))}) \end{cases} \qquad [7.39]$$

Here, the function $max()$ returns the maximum of the levels for two given components of the same pixel, and not the maximum for all pixels in the region.

This proof can be applied to all color characteristics based on the ratio between the levels of different components of the same pixel. This is true, for example, for normalized components:

$$\begin{cases} C^r(P) = \frac{C^R(P)}{C^R(P)+C^G(P)+C^B(P)} \\ C^g(P) = \frac{C^G(P)}{C^R(P)+C^G(P)+C^B(P)} \\ C^b(P) = \frac{C^B(P)}{C^R(P)+C^G(P)+C^B(P)} \end{cases} \qquad [7.40]$$

Finlayson *et al.* pointed out that two different models were required to obtain color characteristics that are invariant to both the color and the direction of illumination [FIN 98]. Thus, the characteristics proposed by Funt *et al.* [FUN 95] normalized the color components with respect to the color of the illumination, whereas the normalized components $\{C^r(P), C^g(P), C^b(P)\}$ are invariant with respect to the direction of illumination and hence to the orientation of the surface in question. They, therefore, proposed an iterative normalization of the color components for each pixel, converging rapidly to color characteristics that are invariant to both the color and the direction of illumination [FIN 98]. This normalization simply involves alternating the normalization proposed by Funt *et al.* [FUN 95] with the normalization used to obtain the normalized color components $\{C^r(P), C^g(P), C^b(P)\}$.

*- Approach of Finlayson et al. [FIN 01a]*

Finlayson *et al.* proposed invariant characteristics based on the following three hypotheses:

– Lambert's model of color formation (see equation [7.6]): $C_{Lambert}(\mathbf{x}, \lambda) = \beta(\mathbf{x}, \lambda)E(\mathbf{x}, \lambda)$;

– narrow spectral bandwidth sensors (see equation [7.10]): $\int_\lambda k(\lambda)d\lambda = k(\lambda_k)$;

– Planck equation for the illumination (see equation [7.14]): $E(\mathbf{x}, \lambda) = \frac{e(\mathbf{x})c_1}{\lambda^5 exp(\frac{c2}{T(\mathbf{x})\lambda})}$.

Thus, using the same notation as in the previous section, the color components $C^k(P)$, $k = R, G, B$, for a pixel $P$ observing the surface element at $\mathbf{x}$ can be estimated as:

$$C^k(P) = \beta(\mathbf{x}, \lambda_k).\frac{e(\mathbf{x})c_1}{\lambda_k^5 exp(\frac{c2}{T(\mathbf{x})\lambda_k})}.k(\lambda_k) \qquad [7.41]$$

If we then take the natural logarithm of this equation we find:

$$ln(C^k(P)) = ln(e(\mathbf{x})) + ln(\frac{\beta(\mathbf{x}, \lambda_k)c_1 k(\lambda_k)}{\lambda_k^5}) - \frac{c2}{T(\mathbf{x})\lambda_k} \qquad [7.42]$$

This equation can be simplified by writing it in the following manner:

$$ln(C^k(P)) = Int(\mathbf{x}) + Ref_k(\mathbf{x}) + T^{-1}(\mathbf{x})L_k \qquad [7.43]$$

where:

– $Int(\mathbf{x}) = ln(e(\mathbf{x}))$ depends on the illumination intensity;

– $Ref_k(\mathbf{x}) = ln(\frac{\beta(\mathbf{x}, \lambda_k)c_1 k(\lambda_k)}{\lambda_k^5})$ depends on the reflectance properties of the surface $\mathbf{x}$, as well as the dominant wavelengths $\lambda_k$ of the acquisition sensors;

– $T^{-1}(\mathbf{x})L_k = -\frac{c2}{T(\mathbf{x})\lambda_k}$ depends on the color of the illumination and on the acquisition sensors.

If we now consider a second component $k' \neq k$, then we can calculate the logarithmic difference, which depends only on the intensity of the illumination:

$$ln(C^k(P)) - ln(C^{k'}(P)) = ln(\frac{C^k(P)}{C^{k'}(P)}) = Ref_k(\mathbf{x}) - Ref_{k'}(\mathbf{x})$$

$$+ T^{-1}(\mathbf{x})(L_k - L_{k'})$$

$$[7.44]$$

In the same way, if we consider components $k''$ and $k'$, we obtain:

$$ln(\frac{C^{k''}(P)}{C^{k'}(P)}) = Ref_{k''}(\mathbf{x}) - Ref_{k'}(\mathbf{x}) + T^{-1}(\mathbf{x})(L_{k''} - L_{k'}) \quad [7.45]$$

If we consider these last two equations, we can see that as the illumination color $T(\mathbf{x})$ changes for a surface $\mathbf{x}$ observed by a pixel $P$, the corresponding points in the space $(ln(\frac{C^k(P)}{C^{k'}(P)}), ln(\frac{C^{k''}(P)}{C^{k'}(P)}))$ move along a line whose direction depends on the characteristics of the acquisition sensors. As a result, for the case where the characteristics of the acquisition sensors are known, Finlayson *et al.* proposed to calculate this direction and project all points in the space $(ln(\frac{C^G(P)}{C^R(P)}), ln(\frac{C^B(P)}{C^R(P)}))$ onto a straight line orthogonal to this direction. They showed that the resultant coordinates do not depend either on the intensity or the color of the illumination. They also showed that shadows can be eliminated from images through the use of this projection. The difference between these characteristics and the previous ones is that there is just one color invariant characteristic per pixel, rather than three.

In subsequent work, Finlayson *et al.* showed that it was not necessary to know the characteristics of the acquisition sensor to define the direction of the straight line onto which all such points are projected [FIN 04a]. They, in fact, showed that this direction is the one that minimizes the entropy of the resultant invariant image.

### 7.3.2. *Transformations based on analysis of colorimetric distributions*

#### 7.3.2.1. *Pixel rank measures – Finlayson et al.*

Finlayson *et al.* [FIN 05] proposed a model based on the hypothesis that a change in illumination can be modeled by the application of a strictly increasing function to each component (see equation [7.22]).

The aim of this was to sort the pixels belonging to a given region of the image in increasing order of their levels for each component. The colorimetric rank measure $\mathrm{Rc}^k(P)$ for component $k$ of pixel $P$ is the ratio between the number of pixels with a level less than or equal to that of $P$ and the total number of pixels in the region. This measure of colorimetric rank is therefore defined in such a way that it will be close to 0 for the first pixels (smallest levels) and equal to 1 for the last pixels (highest levels).

Consider two pixels $P_1$ and $P_2$ in a region extracted from a point of interest. If the color components of these pixels are such that $C^k(P_1) > C^k(P_2)$, then, under different lighting conditions, we will have $f^k(C^k(P_1)) > f^k(C^k(P_2))$ since the change in illumination is modeled by a strictly increasing function $f^k$ for each component. In other words, as long as the hypothesis of Finlayson *et al.* is satisfied, the order of pixel levels will not be modified by a change in illumination. As a consequence, the rank measures for each pixel are conserved under changes in illumination. Finlayson *et al.* therefore proposed to characterize the pixels of a region not by their color component levels $C^k(P)$ but by their colorimetric rank measures $\mathrm{Rc}^k(P)$, $k = R, G, B$, in this region. This is equivalent to performing an independent histogram equalization for each component within the region. Finlayson *et al.* showed that this normalization results in color characteristics that are invariant under changes in acquisition sensor or color of illumination.

#### 7.3.2.2. *Normalizations based on transformations of the colorimetric distribution*

Various authors proposed to normalize the color distribution within an image (or a region of an image) in the RGB color space to deduce illumination-invariant characteristics.

Lenz *et al.* [LEN 99] assumed that a change in illumination can be modeled by an affine transformation associated with a $3 \times 3$ matrix (see equation [7.22]). They calculated the impact of this transformation on the pixel color distribution in the RGB color space and used this to determine normalization in a color space that is invariant under this affine transformation. This normalization first requires that the distribution be normalized in such a way that its matrix of second-order moments is equal to the unit matrix. Then, a rotation is applied so that the third-order moments are normalized.

Along similar lines, Healey *et al.* assumed that a change in illumination could be modeled by the application of a $3 \times 3$ affine transformation to the color distribution in the RGB space [HEA 95]. They then proposed to normalize the color distribution in such a way that the eigenvalues of the matrices of moments were invariant under changes in illumination color.

Both these normalizations lead to characteristics that are invariant to changes in intensity and illumination color. More generally, they are invariant under the application of an affine $3 \times 3$ transformation of the pixel color (see equation [7.22]).

Finlayson *et al.* [FIN 05] showed that the diagonal-offset model gives a good representation of the consequences of changes in illumination (see equation [7.21]). In this case, normalization of the colorimetric distribution, which requires a mean of zero and a standard deviation of 1 to be imposed, can be used to render the pixel components invariant under this type of change in illumination. The associated color invariant characteristics are defined by the following equations:

$$
\left\{
\begin{array}{l}
X^1(P) = \frac{C^R(P) - \mu(C^R(P_i))}{\sigma(C^R(P_i))} \\
X^2(P) = \frac{C^G(P) - \mu(C^G(P_i))}{\sigma(C^G(P_i))} \\
X^3(P) = \frac{C^B(P) - \mu(C^B(P_i))}{\sigma(C^B(P_i))}
\end{array}
\right.
\qquad [7.46]
$$

where $\mu(C^k(P_i))$ and $\sigma(C^R(P_i))$ represent respectively the mean and the standard deviation of the pixels $P_i$ belonging to the region in question.

It can be easily shown that subtraction of the mean can be used to eliminate the offset effect resulting from changes in illumination, while dividing by the standard deviation can be used to remove the unwanted coefficients of the diagonal matrix.

These characteristics are invariant under changes in intensity and illumination color, as well as variations associated with the ambient lighting term (see page 248).

### 7.3.2.3. *Color invariant moments – Mindru et al.*

The moments of the color distribution do not contain any information about the spatial distribution of pixels in an image. Mindru *et al.* therefore suggested the use of generalized color moments to overcome this shortcoming. They are defined in the following manner:

$$M_{pq}^{abc} = \int_y \int_x x^p y^q C^R (P_{xy})^a C^G (P_{xy})^b C^B (P_{xy})^c dx dy \quad [7.47]$$

where $(x, y)$ is the position of pixel $P_{xy}$ in the image under consideration.

Thus, $M_{pq}^{abc}$ is known as the generalized color moment of order $p + q$ and degree $a + b + c$. Mindru *et al.* then proposed to consider generalized color moments of order less than or equal to 1 and of degree less than or equal to 2. They then considered three models of photometric and radiometric variation: the diagonal model (see equation [7.18]), the diagonal-offset model (see equation [7.19]), and the affine transformation plus offset (see equation [7.21]), and they show that in each case it is possible to find several combinations of these generalized moments that are invariant under this transformation. Given that the pixel positions in the image are also taken into account, they also suggested combinations that are invariant under various geometric transformations.

### 7.3.3. *Invariant derivatives*

### 7.3.3.1. *Spectral derivatives - Geusebroek et al. [GEU 01]*

Geusebroek *et al.* proposed color invariant characteristics based on spectral derivatives of the reflectances of surface elements. To construct these, they made three hypotheses that are common to all their color invariant characteristics:

– Kubelka-Munk model of color formation (see equation [7.3]):
$C_{Kub-Munk}(\mathbf{x}, \lambda) = (1 - F_{spec}(\mathbf{x}, \lambda))^2.\beta(\mathbf{x}, \lambda).E(\mathbf{x}, \lambda) + F_{spec}(\mathbf{x}, \lambda).E(\mathbf{x}, \lambda)$;

– the transformation of RGB components from an arbitrary camera into the CIE 1964 XYZ components can be modeled by applying a $3 \times 3$ matrix (see equation [7.11]). If the camera sensor responses are known, this transform can be refined;

– neutral specular reflection (see equation [7.7]): $F_{spec}(\mathbf{x}, \lambda) = F_{spec}(\mathbf{x})$.

Geusebroek *et al.* then proposed to use the Gaussian color model to define color invariant characteristics. Let us consider the color stimulus $C(\mathbf{x}, \lambda)$ reflected by a surface element $\mathbf{x}$ and observed by a pixel $P$. The Gaussian color model considers three sensors $G$, $G_\lambda$, and $G_{\lambda\lambda}$, with spectral responses that are the 0th, 1st, and 2nd order derivatives of a Gaussian function $G(\lambda)$ with a central wavelength $\lambda_0 = 520$ nm and width $\sigma_\lambda = 55$ nm [GEU 00]. Geusebroek *et al.* showed that color components expressed in this Gaussian space represent the successive coefficients of the Taylor expansion of the color stimulus $C(\mathbf{x}, \lambda)$, weighted by the Gaussian $G(\lambda)$. In other words, these components represent the successive spectral derivatives of the color stimulus in question. The color components $\{C^{G(P)}, C^{G_\lambda}(P), C^{G_{\lambda\lambda}}(P)\}$ of a pixel $P$ in this Gaussian space can be approximated using the color components of this pixel expressed in the CIE 1964 XYZ space using the following transformation:

$$\begin{bmatrix} C^G(P) \\ C^{G_\lambda}(P) \\ C^{G_{\lambda\lambda}}(P) \end{bmatrix} = \begin{pmatrix} -0.48 & 1.2 & 0.28 \\ 0.48 & 0 & -0.4 \\ 1.18 & -1.3 & 0 \end{pmatrix} \begin{bmatrix} C^X(P) \\ C^Y(P) \\ C^Z(P) \end{bmatrix} \qquad [7.48]$$

Thus, according to the hypothesis by which the XYZ components are estimated from the RGB components of the camera (see equation [7.11]), the global transformation used to convert the components defined in the

RGB space of the acquisition sensors into components defined in the Gaussian color space is as follows:

$$\begin{bmatrix} C^{G(P)} \\ C^{G_\lambda}(P) \\ C^{G_{\lambda\lambda}}(P) \end{bmatrix} = \begin{pmatrix} 0.06 & 0.63 & 0.27 \\ 0.3 & 0.04 & -0.35 \\ 0.34 & -0.6 & 0.17 \end{pmatrix} \begin{bmatrix} C^R(P) \\ C^G(P) \\ C^B(P) \end{bmatrix} \qquad [7.49]$$

Based on these results, Geusebroek *et al.* defined new color-invariant characteristics based on the spectral derivatives of the color stimulus $C_{Kub-Munk}(\mathbf{x}, \lambda)$ provided by the Kubelka-Munk model.

*- Color invariant characteristic H [GEU 01]*

For the $H$ invariant characteristic, Geusebroek *et al.* added the further hypothesis of white illumination to the three existing hypotheses (see equation [7.17]): $E(\mathbf{x}, \lambda) = E(\mathbf{x})$.

Under all these conditions, the color stimulus $C_{Kub-Munk}(\mathbf{x}, \lambda)$ reflected by the surface element $\mathbf{x}$ is defined by the following equation:

$$C_{Kub-Munk}(\mathbf{x}, \lambda) = (1 - F_{spec}(\mathbf{x}))^2.\beta(\mathbf{x}, \lambda).E(\mathbf{x})$$
$$+ F_{spec}(\mathbf{x}).E(\mathbf{x}) \qquad [7.50]$$

Thus, the first and second spectral derivatives of this signal are:

$$C_{Kub-Munk_\lambda}(\mathbf{x}, \lambda) = (1 - F_{spec}(\mathbf{x}))^2.\frac{\partial\beta(\mathbf{x}, \lambda)}{\partial\lambda}.E(\mathbf{x}) \qquad [7.51]$$

and:

$$C_{Kub-Munk_{\lambda\lambda}}(\mathbf{x}, \lambda) = (1 - F_{spec}(\mathbf{x}))^2.\frac{\partial^2\beta(\mathbf{x}, \lambda)}{\partial\lambda^2}.E(\mathbf{x}) \qquad [7.52]$$

The ratio between the first and second derivatives of the color stimulus only depends on the spectral reflectance of the surface element being observed. The Gaussian color model can be used to obtain these derivatives and Geusebroek *et al.* therefore introduced the following color invariant characteristic [GEU 01]:

$$X^H(P) = \frac{C^{G_\lambda}(P)}{C^{G_{\lambda\lambda}}(P)} \qquad [7.53]$$

Thus, in the case of neutral specular reflection and white illumination Geusebroek *et al.* showed that for a given pixel $P$, the ratio between its $C^{\mathbb{G}_\lambda}(P)$ component and its $C^{\mathbb{G}_{\lambda\lambda}}(P)$ component does not depend on the intensity or direction of illumination, the angle of observation, or any reflections that may be present.

*- Color invariant characteristic C [GEU 01]*

For the $C$ invariant characteristic, Geusebroek *et al.* added the two following hypotheses to the three original hypotheses:

– matte surface (see equation [7.8]): $F_{spec}(\mathbf{x}, \lambda) = 0$. In this case, the hypothesis of neutral specular reflection is not necessary;

– white illumination (see equation [7.17]): $E(\mathbf{x}, \lambda) = E(\mathbf{x})$.

Under all these conditions, the color stimulus $C_{Kub-Munk}(\mathbf{x}, \lambda)$ reflected by the surface element $\mathbf{x}$ is defined by the following equation:

$$C_{Kub-Munk}(\mathbf{x}, \lambda) = \beta(\mathbf{x}, \lambda).E(\mathbf{x}) \qquad [7.54]$$

Similarly, the first spectral derivative of this signal gives:

$$C_{Kub-Munk_\lambda}(\mathbf{x}, \lambda) = \frac{\partial \beta(\mathbf{x}, \lambda)}{\partial \lambda}.E(\mathbf{x}) \qquad [7.55]$$

The ratio between the first spectral derivative of the color stimulus and the stimulus itself only depends on the reflectance of the surface element being observed. Geusebroek *et al.* therefore introduced the following color invariant characteristic:

$$X^C(P) = \frac{C^{\mathbb{G}_\lambda}(P)}{C^{\mathbb{G}}(P)} \qquad [7.56]$$

Thus, in the case of a matte surface and white illumination, Geusebroek *et al.* showed that for a given pixel $P$, the ratio between its $C^{\mathbb{G}_\lambda}(P)$ component and its $C^{\mathbb{G}}(P)$ does not depend on the intensity or direction of illumination or the angle of observation.

*- Color invariant characteristic W [GEU 01]*

The $W$ invariant characteristic is the odd one out in this section since it is does not result from a spectral derivative but rather from a spatial derivative. However since it is based on the components in the Gaussian space, we have included it in the present section. For this invariant characteristic, Geusebroek *et al.* added the three following hypotheses to the three original hypotheses:

– matte surface (see equation [7.8]): $F_{spec}(\mathbf{x}, \lambda) = 0$. In this case, the hypothesis of neutral specular reflection is not necessary;

– white illumination (see equation [7.17]): $E(\mathbf{x}, \lambda) = E(\mathbf{x})$;

– locally constant illumination (see equation [7.16]): $E(\mathbf{x}, \lambda) = E(\lambda)$. When this hypothesis and the previous one hold true, we have: $E(\mathbf{x}, \lambda) = E$.

Under all these conditions, the color stimulus $C_{Kub-Munk}(\mathbf{x}, \lambda)$ reflected by the surface element $\mathbf{x}$ is defined by the following equation:

$$C_{Kub-Munk}(\mathbf{x}, \lambda) = \beta(\mathbf{x}, \lambda).E \qquad [7.57]$$

Similarly, the first spatial derivative of this signal becomes:

$$C_{Kub-Munk_{\mathbf{x}}}(\mathbf{x}, \lambda) = \frac{\partial \beta(\mathbf{x}, \lambda)}{\partial \mathbf{x}}.E \qquad [7.58]$$

The ratio between the first spatial derivative of the color stimulus and the stimulus itself therefore only depends on the reflectance of the surface element being observed. Geusebroek *et al.* therefore introduced the following color invariant characteristic [GEU 01]:

$$X^{W}(P) = \frac{C^{\mathbb{G}_{\mathbf{x}}}(P)}{C^{\mathbb{G}}(P)} \qquad [7.59]$$

where $C^{\mathbb{G}_{\mathbf{x}}}(P) = \frac{\partial C^{\mathbb{G}}(P)}{\partial \mathbf{x}}$ represents the spatial derivative of component $C^{\mathbb{G}}(P)$ at $P$. There, it is assumed that spatial derivatives in the 3D scene space can be approximated by spatial derivatives in the image space.

Thus, in the case of a matte surface, and illumination that is both white and locally constant, Geusebroek *et al.* showed that for a given pixel $P$ the ratio between the spatial derivative of its component $C^{\mathbb{G}}(P)$ and the original component $C^{\mathbb{G}}(P)$ itself does not depend on the intensity of illumination.

- *Color invariant characteristic N [GEU 01]*

For the $N$ invariant characteristic, Geusebroek *et al.* added the two following hypotheses to the three original hypotheses:

– matte surface (see equation [7.8]): $F_{spec}(\mathbf{x}, \lambda) = 0$. In this case, the hypothesis of neutral specular reflection is not necessary;

– locally constant illumination color (see equation [7.15]): $E(\mathbf{x}, \lambda) = e(\mathbf{x}).E(\lambda)$.

Under all these conditions, the color stimulus $C_{Kub-Munk}(\mathbf{x}, \lambda)$ reflected by the surface element $\mathbf{x}$ is defined by the following equation:

$$C_{Kub-Munk}(\mathbf{x}, \lambda) = \beta(\mathbf{x}, \lambda).e(\mathbf{x}).E(\lambda) \qquad [7.60]$$

Similarly, taking first spectral derivative of this signal gives:

$$C_{Kub-Munk_\lambda}(\mathbf{x}, \lambda) = e(\mathbf{x})[\frac{\partial \beta(\mathbf{x}, \lambda)}{\partial \lambda}.E(\lambda) + \frac{\partial E(\lambda)}{\partial \lambda}.\beta(\mathbf{x}, \lambda)] \quad [7.61]$$

The ratio between the first spectral derivative of the color stimulus and the stimulus itself is equal to:

$$\frac{C_{Kub-Munk_\lambda}(\mathbf{x}, \lambda)}{C_{Kub-Munk}(\mathbf{x}, \lambda)} = \frac{1}{\beta(\mathbf{x}, \lambda)}\frac{\partial \beta(\mathbf{x}, \lambda)}{\partial \lambda} + \frac{1}{E(\lambda)}\frac{\partial E(\lambda)}{\partial \lambda} \qquad [7.62]$$

As a result, if we differentiate this equation with respect to $\mathbf{x}$, then the illumination-dependent part will disappear and we will obtain a quantity that depends only on the spectral reflectance of the surface element:

$$\frac{\partial}{\partial \mathbf{x}}\{\frac{C_{Kub-Munk_\lambda}(\mathbf{x}, \lambda)}{C_{Kub-Munk}(\mathbf{x}, \lambda)}\} = \frac{\partial}{\partial \mathbf{x}}\{\frac{1}{\beta(\mathbf{x}, \lambda)}\frac{\partial \beta(\mathbf{x}, \lambda)}{\partial \lambda}\} \qquad [7.63]$$

Geusebroek *et al.* therefore introduced the following invariant characteristic:

$$X^N(P) = \frac{C^{\mathbb{G}\lambda\mathbf{x}}(P)C^{\mathbb{G}}(P) - C^{\mathbb{G}\lambda}(P)C^{\mathbb{G}\mathbf{x}}(P)}{(C^{\mathbb{G}}(P))^2} \qquad [7.64]$$

where $C^{\mathbb{G}\mathbf{x}}(P) = \frac{\partial C^{\mathbb{G}}(P)}{\partial \mathbf{x}}$ and $C^{\mathbb{G}\lambda\mathbf{x}}(P) = \frac{\partial C^{\mathbb{G}\lambda}(P)}{\partial \mathbf{x}}$.

Thus, in the case of a matte surface and locally constant illumination, Geusebroek *et al.* showed that for a given pixel $P$ the spatial derivative of the ratio between its component $C^{\mathbb{G}\lambda}(P)$ and its component $C^{\mathbb{G}}(P)$ does not depend on the intensity, direction, or color of illumination, and neither does it depend on the angle of observation.

### 7.3.3.2. *Spatial derivatives of van de Weijer et al.*

Van de Weijer *et al.* introduced invariant characteristics based on the four following hypotheses:

– Shafer's dichromatic model (see equation [7.4]): $C_{Shafer}(\mathbf{x}, \lambda) = m_{diff}(\theta).\beta(\mathbf{x}, \lambda).E(\mathbf{x}, \lambda) + m_{spec}(\theta, \alpha).F_{spec}(\mathbf{x}, \lambda).E(\mathbf{x}, \lambda)$;

– neutral specular reflection (see equation [7.7]): $F_{spec}(\mathbf{x}, \lambda) = F_{spec}(\mathbf{x})$;

– locally constant illumination color (see equation [7.15]): $E(\mathbf{x}, \lambda) = e(\mathbf{x}).E(\lambda)$;

– to determine the invariant characteristics, they assumed that the illumination color was known (hypothesis 13, page 252), but that its intensity was not. If the color was not known, they assumed the illumination to be white (see equation [7.17]): $E(\mathbf{x}, \lambda) = E(\mathbf{x})$. For the rest of the proof, we will use the assumption of a known but non-flat spectrum.

Thus, the color components $C^k(P)$, $k = R, G, B$, of a pixel $P$ observing the surface element at $\mathbf{x}$ can be estimated as:

$$C^k(P) = \int_\lambda m_{diff}(\theta).\beta(\mathbf{x}, \lambda).e(\mathbf{x}).E(\lambda)$$

$$+ m_{spec}(\theta, \alpha).F_{spec}(\mathbf{x}).e(\mathbf{x}).E(\lambda)d\lambda$$

$$= m_{diff}(\theta)e(\mathbf{x})\int_\lambda \beta(\mathbf{x}, \lambda).E(\lambda)d\lambda$$

$$\text{[7.65]}$$

$$+ m_{spec}(\theta, \alpha).F_{spec}(\mathbf{x}).e(\mathbf{x})\int_\lambda E(\lambda)d\lambda$$

$$= m_{diff}(\theta)e(\mathbf{x})C^k_{diff}(P) + n_{spec}(\theta, \alpha, \mathbf{x}).e(\mathbf{x}).C^k_{spec},$$

$$= e(\mathbf{x})(m_{diff}(\theta)C^k_{diff}(P) + n_{spec}(\theta, \alpha, \mathbf{x})C^k_{spec})$$

where:

$$\begin{cases} C^k_{diff}(P) = \int_\lambda \beta(\mathbf{x}, \lambda).E(\lambda).k(\lambda)d\lambda \\ C^k_{spec} = \int_\lambda E(\lambda).k(\lambda)d\lambda \\ n_{spec}(\theta, \alpha, \mathbf{x}) = m_{spec}(\theta, \alpha).F_{spec}(\mathbf{x}) \end{cases} \quad \text{[7.66]}$$

Differentiating this expression with respect to $\mathbf{x}$, we obtain:

$$C^k_{\mathbf{x}}(P) = e_{\mathbf{x}}(\mathbf{x})(m_{diff}(\theta)C^k_{diff}(P) + n_{spec}(\theta, \alpha, \mathbf{x})C^k_{spec})$$

$$+ e(\mathbf{x})(m_{diff_{\mathbf{x}}}(\theta)C^k_{diff}(P) + m_{diff}(\theta)C^k_{diff_{\mathbf{x}}}(P)$$

$$+ n_{spec_{\mathbf{x}}}(\theta, \alpha, \mathbf{x})C^k_{spec}),$$

$$\text{[7.67]}$$

$$= (e(\mathbf{x})m_{diff}(\theta))C^k_{diff_{\mathbf{x}}}(P)$$

$$+ (e_{\mathbf{x}}(\mathbf{x})m_{diff}(\theta) + e(\mathbf{x})m_{diff_{\mathbf{x}}}(\theta))C^k_{diff}(P)$$

$$+ (e_{\mathbf{x}}(\mathbf{x})n_{spec}(\theta, \alpha, \mathbf{x}) + e(\mathbf{x})n_{spec_{\mathbf{x}}}(\theta, \alpha, \mathbf{x}))C^k_{spec}$$

where the subscript $\mathbf{x}$ represents the spatial derivative.

It then follows that the spatial derivative $\mathbf{C_x}(P) = (C^R_{\mathbf{x}}(P),$ $C^G_{\mathbf{x}}(P), C^B_{\mathbf{x}}(P))$ of the color vector $\mathbf{C}(P) = (C^R(P), C^G(P),$ $C^B(P))$ of a pixel $P$ observing the surface element at $\mathbf{x}$ can be written as:

$$\mathbf{C_x}(P) = (e(\mathbf{x})m_{diff}(\theta))\mathbf{C}_{diff_\mathbf{x}}(P)$$
$$+ (e_\mathbf{x}(\mathbf{x})m_{diff}(\theta) + e(\mathbf{x})m_{diff_\mathbf{x}}(\theta))\mathbf{C}_{diff}(P) \qquad [7.68]$$
$$+ (e_\mathbf{x}(\mathbf{x})n_{spec}(\theta,\alpha,\mathbf{x}) + e(\mathbf{x})n_{spec_\mathbf{x}}(\theta,\alpha,\mathbf{x}))\mathbf{C}_{spec}$$

This indicates that the spatial derivative of the color vector in an image is the weighted sum of three vectors. Van de Weijer *et al.* associated each of the three corresponding directions with a physical phenomenon:

– $(e(\mathbf{x})m_{diff}(\theta))\mathbf{C}_{diff_\mathbf{x}}(P)$ is associated with the difference in spectral reflectance of the surfaces being considered in the derivative;

– $(e_\mathbf{x}(\mathbf{x})m_{diff}(\theta) + e(\mathbf{x})m_{diff_\mathbf{x}}(\theta))\mathbf{C}_{diff}(P)$ is associated with the difference in shadowing of the surfaces in question. Shadowing may be explained by the presence of an object between the illumination and the surface. Van de Weijer *et al.* associated this effect with the scalar $e_\mathbf{x}(\mathbf{x})m_{diff}(\theta)$, but it can also be explained by a variation in $\theta$, the angle formed by the light ray and the surface normal, and van de Weijer *et al.* associated this effect with the scalar $e(\mathbf{x})m_{diff_\mathbf{x}}(\theta)$. We note that if there is no specular reflection from the surfaces in question, then the color vector for pixel $P$ is $\mathbf{C}(P) = e(\mathbf{x})(m_{diff}(\theta)\mathbf{C}_{diff}(P)$. It then follows that the vector $(e_\mathbf{x}(\mathbf{x})m_{diff}(\theta) + e(\mathbf{x})m_{diff_\mathbf{x}}(\theta))\mathbf{C}_{diff}(P)$, explained by differences in shadowing between the surfaces, has the same direction as the color vector of the surface in question, in the case of a matte surface (no specular reflection);

– $(e_\mathbf{x}(\mathbf{x})n_{spec}(\theta,\alpha,\mathbf{x}) + e(\mathbf{x})n_{spec_\mathbf{x}}(\theta,\alpha,\mathbf{x}))\mathbf{C}_{spec}$ is associated with the difference in specular reflection between the surfaces in question. In the same way, this variation can be explained in terms of two effects. The scalar $e_\mathbf{x}n_{spec}(\theta,\alpha,\mathbf{x})$ represents a shadow contour superimposed on a specular reflection, whereas the scalar $e(\mathbf{x})n_{spec_\mathbf{x}}(\theta,\alpha,\mathbf{x})$ represents a variation of one or more of the following angles: direction of illumination, viewpoint, or surface orientation. Since $C_{spec}^k = \int_\lambda E(\lambda).k(\lambda)d\lambda$, we can deduce that the direction of this vector associated with the difference in specular reflection is that of the illumination color.

Through this analysis, van de Weijer *et al.* showed that it is possible to use the pixel color $\mathbf{C}(P) = (C^R(P), C^G(P), C^B(P))$ and the illumination color $(\int_\lambda E(\lambda).R(\lambda)d\lambda, \int_\lambda E(\lambda).V(\lambda)d\lambda, \int_\lambda E(\lambda).B(\lambda)d\lambda) = (E^R, E^G, E^B)$ to calculate the direction (in color space) of two of the causes of a contour:

– shadow direction: $\mathbf{O}(P) = \dfrac{(C^R(P), C^G(P), C^B(P))}{\sqrt{C^R(P)^2 + C^G(P)^2 + C^B(P)^2}}$;

– specular direction: $\mathbf{S} = \dfrac{(E^R, E^G, E^B)}{\sqrt{(E^R)^2 + (E^G)^2 + (E^B)^2}}$.

Based on these two directions, it is then possible to generate a third direction $\mathbf{H}$ that is perpendicular to both these vectors; van de Weijer *et al.* referred to this as the hue direction: $\mathbf{H} = \frac{\mathbf{O} \times \mathbf{S}}{|\mathbf{O} \times \mathbf{S}|}$, where $\times$ denotes the vector product. Van de Weijer *et al.* noted that this direction is not necessarily the one associated with the difference in spectral reflectance that was mentioned earlier, but that they could use the above analysis to deduce that variations in the hue direction $\mathbf{H}$ can only be due to a change in spectral reflectance of the surfaces in question. Klinker *et al.* [KLI 91] had already defined these directions in the context of image segmentation.

*- Shadow invariance [WEI 06]*

If the contours associated with a variation in shadowing have a direction (in color space) that is the same as the shadow direction $\mathbf{O}$, then when we calculate the color derivative $\mathbf{C_x}(P)$ for a pixel $P$, the projection of the vector $\mathbf{C_x}(P)$ onto the vector $\mathbf{O}(P)$: $(\mathbf{C_x}(P).\mathbf{O}(P))\mathbf{O}(P)$ gives us the part of the contour that can be explained by variations in shadowing. If this projection is subtracted from the derivative vector $\mathbf{C_x}(P)$, then the result will be independent of shadowing. Then, to determine a color characteristic $\mathbf{X}^{oq}(P)$ that is shadow invariant, van de Weijer *et al.* proposed to project the derivative of the color vector onto the shadow direction $\mathbf{O}(P)$ and to subtract this result from the derivative:

$$\mathbf{X}^{oq}(P) = \mathbf{C_x}(P) - (\mathbf{C_x}(P).\mathbf{O}(P))\mathbf{O}(P) \qquad [7.69]$$

This characteristic represents that part of the derivative that is not caused by a shadow contour, so it represents only spectral reflectance contours and specular reflection contours.

Van de Weijer *et al.* showed that this characteristic can be obtained by taking the spatial derivative of the components in the spherical color space $r\theta\varphi$ [WEI 06].

In addition, to render this characteristic invariant to the direction and intensity of illumination, they proposed to divide it by the norm of the color vector of the pixel in question [WEI 06]:

$$\mathbf{X}^{of}(P) = \frac{\mathbf{X}^{oq}(P)}{|\mathbf{C}(P)|} \tag{7.70}$$

The characteristic $\mathbf{X}^{of}(P)$ is known as the *shadow-shading full invariant*, while $\mathbf{X}^{oq}(P)$ is known as the *shadow-shading quasi-invariant* [WEI 06]. The authors showed that the *quasi-invariants* are more stable than the *full invariants* in the presence of noise and are more suitable for the extraction of key points than for the description of local regions around such points.

*- Reflection invariance [WEI 06]*

To determine a color characteristic $\mathbf{X}^{sq}(P)$ that is invariant under changes in reflections, van de Weijer *et al.* suggested projecting the derivative of the color vector onto the specular direction $\mathbf{S}$ and subtracting this results from the derivative:

$$\mathbf{X}^{sq}(P) = \mathbf{C_x}(P) - (\mathbf{C_x}(P).\mathbf{S}(P))\mathbf{S}(P) \tag{7.71}$$

This characteristic represents that part of the derivative that is not caused by a specular reflection contour, so it represents only spectral reflectance and shadow contours.

Van de Weijer *et al.* showed that this characteristic can be obtained by taking the spatial derivative of the components of the opponent color space o1o2o3 [WEI 06].

*- Shadow and reflection invariance [WEI 06]*

To determine a color characteristic $\mathbf{X}^{soq}(P)$ that is invariant under changes in shadowing and reflections, van de Weijer *et al.* suggested projecting the derivative of the color vector onto the hue direction $\mathbf{H}(P)$ [WEI 06]:

$$\mathbf{X}^{soq}(P) = (\mathbf{C_x}(P).\mathbf{H}(P))\mathbf{H}(P) \tag{7.72}$$

This characteristic represents that part of the derivative that is not caused either by a shadow contour or by a specular reflection contour, so it represents only spectral reflectance contours.

Van de Weijer *et al.* showed that this characteristic can be obtained by taking the spatial derivatives of the components of the HSI color space [WEI 06].

In addition, to render this characteristic invariant to the direction and intensity of illumination and to the viewpoint of the observer, they proposed to divide it by the saturation of the color of the pixel in question. The saturation is defined as the norm of the color vector $\mathbf{C}(P)$ after projection onto the plane perpendicular to the specular direction $\mathbf{S}$:

$$\mathbf{X}^{sof}(P) = \frac{\mathbf{X}^{soq}(P)}{|\mathbf{C}(P) - (\mathbf{C}(P).\mathbf{S})\mathbf{S}|} \tag{7.73}$$

The $\mathbf{X}^{sof}(P)$ characteristic is known as the *shadow-shading-specular full invariant*, while $\mathbf{X}^{soq}(P)$ is known as the *shadow-shading-specular quasi-invariant*.

In this section, we have listed most of the color-invariant characteristics used in object recognition applications, and in Appendix A, we list each characteristic along with its underlying hypotheses and the photometric variations under which they are invariant.

## 7.4. Conclusion

This chapter describes the latest color invariant characteristics used in the field of object recognition. Color information is crucial for object recognition since it increases the discriminating power of the system, while enabling descriptors to be normalized with respect to radiometric and photometric variations. However, this normalization must be adapted to the application so as to provide only those types of invariance that are necessary for the system, since any unnecessary normalization reduces the discrimination abilities of the characteristic. We have shown the ways in which color can be normalized to determine characteristics that are insensitive to certain photometric or radiometric variations. This normalization is based on hypotheses on color formation, the reflective properties of surface elements, the response of the sensors used in the acquisition system, the illumination characteristics, or directly on the model of photometric and radiometric variation. We have provided a list of color characteristics, which under these hypotheses, can be used to achieve insensitivity to a range of different types of variation.

We have seen that the first two stages in the process of image searching involve the extraction of key points and the construction of a description of their neighborhood. In the next chapter, we will see how the various detectors and descriptors make use of the colorimetric invariances discussed in this chapter.

## 7.5. Bibliography

[BAR 02] BARNARD K., MARTIN L., COATH A., FUNT B., "A comparison of computational color constancy algorithms II. experiments with image data", *IEEE Transactions on Image Processing*, vol. 11, no. 9, p. 985-996, 2002.

[BEC 87] BECKMANN P., SPIZZICHINO A., *The Scattering of Electromagnetic Waves from Rough Surfaces*, Artech House Inc, 2nd edition, 1987.

[CIO 01] CIOCCA G., MARINI D., RIZZI A., SCHETTINI R., ZUFFI S., "On pre-filtering with Retinex in color image retrieval", *Proceedings of the SPIE Conference on Internet Imaging II*, vol. 4311, p. 140-147, 2001.

[FIN 94a] FINLAYSON G.D., DREW M.S., FUNT B.V., "Spectral sharpening: sensor transformations for improved color constancy", *Journal of the Optical Society of America*, vol. 11, no. 5, p. 1553-1563, 1994.

[FIN 94b] FINLAYSON G., DREW M., FUNT B., "Color constancy: generalized diagonal transforms suffice", *Journal of the Optical Society of America*, vol. 11, no. 11, p. 3011-3020, 1994.

[FIN 95] FINLAYSON G., CHATTERJEE S., FUNT B., "Color angle invariants for object recognition", *Proceedings of the 3rd IS&T/SID Color Imaging Conference*, p. 44-47, 1995.

[FIN 98] FINLAYSON G., SCHIELE B., CROWLEY J., "Comprehensive colour image normalization", *Lecture Notes in Computer Science*, vol. 1406, p. 475-490, 1998.

[FIN 01a] FINLAYSON G., HORDLEY S., "Colour constancy at a pixel", *Journal of the Optical Society of America*, vol. 18, no. 2, p. 253-264, 2001.

[FIN 01b] FINLAYSON G., HORDLEY S., HUBEL P., "Color by correlation: a simple, unifying framework for color constancy", *IEEE Transactions on Pattern Analysis and Machine Intelligence*, vol. 23, no. 11, p. 1209-1221, 2001.

[FIN 04a] FINLAYSON G., DREW M., LU C., "Intrinsic images by entropy minimization", *Proceedings of the European Conference on Computer Vision*, p. 582-595, 2004.

[FIN 04b] FINLAYSON G.D., TREZZI E., "Shades of gray and color constancy", *Proceedings of Color Imaging Conference*, p. 37-41, 2004.

[FIN 05] FINLAYSON G., HORDLEY S., SCHAEFER G., TIAN G.Y., "Illuminant and device invariant colour using histogram equalisation", *Pattern Recognition*, vol. 38, p. 179-190, 2005.

[FUN 95] FUNT B., FINLAYSON G., "Color constant color indexing", *IEEE Transactions on Pattern Analysis and Machine Intelligence*, vol. 17, no. 5, p. 522-529, 1995.

[FUN 99] FUNT B., CARDEI V.C., BARNARD K., Method of estimating chromaticity of illumination using neural networks, United States Patent, no. 5,907,629, USA, 1999.

[GER 88] GERSHON R., JEPSON A.D., TSOTSOS J.K., "From [R,G,B] to surface reflectance: computing color constant descriptors in images", *Perception*, p. 755-758, 1988.

[GEU 00] GEUSEBROEK J.-M., VAN DEN BOOMGAARD R., SMEULDERS A.W.M., DEV A., "Color and scale: the spatial structure of color images", *Proceedings of the European Conference on Computer Vision*, p. 331-341, 2000.

[GEU 01] GEUSEBROEK J.M., VAN DEN BOOMGAARD R., SMEULDERS A.W.M. GEERTS H., "Color invariance", *IEEE Transactions on Pattern Analysis and Machine Intelligence*, vol. 23, no. 12, p. 1338-1350, 2001.

[GEV 99] GEVERS T., SMEULDERS A., "Color-based object recognition", *Pattern Recognition*, vol. 32, p. 453-464, 1999.

[HEA 95] HEALEY G., SLATER D., "Global color contancy: recognition of objects by use of illumination invariant properties of color distributions", *Journal of the Optical Society America*, vol. 11, no. 11, p. 3003-3010, 1995.

[ITU 90] (ITU) I. R. C. C., Basic Parameter Values for the HDTV Standard for the studio and for International Programme Exchange, Report no. 709-2, CCIR Recommendation, 1990.

[KLI 91] KLINKER G., SHAFER S., KANADE T., "A physical approach to color image understanding", *International Journal of Computer Vision*, vol. 4, no. 1, p. 7-38, 1991.

[KOU 00] KOUBAROULIS D., MATAS J., KITTLER J., "The multimodal signature method: an efficiency and sensitivity study", *Proceedings of the 15th International Conference on Pattern Recognition*, vol. 3, Los Alamitos, USA, IEEE Computer Society Press, p. 379-382, 2000.

[KRI 70] VON KRIES J., "Influence of adaptation on the effects produced by luminous stimuli", MACADAM D.L. (ed.), *Sources of Color Vision*, MIT Press, Cambridge, 1970.

[KUB 48] KUBELKA P., "New contribution to the optics of intensity light-scattering materials, part I", *Journal of the Optical Society of America A*, vol. 38, no. 5, p. 448-457, 1948.

[LAN 77] LAND E., "The retinex theory of color vision", *Scientific American*, p. 108-129, 1977.

[LEN 99] LENZ R., TRAN L., MEER P., "Moment based normalization of color images", *IEEE Workshop on Multimedia Signal Processing*, p. 129-132, 1999.

[MIN 04] MINDRU F., TUYTELAARS T., GOOL L.V., MOONS T., "Moment invariants for recognition under changing viewpoint and illumination", *Computer Vision and Image Understanding*, vol. 1, no. 3, p. 3-27, 2004.

[MUS 07] MUSELET D., FUNT B., MACAIRE L., "Object recognition and pose estimation across illumination change", *Proceedings of the 2nd International Conference on Computer Vision Theory and Applications*, p. 264-267, 2007.

[NAY 96] NAYAR S., BOLLE R., "Reflectance based object recognition", *International Journal of Computer Vision*, vol. 17, no. 3, p. 219-240, 1996.

[SHA 85] SHAFER S.A., "Using color to separate reflection components", *Color Research and Application*, vol. 10, no. 4, p. 210-218, 1985.

[SWA 91] SWAIN M.J., BALLARD D.H., "Color indexing", *International Journal of Computer Vision*, vol. 7, no. 1, p. 11-32, 1991.

[WEI 05]  VAN DE WEIJER J., GEVERS T., GEUSEBROEK J.-M., "Edge and corner detection by photometric quasi-invariants", *IEEE Transactions on Pattern Analysis and Machine Intelligence*, vol. 27, no. 4, p. 625-630, 2005.

[WEI 06]  VAN DE WEIJER J., GEVERS T., SMEULDERS A., "Robust photometric invariant features from the colour tensor", *IEEE Transactions on Image Processing*, vol. 15, no. 1, p. 118-127, 2006.

Chapter 8

# Color Key Point Detectors
# and Local Color Descriptors

## 8.1. Introduction

In this chapter, we will continue the theme of the previous chapter, that of object recognition in non-controlled conditions (multiple objects, occlusions, changes of viewpoint, and illumination). We have seen that, in this case, the classical solution involves describing the content of an image in terms of a set of local descriptors extracted around key points. There are many different possible key point (or region) detectors [LI 08, MIK 05b, TUY 08] as well as a range of local descriptors [LI 08, MIK 05a] that operate purely using pixel gray levels within an image. The aim of this chapter is to show how color information can be integrated into the very first stages of the description of a color image to increase the effectiveness of an object recognition system. For this, we propose to discuss key point detectors and region detectors in the first part of this chapter, and discuss descriptors in the second part.

---

Chapter written by Damien MUSELET and Xiaohu SONG.

## 8.2. Color key point and region detectors

We will show how color information can be taken into account during the key point or region detection phase, as well as consider the advantages of this information compared to simple gray levels. For this, we will compare different detectors. We will first briefly recall the main quality criteria that can be used to evaluate a detector. We will then consider key point detection. In particular, we will discuss the extension of first and second order partial derivative matrices to include color, as well as the curvature of iso-intensity lines. We will then consider the detection of characteristic color regions, a problem which largely consists of finding regions whose boundaries are stable over a wide range of variations of some parameters. It is difficult to treat key region detection without considering the problem of visual attention. Since the human visual system has a tendency to systematically focus on certain regions within an image, a number of methods propose to make use of this visually emergent information to reproduce this behavior and use it to extract the most relevant regions. We will show how this information can be exploited and the importance of including color information in this process. Finally, we will show how color can be integrated into a learning phase that can be used to improve the detection of key regions within images.

### 8.2.1. *Detector quality criteria*

A very large number of key point or region detectors have been reported in the literature, and although some are much more widely used than others, none of them give excellent results under all circumstances. The choice of detector must be made on the basis of the specification for a particular application. It is therefore necessary to know the strengths and weaknesses of each detector to make the best choice for a given problem. A number of different detector quality criteria exist [TUY 08], and we will not cover all of them in this chapter. Instead, we propose to group them into three main criteria: repeatability, discriminating power, and complexity.

A detector is said to be *repeatable* if it detects the same points (or regions) in two images, both depicting the same scene, but acquired under different conditions. These might include a change in illumination, viewpoint, or different acquisition sensors. Repeatability therefore measures the robustness of the detector in the face of variations in acquisition conditions.

The *discriminating power* of a detector describes the quantity of discriminating information that is contained within the regions around these points. There are several different methods for comparing the quantity of discriminating information. The first method involves testing different detectors for a given application, keeping all the other elements of the object recognition system (image database, local descriptor, comparison measure) constant, and comparing the recognition levels that are achieved [STO 07]. The greater the recognition level, the greater is the quantity of discriminating information provided. The second method is based on information theory, which measures the quantity of information using entropy. Thus, by choosing a local descriptor and an image database, the relative discriminating powers of the detectors being tested are estimated by comparing their associated entropies [SEB 06b]. The final method uses principal component analysis (PCA) over windows surrounding the detected points [HEI 04]. All these windows are scaled to the same size and expressed in vector form via a raster scan. The windows extracted by a detector are therefore presented in the form of a set of vectors, to which the PCA is applied. The most discriminating principal components give an idea of the content of the set of windows. The discriminating power of a detector is then estimated by comparing its principal components to those obtained by extracting random windows from within the same image database. If the principal components of a detector are similar to those obtained randomly, the detector is not considered to be a good discriminator [HEI 04].

The *complexity* is a measure of the calculation time required for the detection of key points within an image.

Tuytelaars *et al.* introduced other criteria such as locality or localization [TUY 08]. Locality is based around the fact that the detector should use very local information without extending the neighborhood too widely, thereby making it more robust in the face of occlusions. Localization considers whether the detector precisely identifies the elements for which it has been defined. A corner detector must extract corners from an image effectively. These last criteria will not be taken into account in our analysis.

### 8.2.2. *Color key points*

We will discuss the main approaches for key point detection using color information, and we will see that most of these are extensions of gray level detectors based on the Harris matrix or the Hessian matrix.

#### 8.2.2.1. *Color Harris detector*

To understand the color Harris detector, we should first recall the gray level Harris detector [HAR 88], which is itself an extension of the Moravec detector [MOR 77]. The Moravec detector measures the similarity between a local window and the windows of the same size around it. It is based on the principle that if we are positioned in a homogeneous region, there will be high similarity in all directions. If instead we are on a contour, the similarity will be high along the direction of a contour and low in the direction perpendicular to the contour. Finally, the similarity will be low in all directions if we are in a corner. For each image pixel, Moravec therefore calculates the differences between the window around the pixel being considered and the windows around the neighboring pixels in all directions. Each pixel is then characterized by the minimum value of these sum-squared differences around it. Corners are extracted by detection of local *maxima* within this new image.

Based on the principle that the Moravec detector analyzes correlations between neighboring windows, Harris and Stephens proposed the use of the autocorrelation matrix [HAR 88]. This matrix $M$ consists of the first-order local partial derivatives of the image:

$$M = \begin{pmatrix} I_x^2 & I_x I_y \\ I_x I_y & I_y^2 \end{pmatrix} \qquad [8.1]$$

where $I_x$ and $I_y$ are the partial derivatives of the image calculated along the $x$ and $y$ directions, respectively. Here, we present a simplified version of this matrix, since we have not mentioned the scales of the derivative and the smoothing (Gaussian).

The eigenvalues of this matrix represent the main variations along two orthogonal directions (the eigenvectors) in the neighborhood in question. Thus, if both eigenvalues are small, then we are in a homogeneous region; if one is high and the other is low then we are on a contour; and if both are high then we are on a corner. In practice, rather than calculating the eigenvalues in each neighborhood, which may be very costly in terms of computation time Harris and Stephens suggested a measure based on the determinant and the trace of the matrix $M$, which is high in the presence of a corner.

The Harris detector is the best known and most widely used key point detector. One of its advantages is that it only uses the first derivatives of the image, which makes it less sensitive to noise then detectors that use higher-order derivatives. However, Harris and Stephens applied their detector to gray level images, and it is not trivial to extend the matrix to color images. Montesinos $et$ $al.$ proposed an autocorrelation matrix that takes into account the 3D nature of the color coordinates of each pixel [MON 98]:

$$M_{Mont} = \begin{pmatrix} R_x^2 + G_x^2 + B_x^2 & R_x R_y + G_x G_y + B_x B_y \\ R_x R_y + G_x G_y + B_x B_y & R_y^2 + G_y^2 + B_y^2 \end{pmatrix} \quad [8.2]$$

where $R_x$, $G_x$, $B_x$ and $R_y$, $G_y$, $B_y$ are the red, green, and blue partial derivatives of the image, calculated along the $x$ and $y$ axes, respectively.

This color Harris detector is the most widely used color corner detector [GAB 05, MON 98, MON 00, GOU 00, STO 07, SEB 06b, SEB 06a, WEI 05]. Its use in all these references demonstrates the advantages of using color in key point detection. Thus, by comparing the gray level Harris detector with the color Harris detector, we can quantify the advantages and disadvantages of considering color information.

Gouet $et$ $al.$ carried out a study comparing the color Harris detector with the gray level Harris detector [GOU 00]. They tested both these detectors on synthetic images to be able to verify precisely the accuracy of the points that were detected. In this study, they showed that color can improve the repeatability of the Harris detector in cases where the image undergoes a 2D rotation, variations in illumination and changes in viewpoint.

Although the initial color Harris detector was defined in the RGB space, Sebe *et al.* also tested it in two other spaces [SEB 06b]: the opponent color space o1o2o3 [WEI 05] and the invariant space obtained by calculating the ratios of components between neighboring pixels [GEV 99] (see section 7.3.1.2). They also applied the *color boosting* method, which we will discuss later in this chapter. They performed their tests using an image database of realistic scenes [MIK 04]. Their findings were as follows:

– repeatability: for certain variations, such as changes in illumination or JPEG compression, the gray level Harris detector gave better results than color detectors. For other types of variation (blurring, rotation, change in viewpoint, or scale) the results were generally rather similar for both the color and gray level variants;

– discriminating power: for this criterion, there is no doubt in the advantages of color. Having said that, as we emphasized earlier, the outcome of tests of discriminating power depend strongly on the descriptor that is used. In their analysis, Sebe *et al.* therefore tested two descriptors, one, gray level and the other, color. They showed that color detection improves the discriminating power compared to a gray level detector only if the descriptor being used makes use of color information, and it does not lead to an improvement if the descriptor only makes use of gray level information. This test can also be used to demonstrate that the more repeatable a detector is, the less good it will be at discrimination. A compromise is therefore required between repeatability and discriminating power;

– complexity: color point detector necessarily results in a higher complexity than gray level detection. Having said that, the analysis of Sebe *et al.* showed that fewer points are required in the color case to obtain equivalent results in terms of discriminating power compared to what is seen with gray level-only results. The increase in complexity required for the extraction can therefore be partially offset by a reduction in the number of points that need to be detected.

### 8.2.2.2. *Color Hessian*

An alternative to the Harris detector is a detector based on the Hessian matrix [BEA 78]. The Hessian matrix $H$ is obtained from the Taylor expansion of the image function $I$:

$$H = \begin{pmatrix} I_{xx} & I_{xy} \\ I_{xy} & I_{yy} \end{pmatrix} \qquad [8.3]$$

where $I_{xx}$, $I_{xy}$, and $I_{yy}$ are the second partial derivatives along $xx$, $xy$, and $yy$. These derivatives contain shape information since they describe the variations of iso-surface normals. As with the Harris matrix, here we have shown a simplified version of the Hessian matrix without discussing the scales of the differentiation and (Gaussian) smoothing. It should be noted that the trace of the Hessian matrix is the Laplacian of the image. Beaudet [BEA 78] showed that the local *maxima* of the determinant of the Hessian matrix can be used to detect the key points of an image in a rotation-invariant manner.

We will describe three interesting extensions of the original Hessian matrix to color images. The first is that of Ming *et al.* [MIN 07], which uses the second derivatives of a color image as a weighted sum of the second derivatives of each component:

$$H_{Ming} = \begin{pmatrix} rR_{xx} + gG_{xx} + bB_{xx} & rR_{xy} + gG_{xy} + bB_{xy} \\ rR_{xy} + gG_{xy} + bB_{xy} & rR_{yy} + gG_{yy} + bB_{yy} \end{pmatrix} \qquad [8.4]$$

where $R_{xx}$, $G_{xx}$, $B_{xx}$, etc. are the red, green, and blue second partial derivatives of the image calculated along the $xx$ directions and $r$, $g$, and $b$ are the RGB components normalized by their sum, $R + G + B$.

This weighting can be used to intensify color contours of a dominant component while minimizing the derivative of a component whose intensity is less significant compared to the others.

The second color extension of the Hessian matrix is the quaternion Hessian matrix [SHI 08]. In their studies, Shi *et al.* did not use it for corner detection but rather for the detection of elongated objects (vessels, tubes, etc.) in color images. This type of object can be extracted using eigenvalue analysis of the Hessian matrix, and Shi *et al.* suggested basing this on the quaternion Hessian matrix. They used the quaternion singular value decomposition (QSVD) to obtain these eigenvalues and extract elongated objects in a more efficient way than would be possible using the gray level Hessian matrix.

The third extension was suggested by Rojas Vigo *et al.* [VIG 10]. It involves replacing the scalar elements of the Hessian matrix with vectors, calculating the vector determinant of this matrix and detecting the local *maxima* of the norm of these vector determinants. Since the determinant of the gray level Hessian matrix used by Beaudet is defined as $Det_{gray} = I_{xx} * I_{yy} - I_{xy}^2$, Rojas Vigo *et al.* suggested extending this detector to color images by replacing the scalars $I_{xx}$, $I_{yy}$, and $I_{xy}$ with the vectors $(R_{xx} G_{xx} B_{xx})^T$, $(R_{yy} G_{yy} B_{yy})^T$ and $(R_{xy} G_{xy} B_{xy})^T$, respectively and calculating the norm of the vector obtained using this process: $Det_{col} = ||(R_{xx} R_{yy} G_{xx} G_{yy} B_{xx} B_{yy})^T - (R_{xy}^2 G_{xy}^2 B_{xy}^2)^T||$.

### 8.2.2.3. *Color Harris-Laplace and Hessian-Laplace*

The Harris and Hessian detectors identify corners in an image, but do not provide any information on the size of the region that is to be characterized around these points. The resultant descriptors are very sensitive to scale variation in images. Mikolajczyk *et al.* [MIK 04] therefore introduced detectors known as Harris-Laplace and Hessian-Laplace detectors, which can automatically detect the scale associated with the corners extracted by these algorithms. Their approach involves smoothing the image around each detected corner using a Gaussian filter, before convolving the result with a Laplacian filter. These Laplacian and Gaussian filters can be combined together in advance to produce a "Laplacian of Gaussian" (LoG) filter. Thus, for a given corner, if we use different values for the variance of the Gaussian, we can obtain a sequence of different values using the LoG convolution filter. If this sequence of values shows a significant local maximum, i.e. one greater than a specific threshold, then the variance associated with this maximum is used as a measure of the scale of this particular corner. If there is no local maximum, or it is too low, the corner is removed from the list of corners. These Harris-Laplace and Hessian-Laplace detectors were themselves first defined for gray level images. Stoettinger *et al.* [STO 07] suggested using color information for this automatic scale detection. Since the Laplacian method for automatic scale extraction works on 1D data (pixel gray levels), the authors suggested converting 3D color information into 1D using principal component analysis (PCA), keeping only the eigenvector with the largest associated eigenvalue. This PCA is applied to the 3D color vectors of every pixel in the input image. Stoettinger *et al.* argued that it is better to determine the scale using this principal component, which represents the axis with the greatest variation in pixel color within the image, rather than the greatest variation in gray level.

Ming *et al.* [MIN 07] also proposed a way of extending automatic scale detection to include color information. They elected to replace the gray level Laplacian with the trace of the color Hessian matrix that they defined as:

$$Laplace_{Ming} = rR_{xx} + gG_{xx} + bB_{xx} + rR_{yy} + gG_{yy} + bB_{yy} \quad [8.5]$$

### 8.2.3. *Color key regions*

The methods that we will describe in this section are based on region analysis (rather than point analysis) in images.

#### 8.2.3.1. *Searching for the most stable color regions*

This approach, known as MSER for *Maximally Stable Extremal Region* was introduced for gray level imaging by Matas *et al.* [MAT 02]. It involves selecting a threshold $t$ and extracting the regions of connected pixels that contain a gray level greater than this threshold. By increasing the threshold value $t$, the regions will change, and the regions that are retained are the ones that are most stable (in terms of number of pixels) over the greatest ranges of variation in $t$. Forssén [FOR 07] extended this approach to color images using a slightly different method. To begin with, he calculated a color distance $(Chi^2)$ between each neighboring pixel pair $(P_1, P_2)$ in the image. Next, he created regions of connected pixels within the image by successively combining neighboring pixels whose color distance is less than or equal to a threshold $t$. Then, in the same way as with the MSER method, he increased the threshold value $t$ and examined how the regions changed. The regions he kept were those that remained stable over a large range of variation of $t$.

### 8.2.3.2. *Hierarchical color segmentation*

Vázquez-Martin *et al.* developed a color region detector based on image segmentation [VÁZ 09]. This consists of two different stages. The first uses a hierarchical algorithm (a pyramid algorithm) to extract homogeneous color regions. They calculated a simple distance in RGB color space to decide whether or not two sub-windows should be associated with the same region. This first stage returns a vastly over-segmented image, and the second stage involves fusing neighboring regions on the basis of three criteria:

– the mean colors of the two regions. Here, the colors are represented in L*a*b* space and the Euclidean distance is calculated to decide whether the two regions should be fused;

– the number of edge pixels found by the Canny edge detector along the boundary between two regions. For this criterion, the Canny detector is applied to the image, and the regions are fused if the number of contour pixels along the boundary between the two regions is small;

– the stereo disparity between the two regions. In the application described by Vázquez-Martin *et al.* the images were acquired by a stereo vision system and neighboring regions were fused if the values of the disparities (indicative of depth) for both regions were similar. In the case of a monocular acquisition system, only the first two criteria are used.

The authors therefore used these three parameters for their dissimilarity criterion between the two regions. They showed that this criterion can be used to extract regions with a great deal of stability in the face of variations in acquisition conditions.

Forssén *et al.* used a similar approach for region detection in color images [FOR 09]. They created a pyramid structure from the image, where at each higher layer, sets of connected pixels with similar mean colors at the previous layer were combined together. Each resultant region was represented by an ellipse whose parameters (major axis, minor axis, and orientation) were estimated from the inertia matrix representing the shape of the region. The color distance used to compare the means of each pixel set was calculated in the YCbCr space.

### 8.2.4. *Simulation of human visual system*

The human visual system is able to extract an extremely large quantity of information from an image in a short period of time (a few ocular saccades), since it is able to quickly process information-rich regions known as visually salient regions [ITT 98]. A number of studies have attempted to reproduce this behavior automatically to identify the salient regions within an image [ITT 98, DIN 08]. Some of these studies have shown that the use of such visual saliency information could improve the performance of object recognition systems [RUT 04, WAL 05]. Since the majority of visual saliency maps are based, among other criteria, on color [JOS 05], we propose to show in this section how visual attention can be integrated into a system for identifying the most significant key points or regions.

Gao *et al.* and Walther *et al.* [GAO 08, WAL 05] worked from the principle that the human visual system first makes use of information extracted from salient regions in images to recognize objects, and so the key points must themselves be extracted from these regions. They, therefore, proposed to apply the model of Itti *et al.* [ITT 98] to color images, which they analyzed to extract the visually salient regions and only retained key points that lay within those regions. To do this, they applied the well-known SIFT point detector, based on a difference of Gaussians (DoG) approach, to the salient regions. This detector only uses gray level information, but the Itti model takes into account color information to extract the salient regions. Thus, the authors showed that by retaining less than 8% of the key points within an image (those in the salient regions), they were still able to obtain the same results as if they had included all the originally detected points.

In a similar way, Walther *et al.* [WAL 05] compared a random selection of SIFT points to a selection based on visual saliency. They showed that the performance (measured in terms of correct associations of detected regions) increased from 12% to 49% when visual saliency was used as a criterion. Both these studies showed that, following gray level-based key point detection, it is convenient to use color (in the context of visual saliency) to filter these points and only retain the most pertinent ones. In the same context, Marques *et al.* [MAR 06] suggested extracting the most salient regions within an image by combining two different models of visual saliency. Their approach involved extracting the centers of the salient regions obtained using the Itti model and performing a region-growing process seeded from these points but based on boundaries obtained using the Stentiford model [STE 03].

Würz *et al.* [WUR 00] attempted to simulate the human visual system for color corner detection. They initially worked not with red, green, and blue components but with the achromatic and chromatic opponent red-green and yellow-blue components. They then applied Gabor filters to each component image, with different scales and different orientations, to simulate the *simple cells* and *complex cells* found in the primary visual cortex. The output from these filters was differentiated in the direction perpendicular to the orientation of the Gabor filter that was used. The first derivative is calculated to simulate *single end-stopped cells*, and the second derivative is used to simulate *double end-stopped cells*. Since it has been shown that end-stopped cells respond very strongly to corners, Würz *et al.* suggested extracting the local *maxima* of these derivatives as a method of corner detection.

More recently, Heidemann [HEI 04] suggested extracting the centers of local color symmetry from images as points of interest. The motivation for this was based on the results from a study by Locher *et al.* [LOC 87] showing that the eye is attracted by symmetric patterns within images. Reisfeld *et al.* [REI 95] had previously developed a center of symmetry detector for gray level images, and Heideman extended this approach to color images. This approach identified symmetries not only between color contours within a single component (red-red, green-green, or blue-blue), but also between color contours across different components (for example red-green symmetry). The symmetry value for a point is then the sum of the symmetries for all combinations of color components. Heidemann showed that the points detected by this method are very robust to changes in illumination between two images. This is because a point that is the center of local symmetry under one set of lighting conditions will still be the center of symmetry under different lighting, even if the colors around it are different.

**8.2.5.** *Learning for detection*

The methods in the previous section use ascending mechanisms to detect key regions in images. These ascending mechanisms are analogous to the process of unconscious visual attention in the human brain. Distinct from this is the concept of conscious visual attention, which is determined by the task being performed. For example, when we are behind the wheel of a car, our attention is drawn more to road signs than when we are on foot, even when presented with the same view in front of us. In the context of object recognition, the task is simple: we must detect as quickly as possible the regions that will enable us to identify a given object. To simulate these descending mechanisms, a number of researchers have suggested that a learning phase be used to detect key regions or points. Here, we will describe various approaches that use color in this context.

Van de Weijer *et al.* [VAZ 10, WEI 06a] suggested applying color preprocessing to images, with the aim of increasing the discriminating power of the points extracted by classical detectors. Specifically, the authors made use of the information theory, which states that the rarer an event, the more pertinent the information that it contains. Thus, for a given image database, they calculated the marginal derivatives (red, green, and blue) over a large number of pixels and plotted their amplitudes in 3D RGB color space. They observed that iso-probability (iso-frequency) surfaces formed ellipsoids in this space, rather than spheres. This indicates that the amplitude of the gradient at a given pixel cannot be used to determine the probability that this gradient will be encountered, i.e. the discriminating power of the key point in question. Its discriminating power will depend on the shape of the ellipsoid that is formed. To directly link the amplitude of the color gradient at a particular point with its discriminating power, van de Weijer *et al.* proposed applying a linear transformation to the RGB pixel components to transform these ellipsoids into spheres centered on $(0, 0, 0)$. Then, following this transformation, the amplitude of the color gradient at a particular point will be directly related to the probability that this value will appear, and hence to the discriminating power of that particular point. Following this preprocessing stage, the color Harris detector can be applied to detect corners with strong discriminating powers, since the

Harris detector detects pixels that have a high gradient along particular directions. Experimental results have shown that this preprocessing, known as *color boosting*, can be used to significantly improve object recognition results for the image databases that were studied.

Both the approaches make use of a training phase to enable the system to classify image pixels into two categories: pixels representing an object and pixels representing the background. Only the pixels representing an object will be used when describing the content of the image. Moosmann *et al.* [MOO 06] suggested that the training phase should take place in the Hue-Luminance-Saturation (HLS) color space, and that wavelet transforms should be calculated for each color plane over a randomly-sized window around pixels that are themselves drawn randomly from all the images in the database. All these windows were resized into $16 \times 16$ windows, which resulted in a color descriptor with 768 elements ($16 \times 16 \times 3$) for each window. All the training images were annotated, so that each random window had a known class (background or object). Moosmann *et al.* then created decision trees that could be used to rapidly classify each pixel into background or object for a new unknown image. This method enabled them to detect object pixels within an image and limit the information extraction to these pixels without degrading the object recognition results.

Alexe *et al.* [ALE 10] suggested reducing the size of the local descriptors used to perform the classification into background or object windows. They proposed to use four parameters to describe an object window. The first of these is a form of visual saliency since it detected regions that appeared only rarely in the image. It was based on the spectral residual of the Fourier transform applied to each color plane. The second is known as color contrast, and is based on the distance between the color histograms of the window in question and the neighboring windows. The histograms were calculated in L*a*b* space. The third parameter uses contour density information along the boundaries of the window. The contours were extracted using the Canny detector. The final parameter requires the image to first be segmented, and counts the number of the resultant regions that intersect the boundaries of the window. If this number is high, it indicates that the window contains just part of the object. This parameter can be used to extract object windows that contain complete objects. The authors then proposed to train their algorithm on these parameters using an annotated image database containing objects and background. They then showed that the trained model could be used to detect objects within images, thereby limiting the number of local descriptors that need to be extracted by restricting the calculation to object windows.

## 8.3. Local color descriptors

Once the key points (or regions) have been detected, local descriptors must be extracted from the regions around these points. For this stage, SIFT is the most commonly-used descriptor [LOW 04]. It consists of local histograms of gradient orientation, so it mainly uses shape information. A recent study compared the levels of object recognition using the SIFT descriptor with classical color descriptors such as color histograms calculated in different color spaces and color moments. The results showed the superiority of the SIFT descriptor [SAN 10a]. However, the images used to test the descriptors were of objects for which color information would also appear to be a useful discriminator. It therefore seems sensible to combine color information and shape information together to improve the level of successful recognition. In this section, we will discuss how color information can be integrated into an object recognition system. We will highlight four main approaches that can be used to combine color and shape information. The first simply involves calculating a shape descriptor and a color descriptor and concatenating the two. The second involves two successive image comparison stages – one using color information and the other, shape information. The third compares the images using a shape descriptor and a color descriptor in parallel, most commonly using them independently, and then in the final stage the shape and color distances are fused. The final approach makes use of spatio-colorimetric descriptors, which are structured so as to describe both the color and shape of objects. It should be noted in the following sections that many color descriptors make use of the colorimetric invariances described in the previous chapter. We will refer to these invariants, listing the page on which they can be found in the preceding chapter.

### 8.3.1. *Concatenation of two types of descriptors*

We will begin by describing some methods that simply combine the two different descriptor families by concatenation.

Quelhas *et al.* [QUE 06], along with the majority of other authors, suggested using the SIFT descriptor to represent local shape information. Since the SIFT descriptor is 128 elements in size, Quelhas *et al.* suggested applying a principal component analysis (PCA) to reduce this size to 44 elements. The color information within the region is summarized in the form of 6 values: its mean and standard deviation as calculated for each of the color components in L*u*v* space. The authors suggested weighting the two descriptors during the concatenation process to ascribe more or less importance to color relative to shape, and following various tests on the database used by Vogel *et al.* [VOG 04] they selected a weight of 0.8 for shape and 0.2 for color. With this procedure, recognition rates were of the order of 63% when using shape alone, 54% using color alone, and 66.5% for the combination they suggested.

Van de Weijer *et al.* [WEI 06b] also suggested concatenating the SIFT descriptor with a range of local color histograms. These histograms are calculated based on various color components:

– the normalized color components $C^r$, $C^g$ (2D) (see page 263);

– hue (1D);

– the opponent angle (1D) [WEI 05], based on the ratio of derivatives in the opponent color space $o_1$ $o_2$ $o_3$ (see page 278);

– the spherical angle (1D) [WEI 05], based on the ratio of derivatives in spherical color space $r\theta\varphi$ (see page 278);

– the normalized components using Finlayson's method [FIN 98] (see page 263).

In addition, the authors suggested that to obtain robust histograms, each occurrence of these components should be weighted according to their instability. They retained the 128 elements of SIFT and expressed the histograms in terms of 37 or 121 elements, depending on whether 1D or 2D data were being considered. The SIFTs were combined into a single color histogram each time, thereby giving five combinations to be tested. Experimentally, they used weights of 1 for shape and 0.6 for color. They tested the performance of the descriptors under three different conditions: 1) Variable illumination and fixed viewpoint; 2) Fixed illumination and variable viewpoint; 3) Illumination and viewpoint both variable. In the first case, they showed that addition of color information to the shape descriptor provided very little additional information. In the second case, the color descriptor gave better results than the shape descriptor, and the addition of shape information to the color information did not result in increased performance. In the third case, the authors showed that the best descriptor is the one that combines both color and shape.

Dahl *et al.* [DAH 08] decided to summarize the color information in a detected region in terms of its mean in the RGB space. They recommended first applying a equalization histogram to each component to obtain values that were less sensitive to illumination [FIN 05] (see page 266 for justification). Their proposed descriptor is a concatenation of SIFTs whose dimension has been reduced to 12 and a 3D color descriptor, with equal weightings of 0.5 for shape and 0.5 for color. Their tests were performed on the image database provided by H. Stewénius and D. Nistér[1], and the tests revealed that even very simplistic color information can improve by 7% on the best results obtained using SIFT alone.

Like van de Weijer *et al.*, Zhang *et al.* combined SIFT descriptors with local color histograms [ZHA 07], electing to work with the following color components:

– the normalized components $C^r$, $C^g$, each quantized into nine levels;

– hue, quantized into 36 levels;

– the $l_1$, $l_2$ components [GEV 99], each quantized into nine levels (see page 260).

---

1 http://www.vis.uky.edu/stewe/ukbench/.

To add spatial information to the colorimetric descriptor, the authors proposed to divide the circular region around the key points that were detected into three concentric rings, and to calculate the histograms for each of these rings. The color descriptor here is a concatenation of these three color histograms, resulting in a descriptor with 594 elements ($3 \times 9 \times 9 + 3 \times 36 + 3 \times 9 \times 9$). PCA can be used to reduce this to 60 dimensions. The shape-color descriptor is a concatenation of the SIFT descriptor and this color descriptor, yielding a 188 element descriptor. The weighting used here was 1 for shape and 0.2 for color. Experimental tests revealed that for the INRIA database[2] the addition of color to the SIFT descriptor led to an increase of 45% in the number of correct image pairings identified.

### 8.3.2. *Two successive stages for image comparison*

Let us now consider approaches that could be described as sequential. The three following methods use color in an initial stage in which the regions having the same colorimetric characteristics in both the images being compared are identified. In the second phase, shape descriptors are then calculated to verify that these regions also have similar shape characteristics.

The first method, proposed by Khan *et al.* [KHA 09, VIG 10], uses a local analysis of the color distribution. More specifically, the authors proposed to characterize a region by its hue histogram or by a histogram of specific colors (Color Names) obtained through training [WEI 07]. Object recognition is then based on a bag-of-words approach using two dictionaries, one for color and one for shape. A bag-of-words is a histogram of quantized local features (visual words). The idea of Khan *et al.* is to weight the probability that each shape word belongs to the target object by a value determined by each color word. An interesting aspect of this approach is that if the color is not discriminative for a particular target object, the "color probabilities" will be uniformly spread over all the shape words, with the result being that only shape will be used in

---

2 http://lear.inrialpes.fr/data.

recognizing the object. In this way, the challenge involved in defining optimal shape/color weightings for each database is avoided.

In the same context, Elsayad *et al.* [ELS 10] and Chen *et al.* [CHE 09] suggested using a bag-of-words based on shape-related words and weighting the contribution of shape descriptors within these bags-of-words by values determined using color information. Their approaches were similar since they proposed to work in a five-dimensional space representing the three color components and the two spatial coordinates of each pixel. They then tried to determine the parameters of the Gaussian mixture that was closest to the pixel distribution in this five-dimensional space. The probabilities of membership to these Gaussians were then the weights used in the shape-based bag-of-words.

The second method of sequential combination, described by Farag *et al.* [FAR 04], was implemented for recognition of road signs. For this, they used a Bayesian classification based on hue information to detect the pixels in an image that might be part of a road sign. In this way, one or more road signs could be associated with an image, following this first stage that was entirely color-based. Then, the SIFT descriptors for each region were extracted and compared to those for the signs in the database that might be present in the image. Thus, color was used to restrict the number of signs to be compared with the image, and shape information was used to settle on a final decision. In the same way, Wu *et al.* used a method that involved establishing an initial region pairing between two images of objects to be compared, using color information [WU 08a], with this choice being confirmed or rejected by comparing the SIFT descriptors of each region. The color description that they used consisted of the means and standard deviations for each region for the a*b* components in the L*a*b* space.

The next two methods propose the use of color in a second phase that follows point matching on the basis of shape information. Ancuti *et al.* assumed that the number of key points matched following the use of the SIFT descriptor would be too small to compare two images [ANC 07]. They therefore proposed to expand the number of pairings by using color information. The first stage involves using the method introduced by Lowe to pair up key points using shape information [LOW 04]. However, since the rejection criteria in this method were too strict according to the authors, they suggested retaining unpaired points and attempting to match them by using color information. The color descriptor that they used was the color co-occurrence histogram introduced by Chang [CHA 99]. This histogram counts the number of co-occurrences of color pairs in a given neighborhood. The authors showed that the use of a simple threshold on the intersection between these local histograms could be used to add pairings between two images without increasing the number of false matches. In contrast to Ancuti *et al.*, Goedeme *et al.* [GOE 05] instead believed that Lowe's matching method led to an unacceptably large number of false pairings, and so they suggested verifying each shape-based pairing by taking into account color information. The color descriptor that they chose in this case was based on the color moments approach of Mindru *et al.* [MIN 99].

### 8.3.3. *Parallel comparisons*

We will now describe methods that make simultaneous use of shape and color descriptors.

Inspired by van de Weijer *et al.* [WEI 06b], Hegazy *et al.* [HEG 08] proposed to combine the SIFT descriptor with the histogram of opponent angles (37-D) [WEI 05]. However, rather than concatenating these two descriptors, the authors proposed to calculate the probabilities of the presence of an object in an image by considering both the SIFT descriptor and the color descriptor separately. The final decision was made using an Adaboost classifier that combines these two probabilities. Classification tests on the Caltech[3] and Graz02[4] databases showed that this combination of descriptors always gave better results than the use of either descriptor on its own.

---

3 http://www.vision.caltech.edu/html-files/archive.html.
4 http://www.emt.tugraz.at/ pinz/data/GRAZ_02/.

Wu *et al.* [WU 08b] suggested combining a SIFT descriptor with a color histogram calculated in the HSV space ($6^3 = 216$–D) for object tracking. The tracking method was based on a particle filter for which the particle weights were updated iteratively, making alternate use of the color descriptor and the shape descriptor. The tracking results revealed that simultaneous use of color and shape information led to better results than when color alone was used.

Hu *et al.* [HU 08] used auto-correlograms as color descriptors. An auto-correlogram is a two-dimensional table where one axis lists colors $C_i$ and the other axis lists distances $d_j$ [HUA 97]. The entry at coordinate $(i, j)$ represents the number of times that a pair of pixels of color $C_i$ can be found at a distance $d_j$ from each other. This descriptor therefore represents the evolution of pairs of pixels of the same color as a function of distance within the image. Thus Hu *et al.* calculated the similarity between two objects by calculating the ratio of a similarity measure between the sets of SIFT descriptors for the two objects over some distance between their auto-correlograms. The shape and color information is therefore combined during the calculation of the distance between two objects.

Schügerl *et al.* [SCH 07] chose to combine the SIFT descriptor with a color descriptor included in the MPEG-7 video compression standard. This color descriptor divides the detected region into 64 blocks laid out in a $8 \times 8$ grid, each block being described by the mean of its constituent pixels in the YCrCb space. A discrete cosine transform (DCT) is then applied to each color plane, and only the coefficients representing low frequencies are retained for the region descriptor. The descriptor therefore consists of a set of DCT coefficients calculated for the Y, Cb, and Cr planes. For a given target image, both descriptors for each detected local region will be compared to the set of descriptors for the objects in the database, and then each descriptor votes independently for an object. The target image will then be associated with the objects in the database that have received the largest number of votes.

Finally, Nilsback *et al.* [NIL 08] attempted to combine color and shape for identifying flowers in color images. The shape descriptors that they used were SIFT and histograms of gradients (HoG), while the color descriptor was the histogram calculated in the HSV space. Like most image classification studies, the authors proposed the use of a visual bag-of-words to characterize the content of each image. They, therefore, extracted shape-based and color-based local features from the images and applied clustering in each of these local feature spaces. This was to get shape-based visual words and color-based visual words. The visual words are the cluster representatives in the space considered and constitute a dictionary. Then, for each image, they evaluate two histograms, one for each dictionary (shape and color). They then proposed to use an SVM classifier with multiple kernels, each kernel corresponding to a dictionary. The final kernel was then a linear combination of the different kernels. The weights used for the combination are defined experimentally. In the context of classification of flower images, Nilsback *et al.* showed that by combining shape and color, it was possible to significantly improve on the results that would be obtained from either characteristic on its own.

### 8.3.4. *Spatio-colorimetric descriptors*

We will now conclude this section by discussing spatio-colorimetric approaches.

The methods in this category are based on the extraction of spatio-colorimetric descriptors, i.e. descriptors where each dimension contains both color and shape information. The most widely used spatio-colorimetric descriptor is the color SIFT. SIFT was initially defined for gray level images, and its structure is not directly suitable for multi-component images. The color SIFT is therefore simply the result of marginal application of classical SIFTs to each color component. The only element of originality in studies discussing the use of the color SIFT is the choice of color invariant components used to extract these descriptors. The drawback of these approaches is that the already significant size of the SIFT (128 dimensions) is multiplied by the number of color components present. For example, Bosch *et al.* [BOS 06] suggested extracting the SIFT in the HSV color space and showing that the recognition results were better than those obtained using SIFTs extracted from gray level images. To extract their color SIFT descriptors, Abdel-Hakim *et al.* [ABD 06] and Burghouts *et al.* [BUR 09] proposed using the color invariants introduced by Geusebroek *et al.* [GEU 01], based on the Gaussian color space (see page 268). Through a comparative study of the various gray levels, colors, shapes and spatio-colorimetric descriptors, Burghouts *et al.* showed that the SIFT descriptor based on the "C" invariant component (see page 271) gave the best results. Van de Sande *et al.* [SAN 10b] also tested a range of local colors, shapes and spatio-colorimetric descriptors, and showed that the SIFTs extracted from the opponent color space (see page 278) gave the best performance as a general rule. SIFT descriptors drawn from Gaussian color space were not included in these tests. Finally, Chu *et al.* [CHU 10] showed that SURF gray level descriptors could also be applied to different color planes, yielding good results. In particular, they showed that SURF descriptors based on the "C" invariant component (see page 271) gave results that were very slightly better than SURF that made use of the opponent color space $o_1$ $o_2$ $o_3$.

Other approaches have also been proposed for extracting spatio-colorimetric descriptors from images. Luke *et al.* drew their inspiration from the structure of SIFT, which is a concatenation of amplitude-weighted histograms of gradient directions, and proposed to characterize the content of a local region by using a concatenation of directional histograms of hues, weighted by the saturation [LUK 08]. The idea here was that the hue of a pixel is more relevant in the case of higher saturations. The authors showed that this descriptor gives better results than the gray level SIFT. Inspired by the work of Matas *et al.* [MAT 00], Naik *et al.* suggested describing an image using a set of local color descriptors [NAI 07]. Specifically, they detected all the regions that contained multiple colors, and each region was characterized by the set of colors contained within it. Pairs of the resultant regions, extracted from a given image, were compared using their Hausdorff distance with the aim of only retaining a set of distinct regions. The set of local descriptors that describe the image therefore represents the way in which the colors are locally structured within the image. Geusebroek [GEU 06] also described invariant local color descriptors based on spatial derivatives calculated in Gaussian color space [GEU 00]. They proposed to characterize each region using twelve Weibull parameters drawn from the histograms of these derivative components and showed that these descriptors are fairly insensitive to rotations of the object in space. This is because they are in contrast to SIFT and not based on the gradient directions in image space. The most intuitive way of combining color and shape on a local basis involves reorganizing each $N \times N$ square region into a $3N^2$-element vector, where the number 3 comes from the number of color components that each pixel has. Qiu [QIU 02] suggested using this representation in combination with the YCrCb color space. For this, they under-sampled all the square regions that were detected, to give $4 \times 4$ image thumbnails from which they extracted luminance information (Y) to give a 16D achromatic vector. They then further under-sampled the image to give a $2 \times 2$ image, extracting the resultant chrominance components Cr and Cb to give two 4D chromatic vectors. Then, they applied vector quantization in the 16D and 4D descriptor spaces to extract the chromatic and achromatic visual words. They, therefore, characterized an image in terms of histograms of visual chromatic and achromatic words (bag-of-words). Qiu showed that this representation gave better results than color auto-correlograms for two different color image databases. Finally, Song *et al.* [SON 09] proposed a local descriptor used to characterize the way in which colors are spatially distributed. The idea consisted of defining an affine transformation applied to the pixels of the local region detected in the 2D image space so that they move to a position that corresponds to their current RGB coordinates in a 3D color space. The application of this transformation from the image space to the color space provides new RGB coordinates that depend both on the colors present in the considered region and on their spatial distribution in the image. The descriptor was formed from the positions of three specific pixels after the transformation. In the same way, the authors showed that this description is less sensitive to 3D rotations of the object than the SIFT descriptor.

## 8.4. Conclusion

In this chapter, we have described the first two stages of the process of image comparison in the context of object recognition: key point detection and the description of the regions around these points. The idea was to show how color can be introduced into these two stages and the benefits of having access to such information.

The general conclusion has been that the introduction of color information into the process of key point (or region) detection can increase the discriminating power of the descriptors extracted around these points. In addition, the use of colorimetric invariants in the detection process can make it robust in the face of variations in acquisition conditions. In the same way, local descriptors extracted from around these points make use of the various invariant components described in the previous chapter, to characterize the content of an image by using values that are relatively insensitive to acquisition condition variations. We have seen that the majority of color descriptors in current use draw on information on both the shape and color of objects. Certain descriptors also allow the possibility of weighting the contributions of these two different sources of information, and we have seen that the values recommended for these weightings vary considerably among different authors. The optimal fusion of diverse types of information within a single descriptor is still an open problem, and the various approaches presented in this chapter give an idea of the wide range of possible solutions.

## 8.5. Bibliography

[ABD 06]  ABDEL-HAKIM A., FARAG A., "CSIFT: a SIFT descriptor with color invariant characteristics", vol. 2, p. 1978-1983, 2006.

[ALE 10]  ALEXE B., DESELAERS T., FERRARI V., "What is an object?", *Computer Vision and Pattern Recognition, IEEE Computer Society Conference on*, p. 73-80, IEEE Computer Society, 2010.

[ANC 07]  ANCUTI C., BEKAERT P., "SIFT-CCH: increasing the SIFT distinctness by color co-occurrence histograms", *Proceedings of the 5th International Symposium on Image and Signal Processing and Analysis*, p. 130-135, Istanbul, Turkey, 2007.

[BEA 78]  BEAUDET P.R., "Rotationally invariant image operators", *Proceedings of the International Conference on Pattern Recognition*, p. 579-583, 1978.

[BOS 06]  BOSCH A., ZISSERMAN A., MUNOZ X., "Scene classification via pLSA", p. 517-530, 2006.

[BUR 09]  BURGHOUTS G., GEUSEBROEK J.-M., "Performance evaluation of local colour invariants", *Computer Vision and Image Understanding*, vol. 113, no. 1, p. 48-62, 2009.

[CHA 99] CHANG P., KRUMM J., "Object recognition with color cooccurrence histograms", *IEEE Conference on Computer Vision and Pattern Recognition (CVPR)*, vol. 2, p. 504-509, 1999.

[CHE 09] CHEN X., HU X., SHEN X., "Spatial weighting for bag-of-visual-words and its application in content-based image retrieval", *Advances in Knowledge Discovery and Data Mining*, vol. 5476 of *Lecture Notes in Computer Science*, p. 867-874, 2009.

[CHU 10] CHU D.M., SMEULDERS A.W.M., "Color invariant SURF in discriminative object tracking", *ECCV Workshop on Color and Reflectance in Imaging and Computer Vision*, 2010.

[DAH 08] DAHL A., AANAES H., "Effective image database search via dimensionality reduction", *Computer Vision and Pattern Recognition Workshops, CVPRW '08*, p. 1-6, 2008.

[DIN 08] DINET E., KUBICKI E., "A selective attention model for predicting visual attractors", *Proceedings of IEEE International Conference on Acoustics, Speech, and Signal Processing*, p. 697-700, USA, 2008.

[ELS 10] ELSAYAD I., MARTINET J., URRUTY T., DJERABA C., "A new spatial weighting scheme for bag-of-visual-words", *Proceedings of the International Workshop on Content-Based Multimedia Indexing (CBMI 2010)*, p. 1-6, 2010.

[FAR 04] FARAG A., ABDEL-HAKIM A., "Detection, categorization and recognition of road signs for autonomous navigation", *Proceedings of Advanced Concepts in Intelligent Vision Systems*, p. 125-130, Brussels, Belgium, 2004.

[FIN 98] FINLAYSON G., SCHIELE B., CROWLEY J., "Comprehensive colour image normalization", *Lecture Notes in Computer Science*, vol. 1406, p. 475-490, 1998.

[FIN 05] FINLAYSON G., HORDLEY S., SCHAEFER G., TIAN G.Y., "Illuminant and device invariant colour using histogram equalisation", *Pattern Recognition*, vol. 38, p. 179-190, 2005.

[FOR 07] FORSSÉN P.-E., "Maximally stable colour regions for recognition and matching", *IEEE Conference on Computer Vision and Pattern Recognition*, Minneapolis, USA, IEEE Computer Society, 2007.

[FOR 09] FORSSÉN P., MOE A., "View matching with blob features", *Image and Vision Computing*, vol. 27, no. 1-2, p. 99-107, 2009.

[GAB 05] GABRIEL P., HAYET J.-B., PIATER J., VERLY J., "Object tracking using color interest points", *Advanced Video and Signal Based Surveillance, IEEE Conference on*, p. 159-164, IEEE Computer Society, 2005.

[GAO 08] GAO K., LIN S., ZHANG Y., TANG S., REN H., "Attention model based SIFT keypoints filtration for image retrieval", *Proceedings of Seventh IEEE/ACIS International Conference on Computer and Information Science*, p. 191-196, Washington, USA, 2008.

[GEU 00] GEUSEBROEK J.-M., VAN DEN BOOMGAARD R., SMEULDERS A. W.M., DEV A., "Color and scale: the spatial structure of color images", *Proceedings of the European Conference on Computer Vision*, p. 331-341, 2000.

[GEU 01] GEUSEBROEK J.M., VAN DEN BOOMGAARD R., SMEULDERS A.W.M. GEERTS H., "Color invariance", *IEEE Transactions on Pattern Analysis and Machine Intelligence*, vol. 23, no. 12, p. 1338-1350, 2001.

[GEU 06] GEUSEBROEK J., "Compact object descriptors from local colour invariant histograms", *British Machine Vision Conference*, vol. 3, p. 1029-1038, 2006.

[GEV 99] GEVERS T., SMEULDERS A., "Color-based object recognition", *Pattern Recognition*, vol. 32, p. 453-464, 1999.

[GOE 05] GOEDEMÉ T., TUYTELAARS T., GOOL L.V., "Omnidirectional sparse visual path following with occlusion-robust feature tracking", *6th Workshop on Omnidirectional Vision, Camera Networks and Non-classical Cameras, OMNIVIS05, in Conjunction with ICCV 2005*, 2005.

[GOU 00] GOUET V., MONTESINOS P., DERICHE R., PELÉ D., "Evaluation de détecteurs de points d'intérêt pour la couleur", *Proc. Congrès Francophone AFRIF-AFIA, Reconnaissance des Formes et Intelligence Artificielle*, vol. 2, p. 257-266, Paris, 2000.

[HAR 88] HARRIS C., STEPHENS M., "A combined corner and edge detector", *Proceedings of the 4th Alvey Vision Conference*, p. 147-151, 1988.

[HEG 08] HEGAZY D., DENZLER J., "Boosting colored local features for generic object recognition", *Pattern Recognition and Image Analysis*, vol. 18, no. 2, p. 323-327, 2008.

[HEI 04] HEIDEMANN G., "Focus-of-attention from local color symmetries", *IEEE Transactions on Pattern Analysis and Machine Intelligence*, vol. 26, no. 7, p. 817-830, 2004.

[HU 08] HU L., JIANG S., HUANG Q., GAO W., "People re-detection using Adaboost with sift and color correlogram", *Proceedings of the IEEE International Conference on Image Processing*, vol. 1, p. 1348-1351, San Diego, USA, 2008.

[HUA 97] HUANG J., KUMAR S.R., MITRA M., ZHU W., ZABIH R., "Image indexing using color correlogram", *IEEE Conference on Computer Vision and Pattern Recognition*, p. 762-768, 1997.

[ITT 98] ITTI L., KOCH C., NIEBUR E., "A model of saliency-based visual attention for rapid scene analysis", *IEEE Transactions on Pattern Analysis and Machine Intelligence*, vol. 20, no. 11, p. 1254-1259, 1998.

[JOS 05] JOST T., OUERHANI N., VON WARTBURG R., MURI R., HUGLI H., "Assessing the contribution of color in visual attention", *Computer Vision and Image Understanding*, vol. 100, p. 107-123, 2005.

[KHA 09] KHAN F., VAN DE WEIJER J., VANRELL M., "Top-down color attention for object recognition", *Proceedings of the International Conference on Computer Vision*, Japan, p. 979-986, 2009.

[LI 08]  LI J., ALLINSON N.M., "A comprehensive review of current local features for computer vision", *Neurocomputing*, vol. 71, no. 10-12, p. 1771-1787, Elsevier Science Publishers B.V., 2008.

[LOC 87]  LOCHER P., NODINE C., *Symmetry catches the eye. Eye Movements: From Physiology to Cognition*, North-Holland Press, Amsterdam, 1987.

[LOW 04]  LOWE D., "Distinctive image features from scale-invariant keypoints", *International Journal of Computer Vision*, vol. 60, no. 2, p. 91-110, 2004.

[LUK 08]  LUKE R.H., KELLER J.M., CHAMORRO-MARTINEZ J., "Extending the scale invariant feature transform descriptor into the color domain", *Proceedings of the ICGST International Journal on Graphics, Vision and Image Processing, GVIP*, vol. 8, p. 35-43, 2008.

[MAR 06]  MARQUES O., MAYRON L., BORBA G., GAMBA H., "Using visual attention to extract regions of interest in the context of image retrieval", *Proceedings of the 44th Annual Southeast Regional Conference*, ACM-SE 44, ACM, p. 638-643, 2006.

[MAT 00]  MATAS J., KOUBAROULIS D., KITTLER J., "Colour image retrieval and object recognition using the multimodal neighbourhood signature", *Proceedings of the European Conference on Computer Vision*, Berlin, Germany, p. 48-64, 2000.

[MAT 02]  MATAS J., CHUM O., MARTIN U., PAJDLA T., "Robust wide baseline stereo from maximally stable extremal regions", *Proceedings of the British Machine Vision Conference*, p. 384-393, 2002.

[MIK 04]  MIKOLAJCZYK K., SCHMID C., "Scale & affine invariant interest point detectors", *International Journal of Computer Vision*, vol. 60, p. 63-86, Kluwer Academic Publishers, 2004.

[MIK 05a]  MIKOLAJCZYK K., SCHMID C., "A performance evaluation of local descriptors", *IEEE Transactions on Pattern Analysis and Machine Intelligence*, vol. 27, p. 1615-1630, 2005.

[MIK 05b]  MIKOLAJCZYK K., TUYTELAARS T., SCHMID C., ZISSERMAN A., MATAS J., SCHAFFALITZKY F., KADIR T., GOOL L.V., "A comparison of affine region detectors", *International Journal of Computer Vision*, vol. 65, no. 1/2, p. 43-72, 2005.

[MIN 99]  MINDRU F., MOONS T., VAN GOOL L., "Recognizing color patterns irrespective of viewpoints and illuminations", *IEEE Conference on Computer Vision and Pattern Recognition (CVPR)*, p. 368-373, 1999.

[MIN 07]  MING A., MA H., "A blob detector in color images", *Proceedings of the 6th ACM International Conference on Image and Video Retrieval*, CIVR '07, p. 364-370, New York, USA, ACM, 2007.

[MON 98]  MONTESINOS P., GOUET V., DERICHE R., "Differential invariants for color images", *Proceedings of the International Conference on Pattern Recognition*, vol. 1, p. 838-840, Brisbane, Australia, 1998.

[MON 00] MONTESINOS P., GOUET V., DERICHE R., PELÉ D., "Matching color uncalibrated images using differential invariants", *Image and Vision Computing*, vol. 18, no. 9, p. 659-671, 2000.

[MOO 06] MOOSMANN F., LARLUS D., JURIE F., "Learning saliency maps for object categorization", *ECCV International Workshop on the Representation and Use of Prior Knowledge in Vision*, 2006.

[MOR 77] MORAVEC H., "Towards automatic visual obstacle avoidance", *Proceedings of the 5th International Joint Conference on Artificial Intelligence*, p. 584-588, 1977.

[NAI 07] NAIK S.K., MURTHY C.A., "Distinct multicolored region descriptors for object recognition", *IEEE Transactions on Pattern Analysis and Machine Intelligence*, vol. 29, p. 1291-1296, IEEE Computer Society, 2007.

[NIL 08] NILSBACK M.-E., ZISSERMAN A., "Automated flower classification over a large number of classes", *Proceedings of the Indian Conference on Computer Vision, Graphics Image Processing (ICVGIP 2008)*, p. 722-729, 2008.

[QIU 02] QIU G., "Indexing chromatic and achromatic patterns for content-based colour image retrieval", *Pattern Recognition*, vol. 35, no. 8, p. 1675-1686, 2002.

[QUE 06] QUELHAS P., ODOBEZ J., "Natural scene image modeling using color and texture visterms", *Proceedings of Conference on Image and Video Retrieval*, p. 411-421, Phoenix, USA, 2006.

[REI 95] REISFELD D., WOLFSON H., YESHURUN Y., "Context-free attentional operators: the generalized symmetry transform", *International Journal of Computer Vision*, vol. 14, p. 119-130, Springer, 1995.

[RUT 04] RUTISHAUSER U., WALTHER D., KOCH C., PERONA P., "Is bottom-up attention useful for object recognition", *IEEE Conference on Computer Vision and Pattern Recognition (CVPR)*, p. 37-44, 2004.

[SAN 10a] VAN DE SANDE K., GEVERS T., SNOEK C., "Evaluating color descriptors for object and scene recognition", *IEEE Transactions on Pattern Analysis and Machine Intelligence*, vol. 32, p. 1582-1596, IEEE Computer Society, 2010.

[SAN 10b] VAN DE SANDE K.E., GEVERS T., SNOEK C.G., "Evaluating color descriptors for object and scene recognition", *IEEE Transactions on Pattern Analysis and Machine Intelligence*, vol. 32, p. 1582-1596, IEEE Computer Society, 2010.

[SCH 07] SCHÜGERL P., SORSCHAG R., BAILER W., THALLINGER G., "Object re-detection using SIFT and MPEG-7 color descriptors", *Proceedings of the International Workshop on Multimedia Content Analysis and Mining*, p. 305-314, 2007.

[SEB 06a] SEBE N., GEVERS T., DIJKSTRA S., VAN DE WEIJE J., "Evaluation of intensity and color corner detectors for affine invariant salient regions", *Proceedings of the 2006 Conference on Computer Vision and Pattern Recognition Workshop, CVPRW '06*, Washington, USA, IEEE Computer Society, p. 18-25, 2006.

[SEB 06b]  SEBE N., GEVERS T., VAN DE WEIJER J., DIJKSTRA S., "Corners detectors for affine invariant salient regions: is color important?", *Proceedings of Conference on Image and Video Retrieval*, p. 61-71, Phoenix, USA, 2006.

[SHI 08]  SHI L., FUNT B., HAMARNEH G., "Quaternion color curvature", *Proceedings IS&T Sixteenth Color Imaging Conference*, p. 338-341, Portland, 2008.

[SON 09]  SONG X., MUSELET D., TREMEAU A., "Local color descriptor for object recognition across illumination changes", *Proceedings of the Conference on Advanced Concepts for Intelligent Vision Systems (ACIVS '09)*, p. 598-605, Bordeaux, France, 2009.

[STE 03]  STENTIFORD F. W.M., "An attention based similarity measure with application to content-based information retrieval", *Proceedings of the Storage and Retrieval for Media Databases Conference, SPIE Electronic Imaging*, 2003.

[STO 07]  STOETTINGER J., HANBURY A., SEBE N., GEVERS T., "Do colour interest points improve image retrieval?", *Proceedings of the IEEE International Conference on Image Processing*, vol. 1, p. 169-172, San Antonio, USA, 2007.

[TUY 08]  TUYTELAARS T., MIKOLAJCZYK K., "Local invariant feature detectors: a survey", *Foundations and Trends® in Computer Graphics and Vision*, vol. 3, no. 3, p. 177-280, 2008.

[VÁZ 09]  VÁZQUEZ-MARTIN R., MARFILA R., NEZ P.N., BANDERA A., SANDOVAL F., "A novel approach for salient image regions detection and description", *Pattern Recognition Letters*, vol. 30, p. 1464-1476, 2009.

[VAZ 10]  VAZQUEZ E., GEVERS T., LUCASSEN M., VAN DE WEIJER J., BALDRICH R., "Saliency of color image derivatives: a comparison between computational models and human perception", *Journal of the Optical Society of America A*, vol. 27, no. 3, p. 613-621, OSA, 2010.

[VIG 10]  VIGO D. A.R., KHAN F.S., VAN DE WEIJER J., GEVERS T., "The impact of color on bag-of-words based object recognition", *International Conference on Pattern Recognition*, p. 1549-1553, 2010.

[VOG 04]  VOGEL J., SCHIELE B., "A semantic typicality measure for natural scene categorization", RASMUSSEN C.E., BÜLTHOFF H.H., SCHÖLKOPF B., GIESE M.A., (eds), *Pattern Recognition*, vol. 3175 of *Lecture Notes in Computer Science*, p. 195-203, Springer Berlin / Heidelberg, 2004.

[WAL 05]  WALTHER D., RUTISHAUSER U., KOCH C., PERONA P., "Selective visual attention enables learning and recognition of multiple objects in cluttered scenes", *Computer Vision and Image Understanding*, vol. 100, p. 41-63, 2005.

[WEI 05]  VAN DE WEIJER J., GEVERS T., GEUSEBROEK J.-M., "Edge and corner detection by photometric quasi-invariants", *IEEE Transactions on Pattern Analysis and Machine Intelligence*, vol. 27, no. 4, p. 625-630, 2005.

[WEI 06a]  VAN DE WEIJER J., GEVERS T., BAGDANOV A., "Boosting color saliency in image feature detection", *IEEE Transactions on Pattern Analysis and Machine Intelligence*, vol. 28, no. 1, p. 150-156, 2006.

[WEI 06b] VAN DE WEIJER J., SCHMID C., "Coloring local feature extraction", *Proceedings of the Ninth European Conference on Computer Vision*, vol. 3954, p. 334-348, Graz, Austria, 2006.

[WEI 07]  VAN DE WEIJER J., SCHMID C., "Applying color names to image description", *Proceedings of the IEEE International Conference on Image Processing*, vol. 3, p. 493-496, San Antonio, USA, 2007.

[WU 08a]  WU P., KONG L., LI X., FU K., "A hybrid algorithm combined color feature and keypoints for object detection", *Proceedings of the 3rd IEEE Conference on Industrial Electronics and Applications*, p. 1408-1412, Singapore, 2008.

[WU 08b]  WU P., KONG L., ZHAO F., LI X., "Particle filter tracking based on color and SIFT features", *Proceedings of the International Conference on Audio, Language and Image Processing*, Shanghai, 2008.

[WUR 00]  WURTZ R., LOURENS T., "Corner detection in color images through a multiscale combination of end-stopped cortical cells", *Image and Vision Computing*, vol. 18, no. 6-7, p. 531-541, 2000.

[ZHA 07]  ZHANG D., WANG W., GAO W., JIANG S., "An effective local invariant descriptor combining luminance and color information", *Proceedings of IEEE International Conference on Multimedia and Expo*, p. 1507-1510, Beijing, China, 2007.

Chapter 9

# Motion Estimation in Color Image Sequences

## 9.1. Introduction

Motion estimation in image sequences and in video is traditionally performed on one single color component of the image representation in color spaces. Typically, the YUV (YCrCb) space is used for motion estimation, which is applied to the Y component as it contains the most information about the image. Studies using all components of a color system for motion estimation are relatively few and far between. If we consider the different approaches taken for motion estimation in color image sequences, we find two main trends. The first involves introducing color component information during the dense estimation of motion fields, while the second focuses on sparse estimation of these motion fields. In the sparse case, similar measures are used between image primitives that make use of color descriptors. In the dense case, methods are based on solving the optical flow equation, extended to color image spaces. In this chapter, we will analyze a number of such methods.

Chapter written by Bertrand AUGEREAU and Jenny BENOIS-PINEAU.

## 9.2. Extension of classical motion estimation techniques to color image spaces

Object motion in an animated scene is entirely defined by the displacement field, which takes the form of a vector field in the 3D space. This defines the velocity vectors for the surface elements of objects at each point in space. Since a video sequence represents the projection of a dynamic 3D scene into the 2D space associated with the focal plane of the camera, the dense displacement field is projected into the 2D space to produce what is commonly referred to as "image flow" [GOL 97] or "projected true motion". Nevertheless, this true motion cannot always be perfectly estimated using its 2D projection, for reasons of insufficiency or inconsistency such as the aperture problem (ambiguity in local motion perception) and occlusions [TEK 95]. Only the motion perceived via changes in image values, either in terms of luminance or color, known as the "apparent motion" or "optical flow" can be estimated.

### 9.2.1. Luminance images and optical flow

We can express the problem of optical flow estimation by using luminance measurements as follows.

Let $(x, y)$ be the coordinates of the spatial projection onto the image plane of a point in the scene observed at time $t$. After a time interval $dt$, the image of the point has moved to the position $(x + dx, y + dy)$.

The fundamental hypothesis requires us to assume that in the absence of occlusions, noise, and changes in scene illumination, the measurement (luminance) of the point image is conserved. This hypothesis can be expressed in the form of the following equation:

$$I(x, y, t) = I(x + dx, y + dy, t + dt) \qquad [9.1]$$

where $I$ is the luminance measured in the image plane. Using a first-order Taylor series expansion we find:

$$I(x, y, t) = I(x, y, t) + \frac{\partial I}{\partial x} dx + \frac{\partial I}{\partial y} dy + \frac{\partial I}{\partial t} dt + o^2(dx, dy, dt)$$

$$[9.2]$$

From this equation we can derive:

$$\frac{\partial I}{\partial x}\frac{dx}{dt} + \frac{\partial I}{\partial y}\frac{dy}{dt} + \frac{\partial I}{\partial t} = 0 \qquad [9.3]$$

By taking this to its infinitesimal limit, we then obtain an equation constraining the apparent motion, more commonly known as the Optical Flow Equation (OFE):

$$\frac{\partial I}{\partial x}\bar{u} + \frac{\partial I}{\partial y}\bar{v} + \frac{\partial I}{\partial t} = 0 \qquad [9.4]$$

where the components of the displacement field are denoted by $\bar{u}$ and $\bar{v}$, anticipating the concept of normalized displacement that we will introduce later on. It should also be noted that this equation can be written in the following form:

$$\bar{\delta} \cdot \nabla I = 0 \qquad [9.5]$$

using a normalized displacement vector $\bar{\delta}^T = (\bar{u}, \bar{v}, 1)$, where $\nabla I = \left(\frac{\partial I}{\partial x}, \frac{\partial I}{\partial y}, \frac{\partial I}{\partial t}\right)$ is the gradient vector of the spatio-temporal image. In this form, it can easily be seen that only the velocity component orthogonal to the luminance gradient can be determined from the OFE. Thus, the problem of motion estimation is ill-posed, and indeed has an infinite number of solutions. An initial regularization method used to obtain a unique solution was proposed by Horn and Shunck [HOR 81]. This involved finding the function $\bar{\delta}$ that minimizes the functional:

$$E(\bar{\delta}) = \iint \left(\left(\bar{\delta} \cdot \nabla I\right)^2 + \lambda^2 \left(\|\nabla \bar{u}\|^2 + \|\nabla \bar{v}\|^2\right)\right) dx\, dy \qquad [9.6]$$

The first term in the functional represents the error in the OFE [9.5], and the second is the smoothing term for the displacement field, where the $\lambda^2$ parameter determines the "smoothing force". The resultant fields satisfy the constraint of minimal variation in the displacement vectors around the point in question.

### 9.2.2. Estimation of optical flow in color spaces

We should first point out that the vast majority of methods for color optical flow estimation are more or less direct analog of methods for solving the OFE, extended to the multi-valued case.

To ensure that we use consistent notations in the rest of this chapter, we will represent a sequence of color images in the following way:

$$I: x = (x_i)_{i=1...3} \in R^3 \longrightarrow I(x) = (I_j(x)_{j=1...3}) \in R^3 \qquad [9.7]$$

where $x_1$ and $x_2$ represent the spatial coordinates and $x_3$ the time coordinate of a point $x$ in the sequence. The subscript $j$ represents the color components of the image representation. The conventional extension of the OFE then involves simultaneous application of equation [9.4] to the three different color planes $j = 1 \ldots 3$ of the image [OHT 89]:

$$\begin{cases} \partial_1 I_1 \bar{u} + \partial_2 I_1 \bar{v} + \partial_3 I_1 = 0 \\ \partial_1 I_2 \bar{u} + \partial_2 I_2 \bar{v} + \partial_3 I_2 = 0 \\ \partial_1 I_3 \bar{u} + \partial_2 I_3 \bar{v} + \partial_3 I_3 = 0 \end{cases} \qquad [9.8]$$

where $\partial_i I_j$ represents the partial derivative at point $x$ of the component or color plane $I_j$ with respect to coordinate $x_i$.

Clearly, the system of equations in [9.8] is over-determined, and a range of different strategies is available for solving it.

### 9.2.2.1. Selection strategies

By choosing two independent equations in [9.8] and using Gaussian elimination [OHT 89], it is possible to estimate $\bar{\delta}$ directly. For example, the two equations that are chosen can be the ones corresponding to the chromatic components in the HSV space [BAR 02, GOL 97], YUV, UCS, or YCbCr space, etc. In [GOL 97], the authors assumed that the quantities representing color information remained invariant under constant illumination conditions, and could therefore be used for apparent motion estimation. The authors therefore proposed the use of normalized color systems such as rgb or HSV where the two chromatic components are independent. Thus, the assumption of conservation of color can be expressed in the form of a determined system based on the independence of the estimated gradients for each color component:

$$\begin{cases} \partial_1 H_1 \bar{u} + \partial_2 H_1 \bar{v} + \partial_3 H_1 = 0 \\ \partial_1 H_2 \bar{u} + \partial_2 H_2 \bar{v} + \partial_3 H_2 = 0 \end{cases} \qquad [9.9]$$

where $H_1$ and $H_2$ are the two chromatic components chosen.

## 9.2.2.2. *Global strategies*

The fields can be estimated in this case by solving the system of equations in [9.8] globally, either by least-squares methods or by pseudo-inverse methods [BAR 02, OHT 89, WEI 04]. In fact, this can be considered as an extension of the work of Lucas and Kanade [LUC 81]. Turning our attention back to [GOL 97], the authors defined a matrix $A$ and a vector $b$:

$$A = \begin{pmatrix} \partial_1 I_1 & \partial_2 I_1 \\ \partial_1 I_2 & \partial_2 I_2 \\ \partial_1 I_3 & \partial_2 I_3 \end{pmatrix}, \qquad b = \begin{pmatrix} -\partial_3 I_1 \\ -\partial_3 I_2 \\ -\partial_3 I_3 \end{pmatrix} \qquad [9.10]$$

which enabled them to rewrite equations [9.8] in the form of a matrix equation:

$$A \begin{pmatrix} \bar{u} \\ \bar{v} \end{pmatrix} = b \qquad [9.11]$$

and thus to obtain a solution in the least-squares sense:

$$\begin{pmatrix} \bar{u} \\ \bar{v} \end{pmatrix} = (A^T A)^{-1} A^T b \qquad [9.12]$$

when the matrix $A^T A$ is non-singular. The authors [GOL 97] reported this method to be very stable in the case of planar motion, i.e. when the objects are undergoing translational motion within the image plane, orthogonal to the viewing axis.

In the case of more complex motion, the authors then proposed to model the RGB color components by decomposing them into terms that depend on the geometry of the reflecting surface and terms based on the illuminating light spectrum. Thus, a color component is expressed as a product with the following form:

$$I_j = C_j c(\phi, \theta, \gamma) \qquad [9.13]$$

In equation [9.13], $C_j$ represents the spectral reflectance of the surface element. $c(\phi, \theta, \gamma)$ is a term that depends on the geometry and in particular on the angles of incidence $\phi$ and observation $\theta$ (angles between the incident and reflected light and the surface normal), and on the phase angle $\gamma$ (the angle between the incident and reflected light). This term does not change if the light source is uniform or parallel to the image plane. In this case, the geometrical conditions on the reflection of the light do not change, and methods based on the assumption of conservation of luminance intensity give good results. In the case of more complex motion, the geometric conditions will change, but the $C_j$ term, which depends only on the spectrum of the light, will remain invariant. The $C_j$ terms cannot be directly observed. Nevertheless, we can deduce from equation [9.13] that the ratios of any two linear combinations of color components $I_j$ are equal to the ratios of these same linear combinations applied to the coefficients $C_j$. This is equivalent to using two components of the rgb or HSV systems as our invariants, quantities that are observable. This, may, however lead to singularities in the case of small values.

### 9.2.2.3. *Fusion strategies*

This approach involves calculating the displacement fields separately for each component, with the help of some scalar extraction method, and then fusing the results that are obtained into a single consistent field.

For example, in [AND 04] the author proposed several methods for solving the color optical flow directly, using an over-determined system of equations [9.8]. One of the proposed methods involves considering the pixel values within a $3 \times 3 \times 3$ spatial neighborhood and solving equations [9.8] by using the method of least squares. This method is effective if the observations (time derivatives) are homogeneous in the sense of their consistency with the underlying model. Nevertheless, if anomalous values are present, then robust statistical estimation must be used. For this approach, the author proposed to calculate the parameters of 54 constraint lines defined using equation [9.8] and associated with each point in the neighborhood. The intersections of these lines correspond to 27 velocity vectors. The coordinates of the resultant vectors are calculated as the marginal medians.

Another solution involves rejecting the 20% of the vectors representing the largest and smallest values, and obtaining the resultant velocity vector as the vector mean of the remaining vectors.

Finally, a more local solution that does not take into account the spatial neighborhood involves fusing the results of optical flow estimation obtained by applying the basic method of Horn and Shunk [HOR 81] to each plane of the chosen color space separately. Two fusion methods have been described:

– using the vectors estimated for each color plane separately, choosing the vector that gives the minimal reconstruction error;

– using the vector that results from linearly combining the vectors estimated for each individual color plane.

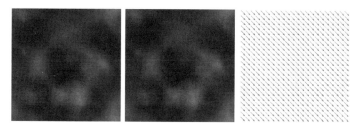

**Figure 9.1.** *Optical flow estimation on test sequence "Translating Clouds". From left to right: color frame at t, color frame at t+1, estimated motion field. (For a color version of this figure, see www.iste.co.uk/fernandez/colorimag.zip)*

Note also that to evaluate the quality of their methods, the authors in [AND 03] proposed to measure the error on the norm and angle of their vectors relative to the available "ground truth":

$$M_{err} = |\,\|G\| - \|Q\|\,|, \quad \theta_{err} = \arccos(G \cdot Q) \qquad [9.14]$$

where $M_{err}$ and $\theta_{err}$ are the error matrices between the estimated vectors $G$ and those of the ground truth $Q$. Global measures such as the mean, RMS (root of mean square error or MSE), and standard deviation are calculated for these matrices, and give a global characterization of the quality of estimation. The best performance is obtained using the method of constraint line intersection, with filtering of anomalous values (trimmed median and mean) and over a synthetic sequence known as *Translating Clouds*, illustrated in Figure 9.1 and also used in [JI 07].

## 9.3. Apparent motion and vector images

A brief analysis of these methods based on equations [9.8] reveals that any solution vector must also be a potential solution to the OFE as applied to each individual component in isolation. Thus, in addition to the problems associated with the over-determined nature of the system, we can observe that by its very nature, this approach can only result in quasi-marginal methods.

In fact, attempts to obtain a vector solution, i.e. a solution that takes into account the vector nature of color images, must involve a geometric interpretation of the optical flow equation [9.4]. This indicates that the displacement vector must necessarily be orthogonal to the gradient vector. We will see how the extension of this property to the vector case leads to a solution referred to as the generalized optical flow equation (GOFE), which we will introduce in the following section.

### 9.3.1. *Motion and structure tensor in the scalar case*

Before developing the approach that will lead us to a vector approach to the solution of the GOFE, let us return to considering the geometrical interpretation of the OFE. In the simplified context of scalar images, the first order differential element, known as the gradient:

$$\nabla I^T = (\partial_1 I, \partial_2 I, \partial_3 I) \qquad [9.15]$$

can be used to generate a structure tensor $\mathcal{S}$ given by:

$$\mathcal{S} = \nabla I \, \nabla I^T = \begin{pmatrix} \partial_1 I^2 & \partial_1 I \, \partial_2 I & \partial_1 I \, \partial_3 I \\ \partial_1 I \, \partial_2 I & \partial_2 I^2 & \partial_2 I \, \partial_3 I \\ \partial_1 I \, \partial_3 I & \partial_2 I \, \partial_3 I & \partial_3 I^2 \end{pmatrix} \qquad [9.16]$$

The spectral elements of $\mathcal{S}$ have the eigenvalues:

$$\begin{cases} \lambda_1 = \partial_1 I^2 + \partial_2 I^2 + \partial_3 I^2 \\ \lambda_2 = \lambda_3 = 0 \end{cases} \qquad [9.17]$$

As for the eigenvectors, the one associated with $\lambda_1$ can be obtained immediately, and is the gradient vector $V_1 = \nabla I$. The subspace defined by the two eigenvectors $V_2$ and $V_3$ associated with the two null eigenvalues is orthogonal to $V_1$. Any vector from the kernel of $\mathcal{S}$ can therefore be a potential solution to the OFE. However, it is particularly convenient to use the classical properties of differential geometry to ensure that the three eigenvectors form a Frenet basis at all points $x$, i.e. a direct orthogonal basis of the vector space:

$$
V_1 = \begin{pmatrix} \partial_1 I \\ \partial_2 I \\ \partial_3 I \end{pmatrix}, \quad V_2 = \begin{pmatrix} \partial_2 I \\ -\partial_1 I \\ 0 \end{pmatrix}, \quad V_3 = \begin{pmatrix} \partial_1 I\, \partial_3 I \\ \partial_2 I\, \partial_3 I \\ -(\partial_1 I^2 + \partial_2 I^2) \end{pmatrix}
$$

[9.18]

As shown in [JÄH 98], the $V_3$ vector can then be taken as a local non-normalized solution to the OFE, with the normalized solution given by:

$$
\bar{\delta}^T = \left( -\frac{\partial_1 I\, \partial_3 I}{\partial_1 I^2 + \partial_2 I^2}, \quad -\frac{\partial_2 I\, \partial_3 I}{\partial_1 I^2 + \partial_2 I^2}, \quad 1 \right)
$$

[9.19]

Of course, in this entirely local approach, the optical flow does not resolve the aperture problem, which is encountered in the context of apparent motion estimation. It is for this reason that many authors (such as [BRU 02, LAU 04]) suggest combining the OFE solution with a diffusion process to determine the apparent motion. Whatever solution is chosen, we will not discuss this important question any further, and we will continue to concentrate on our initial objective, namely a vector approach to the extraction of displacement fields.

### 9.3.2. Stability of tensor spectral directions

Before we continue, to ensure we retain clarity throughout, we propose to introduce a generic property of tensors, a property that we will make considerable use of later on. Consider then a vector $U^T = (a, b, c)$ and the related tensor $\mathcal{T} = U\, U^T$. The eigenvalues of $\mathcal{T}$ are:

$$
\begin{cases} \lambda_1(\mathcal{T}) = a^2 + b^2 + c^2 \\ \lambda_2(\mathcal{T}) = \lambda_3(\mathcal{T}) = 0 \end{cases}
$$

[9.20]

with associated eigenvectors that are chosen to be:

$$V_1(T) = \begin{pmatrix} a \\ b \\ c \end{pmatrix}, \quad V_2(T) = \begin{pmatrix} b \\ -a \\ 0 \end{pmatrix}, \quad V_3(T) = \begin{pmatrix} ab \\ bc \\ -(a^2 + b^2) \end{pmatrix}$$

[9.21]

respectively, to form a direct orthogonal basis, as we saw in equations [9.17] and [9.18]. It can be seen quite easily that the tensor $T_1 = V_1(T)\, V_1(T)^T$ is just the original tensor $T$, and as a consequence, the eigenvectors of $T_1$ will be $V_1(T_1) = U = V_1(T)$, $V_2(T_1) = V_2(T)$ and $V_3(T_1) = V_3(T)$.

Similarly, if we consider the tensor $T_3 = V_3(T)\, V_3(T)^T$, we obtain the following eigenvalues:

$$\begin{cases} \lambda_1(T_3) = (a^2 + b^2)(a^2 + b^2 + c^2) \\ \lambda_2(T_3) = \lambda_3(T_3) = 0 \end{cases}$$

[9.22]

and their respective eigenvectors:

$$V_1(T_3) = \begin{pmatrix} ab \\ bc \\ -(a^2 + b^2) \end{pmatrix}, \quad V_2(T_3) = \begin{pmatrix} b \\ -a \\ 0 \end{pmatrix}, \quad V_3(T_3) = \begin{pmatrix} a \\ b \\ c \end{pmatrix}$$

[9.23]

Finally, since we have the following relationships:

$$V_3(T_1) = V_1(T_3), \quad V_2(T_1) = V_2(T_3), \quad V_1(T_1) = V_3(T_3) \qquad [9.24]$$

we will refer to this property as the *property of spectral directional stability* of the tensor $T$.

### 9.3.3. *Vector approach to optical flow*

Since the aim is to obtain the displacement fields from a color image sequence while taking into account the details of the color space used to represent it, we must avoid any sort of marginal approach. To this end, we have already mentioned that we should find a vector solution to the OFE [9.5], or more exactly a solution to what we have already designated as the generalized optical flow equation (GOFE) and which can be written as:

$$\delta \cdot \vec{\nabla} I = 0 \tag{9.25}$$

where $\delta = (v_1, v_2, v_3)$ represents an un-normalized displacement vector and the term $\vec{\nabla} I$ is not the gradient of the vector function $I$, but rather its conventional extension given by the spectral elements of the first fundamental form [TRE 04]. This is in the direction of strongest variation in the component space and is referred to as the Di Zenzo gradient in the case of a simple color image. We note that the vector function $I$ is defined in a 3D space here, but all the results that follow are directly applicable to a space with any number of dimensions.

### 9.3.3.1. *From the structure tensor to the displacement tensor*

For each component $I_j$, we have a first-order differential element, the gradient vector $\nabla I_j$. This leads to a global first-order differential characteristic, the $(3 \times 3)$ matrix:

$$g = (\nabla I_1 \ \nabla I_2 \ \nabla I_3) \tag{9.26}$$

A natural extension of the scalar case then involves forming a structure tensor $\mathcal{G}$ and examining its eigenvalues and eigenvectors. Thus we have:

$$\mathcal{G} = gg^T, \quad \mathcal{G} = \sum_{j=1}^{3} \nabla I_j \, \nabla I_j{}^T, \quad \mathcal{G} = \sum_{j=1}^{3} \mathcal{S}_j \tag{9.27}$$

where $\mathcal{S}_j$ is the structure tensor [9.16] of the $I_j$ component. This structure tensor $\mathcal{G}$ is, except in special cases, a full rank matrix, meaning that it has three real eigenvalues, generally positive and distinct. Thus the dominant eigenvalue $\lambda_1(\mathcal{G})$ and its associated eigenvector $V_1(\mathcal{G})$ represent the value and direction of maximum variation. These elements are then often considered as the extension of the concept of gradient to the case of color image sequences [TSC 02], which allows us to write:

$$\vec{\nabla} I = V_1(\mathcal{G}) \tag{9.28}$$

We can then also state that the displacement vector $\delta$ in the GOFE [9.25] must necessarily lie in the orthogonal subspace generated by the two other eigenvectors $V_2(\mathcal{G})$ and $V_3(\mathcal{G})$. Unfortunately, difficulties appear when constructing a combination that will give the displacement as a function of these two vectors. In particular, we find that there is nothing we can do to ensure that $\delta$ will lie entirely along the $V_3(\mathcal{G})$ direction associated with the smallest eigenvalue.

To overcome this obstacle, we must use the stability property of the eigenvectors [9.24]. In this way, we define a displacement tensor for each color component $I_j$:

$$\mathcal{D}_j = V_3(\mathcal{S}_j)\, V_3(\mathcal{S}_j)^T \qquad\qquad [9.29]$$

where $V_3(\mathcal{S}_j)$ [9.18] is equal to the displacement vector $\delta_j$ given by the structure tensor $\mathcal{S}_j$ of color component $I_j$. From equations [9.24], [9.18] and [9.28] we determine that:

$$V_1(\mathcal{D}_j) = \begin{pmatrix} \partial_1 I_j\, \partial_3 I_j \\ \partial_2 I_j\, \partial_3 I_j \\ -(\partial_1 I_j{}^2 + \partial_2 I_j{}^2) \end{pmatrix} = \delta_j$$

$$V_3(\mathcal{D}_j) = \begin{pmatrix} \partial_1 I_j \\ \partial_2 I_j \\ \partial_3 I_j \end{pmatrix} = \nabla I_j$$

$$[9.30]$$

### 9.3.3.2. *Displacement field in a color space*

Now, we just need to construct a global displacement tensor $\mathcal{D}$ from the individual component tensors $\mathcal{D}_j$ [9.29], giving us:

$$\mathcal{D} = \sum_{j=1}^{3} \mathcal{D}_j, \quad \mathcal{D} = \sum_{j=1}^{3} \delta_j\, \delta_j{}^T \qquad\qquad [9.31]$$

and take the eigenvector $V_1(\mathcal{D})$ associated with the maximum eigenvalue $\lambda_1(\mathcal{D})$ to be the expression for the displacement vector. It can also be seen that in this method, the displacement vector $\delta$ can be calculated directly from the displacements associated with each individual component, thus in a sense combining certain techniques that are useful for solving equation [9.8] while at the same time preserving the vector nature of the color spaces [AUG 05].

We can then immediately verify the validity of our approach by considering some results from calculations of displacement fields[1]. Figure 9.2 shows the images that will be used to determine the various displacement fields that we will discuss below. It should be noted that in this case, the apparent motion results from a combination of a zooming out of the camera, perceptible at the top of the doorway, and motion produced by the movement of the person.

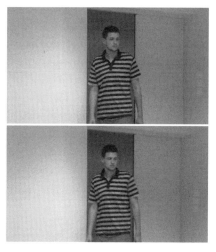

**Figure 9.2.** *Test images for determination of displacement fields in different color spaces; sequence taken from the LABRI-ANR ICOS-HD database available at www.open-video.org*

We should specify that for reasons of visibility, the vectors of these dense fields will be represented using a color coding system

---

1 We will use the *VISUZoomOut_clip1* sequence from the *LABRI-ANR ICOS-HD* database available at *www.open-video.org*.

(see Figure 9.3) where the chrominance is a function of the orientation of the displacement vector and the luminance is a function of its norm.

**Figure 9.3.** *Chrominance/orientation and luminance/norm coding scheme used for vectors. (For a color version of this figure, see www.iste.co.uk/fernandez/colorimag.zip)*

The displacement fields were then estimated for the image on the right of Figure 9.2, in six different color spaces: HSV, L\*a\*b\*, RGB, rgb, XYZ and YUV. To do this, the dominant eigenvalue and eigenvector of the displacement tensors [9.31] were determined, approximating the partial derivatives using the coefficients of the projection of the sequence onto 1 degree polynomials from an a-complete Hermite-Laguerre basis with a support of $7 \times 7 \times 3$. This technique makes it possible to perform $7 \times 7$ Gaussian spatial smoothing to each image while simultaneously rapidly reducing the influence of previous frames in the sequence, limiting this influence to the three images taken into account at a given point in time.

The results are shown in Figure 9.4, where first impressions confirm that these results are all fairly similar. This is not too surprising since as soon as we make the decision to use a vector method, we will be treating color information in a global manner. This information itself will remain quasi-independent of the representation space that is used for it – as long as we respect the condition that it should not be based on irreversible transformations. In addition, and as indicated previously, the symptomatic perception of the effects of zooming out can be seen very prominently on the door frame.

To conclude, we will present an example demonstrating both the relevance of color information and the importance of using a vector method for displacement field estimation. To this end, we will use the *voitures_balles_clip2* sequence from the *LABRI-ANR ICOS-HD* database, and more specifically the images in Figure 9.5.

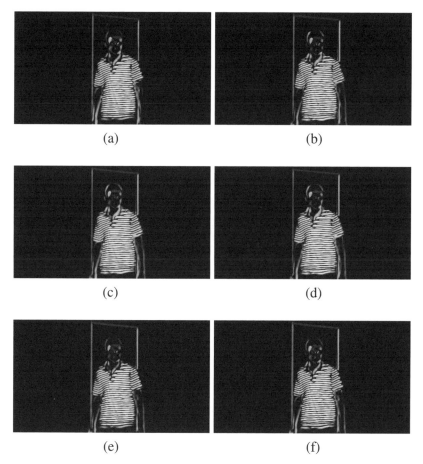

(a)                                    (b)

(c)                                    (d)

(e)                                    (f)

**Figure 9.4.** *Displacement fields determined for Figure 9.2: a) HSV, b) L\*a\*b\*, c) RGB, d) rgb, e) XYZ, and f) YUV. (For a color version of this figure, see www.iste.co.uk/fernandez/colorimag.zip)*

The fields are determined under the same conditions as in the previous example, and this time we will focus our attention on the displacements associated with the tennis ball in the right foreground, within the regions marked in Figure 9.5, with Figure 9.6 showing a magnified view of this ball. We note that the apparent motion results from a combination of the true displacement of the ball, which is rolling from right to left, and a left-right dolly movement of the camera.

**Figure 9.5.** *Test images for investigating the use of color and vector methods in determining displacement fields; sequence from the LABRI-ANR ICOS-HD database available at www.open-video.org*

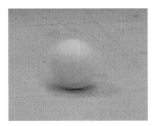

**Figure 9.6.** *Detailed view of the tennis ball image*

Figure 9.7 shows a visualization of the field vectors for the image on the right of Figure 9.5, for the six different color spaces mentioned previously: HSV, L*a*b*, RGB, rgb, XYZ, and YUV.

It can be immediately seen that the fields calculated in the RGB, XYZ, and YUV spaces are very similar because it is possible to convert from one space to the other using linear transformations. In this case, and as we emphasized earlier, the overall information remains identical, and a truly vector-based method must inevitably give similar results in all three cases. Next, we can observe that the field obtained from the HSV representation is particularly different from the others. In fact, the image in Figure 9.6 can be used to identify the presence of motion blur (on the left and right sides of the ball), which has a significant effect on the highest-amplitude component, which is the *Value* component; this then destroys the information available from the other components. Finally, note the similarity between the fields obtained using the two normalized spaces L\*a\*b\* and rgb, with normalization of color differences tending to reduce the perceived displacements in shadowed areas.

On this subject it is interesting to compare the field extracted from the YUV version of Figure 9.7f with the fields in Figure 9.8 which have been computed under similar conditions. First, we notice that the field

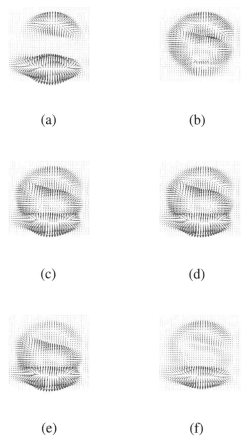

(a)                                (b)

(c)                                (d)

(e)                                (f)

**Figure 9.7.** *Displacement fields obtained for Figure 9.5:*
*a) HSV, b) L\*a\*b\*, c) RGB, d) rgb, e) XYZ and f) YUV*

obtained for the Y component, Figure 9.8a, is equivalent to what would be observed for the gray scale. Moreover, the result obtained for the UV components, Figure 9.8b, shows the expected property: being insensitive to the presence of shadows.

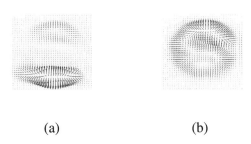

(a)                                        (b)

**Figure 9.8.** *Displacement fields for Figure 9.5: a) Y component, b) UV components*

Finally, in Figure 9.9, we show the fields calculated in three different spaces (L*a*b*, RGB, and YUV) using three of the methods described in section 2. These consist of a selection strategy (f) applied to the UV components, two examples of global strategies applied (b) to RGB and (d) to L*a*b, along with three examples of the fusion strategy applied (a) to RGB, (c) to L*a*b, and (e) to YUV. Of course, to avoid giving misleading results, in this case, the partial derivatives were again estimated by projection onto a Hermite-Laguerre basis with a support of $7 \times 7 \times 3$. These examples illustrate the advantages of using a truly vector approach, in terms of both its stability under changes in color representation and the intrinsic consistency of the results.

## 9.4. Conclusion

As our analysis has revealed, the literature is fairly sparse on the subject of motion estimation in color image sequences. This is undoubtedly because these methods have not yet found practical applications (due to the additional computational cost associated with them) in areas of strong industrial interest, such as video coding. However, the contribution of color information to improved motion

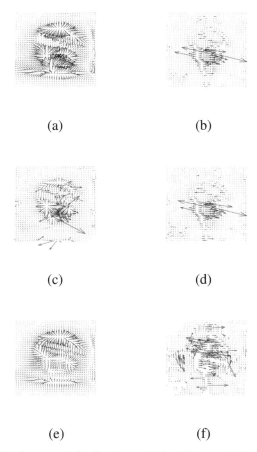

(a)                          (b)

(c)                          (d)

(e)                          (f)

**Figure 9.9.** *Displacement fields for Figure 9.5 for different calculation strategies and different color spaces: a) RGB fusion, b) global RGB, c) L\*a\*b\* fusion, d) global L\*a\*b\*, e) YUV fusion, f) UV selection*

estimation cannot be denied in cases where there is a need for more detailed analysis of the perceived motion in multi-component images. Recently, another trend has appeared in the literature [HUA 07], considering color regions in the image plane and integrating their color descriptors into the energy function to be minimized, using an approach similar to that of Horn and Shunk. Although these methods are still to prove their worth, this trend appears to be a promising avenue for future research.

## 9.5. Bibliography

[AND 03]  ANDREWS R., LOVELL B., "Color optical flow", *Workshop on Digital Image Computing*, p. 135-139, Brisbane, Australia, 2003.

[AND 04]  ANDREWS R., Early Investigations in Optical Flow from Colour Images, PhD thesis, School of Information Technology and Electrical Engineering, The University of Queensland, Australia, 2004.

[AUG 05]  AUGEREAU B., TREMBLAIS B., FERNANDEZ-MALOIGNE C., "Vectorial computation of the optical flow in color image sequences", *Thirteenth Color Imaging Conference*, p. 130-134, Scottsdale, USA, 2005.

[BAR 02]  BARRON J., KLETTE R., "Quantitative color optical flow", *16th International Conference on Pattern Recognition*, vol. 4, p. 251-255, Quebec, Canada, 2002.

[BRU 02]  BRUHN A., WEICKERT J., SCHNÖRR C., "Combining the advantages of local and global optic flow methods", *DAGM Symposium on Pattern Recognition*, p. 454-462, London, UK, 2002.

[GOL 97]  GOLLAND P., BRUCKSTEIN A.M., "Motion from color", *Computer Vision and Image Understanding*, vol. 68, no. 3, p. 346-362, 1997.

[HOR 81]  HORN B., SCHUNCK B., "Determining optical flow", *Artificial Intelligence*, vol. 17, no. 1-3, p. 185-203, 1981.

[HUA 07]  HUART J., BERTOLINO P., "Extraction d'Objets-Clés pour l'Analyse de Vidéos", *Colloque GRETSI*, p. 93-96, Troyes, France, 2007.

[JÄH 98]  JÄHNE B., HAUSSECKER H., SCHARR H., SPIES H., SCHMUNDT D., SCHURR U., "Study of dynamical processes with tensor-based spatiotemporal image processing techniques", *European Conference on Computer Vision*, Freiburg, Germany, p. 322-336, 1998.

[JI 07]  JI H., FERMÜLLER C., "Better flow estimation from color images", *EURASIP Journal on Advances in Signal Processing*, vol. 23, p. 9-19, 2007.

[LAU 04]  LAUZE F., KORNPROBST P., LENGLET C., DERICHE R., NIELSEN M., "Sur Quelques Méthodes de Calcul de Flot Optique à partir du Tenseur de Structure : Synthèse et Contribution", *Reconnaissance des Formes et Intelligence Artificielle*, vol. 1, Toulouse, France, p. 283-292, 2004.

[LUC 81]  LUCAS B., KANADE T., "An iterative image registration technique with an application to stereo vision", *7th International Conference on Artificial Intelligence*, Vancouver, Canada, p. 121-130, 1981.

[OHT 89]  OHTA N., "Optical flow detection by color images", *IEEE International Conference on Image Processing*, p. 801-805, 1989.

[TEK 95]  TEKALP A.M., *Digital Video Processing*, Prentice-Hall, Inc., Upper Saddle River, USA, 1995.

[TRE 04] TREMBLAIS B., AUGEREAU B., "A fast multi-scale edges detection algorithm", *Pattern Recognition Letters*, vol. 25, no. 6, p. 603-618, Elsevier, 2004.

[TSC 02] TSCHUMPERLÉ D., PDE-Based Regularization of Multivalued Images and Applications, PhD thesis, Ecole Doctorale Sciences et Technologies de l'Information et de la Communication, University of Nice-Sophia Antipolis, France, 2002.

[WEI 04] VAN DE WEIJER J., GEVERS T., "Robust optical flow from photometric invariants", *IEEE International Conference on Image Processing*, Singapore, p. 1835-1838, 2004.

# Appendix A

# Appendix to Chapter 7: Summary of Hypotheses and Color Characteristic Invariances

Table A.1 summarizes all the invariant characteristics discussed in Chapter 7. Each one has been assigned a shorthand designation of the form $Car_i$, where $i$ is a number between 1 and 21. Table A.2 lists all the hypotheses, each given a shorthand designation of the form $H_j$ for $j$ between 1 and 18. These designations are then used in Tables A.3 and A.4, which summarize the assumptions on which each characteristic is based, and the photometric and radiometric variations to which they are insensitive. Thus, for a given application, it is possible to make the most appropriate choice of characteristic based on criteria such as the image acquisition conditions and the required invariances of the characteristic. We should point out that Table A.4 cannot be used without also referring to Table A.3, since certain invariances are only obtained on the condition that certain hypotheses are satisfied. For example, characteristics satisfying the assumption of a matte surface will be insensitive to changes in viewpoint. This invariance is not obtained by normalization of the chosen color characteristic that is used, but through satisfying the hypothesis. As a result, it is important to check that the assumptions implicit in the use of a particular color

| Designation in subsequent tables | Description and/or reference | Equation and/or page |
|---|---|---|
| $Car_1$ | Component ratios: Funt et al. [FUN 95] | equation [7.26] page 257 |
| $Car_2$ | $m_1, m_2, m_3$ characteristics: Gevers et al. [GEV 99] | equation [7.32] page 260 |
| $Car_3$ | $l_1, l_2, l_3$ characteristics: Gevers et al. [GEV 99] | equation [7.35] page 261 |
| $Car_4$ | $c_1, c_2, c_3$ characteristics: Gevers et al. [GEV 99] | equation [7.39] page 263 |
| $Car_5$ | Entropy minimization: Finlayson et al. [FIN 01, FIN 04] | Page 265 |
| $Car_6$ | Histogram equalization: Finlayson et al. [FIN 05] | Page 266 |
| $Car_7$ | Normalized moments: Lenz et al. [LEN 99] | Page 267 |
| $Car_8$ | Eigenvalue normalization: Healey et al. [HEA 95] | Page 267 |
| $Car_9$ | Normalized mean and standard deviation | equation [7.46] page 267 |
| $Car_{10}$ | Color moments invariant under diagonal model: Mindru et al. [MIN 04] | Page 268 |
| $Car_{11}$ | Color moments invariant under diagonal-offset model: Mindru et al. [MIN 04] | Page 268 |
| $Car_{12}$ | Color moments invariant under affine model: Mindru et al. [MIN 04] | Page 268 |
| $Car_{13}$ | H characteristic: Geusebroek et al. [GEU 01] | equation [7.53] page 270 |
| $Car_{14}$ | C characteristic: Geusebroek et al. [GEU 01] | equation [7.56] page 271 |
| $Car_{15}$ | W characteristic: Geusebroek et al. [GEU 01] | equation [7.59] page 272 |
| $Car_{16}$ | N characteristic: Geusebroek et al. [GEU 01] | equation [7.64] page 274 |
| $Car_{17}$ | quasi-invariant characteristic in presence of shadows: van de Weijer et al. [VAN 05] | equation [7.69] page 277 |
| $Car_{18}$ | full-invariant characteristic in presence of shadows: van de Weijer et al. [VAN 05] | equation [7.70] page 278 |
| $Car_{19}$ | quasi-invariant characteristic in presence of reflections: van de Weijer et al. [VAN 05] | equation [7.71] page 278 |
| $Car_{20}$ | quasi-invariant characteristic in presence of shadows and reflections: van de Weijer et al. [VAN 05] | equation [7.72] page 279 |
| $Car_{21}$ | full-invariant characteristic in presence of shadows and reflections: van de Weijer et al. [VAN 05] | equation [7.73] page 279 |

**Table A.1.** *Color invariant characteristics listed in Chapter 7*

| Designation | Description of hypothesis and page reference |
|---|---|
| $H_1$ | Kubelka-Munk model page 247 |
| $H_2$ | Shafer model page 247 |
| $H_3$ | Lambert model page 248 |
| $H_4$ | Neutral specular reflection page 248 |
| $H_5$ | Matte surface page 249 |
| $H_6$ | Normalized spectral response curves page 249 |
| $H_7$ | Narrow sensor bandwidth page 249 |
| $H_8$ | Transformation from RGB camera space to CIE XYZ space page 250 |
| $H_9$ | Planck equation page 250 |
| $H_{10}$ | Locally constant illumination color page 251 |
| $H_{11}$ | Locally constant illumination page 251 |
| $H_{12}$ | White illumination page 252 |
| $H_{13}$ | Known illumination color page 252 |
| $H_{14}$ | Diagonal model page 253 |
| $H_{15}$ | Diagonal-offset model page 253 |
| $H_{16}$ | Linear transformation page 254 |
| $H_{17}$ | Affine transformation page 254 |
| $H_{18}$ | Monotonically increasing functions page 254 |

**Table A.2.** *Basic hypotheses used in color characteristics*

| Characteristic | $H_1$ | $H_2$ | $H_3$ | $H_4$ | $H_5$ | $H_6$ | $H_7$ | $H_8$ | $H_9$ | $H_{10}$ | $H_{11}$ | $H_{12}$ | $H_{13}$ | $H_{14}$ | $H_{15}$ | $H_{16}$ | $H_{17}$ | $H_{18}$ |
|---|---|---|---|---|---|---|---|---|---|---|---|---|---|---|---|---|---|---|
| $Car_1$ | | | ⊕ | | | | | | | | ⊕ | | | | | | | |
| $Car_2$ | | ⊕ | | | ⊕ | | ⊕ | | | | | | | | | | | |
| $Car_3$ | | ⊕ | | ⊕ | | | ⊕ | | | ⊕ | | ⊕ | | | | | | |
| $Car_4$ | | ⊕ | | | ⊕ | ⊕ | | | | | | ⊕ | | | | | | |
| $Car_5$ | | | ⊕ | | | | ⊕ | | ⊕ | | | | | | | | | |
| $Car_6$ | | | | | | | | | | | | | | | | | | ⊕ |
| $Car_7$ | | | | | | | | | | | | | | | | ⊕ | | |
| $Car_8$ | | | | | | | | | | | | | | | | ⊕ | | |
| $Car_9$ | | | | | | | | | | | | | | ⊕ | ⊕ | | | |
| $Car_{10}$ | | | | | | | | | | | | | | | | | ⊕ | |
| $Car_{11}$ | | | | | | | | | | | | | | | ⊕ | | | |
| $Car_{12}$ | | | | | | | | | | | | | | | | | | |
| $Car_{13}$ | ⊕ | | | | ⊕ | | | ⊕ | | | | ⊕ | | | | | | |
| $Car_{14}$ | ⊕ | | | | ⊕ | | | ⊕ | | | | ⊕ | | | | | | |
| $Car_{15}$ | ⊕ | | | | ⊕ | | | | | | | ⊕ | | | | | | |
| $Car_{16}$ | ⊕ | | | | | | | ⊕ | | | ⊕ | | | | | | | |
| $Car_{17}$ | | ⊕ | | ⊕ | | | | | | ⊕ | | | ⊕ | | | | | |
| $Car_{18}$ | | ⊕ | | ⊕ | | | | | | ⊕ | | | ⊕ | | | | | |
| $Car_{19}$ | | ⊕ | | ⊕ | | | | | | ⊕ | | | ⊕ | | | | | |
| $Car_{20}$ | | ⊕ | | ⊕ | | | | | | ⊕ | | | ⊕ | | | | | |
| $Car_{21}$ | | ⊕ | | ⊕ | | | | | | ⊕ | | | ⊕ | | | | | |

**Table A.3.** *Hypotheses used in each color invariant characteristic*

| Characteristic | Illumination intensity | Illumination color | Illumination direction | Viewpoint | Ambient lighting | Shadows | Reflections |
|---|---|---|---|---|---|---|---|
| $Car_1$ | ⊕ | ⊕ | | ⊕ | | | |
| $Car_2$ | ⊕ | ⊕ | ⊕ | ⊕ | | | |
| $Car_3$ | ⊕ | | ⊕ | ⊕ | | | ⊕ |
| $Car_4$ | ⊕ | ⊕ | ⊕ | ⊕ | | | |
| $Car_5$ | ⊕ | ⊕ | | | | ⊕ | |
| $Car_6$ | ⊕ | ⊕ | | | | | |
| $Car_7$ | ⊕ | ⊕ | | | | | |
| $Car_8$ | ⊕ | ⊕ | | | ⊕ | | |
| $Car_9$ | ⊕ | ⊕ | | | | | |
| $Car_{10}$ | ⊕ | ⊕ | | | ⊕ | | |
| $Car_{11}$ | ⊕ | ⊕ | | | ⊕ | | |
| $Car_{12}$ | ⊕ | ⊕ | | | | | |
| $Car_{13}$ | ⊕ | | ⊕ | ⊕ | | | ⊕ |
| $Car_{14}$ | ⊕ | | ⊕ | ⊕ | | | |
| $Car_{15}$ | ⊕ | | | | | | |
| $Car_{16}$ | ⊕ | ⊕ | ⊕ | ⊕ | | | |
| $Car_{17}$ | ⊕ | | ⊕ | ⊕ | | | |
| $Car_{18}$ | | | | | | ⊕ | ⊕ |
| $Car_{19}$ | | | | | | ⊕ | ⊕ |
| $Car_{20}$ | | | | | | ⊕ | ⊕ |
| $Car_{21}$ | ⊕ | | ⊕ | ⊕ | | ⊕ | ⊕ |

**Table A.4.** *Invariance of each characteristic in the presence of different photometric and radiometric effects*

characteristic (Table A.3) are indeed met, to be confident that the invariance stated in Table A.4 will be obtained. Moreover, we also point out that we have not mentioned invariance to changes in surface orientation, unlike some articles, since this is redundant given that we have considered changes in viewpoint and in illumination direction. If a color characteristic is invariant to the viewpoint and the direction of illumination, it will also be invariant to the orientation of the observed surface.

## A.1. Bibliography

[FIN 01]  FINLAYSON G., HORDLEY S., "Colour constancy at a pixel", *Journal of the Optical Society of America*, vol. 18, no. 2, p. 253-264, 2001.

[FIN 04]  FINLAYSON G., DREW M., LU C., "Intrinsic images by entropy minimization", *Proceedings of the European Conference on Computer Vision*, p. 582-595, 2004.

[FIN 05]  FINLAYSON G., HORDLEY S., SCHAEFER G., TIAN G.Y., "Illuminant and device invariant colour using histogram equalisation", *Pattern Recognition*, vol. 38, p. 179-190, 2005.

[FUN 95]  FUNT B., FINLAYSON G., "Color constant color indexing", *IEEE Transactions on Pattern Analysis and Machine Intelligence*, vol. 17, no. 5, p. 522-529, 1995.

[GEU 01]  GEUSEBROEK J.M., VAN DEN BOOMGAARD R., SMEULDERS A.W.M. GEERTS H., "Color invariance", *IEEE Transactions on Pattern Analysis and Machine Intelligence*, vol. 23, no. 12, p. 1338-1350, 2001.

[GEV 99]  GEVERS T., SMEULDERS A., "Color-based object recognition", *Pattern Recognition*, vol. 32, p. 453-464, 1999.

[HEA 95]  HEALEY G., SLATER D., "Global color contancy: recognition of objects by use of illumination invariant properties of color distributions", *Journal of the Optical Society America*, vol. 11, no. 11, p. 3003-3010, 1995.

[LEN 99]  LENZ R., TRAN L., MEER P., "Moment based normalization of color images", *IEEE Workshop on Multimedia Signal Processing*, p. 129-132, 1999.

[MIN 04]  MINDRU F., TUYTELAARS T., GOOL L.V., MOONS T., "Moment invariants for recognition under changing viewpoint and illumination", *Computer Vision and Image Understanding*, vol. 1, no. 3, p. 3-27, 2004.

[VAN 05]  VAN DE WEIJER J., GEVERS T., GEUSEBROEK J.-M., "Edge and corner detection by photometric quasi-invariants", *IEEE Transactions on Pattern Analysis and Machine Intelligence*, vol. 27, no. 4, p. 625-630, 2005.

# List of Authors

Olivier ALATA
Laboratoire Hubert Curien, UMR CNRS 5516
Saint-Etienne University
France

Jesús ANGULO
Laboratoire CMM-Centre de Morphologie Mathématique
MINES ParisTech
Fontainebleau
France

Bertrand AUGEREAU
Laboratoire XLIM-SIC UMR CNRS 6172
Poitiers University
France

Jenny BENOIS-PINEAU
Laboratoire LABRI UMR CNRS 5800
Bordeaux 1 University
Talence
France

Jean-Christophe BURIE
Laboratoire Informatique Image Interaction (L3i)
La Rochelle University
France

Laurent BUSIN
Laboratoire LISIC
University of the Littoral Opal Coast
Calais
France

Alain CLÉMENT
Laboratoire d'Ingénierie des Systèmes Automatisés (EA 4094)
Angers University
France

Eric DINET
Laboratoire Hubert Curien, UMR CNRS 5516
Jean Monnet University
Saint-Étienne
France

Christine FERNANDEZ-MALOIGNE
Laboratoire Xlim-SIC
Poitiers University
Chasseneuil
France

Christèle LECOMTE
Laboratoire LITIS EA 4108
Rouen University
Saint Etienne Du Rouvray
FRANCE

Sébastien LEFÈVRE
Laboratoire IRISA-UBS
University of South Brittany
Vannes
France

Olivier LEZORAY
Laboratoire GREYC UMR CNRS 6072
University of Caen Lower Normandy
France

Ludovic MACAIRE
Laboratoire LAGIS
Lille 1 University
Villeneuve d'Ascq
France

Henri Maître
Institut Télécom
Télécom ParisTech
Paris
France

Damien Muselet
Laboratoire Hubert Curien, UMR CNRS 5516
Saint-Etienne University
France

Alice Porebski
Laboratoire LISIC
University of the Littoral Opal Coast
Calais
France

Imtnan Qazi
Laboratoire XLIM-SIC UMR CNRS 6172
Poitiers University
France

Frédérique Robert-Inacio
IM2NP - UMR CNRS 6242
ISEN-Toulon
France

Xiaohu Song
Laboratoire Hubert Curien, UMR CNRS 5516
Saint-Etienne University
France

David Tschumperlé
Laboratoire GREYC (CNRS UMR 6072) / Equipe IMAGE
ENSICAEN / Caen University
France

Nicolas Vandenbroucke
Laboratoire LISIC
University of the Littoral Opal Coast
Calais
France

# Index